•IMPERIAL STANDARD•

ENERGY HISTORIES, CULTURES, AND POLITICS

SERIES EDITOR: Petra Dolata, Associate Professor and Tier II Canada
Research Chair, Department of History, University of Calgary

ISSN 2562-3486 (Print) ISSN 2562-3494 (Online)

This series features original research at the intersection of energy and society. It welcomes works that contribute to international discussions on the history, culture, and politics of energy and speaks to the energy humanities and energy social sciences. The series has a strong interest in, but is not limited to, North American issues.

UNIVERSITY OF CALGARY
Press

GRAHAM D. TAYLOR

•IMPERIAL STANDARD•

Imperial Oil, Exxon, and the Canadian Oil Industry from 1880

Energy Histories, Cultures, and Politics Series
ISSN 2562-3486 (Print) ISSN 2562-3494 (Online)

University of Calgary Press
2500 University Drive NW
Calgary, Alberta
Canada T2N 1N4
press.ucalgary.ca

LIBRARY AND ARCHIVES CANADA CATALOGUING IN PUBLICATION

Title: Imperial standard : Imperial Oil, Exxon, and the Canadian oil industry from 1880 / Graham D. Taylor.
Names: Taylor, Graham D., 1944- author.
Description: Series statement: Energy histories, cultures, and politics ; 1 | Includes bibliographical references and index.
Identifiers: Canadiana (print) 20190072881 | Canadiana (ebook) 20190072903 | ISBN 9781773850351 (softcover) | ISBN 9781773850368 (open access PDF) | ISBN 9781773850375 (PDF) | ISBN 9781773850382 (EPUB) | ISBN 9781773850399 (Kindle)
Subjects: LCSH: Imperial Oil Limited—History. | LCSH: Petroleum industry and trade—Canada—History.
Classification: LCC HD9574.C24 I478 2019 | DDC 338.2/72820971—dc23

The University of Calgary Press acknowledges the support of the Government of Alberta through the Alberta Media Fund for our publications. We acknowledge the financial support of the Government of Canada. We acknowledge the financial support of the Canada Council for the Arts for our publishing program.

Copyediting by Kathryn Simpson
Cover image: Imperial Oil Service Station, Oshawa, Ontario, September 1954. Glenbow Archives, IP-12-26-33, Imperial Oil Collection.
Cover design, page design, and typesetting by Melina Cusano

Table of Contents

Illustrations

Acknowledgements

This is not an "official" history of Imperial Oil Ltd. I received no financial support from Imperial Oil, Exxon/Mobil or any of their affiliates, nor for that matter did I seek or receive funding from the Social Sciences and Humanities Council of Canada or any other source. In writing this history I have used material that is available to any researcher, including most particularly the Imperial Oil Ltd. and Royalite records at the Glenbow Museum and Archives in Calgary and the Exxon/Mobil records at the Dolph Briscoe Center for American Studies at the University of Texas at Austin. I would like to acknowledge my appreciation to those companies for having made their business records available to the public.

This is also not a "definitive" history. The records of Imperial Oil are among the largest business archives in Canada, surpassed only by those of the Hudson's Bay Company and the country's transcontinental railways. These records are indeed a vast treasure trove for researchers on a wide range of topics—ranging from the history of the company's large tanker fleet to the technological achievements of its research scientists, and much else in between—and I hope other scholars will find them valuable in understanding Imperial's role in the history of our country. My intent was to sketch the general history of Imperial Oil and its role in that history and to focus on some particular features of the company that are of relevance to the evolution of multinational enterprises as significant players in the world's economic, political, and natural environment over the past two centuries.

This project originated over forty years ago. When I first came to Canada in the 1970s one major controversy (in addition to the status of Quebec) focused on the role of foreign-owned corporations in the Canadian economy. Critics charged that these foreign multinationals undermined Canada's industries, stifled innovation and entrepreneurship, and depleted the country's natural resources. Defenders countered that these companies brought much-needed capital, technology, and management skills, which all contributed to the dramatic growth of the Canadian economy after the Second World War. The debate featured much rhetoric, reams of statistics, and media stories that celebrated their achievements or condemned their depredations.

It seemed to me that as a historian what I could contribute to this ongoing debate was analysis of how multinationals in Canada actually operated in practice: to what extent did parent firms determine not just the strategies but day-to-day functioning of the Canadian companies they owned or controlled? In the longer run did the relationship between the parent firm and subsidiaries evolve over time, as theorists such as Raymond Vernon maintained, from close control to a more diverse, autonomous model? Or was foreign domination so complete that it could only be constrained by government measures to limit and regulate these companies? Or indeed was there some other, more suitable model?

In these years the study of business enterprise was undergoing a transformation as historians such as Alfred D. Chandler Jr. and others explored the internal workings and evolution of large-scale enterprises and highlighted the relationship between corporate strategies and organization. I had the good fortune to discuss my interest and research in Canadian business with Dr. Chandler; I benefited from his advice, and perhaps benefited even more from my conversations with Mira Wilkins, the most accomplished historian of multinational business in our time.

In order to achieve my aim of observing business relationships "from the inside," I sought to find companies whose internal records were available to research, which limited the range of my work to some extent, but allowed for more in-depth analysis. Over the years I developed "case studies" of Canadian affiliates of multinationals, mostly American or British, including Canadian Industries Ltd., Bell Canada, Vickers of Canada, and Great Canadian Oil Sands (now Suncor).

One of the objects of my quest was the "great white whale" of foreign-owned businesses in Canada: Imperial Oil, affiliated since 1899 with Standard Oil of New Jersey (Exxon, now Exxon/Mobil), which was not only one of the largest companies in the country, but one of the most enduring, and one whose significance was felt throughout Canadian history, comparable in many respects to the Hudson's Bay Company and the Canadian Pacific Railway. In the late 1980s I was able to get access to the records of Imperial Oil in the early twentieth century, relating to the presidency of Walter Teagle, who went on to become the chief executive of Standard Oil for many years. When I learned that the Imperial Oil records were available at Glenbow Museum and Archives, I set out to fulfill that quest.

There were several people whose advice and assistance were particularly valuable to me in this endeavour. Robert Taylor-Vaisey had been the corporate archivist at Imperial for many years and in that capacity had systematically organized the company records. When Imperial Oil decided to move its headquarters from Toronto to Calgary, Taylor-Vaisey played a major role in arranging for the disposition of the company records at Glenbow. When I began my work on Imperial, I met with him several times and benefited from not only from his knowledge of the archives but also his insights into the history of the company.

My thanks also go to Douglas Cass, the director of the Glenbow Archives, who is himself an expert on the history of the Canadian oil industry, and who took a great interest in my project, introducing me to various other researchers whose input has also been valuable. I received inestimable help in locating and retrieving relevant material from two archivists at Glenbow responsible for the organization and maintenance of the Imperial Oil records: Tonia Fanella and particularly Lynette Walton who was always prepared to spend extra time chasing down documents I requested. All of the staff at the Glenbow Archives were helpful and courteous, even when working under apparently perpetual financial constraints.

I appreciate the help I received from a wide range of fellow researchers I encountered in writing this book. David Finch provided valuable information about the history of Turner Valley and the Alberta oil industry, through both his books and conversations with me. I had numerous discussions with Debbie McLeod Knall about the career of her grandfather, John McLeod, with Imperial Oil and Royalite. Joyce Hunt shared information about her research on the early history of the oil sands. David Breen provided insights on company-government relations in the Alberta oil industry based on his extensive research and publications on the subject. Timothy Cobban shared research materials on the early history of Imperial Oil in Ontario, drawing on his valuable work, *Cities of Oil*. Professors Stephen Bocking of Trent University and Sean Kheraj of York University provided guidance into the history of environmental law and policies in Canada. I received encouragement from Professor Geoffrey Jones of the Harvard Business School and Dr. Matthias Kipping, Richard E. Waugh Chair in Business History at York University, to seek ways of integrating my work on Canadian business into the growing literature on the history of multinational enterprises. In addition, I appreciate the careful review of my manuscript by the two anonymous peer reviewers for the University of Calgary Press whose comments stimulated me to provide more clarity in explaining the structure and value of my work to the wider audience of historians of Canada and the oil industry.

Perhaps my greatest debt is to Earle Gray, without question the "dean" of historians of Canadian oil, who in addition to providing many insights based on more than half a century of covering the industry, also read every chapter in this book in draft form and made many suggestions as well as providing useful advice on the geology and technology of oil and gas in an effort to correct my misconceptions. Gray is still very active in the field, and we traded drafts of my book for commentary on chapters on his current project, *Fossil Fire*, which will be a valuable contribution to the history of the fossil fuel industries and their impact on the environment.

Finally, my thanks to my wife, Deborah, who not only put up with frequent and extended visits to Calgary, but also provided much help with my research, going through sixty-odd years worth of the tedium of minutes of the board of directors of Imperial Oil, and locating pertinent articles in the *Imperial Oil Review* covering an almost equally long time period. As partial compensation, we spent weekends taking in the remarkable diversity of Alberta, from (melting) glaciers north of Lake Louise to dinosaurs in Drumheller.

Of course I accept responsibility for any errors of omission or commission in this work.

Graham D. Taylor
Professor Emeritus, Trent University
Peterborough, Ontario
August 1, 2018

INTRODUCTION

For one hundred and thirty years, from its establishment in 1880 to 2010, Imperial Oil Company Ltd. was the largest petroleum company in Canada; in 2009, Suncor merged with Petro Canada and Imperial fell to second place. Even so, in 2018 Imperial remained among the top ten non-financial companies in Canada, ranked by revenues and assets. The third ranked company, Enbridge, had been a subsidiary of Imperial when it was the Interprovincial Pipeline Company.[1]

During those years Imperial Oil was the largest company in terms of assets, revenues, and net earnings, towering over others in the Canadian oil and gas sector. In 1948, for example, even before the impact of the Leduc discovery took effect, Imperial's sales revenue and net profits were twice the size of its two largest competitors, British-American Oil (later taken over by Gulf) and Texaco Canada (which Imperial acquired in 1991). Even in the 1990s, Imperial's sales and assets were equal to those its two major rivals, Shell Canada and Petro Canada. Its share of the gasoline market in Canada fell from the 60 per cent position it held in the early 1950s, but it still accounted for one-third of that market.[2]

Not only was it Canada's largest petroleum company, it was also in the proximity of—if not always "present at the creation" of—virtually every major event in the industry after 1900. When demand shifted from kerosene to gasoline in the early 1900s, Imperial acquired patents to the most efficient thermal cracking processes. In 1920 the Northwest Company, an Imperial subsidiary, drilled the first oil well in northern Canada. When gas (and some oil) was discovered in the Turner Valley in Alberta, Imperial arrived shortly thereafter, bought up the largest gas company, and its subsidiary, Royalite, made the largest oil find there in 1924. During the Second World War, Imperial developed oil fields and a refinery in the

Northwest Territories of Canada as part of the war effort. And all this was before Leduc in 1947.

Imperial built the first oil pipeline linking the Alberta oil fields to central Canada in the early 1950s. At one point the company held between one-third and one-half of the assets of every oil pipeline in the country. When the oil sands began to be exploited in the 1960s–70s, Imperial was a founding member of the Syncrude consortium; a decade later Imperial developed its own project at Cold Lake.

Over this same period—from 1899 to the present—between two-thirds and three-quarters of the equity in Imperial Oil has been held by Standard Oil of New Jersey (later Exxon, now Exxon-Mobil). In 2018 Exxon-Mobil was ranked the second largest company in the United States by *Fortune* magazine. In terms of revenues it was surpassed only by the discount retail giant, Walmart. In the same year it was ranked the third largest petroleum company in the world, trailing the surging China National Petroleum Company and its erstwhile rival, Royal Dutch Shell. Exxon-Mobil remained a global power in the industry, serving markets on virtually every continent, and even in a world crowded with government-owned oil producers it maintained reserves in North and South America, Africa, East Asia, and Australia.[3]

Imperial Oil was both one of the largest companies in Canada, which had played a major role in shaping the country's petroleum industry, and a not inconsequential part of one of the world's largest multinational companies: in 2018, it accounted for close to 10 per cent of the $205 million (USD) revenues of Exxon-Mobil. The relationship between Imperial and Exxon was also one of the most enduring examples of a parent company and a foreign affiliate. In 1929 Imperial Oil was the third largest non-financial corporation in Canada. Eighty-nine years later, only five of the twenty largest firms had survived at all, and Imperial was the only company whose status as a foreign-owned entity remained virtually unchanged.[4]

In 1949, Exxon had partially or wholly owned affiliates in virtually every part of the world outside the Soviet Union—many of them larger and more significant to the company than the operations of Imperial Oil in Canada. By the early twenty-first century, although Exxon was ambitiously seeking access to the republics of the former Soviet Union, many of its largest affiliates—particularly in the Middle East and Latin America—had been swept away by nationalizations, and its ventures into new territories in Africa and Asia were fraught with risk, not only in a financial sense but also in terms of the safety of its employees. The survival of Imperial Oil through the (relatively restrained) controversies in Canada over "foreign multinationals" in the 1970s and 1980s contrasted sharply with upheavals in other parts of Exxon's empire. More recently, however, the emerging scientific consensus linking carbon emissions from fossil fuel production to climate change posed challenges to both companies—and particularly to Imperial Oil, whose future had been tied to the development of Alberta's oil sands.[5]

This history of Imperial Oil is intended to address its role as one of the major shapers of Canada's petroleum industry—arguably as important for the nation's economic development in the twentieth century as was the Canadian Pacific Railway in the nineteenth century and the Hudson's Bay Company in the years before Confederation. At the same time I wish to present its dual status as an integrated oil company in Canada and an integral part of the system of continental and then global expansion and dominion that Exxon pursued from its emergence in 1880.

The literature on multinational enterprises is enormous. Even the literature on the history of multinational enterprises is formidable: one recent overview of the field listed over three hundred publications, of varying scope and scale.[6] Many of the works on particular companies focus on the development of the parent firm, its reasons for expansion (or contraction), and its perspective on strategies and organizational evolution. There are of course exceptions, including the multivolume history of Standard Oil of New Jersey, which reviews the development of affiliates and subsidiaries in some depth and has been of inestimable value to this study of Imperial Oil.[7]

Of somewhat more recent vintage are studies that focus on the role and evolution of subsidiaries per se, rather than adjuncts to a larger organization. From this perspective the subsidiary has been analyzed in terms of its relationship to the host country's political and economic environment, cooperative as well as competitive linkages with local businesses, its role in organizations that feature a networked as well as a hierarchical structure, and the development of subsidiary-specific strategies that extend beyond following the lead or direction of the parent company.[8] This approach provides useful insights into the workings of multinational enterprises, but many of these studies reflect analyses of the operations of companies during the 1980s–90s, with features that may be time-bound. In contrast, my approach seeks to view the evolution of a subsidiary over a longer period with changing conditions.

This study is structured as a narrative, tracing the history of the Imperial Oil company and its role in the evolution of the Canadian petroleum industry. At the same time, it seeks to provide an analysis of the relationship between Imperial Oil and the American company that controlled it from 1899 by addressing a series of questions:

- What circumstances led Standard Oil to enter the Canadian market? Since this expansion involved a merger (in effect a takeover) of Imperial Oil, what factors led Imperial to join the American company?

- What was the relationship between Imperial and Standard after the merger? Did it extend beyond financial control through majority ownership? Did Standard exercise control over the management of operations?

- What events marked turning points in the relationship between the companies? Were these the result of strategic decisions made by the parent company (Standard Oil) or developments within the subsidiary (Imperial) or external factors, or a combination of these elements? Did these changes reflect a longer-term alteration of the conditions of the industry as a whole?

- Was there a transfer of technological and managerial capabilities between the parent company and the subsidiary? Were there transfers in the opposite direction? To what extent did Imperial develop its own initiatives and organizational capabilities?

- What was the role and status of Imperial Oil within the larger system of divisions and affiliates controlled by Standard Oil/Jersey Standard/Exxon over time? To what extent was

Imperial able to develop and execute strategies for its own objectives separate from those of the parent company?

- To what extent were the operations of Imperial Oil affected by competitive (and other) conditions in the Canadian market? To what extent did developments in the international economy affect the operations and objectives of Standard Oil, Imperial, or the relationship between them?

- In what ways did measures by either the US or the Canadian government (or provincial governments) in such areas as trade, taxation, labour relations, financial rules, and environmental regulation affect the operations of either or both companies and the relationship between them? In what areas did differences in the legal, policy, and political environment between the US and Canada affect the operations of either or both companies?

In tracing the history of Imperial Oil and its relationship with Jersey Standard/Exxon, I have drawn substantially on the records of Imperial Oil at the Glenbow Museum and Archives in Calgary, Alberta. The minutes of the board of directors from 1899 and the executive committee of the board from 1951 were very valuable in providing insights into the perspectives of Imperial's executives as they dealt with events affecting the Canadian oil and gas industry and the expectations of the majority owner in New York (and more recently, in Texas).

Because of the forty-year rule applied to these particular records, I was unable to access them beyond 1978. My original intention was to end the detailed history in 1980 and provide a brief epilogue with an overview covering events after that time. As I proceeded, however, the need for an expanded epilogue seemed clear, as a number of significant developments affected the company over that forty-year period, including the second energy crisis of 1980–81 and the rise and fall of the Canadian government's National Energy Policy (NEP); Imperial's acquisition of one of its main competitors, Texaco Canada, in 1989–90; and the emergence of environmental issues and particularly the controversy over the relationship between carbon emissions and climate change that roiled the industry from the late 1990s on. In this part, I have drawn on the company's annual reports and related materials, on coverage of developments in the business and petroleum industry media, and works on Exxon, including in particular the history of that company by Joseph Pratt and William Hale that covers the period from 1973 to 2005.[9]

I have organized the book into four major sections:

- The first part (chapters 1 to 3), covering the period from 1880 to 1918, traces the parallel development of Imperial Oil in Canada and Standard Oil in the United States that formed the backdrop to Standard's takeover in 1899, through the reorganization of Imperial under Walter Teagle in 1914–18.

- The second part (chapters 4 to 6), which could be designated the "pre-Leduc era" from 1918 to 1947, covers a period in which Imperial was closely tied in with Jersey Standard's expansion into Latin America after the First World War, and the Canadian company embarked on a thirty-year quest to find oil in Alberta to replace its now-diminished capacity in Ontario.

- The third part (chapters 7 to 10), the "post-Leduc era" from 1948 to 1980, focuses on the expansion of Imperial's role as a major Canadian oil producer as well as its continuing role as the country's largest vertically integrated company in the industry, and traces its efforts at diversification into petrochemicals and related areas, and its involvement in the opening of the oil sands from the 1960s and northern oil and gas exploration in the following decade.

- The epilogue (chapters 11 to 13) carries the history forward beyond 1980, selectively focusing on government-company relations during the energy crises of the 1970s–80s, the consolidations of the 1980s–90s including Imperial's acquisition of Texaco Canada and the Exxon-Mobil merger, and the emergence of environmental issues as a major concern for both Imperial and Exxon.

- The conclusion undertakes a review of Imperial's evolving linkages with Exxon in the context of the broader history of multinational enterprises in the nineteenth through twenty-first centuries, which hopefully will provide a useful contribution to the literature on parent-subsidiary relations.

PROLOGUE

Leduc, Alberta: February 13, 1947

The visiting dignitaries were scheduled to arrive around ten in the morning at the well site, named Leduc Number One after the nearby town: the mayor of Leduc, of course, and the mayor of Edmonton (among others); reporters and photographers; and most critically, Nathan Tanner, Alberta's Minister of Mines. There was some snow on the ground and the temperature was cold, but it was clear—a good sign.

Then, around 4 a.m., Murphy's Law kicked in: Vern Hunter, the chief driller on the well, discovered that a shaft on the cable's swabbing drum that removed excess mud had snapped inside the casing. It would have to be hauled out and replaced, which could take up to half the day. Hunter, who was sensitive about his nickname, "Dry Hole," had been doubtful about inviting official observers in the first place, even though the drill stem tests had indicated that Leduc Number One had a good reservoir of oil at 5,000 feet down. But the public relations department in Toronto wanted to put on a show, and it was hard to keep things secret at this point.

Hunter's boss, Walker Taylor, the head of western production for Imperial Oil, arrived at the site around 8 a.m. and assured Hunter he would try to keep the visitors out of his way. Travel arrangements from Edmonton for the officials were delayed for an hour but by early afternoon when they arrived a crowd had already gathered, including local farmers who had more than a passing interest in the event. Although the province of Alberta owned the subsoil mineral rights, landowners could make some money leasing rights of way to drillers.

By 4 p.m. the repairs were done and the cable began running again. Then a column of liquid and mud (used to lubricate the drilling) shot up

FIGURE 0.1. Leduc #1, 13 Feb 1947. Glenbow Archive IP-6f-18, Imperial Oil Collection.

fifty feet above the pit alongside the drill tower. A Calgary driller, George Coakley, shouted "Here she comes—it's oil!" A fire was lit in the pit that caused a dramatic flaring: a Hollywood moment for the photographers that was to appear in the local newspapers the following day. The flaring formed a giant smoke ring, which oil drillers regarded as a sure sign of success.

A couple of hours passed as the excess gas and mud was being cleared out and many onlookers headed home in the cold. Shortly after 6 p.m. the official ceremonies finally took place. Tanner, joined by Walker Taylor and Vernon Taylor—a geologist who would soon head up western operations for Imperial—turned a valve that released the oil into a storage tank, marking the beginning of Leduc Number One's production history.

No one admitted to having celebrated excessively in Edmonton that evening. The news stories were all positive, a public relations success for Imperial. But company officials were still cautious: one well did not necessarily prove a large field, although seismic information seemed to confirm it. A few days later a second well site, Leduc Number Two, proved temporarily disappointing. Over the next few months, however, four more wells had come in, and by September Imperial's president, Henry Hewetson, announced: "The Leduc field is now recognized as a major one. Our geologists estimate there are 50 million barrels of oil and there may be even more since we do not know the limit of the field yet."

Leduc was just the beginning, of course. In 1948 Imperial opened the Redwater field and a year later there was Golden Spike. By this time other oil majors had arrived in (or in some cases returned to) Alberta: Shell, Texaco, Petrofina, and Mobil, which discovered a field even larger than Leduc at Pembina in 1953. Pipelines sprouted east, west, and south; Calgary and Edmonton boomed, both laying claim to the title of "oil capital." Alberta was no longer a "have not" province. Canada became a net oil and gas exporter. Leduc also left its mark on the company that had found it. Imperial Oil—big, cautious, bureaucratic, risk-averse, the quintessential "Canadian" business enterprise—was transformed as well, in ways that few outside its stolid gray stone walls on St. Clair Avenue in Toronto may have anticipated.[1]

The Road to Leduc

In 1947 Imperial Oil was the largest petroleum company in Canada and one of the ten largest non-financial enterprises in the country. In every dimension it was more than twice the size of its nearest competitors. Imperial refineries were located in every major city in Canada from Halifax to Vancouver. Esso service stations dotted the landscape. Imperial commanded a fleet of tankers, many of which had served in transatlantic convoys in both the First and Second World Wars.

What Imperial did not have, however, was very much oil of its own in Canada. The Petrolia fields in Ontario, which had provided the base for Imperial's founding in 1880, had been declining steadily since the turn of the century. Gas and oil had been exploited in the Turner Valley in Alberta by an Imperial subsidiary, Royalite, since the 1920s but those fields were reaching their limits as well. The largest source of supply came from Ohio through the "Cygnet line," serving the markets of central Canada. A second pipeline, built in 1941, carried oil from Portland, Maine to Montreal. Imperial owned the storage facilities at Cygnet but the oil came from other companies, mostly controlled by Standard Oil of New Jersey (now Exxon/Mobil), the largest successor company to the old Standard Oil Trust of John D. Rockefeller after it was broken up by a US court order in 1911.

Cygnet symbolized another critical feature of Imperial Oil: more than two-thirds of its shares were owned by Jersey Standard. Esso was the brand name for Jersey Standard's products; major decisions (including the development program that led to Leduc) were ultimately submitted for approval in New York; and in many other aspects Imperial was part of a global network of affiliates that made Jersey Standard the largest corporation in the world. Ironically, Imperial had been established to be Canada's defender against the sprawling tentacles of the Standard Oil "octopus" in the 1880s. Imperial's owners were stalwart Conservative supporters of the National Policy tariffs on imported petroleum products and the name of the company was intended to demonstrate its fealty to the empire in which Canada was a dominion. But a number of problems beleaguered the company: Rockefeller's aggressive strategy surrounded Imperial with regional competitors (controlled by Standard Oil); output from the Petrolia fields began to decline; and Imperial failed to acquire technology that would reduce the sulphur content of its product, which unhappy consumers called "skunk oil." The Liberals in Canada systematically dismantled the protectionist measures that had shielded Imperial from the Americans. By the end of 1898 Imperial's owners capitulated and the Standard Trust acquired control of a majority of the shares.

For more than a decade Imperial barely functioned, and was little more than a brand name. The Petrolia refinery was closed, the company records were removed to Buffalo, and the Standard manager there ran operations in Canada, rarely consulting the minority shareholders—who nevertheless did very well financially and so had few complaints. This situation changed, however, in the wake of the breakup of the Standard Oil Trust in 1911. Imperial was assigned to Standard Oil of New Jersey, which dispatched one of its rising stars, Walter Teagle, to reorganize the derelict Canadian operation.

Teagle was worried about threats from Jersey Standard's biggest rival, Royal Dutch Shell, and also envisioned Imperial as a vehicle for offshore activities if the US government continued to hound the American parent. New refineries were built, the Imperial sales force was overhauled, troubled labour-management relations were attended to, and Imperial's board was given a larger role in running the company, although Teagle colonized management with his own protégés. As Imperial's official historian John Ewing put it, Teagle "took Imperial from the vassalage in which had been since 1898 and gave it at least the status of a free man."[2]

Teagle, however, was a Jersey Standard "company man:" Imperial was expected to do its part as a cog in the larger wheel. During the First World War, Teagle arranged for Imperial to set up a subsidiary, International Petroleum Company (IPC), to develop oil production in Peru and Colombia. Ostensibly, IPC's output would supply Canada's oil needs, but in practice a substantial amount of the oil found its way to Jersey Standard's giant refinery in Bayonne, New Jersey. The IPC arrangement may have been intended in part to deflect South American nationalist opposition to the Standard Oil octopus. Once Teagle moved on to become chief executive of Jersey Standard in the 1920s, Imperial's strategic role diminished. In the 1930s Imperial and IPC became essentially "cash cows" for Jersey Standard: virtually all Imperial's earnings from its South

American operations were transferred to the parent company through dividend payments.

Nevertheless, Teagle supported Imperial's aspirations to find a secure oil supply within Canada. Initially his commitment was spurred by the machinations of Royal Dutch Shell: in 1918 that company had approached the Dominion government with a proposal: in return for full access to mineral rights on Crown lands, it would develop western Canadian oil resources and build pipelines to Ontario and Quebec. Little of substance came of this improbable scenario, but Teagle countered it anyway, setting up a subsidiary, the Northwest Company, to explore for oil in northern Alberta and procuring the help of T.O. Bosworth, one of Britain's leading geologists, to head the effort.

Bosworth mounted an ambitious operation, with expeditions ranging from the Calgary region (where natural gas and some crude oil had been discovered in the Turner Valley in 1914) to the Mackenzie River delta, but the results were frustrating. The expeditions were beset with perils: Bosworth feuded with other geologists; there was at least one suicide; an experiment at aerial surveying ended in near disaster. Everitt Sadler, one of Teagle's associates at Exxon, ridiculed the undertaking as "politically motivated"—i.e., to keep Canadian officials happy. There may have been some truth to this view—in 1921 Imperial Oil persuaded the Canadian government to write off the company's expenses on exploration in the west against its mineral leasing fees. But Teagle never imposed a veto on Imperial's exploratory ventures despite its dismal record: Imperial Oil folklore has it that the company drilled 133 "dry holes" before 1947. This was an exaggeration—drillers found some natural gas but only one potentially large oil well.

The most stalwart exponent of western exploration was Ted Link, an American-born geologist who had joined Bosworth's expedition in 1919 as a graduate student at the University of Chicago. During the following summer Link and his group discovered oil near Fort Norman in the Northwest Territories. Although the output was small, Link believed the formations in the area held great promise. "This is the biggest oil field in the world," he told a reporter from Edmonton, "stretching all the way to the Arctic coast."[3] Imperial followed up on this discovery and developed five wells around Fort Norman in the 1920s, but ultimately decided that the site was too remote and the problems of transportation too challenging to merit further expansion.

During the Second World War, however, the US Army approached Imperial with a proposal to reopen the wells near Fort Norman. Fearing a Japanese invasion of the Alaskan islands in 1941–42, the Americans wanted to build a pipeline from Norman Wells to Whitehorse in the Yukon to connect up with an equally ambitious highway between the Yukon and Alaska. When the Japanese threat receded the project foundered amidst US congressional hearings featuring charges of waste, bureaucratic mismanagement, and the malign influence of oil companies. Although the pipeline and the "Alcan highway" were completed, the refinery built at Whitehorse fell into disuse after the war.

Link's hopes for a massive expansion of Imperial's exploration in western Canada were frustrated in the 1920s; nevertheless, he continued to play an important role in the company, and became chief geologist in 1946. By this time pressures were once again mounting for another effort to find oil in western Canada. Postwar demand for auto fuel was sure to increase; the cost of importing oil from the United States was expected to rise with the weakened Canadian dollar; and International Petroleum's wells in Colombia were likely to be nationalized by 1950, cutting off that already limited source. Link became part of a team headed by Dr. O.B. Hopkins of Imperial's board of directors to decide on a strategy for exploration.

Imperial's president Hewetson laid out the alternatives: if the exploration option failed, the company would turn to an alternative-fuel technology, the Fischer-Tropsch process developed in Germany during the 1920s that could convert natural gas to oil, which would of course be more costly and still leave Imperial dependent on imported oil. Hopkins's group produced a report that endorsed one more exploratory venture in Alberta, using improved seismic technology and probing deeper than previous drilling, which had focused on the "Cretaceous" level (3000–4000 feet) from the age of dinosaurs to what was (hopefully) a "Devonian reef" at about 5000 feet containing the remains of much older organic matter. The Leduc area was actually on the edge of the prospective "Devonian reef" but early tests revealed "anomalies," and drilling ultimately led to success.[4]

After Leduc

Leduc's success posed as many challenges to Imperial as failure might have, all of them expensive. There was no refinery near Leduc. As the oil sands companies would discover a generation later, the oil was remote from its markets and transport costs would be formidable. With other companies flocking to Alberta, Imperial would have to expand its exploration investment to keep ahead. Most of Imperial's net earnings over the previous decades had been passed on to its shareholders (principally Exxon); but now Exxon was not prepared to provide capital on the scale required—it had even larger demands on its resources to develop big new fields in South America and the Middle East.

Hewetson moved quickly to address the refining and transport issues. Imperial bought (back) the Whitehorse refinery built in the Second World War by the US Army, dismantled it and shipped it to Edmonton—by July 1948 it was in operation. The Canadian government quickly approved an interprovincial pipeline that would ultimately carry Albertan oil to Wisconsin and then ship it to Imperial's largest refinery in Sarnia, Ontario. The Interprovincial Pipeline Company (now Enbridge) was moving oil by the autumn of 1950. For Imperial, however, the costs of moving so rapidly were high, and financing the projects became the central issue facing the board of directors.

The first step, in the autumn of 1947, was to issue $24 million (CAD) in debenture bonds—a first for Imperial, which had relied on Jersey Standard for financing since 1899. The Royal Bank of Canada quickly took up the subscription, but it proved at best a stopgap. Before the end of the year Hewetson was seeking a longer-term solution, which led to a review of Imperial's other investments and subsidiaries.

The largest of these was International Petroleum with its oilfields in Peru and Colombia. In this case Imperial's dependence on Jersey Standard proved to be a blessing, for the parent company took over the South American properties for $80 million (CAD). In retrospect this was a puzzling decision for Jersey Standard: Colombia was already threatening to nationalize IPC's fields, and would do so in 1951; Peru followed suit a decade later. For Imperial, however, this was a win-win situation, as it could disengage from increasingly troubled overseas operations and focus on developing its Canadian fields.

A second subsidiary and also a somewhat difficult one was Royalite in Alberta. Imperial had taken over that company in 1921 to give it a surreptitious foothold in the Turner Valley oil and gas fields. Although Royalite struck oil in Turner Valley in 1924, for various reasons—the cost of transportation to central Canada, the objections of Alberta politicians to "exporting" their oil—it remained principally a supplier of the local western regional market. In recent years Royalite had become almost a competitor with Imperial in the search for oil beyond Turner Valley. In 1948 Imperial tried to buy out the minority shareholders in Royalite in order to get better control over its operations. When this move failed, Imperial simply sold off its interests for $14 million (CAD).[5]

Today Imperial Oil remains one of the largest oil companies in Canada. Exxon-Mobil still holds more than a two-thirds ownership of the company. In critical ways, however, it changed substantially in the aftermath of Leduc. Imperial became a truly integrated oil company, with its own domestic source of supply. It became more "Canadian," jettisoning the entangling commitments overseas that had been a key feature of its history before 1947. While it remained part of the Exxon network, these features returned Imperial to its original national role. At the same time, Imperial became more "entrepreneurial"—before 1947 many of the executives were managers involved in running a company that functioned like a utility: refining, transporting, and selling oil products that came from somewhere else. After Leduc, Imperial focused on exploration and development of resources, and leadership passed to those whose perspectives were shaped by experiences in the new oil fields of Alberta, and later the Arctic and the oil sands. For that generation, the exploitation of Canada's northern environment became essential to the future of Imperial Oil.

• PART ONE •

FOUNDATIONS 1860–1917

1

ORIGINS

Gesner

Abraham Gesner seemed destined to failure. The son of a Loyalist forced to emigrate from New York to Nova Scotia after the American Revolution, Gesner had tried his hand at horse trading, only to see his investment go down with a ship off Bermuda; Gesner then turned to farming and narrowly avoided debtors' prison. His father-in-law financed an education in medicine at St. Bartholomew's Hospital in London, England; but Gesner did not enjoy the practice. An enthusiastic, self-taught rockhound, in 1837 he wangled a position as "geologist for New Brunswick," but his estimates of the province's coal seams were found to be overly optimistic and he lost the job after his patron, the lieutenant-general of New Brunswick, was removed from power. But Gesner had two redeeming qualities: an insatiable curiosity about the natural world—a common characteristic of Victorian-era gentlemen—and ability as a public lecturer, which enabled him to earn fees to offset losses in other pursuits.

In 1846 Gesner delivered a series of lectures at Charlottetown, Prince Edward Island that covered his geological research in that province and assorted other topics, including the possibility of developing an alternative source of illumination to replace lamps using whale oil and coal oil. Whaling, particularly in New England, was booming, based on the distillation of oil from sperm whales. But Nova Scotia was a minor participant in the industry, and prices were rising for consumers as the depletion of the whale population drove the fleets further afield, into the South Atlantic and beyond. Since the early 1800s a gas distilled from coal had been used in England for illumination, but Gesner believed he could produce a brighter and less hazardous fuel. He maintained that a gas distillate based on a bitumen called "albertite" that he had discovered in New Brunswick could produce a cheaper and more efficient source of lighting which he designated "kerosene," and he presented the audience with a demonstration of his experiments.

Back in Halifax Gesner continued his research—focused, critically, on the use of liquid fuel rather than gas for lighting. His work in this new field was supported by the British Admiral Lord Thomas Cochrane who arranged for supplies of "pitch" (asphaltum) to be shipped to Halifax from Trinidad. In 1850 Gesner and Cochrane set up a company to provide gas lighting in Halifax; but at this point bad luck intervened again. A rival group, the Halifax Gas Company, acquired the franchise, while at the same time he was blocked from mining bitumen in New Brunswick by a coalition of coal owners in that province, including some who had earlier backed his enterprise. He had, however, had the foresight to file as well for a patent in the US, and in 1853 he moved to New York and was hired by the North American Gas Light Company, to produce kerosene based on his process. Gesner designed and built the first kerosene refinery in North America the following year.

But misfortune continued to plague him: James Young, a scientist in Scotland, claimed an earlier US patent to a process similar to Gesner's kerosene; additionally, Gesner had turned over his patent rights to the company and found himself sidelined. In 1857 he lost his position with North American Gas Light Company, replaced by Luther Atwood who had worked with Young. He returned to Nova Scotia where he wrote *A Practical Treatise on Petroleum, Coal and Other Distilled Oils*, published in 1860, which he came to regard as his most lasting contribution. Thereafter he set himself up as a consultant, which took him—among other places—to the petroleum fields that were being exploited in what is now Ontario.[1]

Oil Springs

In 1849, Thomas Sterry Hunt of the Geological Survey of Canada noted the presence of "asphaltum or mineral pitch" in swampy areas of Enniskillen Township. The township was located in Lambton County in the southwestern corner of "Canada West" as it was then designated. As was the case with Gesner's work in New Brunswick, the geological survey was intended, in part, to identify resources with commercial potential; and Hunt's associate, Alexander Murray, provided a more detailed examination of the area over the next two years. The material in the "gum beds" of Enniskillen had been used by the Ojibway in the area to caulk boats and possibly for medicinal purposes, but colonial settlement was sparse because the area was not considered good for farming. The Ojibway had never ceded claims to the land (or its subsurface rights) and would later challenge their exploitation, although by then most of the resources there had been depleted.

Murray was cautious in projecting the economic benefits of the gum beds, but his work attracted the attention of Charles and Henry Tripp of Woodstock, Ontario. They acquired a lot in Enniskillen in 1852, and sent samples for analysis of the asphaltum there to Thomas Antisell, a chemist in Washington, DC who had played a role in procuring the contentious patent for James Young. At the same time they petitioned the provincial government for a charter to establish the International Mining and Manufacturing Company, which was to be capitalized at 1,250 (British) pounds sterling with seven partners, including two Americans. The charter was not issued until 1854, but in the meantime they had expanded their land purchases and begun operations that involved literally digging up the surface bitumen to be processed (minimally) into asphalt for caulking and paving material for roads. Although Antisell's report indicated that the bitumen they were mining was suitable for refining into "fluids and gas for illuminating purposes," the Tripps continued to focus on selling asphalt in a solid state, which proved costly as the Enniskillen oil fields were distant from markets for their products in Hamilton and London: roads were poor and there was no railway connection in the area until 1858.

By this time the Tripps, heavily in debt, had been forced out of business. One of their creditors, James Miller Williams, a successful carriage and wagon maker in Hamilton, bought up the entire 600 acres of gum beds that the Tripps had accumulated and commenced operations there in 1857, with Charles Tripp now working for him. Within a year Williams and Tripp were drawing petroleum in a liquid form beneath the surface, which Williams shipped to Hamilton where he established a refinery in

FIGURE 1.1. Drilling operations in Lambton County, Ontario, 1870s. Glenbow Archive IP-1a-71, Imperial Oil Collection.

1858. Bragging rights to the "first oil well" have been accorded to Williams as his company was bringing in subsurface petroleum for refining at least a year before "Colonel" Edwin Drake successfully drilled his first well in Titusville, Pennsylvania in 1859.

In 1860 Williams incorporated his venture as the Canadian Oil Company, capitalized at $42,000 (CAD), in which he held the controlling shares. By this time he had accumulated over 1,400 acres in what was now being called "Oil Springs." Gesner, who was in Hamilton in 1861, may have acted as a consultant in the development of the refinery there. In the following year his company's entry at the International Exhibition in London won two gold medals, which Williams expected would boost exports outside Canada. Williams's success ignited the first "oil boom" in Canada as hundreds of prospectors flocked to Oil Springs, many of who found they had to lease mineral rights from Williams. By the middle of 1861 over 100 wells had been undertaken in Enniskillen, although few were actually producing much oil. In the following year several producers began following the lead of Pennsylvania oilmen by drilling into the limestone several hundred feet beneath the surface. Drillers discovered several "gushers" producing hundreds of barrels per day, encouraging even more activity.

But problems were emerging. Transportation remained a challenge. Although the Great Western Railway had extended a line to Sarnia, producers in Oil Springs still had to find ways of carrying their crude twelve miles to the railhead. As new wells came in, production outran the capacity of local markets. Crude oil prices fluctuated wildly, falling from 70 cents to 10 cents per barrel in 1861–62. This situation was aggravated by a short-lived oil boom in the nearby community of Bothwell. Producers had to store their excess oil in tanks and barrels, which were often so poorly built that much oil was lost. The oil itself contained impurities, particularly sulphur, which refiners could not eliminate (although Williams claimed to have done so in 1861). Imported kerosene from Pennsylvania made inroads as consumers in British North America rejected locally produced "skunk oil." This issue would continue to plague the Canadian industry for the next forty years.[2]

Then in 1863 the boom at Oil Springs suddenly collapsed as wells began to dry up. Crude prices began to climb again, to more than $1.00 per barrel. Activity shifted to another part of Enniskillen Township, the vicinity of Bear Creek, which would soon be called "Petrolia" and was officially incorporated as a village with that name in 1866. Conditions in Petrolia were somewhat different from Oil Springs: the area of potential development was substantially larger: at twenty-six square miles it was more than ten times the size of the Oil Springs oil fields. But oil wells had to be drilled deeper, between 500 and 1000 feet, while at Oil Springs gushers had been brought up at 200 to 400 feet; more investment was required for equipment. Additionally, some of the more successful producers in Oil Springs had already been acquiring land in Petrolia, notably John H. Fairbank, an American emigrant who emerged as a dominant figure in the town, establishing a general store, supplying equipment to other drillers, and opening a bank as well as producing and refining his own oil. In 1866 Fairbank played a major role in building a spur line to connect Petrolia to the Great Western Railway, a boon to all the producers.

The development of Petrolia was more orderly than at Oil Springs, although the boom and bust atmosphere persisted. When Benjamin King, working for an oil company from Saint Catherine's, struck oil in Petrolia he ignited a new run with a horde of new investors, including John Carling of the London brewing dynasty and a number of Americans from neighbouring Michigan joining in. In 1865 crude oil prices had risen to $5.00 per barrel, surging even higher but then dropping rapidly to less than a dollar per barrel in 1867.[3]

The Refiners

During this period, the refining sector of the industry began to consolidate. In 1858 James M. Williams had established a refinery in Hamilton; in part this was to enable him to develop measures to reduce the sulphur content of Oil Springs crude through the addition of sulphuric acid in the distillation process. This proved to be a short-lived solution, however, as the effects of the treatment diminished when the lamp oil was stored for more than a few weeks. But locating in a larger city was useful, because he could get coopers and stavers to prepare barrels, and with the railway line Hamilton was closer to potential markets.

In the next year Williams joined up with William Spencer, an aspiring refiner from Woodstock, to build a plank road from Oil Springs to the railhead of the Great Western at Wyoming. Both participants would benefit, as the crude oil would be carried to their refineries in locations better suited to reach urban consumers. Within a short time Spencer had moved his operations to London, which was on the Great Western line, and formed a partnership with the Waterman brothers—clothiers from Germany who later split from him and set up their own operation. Refining at this stage was not a particularly capital-intensive operation, so competition thrived in the first decade of the industry. But the booms and busts of the 1860s winnowed the ranks of refiners, and by 1870 the six largest companies were located near London.

Petroleum refining was not exactly a community-friendly activity. Early refineries were hazardous: during the 1860s at least one refinery in Petrolia had burned down and another had exploded. The refining of sulphur-laden crude produced an exceptionally offensive odour that observers at the time likened to a "sea of rotten eggs;" furthermore the refiners, having extracted lamp oil, dumped the remaining waste material in local creeks and waterways. For obvious reasons city dwellers objected to these activities, and the London refiners, seeking to avoid municipal regulations, located beyond urban boundaries whenever possible and resisted efforts at annexation that would result in regulation.[4]

The problem of sulphur continued to bedevil the Canadian oil industry. The US market, which was supplied by lamp oil refined from "sweet" Pennsylvania crude, was off limits. In 1862 Canadian oil was banned from the ports of Liverpool and London in England, and ships carrying it were ordered to keep away from vessels with food cargoes. The limitation imposed on exports was a major cause (although not the only one) of the boom and bust cycle in the Canadian oil business. In 1868, Spencer and a neighbouring refiner in London, William Peters, discovered a new process developed in France that would "sweeten" Petrolia oil by adding an alkaline solution of lead oxide, called "litharge" to the refining. Surprisingly, they shared the process (at a price) with other London refiners, and within two years Canadian oil exports rose from 3,500 barrels to 130,000 barrels, representing more than half of the industry's output, and peaking at about twice that level in 1873. This foothold in the English and European markets provided a degree of stability that had not existed before. The litharge treatment did not in fact address the underlying problem of sulphur content in Canadian crude oil, but it did at least salvage the floundering Canadian oil industry for the next five years.[5]

The advent of Canadian Confederation in 1867 offered an opportunity to address another issue: the continuing threat of American competition. In 1862 the government of Canada (then comprising Ontario and Quebec) had imposed an import duty on kerosene, which extended to crude oil two years later; but this did not cover the Maritime provinces. The new federal government established duties of 15 cents per "wine gallon" on refined oil imports (including naptha and kerosene), although this was offset by an excise tax on refined products exported from Canada. Over the following decade, as its export markets shrank, the industry would become increasingly dependent on tariffs and other barriers to expansion of the "Standard octopus" to the south.[6]

Relative stability encouraged the entry of new and more ambitious investors, most notably Jacob Englehart. Born in Cleveland (John D. Rockefeller's hometown) in 1847, Englehart had what respectable Victorian gentlemen regarded as a "shady career" before he turned up in Petrolia. In

New York, he had been involved with Solomon Sonneborn and others as a whisky salesman—peddling alcohol was a somewhat disreputable and occasionally illegal activity, and in later years Englehart took some pains to suppress his checkered past; but support from Sonneborn and other Jewish business figures in New York would continue to play a role in his ventures into Canadian oil. Still in his teens but articulate, nattily attired and sporting a Van Dyke beard, Englehart went to the oil fields and then to London where he arranged to build a refinery, presumably with financial help from Sonneborn who was then hiding in Canada from US revenue agents investigating charges that he had evaded excise taxes on his whisky sales during the Civil War. Englehart also began buying kerosene from other refiners to be sold through Sonneborn's export house.

Two years later Englehart's refinery was damaged by explosions. Undeterred, he rebuilt it and then joined forces with Ebenezer Higgins of Chicago in an effort to control all the refiners of oil in Canada. Higgins, backed by financiers "notorious to the whiskey trade"[7] from the United States, set out to lease fifty-two refineries in Ontario (including the major ones in London) and simply close them down, hoping to force up the price of refined kerosene by restricting them to production intended only for export. This scheme apparently unravelled: some major refiners joined in, but others did not, and even those who participated simply stockpiled their inventories for sale after the leases expired—although they recognized the benefits of the temporary shutdown, and used the opportunity to improve their refining operations. Higgins apparently made a profit from his venture, but the timing was bad for establishing an enduring cartel as the kerosene trade was picking up in 1869. In the wake of Higgins's departure a group of London refiners set up a cartel to allocate production quotas and coordinate sales, but it lasted little more than a year.

Higgins and Englehart, however, were not the only players contemplating a consolidation of the industry. Oil producers in Oil Springs and Petrolia had been experimenting with cartel arrangements since 1862, but each time agreements to suspend operations fell apart once crude prices began to rise. In 1867–68 Fairbank mounted the most vigorous effort along these lines, and at one point his Crude Oil Association controlled one-third of the output from Petrolia, but once prices rose to $2.25 per barrel, the organization dissolved. A more successful cartel was the Lambton Crude Oil Partnership formed in 1871 with more than 100 Petrolia producers, including Fairbank, as well as some refiners and marketers across Ontario and Quebec, which helped to stabilize domestic prices. When Higgins and Englehart set out to dominate the refining sector, Fairbank financially backed James M. Williams of Hamilton in establishing a new company, the Carbon Oil Company, which would operate outside the control of the London group. In 1871 Fairbank sold his shares in the Carbon Oil Company and set up a new refinery in Petrolia.

After the debacle with Higgins, Englehart sought an alliance with Herman and Isaac Waterman, former partners with William Spencer.

Meanwhile Jonas Sonneborn, uncle of Jacob's former New York associate Solomon, acquired the Carbon Oil Works at a knock-down price after a fire destroyed its refinery. He then formed an alliance with the Watermans and Englehart that eventually controlled two-thirds of the exports of refined oil from Canada, channelled through a New York office of a company run by Solomon Sonneborn and his partner, Abraham Dryfoos. Although Canadian kerosene was still disdained as inferior to the American product, the demand for lamp oil was growing rapidly in Europe in the aftermath of the Franco-Prussian War of 1870–71. Exports doubled between 1870 and 1873; in that year 8 million wine gallons of refined oil went overseas, more than twice the amount sold on the Canadian domestic market.[8]

Crisis

All these dreams of avarice came crashing down in 1873 when the Canadian oil export market virtually collapsed. In part, this was the result of an economic depression that affected the entire industrialized world. But it also was the result of the discovery of large new oil fields in Pennsylvania, which fuelled a strong export drive by American companies, particularly the emerging leader, Standard Oil. Exports of US crude and refined oil almost doubled, rising from 3.4 million barrels in 1871 to 5.4 million barrels in 1873 with 96 per cent headed for Europe, principally Britain, France, and Germany, and more than 90 per cent refined oil. Canada had always been a small player in these markets, but access to them was vital to the industry. Between 1868 and 1873 overall Canadian production rose from 190,000 barrels to 365,000 barrels; in 1874 production shrank to 165,000 barrels and did not regain its earlier scale until the 1880s. As production in Petrolia tailed off, experienced workers—the "hard oilers"—departed, some for distant, even exotic, climes: Central Europe, Mexico, and the Dutch East Indies.[9]

The impact of the downturn was hardest on the companies most tied to exports. The Carbon Oil Company careened toward bankruptcy and Jonas Sonneborn was pursued by creditors accusing him of fraud, as well as US tax collectors. Englehart wisely cut his ties to Sonneborn & Dryfoos and adopted a low profile on the Canadian oil scene for a time. His large London refinery ended up in the hands of the London Refining Company, a partnership that included Frederick A. Fitzgerald, a grocery wholesaler who had gone into oil refining in the 1860s; William Spencer and his son; Thomas and Edward Hodgins, barrel makers for the industry; and John Minhinnick, William English, and John Geary—all of whom would end up as participants in the formation of Imperial Oil six years later. Fairbank challenged this latest foray by establishing the Home Oil Company that combined Petrolia producers and refiners, joined by Williams in Hamilton. The "London Ring" was weakened by both competition from Fairbank and their failure to bring all the London refiners, including the Watermans, into their tent.

In both London and Petrolia, the tactics being deployed by Standard Oil and its rivals in the United States were being observed with interest. The strategic role of railways and pipelines in reaching markets there was becoming apparent. In Canada the Great Western Railway had been operating in the oil region since 1859; and, thanks to Fairbank, the spur line to Petrolia had been established in 1866. The Great Western had a virtual monopoly in transporting oil from Petrolia to London and a dominant role in shipping refined oil to the eastern cities for many years. The company had been careful to maintain a rate structure that would ensure a modest profit without inviting competition from other carriers—particularly the Grand Trunk Railway, which had a line running through London to Windsor. The economic downturn of 1873, however, disrupted this cozy situation and ignited a rate war between the two lines. The London refiners found themselves in a position of leverage in terms of dealing with the railways. In 1874 the Great Western slashed rates on eastbound cargoes of kerosene, but retained a higher rate on shipments of crude oil from Petrolia to London and on direct shipments of illuminating oil from Petrolia.

In that town these policies were perceived to be the result of collusion between the railway and the London refiners, which inaugurated a search for alternative ways of reaching markets. Even before the rate changes, two groups of railway promoters had been seeking charters to challenge the Great Western's position in southwest Ontario. At this point Petrolia oilmen, led by Fairbank, set out to provide the capital needed to achieve their goal. The first railway group, the Erie & Huron, backed out of their project in 1874 when hoped-for provincial subsidies were not approved. The Petrolia group then turned to a more ambitious project: to build a pipeline that would link the oil fields to the Grand Trunk, bypassing the London refiners. Although this dramatic initiative did not occur, a second railway proposal emerged—the Sarnia, Chatham & Erie—that received financial and political backing from Fairbank and his Petrolia associates. Its charter was approved in 1876, and the line inaugurated operations two years later with great fanfare, linking Petrolia to another main line carrier: the Canadian Southern Railway.

At this propitious moment, Jacob Englehart reappeared on the scene. He had now found a new partner: Isaac Guggenheim. Although the Guggenheims had yet to achieve the status of multinational mining barons, they were a wealthy family with a wide range of investments in Europe and the United States, and in 1876 Isaac married Carrie Sonneborn, Solomon's daughter. Backed by $25,000 (USD) of Guggenheim capital, Englehart acquired the defunct Carbon Oil works in Petrolia and rebuilt it as the Silver Star Refinery, with state-of-the-art equipment and a strongly competitive position against the London Refinery Company, boasting a 100,000-barrel reserve capacity. But Englehart's ambitions ranged much wider. He contemplated the amalgamation of the entire Canadian oil industry, much as Rockefeller was undertaking in the United States.[10]

By 1877 the London Refining Company had managed to drive most of the marginal refiners out of business and another effort was mounted to establish stability in the market. The two major surviving London companies (London Refining and Waterman Brothers) entered an agreement with Englehart and Fairbank in Petrolia to set a minimum price for refined kerosene, although the participants would continue to purchase their own crude oil and market their own products. Not surprisingly, this initiative invited a new rival into the refining field, the Mutual Oil Company, led by William English, a former partner in the London Refining Company. More seriously, the "stabilization" of prices was highly unpopular with the consuming public, particularly those in the more distant markets of the Maritimes and British Columbia. Partly in response to this ire, the federal government—under the Liberals who were, at least in theory, committed to "free trade"—reduced import duties on refined oil from 15 cents to 6 cents per wine gallon: between 1877 and 1879 imports of kerosene almost doubled from 570,000 to more than one million wine gallons per year. To the consternation of the refiners' cartel, this increase affected their largest markets in Quebec and Ontario as well as the outlying provinces.

Curiously, the tariff reductions did not extend to crude oil imports, which may have reflected the fact that Liberal Prime Minister Alexander Mackenzie was also MP from Lambton County, the seat of petroleum production; in any case, relatively little crude was imported from the United States. But this measure did little to assuage the dissatisfaction of refiners now leaning toward the Conservatives under John A. Macdonald, who was promising a more protectionist "National Policy." Although swept into office in September 1878, Macdonald was mindful not to be openly associated with the reviled "Oil Lobby." To that end his government introduced, rather surreptitiously, a "non-tariff barrier" in the form of a revision of inspection fees that had been imposed on both domestic and imported refined oil products since 1868. Although the fees were increased for all refined products, they were differentiated so that fees on domestic oil were set at 10 cents, and those on imports at 30 cents.

This measure was exacerbated by a more complex form of discrimination: the combustible potential of refined illuminating oil had been an issue from the early years of the industry, with the great Chicago fire of 1871 cited as an example of the danger. Since the late 1860s governments in the US and Canada had been imposing what was called a "flash test" to determine the temperature at which "an oil gives off enough vapours to form an explosive mixture . . . when ignited by a small flame." At this temperature oil used in a kerosene lamp could catch fire. In 1868 the "flash test" was set in Canada at 115 degrees (F). Under the revised inspection law, the requirement was established that domestic kerosene had to withstand heating up to 105 degrees (F) while imported oil had to meet a standard of 130 degrees (F). The combination of the differential fees and the revised flash test requirements raised the cost of imported oil by 5 cents per gallon.[11]

The government soon came under fire for introducing a protectionist policy under the guise of science, and the law was eventually repealed in 1881, although the inspection fee differential remained. For the refiners, however, the promises of the "National Policy" were not being fulfilled, and south of the border John D. Rockefeller was assembling a powerful new coalition under the Standard Oil banner. After a decade of experiments at controlling the market through agreements and partnerships, the Canadian refiners were still divided, vulnerable to surging American imports. Englehart, with his Guggenheim money, had the second-largest refinery and the largest stake in the creation of a stable environment for the oil business. He was protected against both American invasion and continuing competition among refiners and producers in Canada. In many accounts of the establishment of Imperial Oil, Englehart is credited with introducing the "Rockefeller plan" to replace the unstable cartels with a tight corporate organization of the Canadian oil industry. But Englehart actually anticipated rather than emulated Rockefeller: in 1879–80 the American oilman was still in the process of trying to set up a system of centralized control over the sprawling US oil industry, and the Standard Oil Trust did not emerge until 1881.

In some respects the Canadian legal environment was better suited than the United States to consolidation. In Canada the federal government could issue corporate charters with national scope, while in the US Standard Oil had to build a network across companies chartered in different states. At the same time that Imperial Oil was being formed, an American named Charles Sise was procuring a federal charter in Canada for the Bell Telephone Company of Boston. Canada's Bank Act of 1871 authorized banks to establish branches across the country; in the US even the largest banks were operating under state charters. One of the features that impressed the executives of Standard Oil about Imperial Oil in 1899 was the extraordinary range of powers it held under its charter.

In April 1880 Englehart and the owners of the largest London refineries agreed to form a co-partnership along the lines of the earlier London Refining Company structure. Over the summer they continued to meet, and in September took the further step of undertaking a joint stock enterprise to be capitalized at $500,000 (CAD), distributed in 5000 shares at $100 per share. In addition, each of the original eighteen shareholders contributed to a cash reserve of $25,000 (CAD). The shareholders pooled their resources, which included a dozen refineries, among them the two largest—Englehart's Silver Star in Petrolia and the Victor Refinery in London (which had originally been built by Englehart, and then taken over by Fitzgerald and London Refining). They thus controlled 85 per cent of the refining capacity in Canada, in addition to oil wells in

FIGURE 1.3. Frederick A. Fitzgerald (1890). Glenbow Archive IP-26-5-5c, Imperial Oil Collection.

Petrolia and marketing operations. The charter authorized Imperial Oil Ltd. to "find, produce, refine and distribute petroleum and its production throughout Canada."[12]

The shareholders included (in addition to Englehart and Fitzgerald): the Waterman brothers, Isaac and Herman; William Spencer and his sons, William and Charles; Thomas and Edward Hodgins, who built oil barrels for the refiners; John Geary, Joseph Fallows, and John Minhinnick, partners with Fitzgerald in London Refining; plus William English and John Walker of the former Mutual Oil Association—Walker was also a partner with Thomas Smallwood in a London-based company manufacturing sulphuric acid. The largest shareholders were Englehart, who held 577 shares (20 per cent) of the 2,928 issued, and Fitzgerald, who held 292 shares. Curiously, Fitzgerald was named the first president, and Englehart the vice president, although Englehart was obviously the driving force behind the merger. The board of directors included Isaac Waterman, John Walker, and Thomas Hodgins.[13]

Notably absent from Imperial Oil were two of the most prominent figures in the Canadian oil industry: James Williams and John Fairbank. By the 1870s Williams was involved in a wide range of businesses in Hamilton, including railways, banks, and insurance companies. He had also entered politics—as an alderman for Hamilton, and later as a (Liberal) member of the Ontario legislature. He passed on ownership of the Canadian Oil Company to his son, Charles James Williams, who continued to run it until 1891 when he retired and it was sold to Imperial Oil. Fairbank sold his refinery in Petrolia to the Bushnell Company (a Standard Oil affiliate) in 1896. He continued to maintain his interest in production, and when he died in 1914 he owned 485 operating wells. By that time he was the wealthiest man in Petrolia, with a wide range of businesses, and served as mayor of Petrolia and MP for Lambton East in the 1880s.[14]

Neither Williams nor Fairbank posed a threat to Imperial Oil, but the fact that they remained outside its orbit of control signalled an underlying weakness in the new order of the Canadian oil industry. Imperial never established complete domination of either the producers or the refiners. More seriously, the protectionist measures of the government—which were half-hearted at best—did not impede the entry of American competition. Imperial Oil did not regain the foothold in export markets that had bolstered the Canadian industry in the early 1870s. Within a decade after its formation, Imperial would face new competitors on its home turf, backed this time by a formidable and well-organized juggernaut in the United States—which was a highly desirable situation for the consuming public.

WHEN EMPIRES COLLIDE

Rockefeller and Standard Oil

Conditions in the western Pennsylvania oil fields in the 1860s–70s had much in common with Oil Springs and Petrolia. Although drilling to reach the "rock oil" had been necessary from the beginning, the costs of entry were low, and Drake's success at Titusville in 1859 inaugurated a similar oil rush with predictable consequences: overproduction, the rapid depletion of some of the early well sites, and dramatic swings in the price of crude oil that persisted through the first decade of the industry. The scale of operations and markets were larger in the United States, particularly in the aftermath of the Civil War.

Techniques of production and refining resembled those in Canada in the early years, featuring many small operators relying on relatively simple methods of drilling and distilling. The "Oil Region" of Pennsylvania was also distant from potential markets and dependent on teamsters carrying rough-hewn barrels of crude oil at high prices, although some producers found ways to cut costs by building pipelines from their remote wellheads. By the mid-1860s the refining sector was changing: fractional distilling of crude oil was being replaced by techniques of "cracking" that involved the application of higher degrees of heat, provided by steam power. The application of sulphuric acid and caustic soda reduced impurities and produced more and better quality kerosene. Fractional distilling also produced by-products that included naptha and lubricating oil. Gasoline was still regarded as a waste residue. These technologies were more costly but enabled a much larger rate of production—where early refineries could produce at best 500 barrels per week, those using the new processes could exceed 2,000 barrels per week and by 1866 the largest refineries were able to handle 500 barrels per day.

As in Canada, big refineries thrived in cities connected to the population centres of the east coast, particularly New York and Pennsylvania, and by the mid-1860s New York itself had emerged as a mecca for refining, with one of the largest and most cost-effective producers, the Charles Pratt Company. Pittsburgh, which was close to the "Oil Regions" and had ties to the coal industry, also appeared to be a leader in the refining sector. Yet by the end of the decade a new challenger had come forward from an unlikely quarter: Cleveland, Ohio—and the leading figure was John D. Rockefeller.[1]

Rockefeller was in his early twenties and regarded as little more than a "clerk'" by the Clark brothers, his partners in the hardware business in Cleveland, when he first visited the Pennsylvania oil region in 1861. Although appalled by the anarchic conditions in the oil fields, Rockefeller was intrigued by the potential value of the kerosene industry. Two years later Rockefeller persuaded the Clarks to join him and Samuel Andrews, a self-taught refiner, in setting up the Excelsior refinery in Cleveland—in 1865 he bought out the Clarks and he and Andrews built a second refinery, called the Standard. Rockefeller brought in other partners, including Henry Flagler, an experienced grain merchant, and (perhaps more crucially) Flagler's father-in-law, Samuel Harkness, who had the deep pockets Rockefeller needed to finance his ambitious plans. By that time he had detailed his brother, William, to move to New York to manage kerosene sales on the east coast and the promising export market in Europe.

The post-Civil War era in the United States was a time of optimism for the business community, but for those involved in the oil industry, this optimism was chastened by the boom-and-bust atmosphere: the volatility of prices and costs in the oil regions as producers and refiners proliferated. The period was marked by the rise and fall of numerous cartels formed by producers, pipeline operators, and refiners to bring stability to the market. Rockefeller shared that desire for stability, but took it a step further: he envisioned an industry subjected to centralized control at every phase, achieving efficiencies and economies of scale that would benefit consumers and manufacturers alike—all under the benign control of Rockefeller.

Graham D. Taylor

LAKE HURON
ONTARIO
SARNIA
ST. CLAIR R.
PETROLIA
OIL SPRINGS
LONDON
BOTHWELL
NEW YORK
LAKE ST. CLAIR
CUBA SPRING
LAKE ERIE
OIL CREEK
TITUSVILLE
CLEVELAND
OIL CITY
ALLEGHENY R.
PENNSYLVANIA
OHIO
TARENTUM
PITTSBURGH
WHERE THE OIL INDUSTRY BEGAN
IN NORTH AMERICA

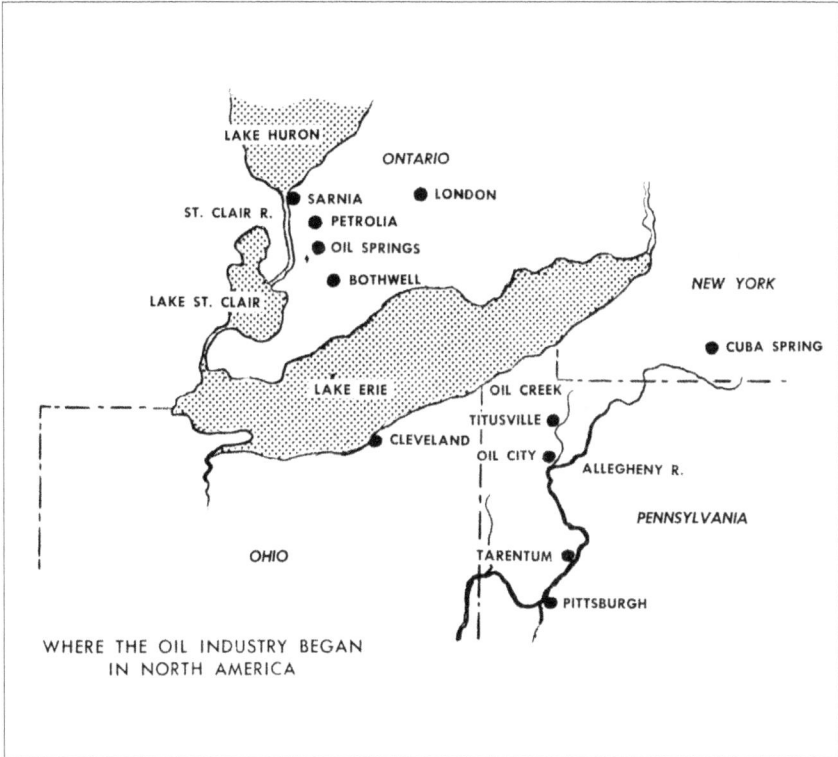

MAP 2.1. Oil in the US and Canada, 1860, G.A. Purdy for Imperial Oil. G.A. Purdy, *Petroleum: Prehistoric to Petrochemicals*. Vancouver: Copp Clark 1957, p. 21. Courtesy of the Glenbow Archive, Imperial Oil Collection.

To achieve these goals, he brought a range of talents: from his father, a travelling salesman, he acquired skills at persuasion and negotiation; from his mother, he was imbued with iron self-discipline and a conviction that his aims reflected God's will.

By 1867 Cleveland was linked to the urban markets of the east coast by multiple rail lines, which provided Rockefeller and his partners with great opportunities. The major railroads—the New York Central under the Vanderbilts, the Erie under Jay Gould, and the Pennsylvania under Thomas Scott—were locked in a struggle for control of transportation links between Chicago and the northeast. Each of these railroads was prepared to offer special deals to large shippers to attract their business or keep them from straying to competitors. Rockefeller skilfully played off the roads against one another, extracting rebates on posted shipping fees from each one—the Erie went so far as to build a special depot in New Jersey for oil shipped from the Standard refineries in Cleveland. With transport costs under control, Rockefeller could buy out other refiners, enhancing his bargaining position with the railroads. The development of tanker cars—replacing barrels, and owned by Rockefeller-connected companies—contributed to falling costs and a larger share for Cleveland in the refinery sector. In 1869 Rockefeller took a further step toward achieving his vision, setting up Standard Oil as a joint stock company, capitalized at $1 million (USD).

But Standard's success attracted more entrants into petroleum refining, and oil producers continued to proliferate, which stalled efforts to stabilize crude oil prices. The railroads were seeking ways of ending their internecine and costly warfare. These circumstances set the scene for the first effort to control the industry as a whole. The scheme, the South Improvement Company, was concocted by Tom Scott of the Pennsylvania Railroad in 1872. It would bring the major competing railroads and the largest oil shippers together into a cartel that would set prices for crude and refined oil and transport costs to benefit those who joined at the expense of everyone else. Rockefeller did not originate this idea, and it conflicted with his preference for centralized control; but he emerged as the leading figure in planning for the operation, and he became the public face of the scheme. Premature release of the new freight fee structure of the South Improvement Company initiated widespread protests throughout the oil region of Pennsylvania; ultimately the railroad leaders retreated in the face of political pressure. The South Improvement venture never actually got off the ground, but it shaped the public perception of Rockefeller and Standard Oil for the next generation, in Canada as well as the United States.

After the South Improvement debacle, Rockefeller resumed his strategy of achieving an integrated oil industry through expansion of Standard Oil rather than cartelization. When Scott tried to undercut him by backing the Empire Transportation Company, which would build pipelines from the Oil Region to the east coast markets, Rockefeller retaliated by building his own pipelines and using every legal tactic possible to block

Empire. By the end of the 1870s Standard Oil had formed alliances with the major refiners in New York, Philadelphia, and Pittsburgh, and had driven many of those who rejected Standard's overtures out of business. Rockefeller's toughest opposition came from producers and small refiners in the Pennsylvania oil fields who dealt him a sharp blow by completing a rival pipeline in 1879; in the meantime, Rockefeller and his associates faced legislative investigations in New York and threats of criminal prosecution in Pennsylvania. Despite these travails, Rockefeller interests controlled close to 90 per cent of the refining capacity of the United States by 1880.[2]

The capstone to Rockefeller's "system" was provided—ironically—by a lawyer who had been an implacable opponent during the wars with the oil producers in the 1870s. Samuel C.T. Dodd had criticized the rebate system that had been the source of Standard's success, but by 1879 he had thrown in his lot with Rockefeller (along with many others). A major problem for Rockefeller was that his confederacy of alliances with refiners in other states was based on "communities of interest," which could easily be breached. In 1881 Dodd came up with a plan that could unify the disparate Rockefeller interests across the country. He set up a Standard Oil "Trust," in which a designated group of individual "trustees" (all tied to Rockefeller) would hold shares in multiple state-chartered corporations. Thus the decrees of the Trust could be assuredly carried out by the various state entities. To this end, Dodd also established state-chartered companies (Standard of New York, Standard of New Jersey, Standard of Indiana, etc.) that would essentially act as determined by their "trustees."

Dodd's proposals established the legal basis for a centralized Standard Oil system, but much was left to be developed at the management level to make it work. Over the years Rockefeller had worked hard to ensure that he had a loyal and competent band of executives who could carry out his wishes. In many cases this involved individuals who had opposed Rockefeller, such as John Archbold and H.H. Rogers. Rockefeller welcomed them aboard and showered them with benefits and incentives. As a result, he produced a strong management group that shared his corporate interest in the success of Standard Oil.

But the Standard Oil system was intended to avoid the hazards of over-centralization. An array of committees was set up to advise the trustees on a range of issues from "cooperage" to "export trade." The committees in turn consulted with state-based organizations. Some companies, such as the Vacuum Oil Company, operated more or less outside the reach of the trustees, as long as they performed well. This was by no means a perfect arrangement, but it reflected the views of those who designed the system, and in many respects helped define the fate of Imperial Oil once it fell into the hands of the Standard octopus.[3]

Opportunities Missed

After a smooth start, Imperial Oil encountered some rocky times. In 1880 the company boasted a net profit of $116,049 (CAD) from $131,700 (CAD) in revenues; shareholders received $114,000 (CAD) in dividends. Revenues rose another 67 per cent in the following year although profits lagged. By 1882 revenues and profits had fallen by more than 50 per cent. No new dividends were issued until 1887. For several years thereafter the dividends took the form of a 6 per cent demand loan; regular payments to stockholders were only restored in the 1890s. These problems reflected both a downturn in the economy and developments in the United States, where the opening of new fields in Pennsylvania and New York drove crude oil prices down, and the formation of the Standard Oil Trust resulted in a dramatic increase in imports into Canada, more than doubling the pre-1880 figures—in terms of both volume and value—despite the continuing protectionist measures.[4]

By 1880 Imperial had closed down seven of the nine refineries it had acquired through the merger, in a deliberate move to reduce production and boost kerosene prices. This left only the two largest operations: the Silver Star refinery in Petrolia, and the Victor works in London (the largest one), which was renamed the "London East Refinery." Imperial set out to construct a pipeline from Petrolia to London, and asked the London city council to provide $20,000 (CAD) to help complete the project; but objections from the council (and taxpayers) to expansion of this source of pollution led to rejection. In 1883 this unpopular refinery was hit by lightning and burned to the ground. Given the bad market conditions, Imperial decided not to rebuild the Victor works and refining was concentrated at Petrolia.[5]

Despite these setbacks, Imperial had accomplished a good deal in its short existence. By 1887 revenues were at $234,000 (CAD) and net profits at $145,000 (CAD), justifying a modest dividend. In 1883 the company set up a branch office in Winnipeg to sell kerosene (and other products) in the western provinces. Lubricating oil, a by-product of the refining process, became increasingly important for railway and industrial uses, offsetting some of the problems Imperial encountered in selling its illuminating oil. After completion of the Canadian Pacific Railway, Imperial Oil barrels became a familiar sight on the prairies—often recycled to hold rainwater.

But fundamental weaknesses continued to undermine Imperial's aspirations. Although it expanded into the west, the Maritimes and Quebec continued to be supplied from American sources, despite the tariff and related import restrictions. The company never established a degree of control over refiners in Canada comparable to Standard in the US. The most formidable holdout was Fairbank in Petrolia, who controlled his own crude oil sources, but he was not the only one. There were five "independents" in 1880, and at least a dozen firms were operating outside Imperial's reach by 1887—including refineries owned by two of their own shareholders: William Spencer and John Minhinnick in London. During 1885–87, Fitzgerald of Imperial was able to form a refiners' syndicate to hold the line against American competition, but by the end of that period its control of domestic refining capacity had shrunk from two-thirds to one-half of the total.[6]

The most egregious error involved the quality of their major product: kerosene. The problem of sulphur content had plagued the Canadian industry since its inception: Imperial had the opportunity to overcome this defect, and lost it. When the company decided to consolidate their refining operations at Petrolia in 1883, they determined to recruit an expert on the most efficient methods of petroleum distilling and refining. This was Herman Frasch, who had emigrated from Germany to the United States in 1868, establishing a chemical consulting lab in Philadelphia: by 1877 he was focusing on oil refining and joined a chemical company in Cleveland that was associated with Standard Oil, bringing with him a patent for improved refining that had the added advantage of more efficient recovery of other by-products, particularly lubricating oil. It was Frasch's work in this regard that persuaded Imperial's directors to enter an agreement in 1884

FIGURE 2.1. Herman Frasch, 1884. Glenbow Archive IP-26-5-4, Imperial Oil Collection.

that licensed Frasch's patent in Canada. The company also set out to bring the inventor to assist them in redesigning the Petrolia refinery. To that end, Frasch was offered a fee of $10,000 (CAD) and Imperial Oil stock. Proving himself to be a shrewd negotiator as well as a talented researcher, Frasch persuaded the company to offer him a position as chief chemist at a fee that matched Fitzgerald's own salary, and also a seat on the board of Imperial Oil.

While Frasch was working at Petrolia, he was persuaded by John Minhinnick, who was something of a renegade on the Imperial board, to join him in a separate venture called the Empire Oil Company: Minhinnick had a dormant refinery in London, which he outfitted as a lab for Frasch to conduct experiments aimed at reducing the sulphur residue in kerosene refined from Petrolia oil. By 1885 Frasch had determined that mixing lead

oxide with the petroleum during the distilling process would not only remove the sulphur odour but also effectively eliminate the sulphur from the
refined product. He later concluded that copper oxide was best for achieving this goal on a large scale, but his patents covered a variety of oxides: in
any case what became known as the Frasch process represented a major
breakthrough in kerosene refining.[7]

It is not clear whether Imperial's board was fully aware of Frasch's
progress; by 1885 he had resigned from Imperial to work full-time at the
London refinery. In the meantime, however, circumstances had changed
dramatically in the United States. Large new oil fields had been discovered
in Ohio, stretching into Indiana in 1885, and Rockefeller had decided to
move Standard into production in the region, overcoming the objections
of fellow Standard trustees. But the "Lima" (Ohio) oil exhibited the same
characteristics as the Petrolia fields: a high sulphur content that could at
best be masked temporarily, but not eliminated. Frasch's experiments
were providential from Rockefeller's point of view, and he lost no time
in setting out to bring him back to the United States. Frasch was offered
a salary higher than that of any other scientist in the country plus an exchange of his shares in the Empire Oil Company for those in Standard
Oil. Frasch also knew that Standard had the financial capability to support
research on a much larger scale than he could acquire in Canada. In July
1886 Frasch rejoined Standard Oil of Ohio.

Frasch was right about the financial requirements of his work. He was
not able to demonstrate the viability of his process for sulphur removal
on a large scale until 1888; but Standard had set up a special unit—the
Solar Refining Company—to support his efforts, at a cost that exceeded
$200,000 (USD). Imperial may not have ever been in a position to match
the kind of incentives available to Rockefeller, but losing Frasch (and
his process) was a major blow to the long-term future of the Canadian
company, as events a decade later would demonstrate. Frasch went on to
become a multimillionaire in his own right as the "sulphur king" in the
mining and refining of sulphur in Louisiana in the early 1900s.[8]

Imperial at Bay

By 1890 Imperial Oil appeared to have surmounted its earlier travails. Revenues and net earnings had tripled since the mid-1880s, and the company issued a $40,000 (CAD) dividend in 1891, the first in three years. Sales in western Canada were increasing, and Petrolia had its best year ever in terms of revenues. The re-election of the Conservatives under MacDonald in 1891 reaffirmed the solidity of the "National Policy" in protecting the country from the depredations of Standard Oil. Not every Imperial board member may have been so sanguine, however, as Standard reported at least one overture about a possible merger that year—setting the tone for a decade of manoeuvres among Canadians, British, and Americans over the future of the oil industry in Canada.

Beneath the surface of growth and prosperity, Imperial had underlying problems. One related to financing. The major shareholders, after a decade in the wilderness, were clamouring for dividends. Imperial was careful to provide a regular flow of dividends throughout the 1890s, but the result was pressure on its capital requirements. Imperial negotiated a short-term loan of $200,000 (CAD) per year from Bank of Montreal in 1891, with a sharp jump in 1894 when it acquired the Premier Oil Co. to increase its refining capacity, carrying an interest rate of 12 per cent. Although net profits stabilized at $350–375,000 (CAD) in 1892–94, the combined effect of dividends and loan interest reduced the company's liquidity and its capacity to respond to changes in the market conditions that would soon emerge. In addition, this situation impeded any consideration of finding new oil fields—an unlikely event, but nevertheless an increasingly troubling circumstance in view of the long-term prospects for the Petrolia oil fields.[9]

Imperial also faced rising challenges in its markets, reflecting in part a concerted strategy by Standard Oil. The Canadian company had never been able to establish a strong position in the Maritimes or Quebec. Through the 1880s Standard had dealt with these regions through long-term contracts with local agencies. In Nova Scotia the Shatford brothers had been selling Standard products since 1882, and another agency under Joseph Bullock was connected to them in New Brunswick. The oldest Standard agency, however, was in Toronto where Samuel Rogers

FIGURE 2.2. Royalite tank wagon, 1906. Glenbow Archive IP-2a-8, Imperial Oil Collection.

had been marketing their kerosene since 1880. The Rogers operation was particularly irritating to Imperial, which established a subsidiary—Royal Oil Co.—in Toronto in 1889, selling its products as "Royalite" (possibly to avoid association with the sulphuric Imperial kerosene). Rogers, however, continued to thrive and joined with Fairbank in 1891, taking over a bankrupt independent refinery in Petrolia. By this time Rogers was the largest wholesale distributor of petroleum products in Ontario.[10]

The next stage of Standard's invasion was prompted less by circumstances in Canada than by events in distant and much larger overseas markets. Large reserves of oil had been discovered in Russia in the late 1870s and two powerful business groups—the Nobels and the Rothschilds—began developing the fields, completing a railway link from the Caspian Sea to the Black Sea by 1883. Alarmed by this threat to their markets in Europe and Britain, Standard cut prices on their exports of refined products, but by 1888 their virtual monopoly over Britain had diminished to 70 per cent, and the Rothschild interests were establishing a marketing company there. Characteristically, Rockefeller responded to this new challenge by reorganizing Standard's export trade organization. The first step in this process was the creation of the Anglo-American Oil Company in 1888, which consolidated all their marketing operations in Britain. Anglo-American reported to Standard of New York, where William Rockefeller had been running the export business for his brother since the 1870s.[11]

These organizational changes were extended to Canada: in 1888, the New Brunswick agency, Joseph Bullock & Sons, was recapitalized at $50,000 (USD) as the Eastern Oil Company with Standard of New York holding almost two-thirds of the shares; shortly thereafter the Shatford Brothers operation in Nova Scotia was folded into the company. Two years later the various marketing agencies selling Standard products in Montreal were consolidated as the Bushnell Company, capitalized at $100,000 (USD); the Bushnell brothers, Thomas and Joseph, had been involved in Standard of New York's export activities since the mid-1880s. In 1892 both of these companies were placed under the Anglo-American Oil Company, possibly as a gesture toward Canada's status as a British Dominion. In practice the general management of the Canadian operations was coordinated by Frank Q. Barstow, a long-time associate of Rockefeller from Standard of Ohio who was now functioning as the head of the manufacturing committee for Standard of New York.

Imperial responded to these challenges by expanding its marketing operations in Toronto and competing with some success against the Eastern Oil Company in the Maritimes; Eastern had no domestic oil supplies and no capacity for bulk storage until 1894. With strong agencies in Winnipeg and British Columbia, Imperial effectively dominated the western market, although Standard of California set up a sales agency in Vancouver in 1893. Imperial did not seek to emulate Standard's organized approach to marketing: Fitzgerald monitored all transactions across Canada from his office in Petrolia, relying on the efforts of travelling salesmen. Similarly, refining continued to be concentrated at Petrolia, under Englehart's direction, although the company acquired an independent— Premier Oil Company—in 1894 to expand its refining capacity.[12]

In the early 1890s Standard Oil was preoccupied with its domestic problems as well as the threat of Russian oil, now under the control of

Marcus Samuel and the Shell Transport Company. A harsh depression gripped the United States between 1893–96, featuring a Wall Street panic, railroad bankruptcies, protracted labour unrest, and increased public hostility toward "big business," with Rockefeller as a handy target. An example of this kind of hostility can be seen in Henry Demarest Lloyd's *Wealth against Commonwealth*, published in 1894, which denounced the Standard Oil "monopoly." In 1890 the US Congress had passed an "antitrust" act that implicitly contemplated the breakup of combines such as the Standard Oil Trust, although the US Supreme Court ensured that the law would be interpreted narrowly, at least for the next two decades. At the state level, however, the oil giant faced more serious challenges. The New York state legislature had conducted investigations of Standard Oil in the late 1880s, and in Pennsylvania arrest warrants were issued against Rockefeller and his associates (which he took seriously enough to avoid entering the state for several years). In Ohio, the Supreme Court issued a ruling in 1892 that questioned the legal division between the trust and various state-level Standard companies that Dodd had designed in 1882, and threatened to cancel the charter of Standard Oil of Ohio.

In response to this danger, the executives of Standard Oil decided to dissolve the "trust" and replace it with a "community of interest" among the Standard companies, achieved by exchanging stock. From this reorganization Standard Oil of New Jersey emerged as the largest entity, recapitalized at $10 million (USD), and with a very broad charter (generously provided by the state of New Jersey—in return for fees) as both an operating enterprise in all phases of the oil business, and a holding company exercising control over a range of subsidiaries including refineries, pipelines, ocean transportation, marketing, and a variety of other functions. Among its largest affiliates was Anglo-American Oil, which now became the coordinator of many of Standard's foreign enterprises including those in Canada. In practice this would lead to confusion for some time, since Standard of New York continued to play a role in managing the affairs of the Canadian companies (including Imperial Oil after 1899) until the US Supreme Court's antitrust decision in 1911. In any case, the turmoil of reorganization occupied the attention of the residents of 26 Broadway in New York (the headquarters of Standard Oil), which provided a temporary respite for their much smaller rivals in Petrolia.[13]

But Imperial would face its own hazards in this period, as the bastion of tariffs and import restrictions that had protected it from Standard came under siege—prompted, in part, by the vigorous lobbying of Standard Oil's affiliates in Canada. Although the Conservatives remained in power in Ottawa, the outer works of the National Policy were fraying, particularly with regard to illuminating oil, where consumers regarded Imperial's products as inferior to those offered by Standard Oil: the highest grade of "white" kerosene offered by Imperial was considered at best comparable to the medium grade of imports from the US; but trade restrictions made the American product more costly. The Liberals were moving away from a doctrinaire commitment to "free trade," and the government, deprived of their "Old Leader" (Macdonald), was more susceptible to moderation on these issues. In 1893 the government reduced import duties on refined oil products from 7.2 cents to 6 cents per wine gallon. More critical, however, were changes in the "non-tariff" barriers.

There had been significant changes in the system of transportation of oil products since 1880. Tank cars for bulk shipping of oil had come into use on American railways in the mid-1880s, vigorously supported by Standard Oil. By the end of that decade tank steamers (ocean-going vessels carrying bulk oil) were appearing, providing the Shell Transport Company with its substantial cost efficiencies in shipping oil from Russia; Standard was following suit. Canadian refiners, principally Imperial Oil, had successfully resisted the entry of either tank cars or steamers into Canada until 1893, even though they were using tank cars for internal transportation by this time. The government maintained the restriction on tanker vessels, but allowed tank cars to enter Canada, although it required the importers to repackage their product in barrels after inspection at the border, a ridiculous and (for importers) expensive process.

When the Liberal government under Wilfrid Laurier came to power in 1896, touting a platform of "Imperial Preference" in contrast with the National Policy, the last shards of protection—at least for Imperial Oil—appeared to be disintegrating. During hearings on tariff reform in 1897, Fitzgerald made the case for continued protection against oil imports. But in 1898 the tariff was cut again from 6 cents to 5 cents per wine gallon on kerosene, and the restrictions on tank vessels and the entry of tank cars were removed.[14]

Meanwhile, Imperial continued to be encircled. On the surface Imperial seemed to have recovered from these setbacks. Revenues rose from $488,000 to $767,000 (CAD) in 1894–98, and dividends continued to flow, averaging $30,000 (CAD) per year to shareholders.[15] But its long-term future looked increasingly bleak. In 1894 Samuel Rogers had joined John Fairbank, Imperial's perpetual foe, in acquiring a defunct refinery in Petrolia. In that same year, Eastern Oil in Halifax and Bushnell in Quebec both established bulk storage facilities. Two years later the Bushnell Company took over the Fairbank-Rogers refinery and joined forces with Rogers to set up the Queen City Oil Company in Toronto, which competed directly with Imperial's Royalite. But Bushnell's most ominous move came in 1897 when it acquired the Alpha refinery in Sarnia and began to use the Frasch process, completely undercutting Imperial's position in the Canadian market.[16]

As early as 1895 Imperial Oil had begun negotiations with a British company—the Colonial Development Corporation—for a takeover. Fitzgerald approached Frederick White, of Colonial Development, while White was visiting Canada. White showed interest, and Fitzgerald responded by sending a good deal of information on Imperial to him. A petroleum geologist was dispatched from England to survey the Petrolia works. Imperial seems to have felt encouraged enough to propose an offer to sell majority shares in the company to Colonial for $585,000 (CAD). But at this point talks stalemated. Colonial sent more investigators to go through Imperial's books; not all of the Imperial board members were enthusiastic about the proposal, and their patience waned as the waiting period extended. Meanwhile, company shareholders benefited from sharply increasing dividends.

By April 1898 it had become clear that negotiations with Colonial had reached a dead end. Fitzgerald, possibly at Englehart's prompting, went to New York to open talks with Standard Oil. An agreement (of sweeping proportions) was quickly worked out. Standard Oil would acquire 75 per cent of Imperial Oil's shares. All plants and inventories held by Standard Oil in Canada (including those of Bushnell, Queen City, and Eastern) would be folded in with Imperial Oil. Imperial's capitalization would be increased to $1 million (USD). In addition, Imperial shareholders would receive a dividend of $93,000 (CAD). This was a remarkably generous takeover (for the shareholders), which prevented many lawsuits from outsiders and criticism from the Canadian press. As usual, Standard had achieved its objectives secretly.[17]

3

RESURRECTION

Nadir

The sale of Imperial Oil to Standard Oil (via Anglo-American) proved to be propitious for the company's Canadian shareholders, who fared very well from the deal. Although the future looked ominous with the shifts in Canada's trade policy, in 1898 Imperial still had a strong competitive position. Its share of the Canadian market had actually increased as smaller refiners departed from the scene, and revenues had almost doubled—from $421 million to $766 million (CAD)—over the preceding five years; dividends increased at the same rate. The Petrolia fields were still productive, although the longer-term outlook was not good. Standard's offer therefore proved generous, netting the "old shareholders" a total of $324 per share (CAD) in three disbursements in 1898–99; this was on top of the final dividend payments made under the old company. Furthermore, they continued to own 25 per cent of the shares, which opened the door to further benefits. Both the American and Canadian economies had recovered from the depression of the mid-1890s, so the reorganized company continued to grow, both in revenues and dividends, which averaged 12 per cent per year. Despite fears of post-amalgamation reductions, managers and salaried employees also experienced increases under the new regime, although wage earners in the refineries were not so fortunate.

In other respects, however, the takeover brought about traumatic changes. At the first meeting of the new board of directors in January 1899, the existing bylaws were terminated, and a new issue of shares was authorized, to be distributed to shareholders in the other amalgamating companies (primarily Bushnell); and, more crucially, to representatives from Standard Oil including Frank Q. Barstow, Horace Chamberlain, Alfred Brainerd, William R. King, and Charles Stillman. Shortly thereafter the board was reorganized: Fitzgerald became chairman, while Barstow became president, with Chamberlain appointed general manager, King the treasurer, and Brainerd the secretary. The only remaining Canadians on the board were Fitzgerald, Jacob Englehart, and William Pratt. Pratt resigned shortly thereafter, to be replaced by James Archbold, the son of John D. Archbold, who had succeeded Rockefeller as president of Standard Oil of New Jersey.[1]

The key figures in this reorganization were Barstow and Chamberlain. Barstow had been involved with Standard Oil since 1871, was secretary of the company's manufacturing committee in the 1880s, and was a close associate of John Archbold. Considered one of Standard's experts on foreign markets, Barstow travelled to Asia and South America as well as negotiating a petroleum concession in Romania in the 1890s. Barstow had also played a role in the establishment of Queen City Oil Co. with Samuel Rogers in Toronto. In 1899 he was appointed to the board of Standard Oil of New Jersey, and functioned in effect as Standard's "proconsul" in Canada. Barstow, however, had many responsibilities and attended relatively few Imperial board meetings. Running the company was left principally to Chamberlain, who was general manager of the Atlas Refining Co. in Buffalo, New York. Chamberlain and Stillman had been involved in setting up the Sarnia refinery for Bushnell, an experience that may have influenced the next major change in the company's affairs.[2]

At its last board meeting the "old board" had reaffirmed that Petrolia was Imperial's "chief place of business"—possibly to stave off fears about the Standard takeover. Three months later, however, the new board announced that the company's headquarters would move to Sarnia. In business terms the move made sense: the Bushnell company had acquired a refinery at Sarnia with generous tax concessions from the municipality (thanks in part to the efforts of William J. Hanna, a lawyer with connections to Standard—and later to Imperial) and Bushnell had laid a pipeline to Petrolia. Furthermore, the Sarnia refinery was closer to potential connections with Standard's pipeline supplies in the United States. Nevertheless, the move presaged the closure of the Petrolia refinery several

FIGURE 3.1. Sarnia refinery, 1906. Glenbow Archive IP-10a-1-4e, Imperial Oil Collection.

years later, which fulfilled fears about the impact of the amalgamation and led to the formation of a new independent refiner in Petrolia, Canadian Oil Companies Ltd., in 1901.[3]

Queen City Oil Co. in Toronto received special treatment, possibly reflecting the previous connections between Samuel Rogers and Barstow. Queen City remained outside Imperial for a time until Anglo-American (Standard) provided financing for its acquisition ($201,000 CAD). Imperial was already carrying a debt of $420,000 (CAD) to Anglo-American, another lever for Standard's control over the Canadian enterprise. Two of the Rogers brothers joined the Imperial board a few years after the merger.

Output from the Petrolia fields began to decline precipitously after 1900—demonstrating the wisdom of moving refining operations to Sarnia: between 1899 and 1904 production fell from 800,000 bbl. to 500,000 bbl./ year. Imperial (and Standard) began to lobby for a reduction in duties on imported oil; this effort was successful in 1904, with duties on crude eliminated and those on refined oil cut in half. At the same time, Standard finally provided Imperial with access to the Frasch process, but charged a royalty of 3 cents (later 5 cents) per barrel for the benefit. The Petrolia output continued its downward spiral, producing less than 300,000 bbl./year by 1911. To offset this decline Imperial began bringing in oil by lake tanker from Ohio Standard's Cygnet pipeline, but of course this tied Imperial closer to US suppliers.

Chamberlain, as head of the Sarnia operations, pressed for expansion of supplies and manufacturing capacity to enable Imperial to develop a Canada-wide market for refined products. But he encountered resistance from the established marketing operations in Standard: Henry Folger, who headed up the parent company's manufacturing committee, maintained that the Maritimes (and western Canada) would be better served by other elements of Standard's supply system, and the local affiliates shared this perspective despite their formal connection to Imperial Oil. Similarly, Chamberlain faced restrictions on Imperial's marketing operations. Sales operations in Canada after 1899 were coordinated from 26 Broadway in New York. H.J. Guthrie, an American who set up a sales agency in Winnipeg for Imperial, lobbied for years (with little success) to reorient the company to provide lubricating oil for farm equipment for the growing market in the Prairies. At the same time, Imperial was constrained to allow Queen City to continue to market its own products in Toronto. Imperial seemed to face an excess of centralization and decentralization at the same time.

Fitzgerald retired in 1905, and Barstow stepped down three years later as president, leaving Chamberlain more or less in control of the management of Imperial. But Chamberlain regarded Imperial as a sideline from his real job as head of Atlas Refining. An "imposing presence of autocratic appearance and manner," Chamberlain ran Imperial as a one-man show. He maintained the Imperial refinery records (and related material) at the Atlas refinery in Buffalo. Chamberlain also feuded with the Canadian board members, particularly Englehart and Rogers. By this time the company had been reduced to a virtual nullity. Its domestic production was declining, sales and marketing policies were determined in New York, refinery operations were set in Buffalo, and board members were reduced to recipients of "fat" dividends. After 1909 even the board meetings were scheduled in New York City. But circumstances were to change soon, and very dramatically.[4]

Graham D. Taylor

The Trust on Trial

In 1899, while new owners were overhauling Imperial, the board of Standard Oil of New Jersey was contemplating its own reorganization. Seven years earlier, in response to an Ohio state court order, Standard Oil had been transformed from a closely held trust to a "community of interest" among various Standard Oil affiliates, with Jersey Standard as the largest component. But these changes had not deterred state-based prosecutors from continuing to pursue the oil giant. Lawsuits were filed against Standard-associated companies in Texas and Pennsylvania, while the US Interstate Commerce Commission conducted an investigation of rebates by railroads to Standard Oil. Once again the most serious challenge came from Ohio: attorney general Frank Monnett charged in 1899 that the 1892 reorganization had not been in compliance with the court order against Standard Oil, and that the companies in Ohio were violating the state's antitrust law (which had been enacted the year before).

Although Monnett's charges were ultimately dismissed, Standard's lawyers and senior executives contemplated replacing the federation with a single holding company that would exercise majority control over all the others. Standard of New Jersey was the obvious choice; not only was it the largest of the Standard companies, but also New Jersey corporation laws were extremely liberal—particularly insofar as they allowed companies to own businesses in other states. Not everyone in the Standard community shared this enthusiasm for a single holding company: Samuel Dodd, the architect of the original trust, was skeptical of the argument that the proposed organization could withstand antitrust prosecution, particularly from the federal government. Dodd's fears proved prescient, but in 1899 both President William McKinley and the US Supreme Court seemed business-friendly, and the reorganization would presumably undermine state prosecutions.[5]

Unfortunately, the new century brought no respite to Standard Oil. Rockefeller had stepped down from his position as chief executive, but he continued to personify the monopolist in the public mind. Prosecutors in a number of states brought suits against Standard, but even more serious—at least in some respects—were the attacks in the media. In a rare show of unity, both Joseph Pulitzer and William Randolph Hearst, the leading newspaper magnates of the day, denounced Standard Oil on a regular basis in their publications. In 1902 Ida M. Tarbell began publishing a series of articles in *McClure's Magazine* that were eventually published as *The History of Standard Oil*. Although not completely negative—one of her chapters was entitled "The Legitimate Contributions of Standard Oil"—the account revisited all of the familiar charges against the company: the South Improvement Company episode; the railroad rebates; the allegations of "predatory pricing" and other sharp dealings with competitors. Tarbell had several advantages over other critics—her father and brother had experience in dealing with Standard Oil in the Pennsylvania oil field battles of the 1880s, and she had the opportunity to interview Henry H. Rogers, a member of the Standard Oil board who believed that he could persuade her to adopt a more sympathetic view of the company. More significantly, her account provided the first coherent narrative of the history of the company—even John D. Rockefeller acknowledged that his son probably learned more about the company from reading Tarbell than from any other source. For the first time in its history Standard Oil had to scramble to develop a public relations policy to offset the impact of Tarbell's story.[5]

Events at the national level posed even greater challenges than did exposés in the media. In 1901 President McKinley was assassinated, and his successor Theodore Roosevelt exhibited a more bellicose attitude on antitrust issues. A railroad amalgamation scheme was blocked in 1903 and shortly thereafter Roosevelt established a Bureau of Corporations in the US Department of Justice with the explicit aim of reinvigorating the Sherman Antitrust Act. In 1906 the US attorney general Charles Bonaparte brought a suit against Standard Oil in the US federal court in St. Louis, Missouri. The case was complex and generated thousands of pages of documents, years of litigation, and hundreds of witnesses (including John D. Rockefeller himself, who adopted a folksy persona—albeit with a short memory). In 1909 the court concluded that Standard Oil was in violation of the Sherman Act, but not because of its predatory practices. Instead the court determined that the establishment of Jersey Standard as a holding company in 1899 was the major issue, because this measure made it impossible for other companies in the Standard group to compete with one another in the future.

Standard's lawyers objected on the grounds that the companies had effectively acted in concert since 1881 when the original trust was established. The case then proceeded to the US Supreme Court, which mulled over the mountains of documents for two more years. In 1911 the Supreme Court finally announced its decision, which reaffirmed the lower court. Although Chief Justice Edward D. White, in handing down the judgment, enunciated what became known as the "rule of reason" in determining antitrust suits, the decision did not hold Standard Oil accountable for bad behaviour. Instead White upheld the lower court's view that the creation of Jersey Standard as a holding company in effect established a monopoly.[6]

The lower court had ordered the breakup of Standard Oil into its constituent units, and even while the appeal wended its way to the Supreme Court, the company, characteristically, began planning for the worst. The final dissolution decree identified thirty-four components to be resurrected as competing companies. The largest of these were Jersey Standard, New York Standard, Indiana Standard, Ohio Standard, California Standard, Vacuum Oil, and Atlantic Refining. One of the peculiar features of the decree was that it did not establish integrated companies (except for Standard of California): some had production facilities but limited access to markets; Jersey Standard had huge refining capacity but no sources of crude oil. Later critics of antitrust policies pointed out that the failure to create independent integrated companies led to collaboration among the sundered elements of the trust, undercutting the presumed intent of the dissolution.

Since the decree did not require the major investors in Standard Oil to divest themselves of their shares, Rockefeller and others ended up with proportionate ownership in all thirty-three companies, and continued to reap the financial benefits of growth of the formerly united oil companies. Eventually the largest of the "successor" companies (particularly New York Standard and California Standard) developed into integrated businesses with multinational operations; but by the end of the twentieth century, with the merger of Jersey Standard (Exxon) and Standard of New York (Mobil), the process of re-amalgamation had resumed. Perhaps the most significant effect of the dissolution was that it opened up opportunities for ambitious younger managers to rise quickly in their respective companies, which accelerated generational changes.[7]

In the normal course of events, Imperial Oil might have ended up as an affiliate of Standard of New York. Its operations had been closely tied to that company through Bushnell Company even before 1899; Chamberlain, who became president of Imperial in 1908, was tied to the New York company through Atlas Refining. But Imperial was a "foreign" entity, aligned with Anglo-American, which was in turn a subsidiary of Jersey Standard. Jersey Standard was the largest of the "survivors" of the dissolution, with 43 per cent of the assets of the former trust; and, more crucially, it had inherited most of the overseas responsibilities of Standard Oil, which were to become more important for the long-term future of the US oil industry. In the immediate situation in 1911, the "international" connection of Jersey Standard brought Walter Teagle to the helm of Imperial Oil.

Teagle at Imperial Oil

Ironically, the antitrust prosecution of Standard Oil took place in an era when changes in markets and the rise of new competition were undermining the once-dominant position of the company in the oil industry. The advent of the electric light cast an ominous shadow over the future of the kerosene market, Standard Oil's major revenue source. By the end of the first decade of the twentieth century the growth of the automobile industry, particularly the development of Henry Ford's mass-produced Model T, stimulated growing demand for gasoline and lubricating oil. In this same period the navies of the Great Powers were hastening to convert their ships from coal to petroleum fuel. But these new markets were only beginning to take effect when Standard Oil faced the dissolution decree.

Standard also faced new competitors both at home and abroad. New oil fields were coming on stream in California and Texas, where the Spindletop oil strike of 1901 triggered the first boom of the new century. For many years Standard Oil was stymied in its efforts to get a foothold in the Texas fields, in part because of vigorous antitrust opposition in the state, which barred the establishment of integrated production and refining companies until 1917. In the meantime other players had entered the field: entrepreneurs like J. Howard Pew (creator of Sun Oil) and Joseph Cullinan, a former Standard Oil employee who abandoned his sponsors to set up the Texas Fuel Co. (later Texaco). The Mellons of

Pittsburgh, a formidable banking family, also got into the market, establishing Gulf Refining Company in Texas in 1901. Eventually Standard established a beachhead in Texas by acquiring Humble Oil in 1919, but during the first decade of the twentieth century Standard was an outsider and a pariah there.[8]

Even more formidable were the new challengers from overseas. During the 1890s oil tankers of the Shell Transport Company carried Russian petroleum to European markets, diminishing Standard's domination there. During that same decade a new player entered the global market as oil fields in the Dutch East Indies came into production. Both Rockefeller and Shell's Marcus Samuel angled for control of the East Indies oil, but they were outmanoeuvred by the head of the Royal Dutch company, Henri Deterding, who orchestrated the merger of Royal Dutch and Shell in 1907, effectively creating a worldwide competitor for Standard Oil.[9]

The rise of Royal Dutch Shell gave Imperial Oil a greater saliency in the minds of Standard Oil's leaders at 26 Broadway. In 1911 a Canadian subsidiary, Shell Company of Canada Ltd., was established and began setting up storage facilities in Montreal and Vancouver. The prospect of Standard's global rival entering North America through the back door was alarming, in part because, as an at least partially British company, Shell had some potential legal advantages over the American-owned firm. This would become apparent later. In such circumstances Jersey Standard moved quickly to counter the Shell threat, sending one of its rising stars to revive the moribund Imperial Oil and reinstate it as a barrier to the Anglo-Dutch threat.

Of Walter Clark Teagle, it could be said that oil flowed through his veins. His mother Amelia Belle Clark was the daughter of Maurice Clark, Rockefeller's partner in his first oil venture. Walter's father John Teagle was an independent refiner in Cleveland from the 1870s, who had resisted Standard's embrace for more than thirty years. Family relations thus played no part in Walter's rise to prominence within Imperial Oil. Born in 1878, Walter Teagle studied chemical engineering at Cornell University, and during the summer breaks worked for his father's company in the refinery. After graduating he became a salesman for his father's company, Scofield, Schurmer & Teagle, which proved so successful that in 1901 Standard Oil decided to buy it—to eliminate a troublesome competitor,

FIGURE 3.2. Walter Teagle, 1917. Glenbow Archive IP26-8b-Teagle-1, Imperial Oil Collection.

but also to acquire the services of his precocious son. Walter soon found himself in the Export Trade Department of Jersey Standard, which enabled him to interact with the major players in international oil, including Henri Deterding, and brought him to the notice of John Archbold, Rockefeller's successor as president of Jersey Standard. Before long, Teagle was a key figure in virtually all of Standard's international negotiations. A formidable figure, with jut-jawed looks, Teagle dominated meetings even though he rarely spoke. He spent time befriending potentially hostile figures, like Deterding, and impressed the Standard Oil chieftains as their best hope for the future—the "boy who could fill John D.'s Shoes."[10]

In 1911 Teagle, at age thirty-three, was appointed to the Jersey Standard board with responsibility for the company's international relations, and also (incidentally) for Imperial Oil Company. Teagle grasped both opportunities with enthusiasm. He initially planned to divide his time between these responsibilities, but pressures on the European scene delayed his plans to formally take up the presidency of Imperial until 1914. Chamberlain retired at the end of 1911. During the hiatus the task of running the company fell to Charles Stillman, the head of the Sarnia refinery, aided by the Rogers brothers and H.J. Guthrie. Guthrie had successfully overhauled Imperial's sales operations, and might have become Chamberlain's successor had the Standard Oil leaders not decided to send in their most promising manager instead. Guthrie left the board shortly after Teagle became president.

Even before his arrival in Canada, however, Teagle's influence was being felt at Imperial Oil and his connections with 26 Broadway were yielding benefits. Chamberlain had persistently pressed (albeit in vain) for an expansion of the Sarnia refinery and improved linkages with US oil suppliers. During 1911–12 Chamberlain and Stillman, with help from W.J. Hanna—Imperial Oil's legal counsel since 1897—took the matter up with Teagle; Teagle, who ultimately supported them, also advocated increasing the company's lake steamer fleet. Jersey Standard's board agreed in principle, but Imperial needed working capital to finance this kind of expansion. Imperial still had $2 million (CAD) in unsubscribed authorized capitalization (which had been increased to $6 million in 1907) but Jersey Standard was reluctant to take up the shares necessary to maintain its proportion.

Teagle was not only able to persuade New York to provide the financing, but also endorsed an expansion of authorized capital to $15 million (CAD); Imperial's directors were empowered to issue new stock as required. With Teagle on the scene as president in 1915, authorized capital was increased to $50 million, and two years later the company was financially reorganized: Imperial Oil Ltd. was established as a $50 million (CAD) operating company, with responsibility for refining and marketing, wholly owned by Imperial Oil Co. Ltd. (which by this time also had subsidiaries in South America).[11]

Once ensconced in office, Teagle initiated even more dramatic changes. With new capital in hand, the capacity of the Sarnia refinery was expanded from 5,000 bbl./day to 13,000 bbl./day; a pipeline was built to link Sarnia to the Cygnet pipeline, enabling Imperial to supply all of Canada outside the Maritimes. Refining capacity was increased again with the construction of refineries in Vancouver in 1914, Montreal in 1916, and Halifax in 1918. In that same year Imperial's headquarters moved to a new building in Toronto; and of course the records and company books were deposited there.

The marketing system was also completely overhauled. In place of the New York office and its three regional agencies, a central sales division was set up in Toronto with branch offices in every major city and town across Canada. Although the old commission agents were retained, they were absorbed into the new organization, under the charge of the sales vice president, G.W. Mayer, who had been brought by Teagle from New York. Mayer moved sales managers frequently to break down the traditional system in which commission agents had established long-term relationships with customers—sometimes inducing them to set up their own independent operations. Mayer's office also tightened up on credit collections, another departure from the more easygoing past. Teagle and Mayer emphasized advertising and public relations: in 1914 Imperial was the first Standard company to make a promotional film, and the company issued specialized publications for its salesmen. In 1917 the company brought out the *Imperial Oil Review* as part of an overhaul of relations with its employees and shareholders.[12]

Teagle's biographers characterize him as "conservative" on issues of labour relations, although in this era even the most "enlightened" business leaders opposed trade unions and challenges to management prerogatives. But Teagle proved reluctant even to follow the lead of Jersey Standard in this area; when Jersey adopted the forty-hour work week in 1915, Teagle resisted introducing a similar change at Imperial, arguing that this would take the company out of step with other Canadian manufacturers. The forty-hour week was only initiated at Imperial in 1918 when Teagle was moving on to 26 Broadway; similarly the Joint Industrial Committees that Jersey set up in the United States during the First World War (based in part on the advice of the future Canadian prime minister Mackenzie King) were extended to Imperial in 1918. Teagle's attitude toward the minority shareholders in Imperial, and the Canadian public, could also be seen as "reactionary:" he ensured that information about the company's sales and profits were kept "secret," and even sought—unsuccessfully—to suppress public knowledge about the extent of Jersey Standard's control of Imperial Oil.[13]

On the other hand, Teagle was prepared to be a pioneer in one area of employee relations: the promotion of employee stock ownership plans that he initiated in 1915. It was not only the first Canadian company to do so, but the first in the Jersey Standard group as well. The opportunity arose as Jersey Standard declined to increase its own investment in Imperial when the authorized capital was raised to $50 million (CAD). In order to encourage employee participation, instalment purchasing was allowed and Imperial drew on its own retained earnings as a reserve to cover the costs involved. When Jersey officials (contradicting their earlier position) objected to the plan on the grounds that the parent company's equity would be diluted, Hanna resorted to a special provision in Imperial's charter that enabled it to issue a "stock dividend" to the shareholders.[14]

Although the stock ownership plan allowed employees to sell their shares, Teagle regarded such actions as disloyal to the company. In an angry letter to an Imperial Pipeline manager, Teagle complained that "when this offer was made to employees it was not with the thought that they would speculate in the company's stock but rather that they would retain it as a permanent investment and thus secure for the company their increased interest and cooperation." Although Teagle emphasized loyalty over speculation, he was also clearly concerned about the possible acquisition of Imperial stock by "outsiders."[15]

Teagle was sensitive to the impact of Canada's involvement in the First World War on Imperial's employees—and sensitive as well to the public relations value of demonstrating that the company was a patriotic supporter of the Canadian war effort, particularly in the years before the United States entered the war. Rumours that Jersey Standard was still trading with Germany abounded. When the government of Canada issued its first War Bond in 1915, Imperial quickly made a $1 million (CAD) subscription and another $1.25 million (CAD) to the Canadian Victory Loan Bond. Employees were encouraged to subscribe for $50 bonds up to 20 per cent of their annual salary (this was particularly intended to demonstrate the support by Imperial's managers for the war effort). A special wartime employee bonus was authorized in August 1917, and extended to Imperial employees who were in military service. Imperial's tanker

FIGURE 3.3. Workers at Dartmouth, NS refinery, 1919. Glenbow Archive IP-10e-1-1, Imperial Oil Collection.

fleet was also seconded to the Royal Canadian Navy during 1916–18. In 1916 the Canadian government introduced a Business Profits War Tax; subsequently Imperial was assessed $1.4 million (CAD) on reported net profits of 13.8 million (CAD) during 1917–20; the tax was paid out over two years.[16]

With the increase in refining capacity, Imperial's sales volume rose from $17 million in 1912 to $27 million (CAD) in 1917. Mayer's tough policies on marketing overhead costs and credit sales, together with improvements in the scale and efficiency of the Sarnia refinery, boosted net earnings from $2.6 million (CAD) in 1912 to $7.4 million (CAD) in 1917. It was a highly creditable record.

For Teagle, however, after restoring Imperial's refining and marketing capabilities the most important tasks were to find new sources of crude oil to offset the declining output of the Petrolia fields—bearing in mind that Jersey Standard also faced the same problem—and to deploy Imperial effectively in Jersey Standard's global search for oil. In particular it was crucial to stymie the efforts of the Royal Dutch Shell. These objectives were to converge and present Teagle with opportunities to help Imperial Oil and Jersey Standard at the same time, although his fundamental loyalties were with the parent company.

Teagle's search for new oil sources for Imperial began even before he appeared in Canada. In 1911, after failing to persuade Jersey Standard to invest in oil wells in Salt Creek, Wyoming, Teagle persuaded Hanna and some other Imperial shareholders to join him in a personal venture. That venture worked out well for the investors, although it never became a big player. After he came to Imperial, Teagle pursued an investment in Midwest Refining Co. (which was tied to the Salt Creek venture) to supply the Canadian company's operations in Regina, Saskatchewan. But at Jersey Standard Archbold vetoed the acquisition of Midwest Refining, and that seems to have ended the initiative, although the investors were not unhappy.[17]

But the search for oil continued. In 1913–14 Teagle orchestrated the acquisition of oil resources in Peru from the British company, London & Pacific. He then created the International Petroleum Company, which would provide Imperial with a source of oil for its west coast markets. Imperial undertook a much larger investment in Colombia four years later. In 1917–18, Teagle learned that Royal Dutch Shell had big plans for exploring and exploiting the oil resources of western Canada. Although little came of this foray by Shell, Imperial began a quest for oil in Alberta that would ultimately lead to the Leduc strike (after thirty years).[18]

In early 1918 Teagle departed from Toronto to become the president of Standard Oil (New Jersey). His resignation from the Imperial board came a few months later, and was the occasion for an unusual outpouring of gratitude from the board: "Upon his acceptance of the office of President in January of 1914, Mr. Teagle initiated a forward policy of development which his infinite capacity for administration and his broad and deeply grounded knowledge of the petroleum industry, his unique executive abilities and his genius for enlisting the co-operation of those of all ranks with whom he was associated, enabled him to implement with singular expedition and success."[19] The sentiments appear to have been heartfelt, particularly in light of the usually terse board minutes.

Teagle left an indelible imprint on the history of Imperial Oil. He had taken a company that was virtually moribund and resuscitated it. Refining capacity was increased, marketing capabilities were substantially improved, and the search for new crude oil resources was well underway. The company's public image was also less negative. Imperial Oil actually functioned as an integrated entity—which was an important feature. Imperial Oil would become a player in its own right, not just a local representative of the Standard Oil octopus. Teagle was of course a "company man" first and foremost—and the company he served was Jersey Standard. Nevertheless, Teagle gave Imperial a new lease on life.

Teagle also left behind a number of managers who would carry forward his ideas, including G.W. Mayer and G. Harrison Smith. Smith became the president of International Petroleum and later Imperial Oil. Like Smith, Mayer was American, but there were Canadians who commanded his support—including R.V. LeSueur, who was a major figure in International Petroleum Co. and became president of Imperial Oil, and Alex McQueen, an "old Petrolia hand" who would be involved in both the South American and Alberta exploration operations in the 1920s–30s. These figures would play a major role in the development of the company through the Second World War.

PART TWO

BEFORE LEDUC 1917–1947

4

ADVENTURES IN THE TROPICS

The Genesis of International Petroleum

Early in 1913, Sir Archibald Williamson and Kenneth Mathieson—representatives of the heirs of the late William Keswick of London—contacted Walter C. Teagle, the vice president and member of the board of directors of Standard Oil of New Jersey, with a proposal to sell the shares owned by Mr. Keswick in the London & Pacific Petroleum Company to Standard. London & Pacific had been established in 1889 by partners in the merchant houses of Jardine Mathieson and Balfour, Williamson, to develop oil fields on the La Brea y Parinas Estate on the northern coast of Peru, based on a ninety-nine-year lease of the mineral rights of the estate. Keswick had been the major investor in the company, and the shares offered would effectively transfer ownership of London & Pacific to the American company.

Over the next few months negotiations ensued and Jersey Standard dispatched a mission headed by John H. Carter—also a Standard director and a veteran of the oil business going back to the development of the Pennsylvania fields in the mid-nineteenth century—to survey the potential costs and benefits of taking over the Peruvian venture, which up to that point had exhibited limited success, producing at most 400 bbl./day by 1913—although that still made Peru the second-largest contemporaneous oil exporter in Latin America, following Mexico. Carter's report was positive, indicating that with the kind of technical and management capabilities that Jersey Standard could provide, production from the proven reserves could be substantially expanded. Teagle advocated a more ambitious plan, which involved acquiring not only the La Brea estate but also the assets of all the other companies operating in the area under sub-leases from London & Pacific.

The parties reached an agreement that took effect on November 2, 1914. The company that acquired these assets, however, was not Jersey Standard but a new entity, the International Petroleum Company Ltd., which was to be a subsidiary of Imperial Oil Ltd. A major issue for both Imperial Oil and Jersey Standard was access to oil reserves. Imperial's output from the Petrolia fields had declined to the point that by 1912 its Sarnia refinery was increasingly dependent on supplies from Cygnet, Ohio. Jersey Standard had a huge refining capacity after the breakup of the Standard Oil Trust, but few new producing fields, and it needed to find alternative sources to serve the East Asian markets. Wearing both his Imperial and Jersey Standard hats, Teagle set out to find new sources. Consequently, the London & Pacific offer was particularly attractive. But for several other reasons, from Teagle's viewpoint orchestrating the acquisition through Canada was useful.

The issue of nationality was a factor, as the British shareholders in London & Pacific preferred to deal with a "British" company rather than the American behemoth.[1] But there were other considerations that Teagle and his Jersey Standard colleagues found persuasive. New Jersey had passed a corporate reform act in 1913 that substantially restricted the ability of companies chartered in that state to hold shares in other enterprises; in addition, in 1909 the US Congress had passed an act establishing a corporate income tax. Jersey Standard could have established a British holding company for the Peruvian fields; but under English law, a company that held undistributed assets could be taxed, and this could have substantially diluted the value of the London & Pacific holdings. Canada's federal tax laws were more lenient in this regard, as income from overseas assets was not taxed. All of these elements reinforced Teagle's interest in using his new fiefdom, Imperial Oil, as the vehicle for the Peruvian investment.[2]

But Teagle's ambitions extended well beyond the acquisition of an oilfield in Peru. In the aftermath of the antitrust suit, and the election of Woodrow Wilson as President (he had been the governor of New Jersey when the state's corporate reform act was passed), there was widespread distrust in the halls of 26 Broadway, Jersey Standard's headquarters, about

The Oil Fields of Peru

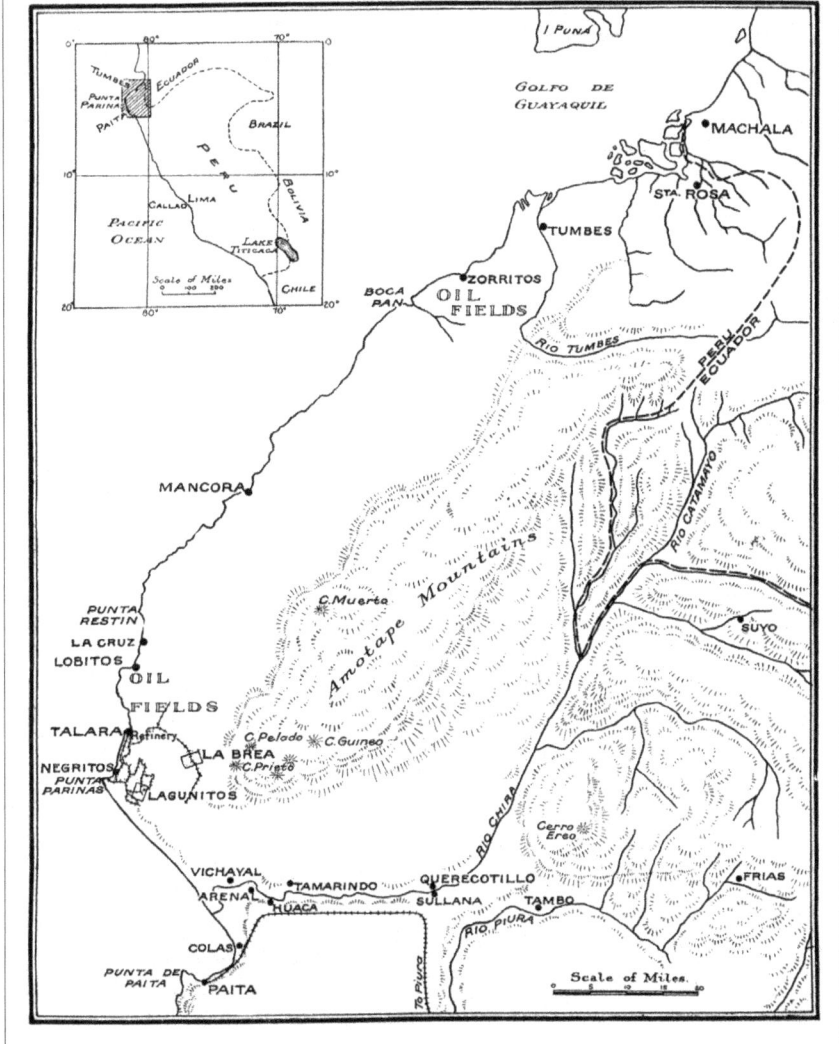

MAP 4.1. Oil Fields in Peru, *Imperial Oil Review*, June 1922, p. 5. Courtesy of the Glenbow Archive, Imperial Oil Collection.

the future intentions of US government policies toward "big business," in particular the possible extension of the Sherman Act to "monopolies in foreign nations."[3] Teagle envisioned an entity, located offshore from the United States, that could manage Jersey Standard's emerging foreign investments; and Imperial Oil could well fit that bill. The scope of Teagle's vision was outlined by his colleague and legal counsel at Imperial, W.J. Hanna, in a letter to T.H. White, the Minister of Finance for the government of Canada, in April 1914: "For some time there has been under consideration the bringing together in one corporation of a number of large commercial interests that are to-day operating in Germany, France, Italy, South America, China and in fact the principal countries of the world. Capitalization when brought together would be upwards of 100 millions . . . There would be between fifty and sixty thousand shareholders, located in different companies that it is intended to bring together."[4] Although International Petroleum did not become the vehicle for all of Jersey Standard's foreign ventures, for Teagle it was a handy device when needed.

In December 1914 Imperial Oil approved the establishment of International Petroleum Company as a subsidiary, acquiring all the La Brea estate and most of the associated enterprises. The company's authorized capital was $20 million (CAD), of which $5.2 million in common stock and $500,000 in preferred shares were issued in early 1915. Teagle was the president, and G. Harrison Smith (who would succeed Teagle as president of IPC in 1917 and later became head of Imperial) was vice president. In its public communications the new company emphasized that IPC was to provide crude oil from Peru to Imperial's Vancouver refinery for western Canadian markets.[5]

Teagle dispatched petroleum engineers and drillers to develop the La Brea fields, most of them Americans since "Imperial had no producing staff at that time."[6] Despite the remote location of the estate, it was close to the coast of Peru, and the wells struck oil quickly, so that production rose by early 1916 from 400 bbl./day to 5,000 bbl./day, and the small refinery at Talara was expanded. Four oil tankers were sub-leased from Imperial's own fleet, one of which was specifically tasked to supply the Peruvian port of Callao for the domestic market.[7]

IPC's relations with the government of Peru, however, were not developing as smoothly as production in the fields. By the second decade of the twentieth century, there was increasing tension throughout much of Latin America over the rapid growth of foreign direct investment in the region, directed both at the foreigners and at the politicians who were perceived as working for them. Admittedly British, French, and German capitalists were very much a part of these developments; nevertheless, a decade of "Big Stick" diplomacy by the United States had encouraged particular animosity toward American business. And although IPC was a "Canadian" subsidiary, it was largely perceived in the countries where it operated as an arm of the Standard Oil octopus.

Revolutionary nationalism and anti-American sentiments were most prevalent in Mexico and Colombia, but Peru was also experiencing political turmoil. In 1914–15, while Jersey Standard and Imperial Oil were setting up IPC, Peru was convulsed by civil strife, a military coup, and eventually the election of a new president, José Pardo y Barreda. Although no radical, Pardo found it politic to cater to the nationalist sentiment that focused on the threat of this new foreign behemoth.[8]

The Pardo government brought forward a series of tax measures, beginning with a revision of the original La Brea concession that increased the mining tax to cover all lands in the estate regardless of whether or not they were developed—this was based on the view that London & Pacific had consistently understated the extent of their development in order to avoid taxation. Next, taxes were proposed on production and exports, both specifically to be imposed on IPC. The company responded in a variety of ways: seeking to negotiate a compromise on the concession issue (which proved fruitless), lobbying against the bills, challenging the proposals in court, demanding that the issue be subject to international arbitration (through Britain, and later the Hague), and threatening to curtail production.[9]

The confrontation reached a critical point in 1918 when the IPC announced that the Canadian government had requisitioned its tankers to serve with the convoys in the Atlantic carrying supplies to Britain. This was in response to Germany's vigorous U-boat campaign, and Imperial Oil had already contributed its own tankers to convoy duty. But to the government of Peru, the move appeared to be another pressure tactic by IPC, which closed down operations for several months, leaving Lima stranded with a limited supply of oil. Many Peruvians viewed IPC's moves with skepticism, since from their perspective the "real" parent of IPC was the American company Standard Oil. Several accounts of this episode indicate that these suspicions were not without substance and that the Canadian government did not specifically requisition two of the IPC tankers.[10]

Proposals were floated to cancel the La Brea concession altogether, and possibly transfer ownership to interested German parties or establish a domestic oil company. Yet in this same time period, the government asked IPC to support its efforts to acquire a $15 million (USD) loan from banks in New York—which unravelled when the bankers demanded that Peru pledge revenues from its export taxes (including those on petroleum) as collateral.[11]

In any case, the shutdown seems to have had the desired effect from IPC's point of view. Shortly after the First World War ended, the Peruvian Congress agreed to submit the La Brea issue to international arbitration. Early in 1919 Pardo was overthrown by another coup, this one staged by Augusto Leguia, who had been president from 1908–12. Leguia, who had been an executive with the New York Life Insurance Company before entering politics, was pro-business and pro-foreign investment. But he also drove a hard bargain, demanding that IPC make a "gift" of $1 million (USD) to the government of Peru. In 1922 the company and the government reached an agreement on the La Brea issue, with Peru confirming IPC's rights to minerals, and levying taxes only on property actually under development; in return IPC accepted a higher tax rate.[12]

Expansion into Colombia

In 1915 Joe Trees and Mike Benedum, two American "wildcatters" (independent oil producers) with a record of successful oil finds in West Texas, Mexico, and Romania, acquired an option to an oil concession in Colombia from a French speculator, Robert De Mares. Ten years earlier De Mares had obtained access to mineral rights in a 2,000 square mile area along the upper reaches of the Magdalena River, deep in the interior of the country, but had been unable to raise the capital to develop the concession. Trees and Benedum set up a company, Tropical Oil, and began drilling in 1916 in what became known as the "Infantas" field. After two

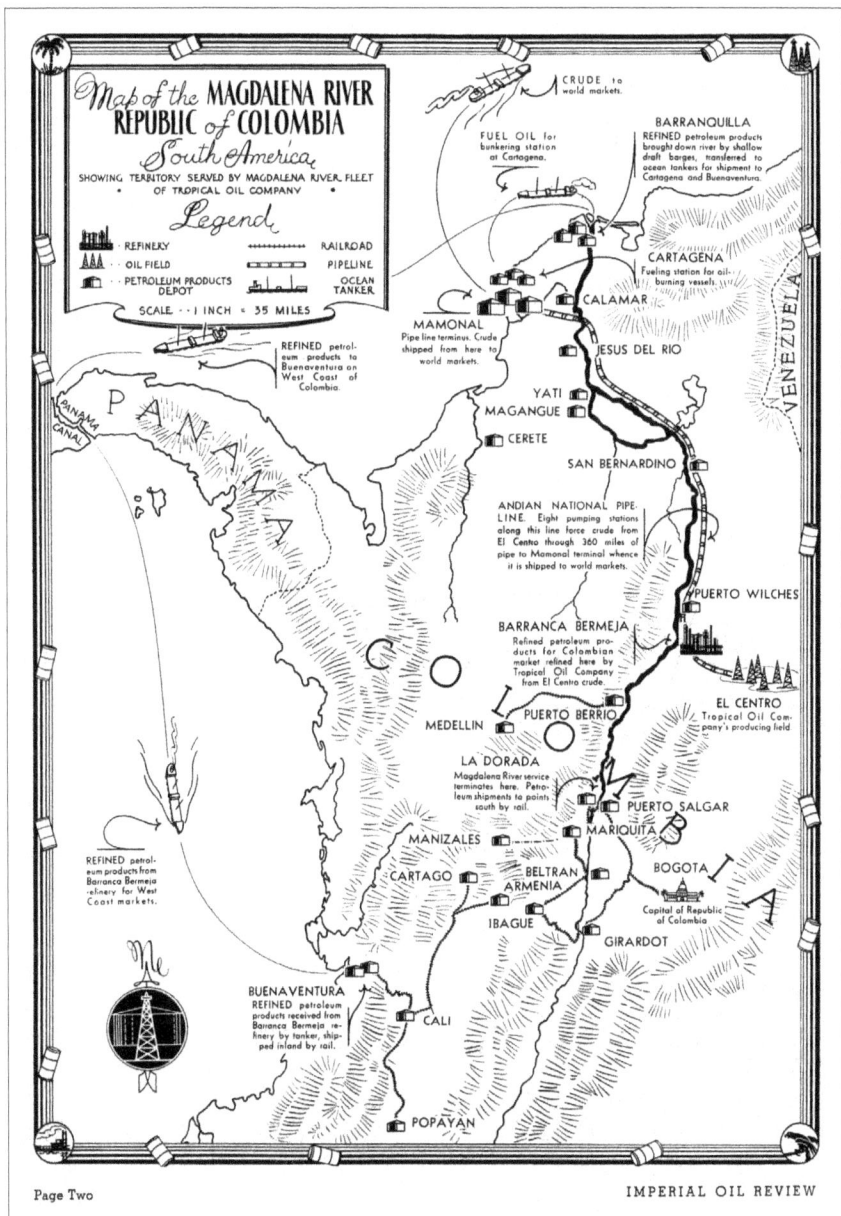

MAP 4.2. Oil in Colombia. *Imperial Oil Review*, Autumn 1937, p. 2. Courtesy of the Glenbow Archive, Imperial Oil Collection.

years of working in the wilderness region with limited resources, they felt confident enough about their prospects to take over the concession.

In the meantime, the government of Colombia had been deliberating on a policy regarding development of potential oil resources. The governing Conservative party was divided between those who supported foreign investment and a more nationalist element that borrowed ideas from revolutionary Mexico. This latter faction prevailed in debates over oil policy: they passed a petroleum law in 1919 that asserted government control over subsoil resources, imposed export taxes, and limited concessions to a thirty-year period, after which the government could take over the assets. Subsequently, the Colombian Supreme Court ruled much of this legislation unconstitutional, but for foreign oil companies contemplating investment in Colombia, it had provided a glimpse of the kind of obstacles they would face. Two potential American competitors—Pure Oil and Sinclair Oil—backed out of earlier commitments in Colombia. More crucially the British firm Pearson & Son, which had a strong position in Mexico and had been wooing the Colombian government for years, also withdrew from the scene.[13]

Nevertheless, Jersey Standard found the De Mares concession attractive. Trees and Benedum had worked with Standard Oil on earlier projects and a geological survey confirmed that the concession was worth at least $5 million (USD). Because the concession predated the 1919 law, it (presumably) was not subject to the restrictions imposed on new investments. Although the prospects for drilling were good, the site was far upriver from any potential market and would require substantial capital investment for development, so that Tropical's owners could be brought to the negotiating table. Teagle, now installed as president of Jersey Standard, was firmly committed to the project, and had both the motive and the means to achieve his aims.[14]

By 1919 Jersey Standard's fears of further antitrust measures had been allayed, and Teagle's original ideas about the uses of International Petroleum were less salient. There were, however, reasons why IPC came to be seen as an appropriate instrument for investment in Colombia. Anti-American resentment over the US role in the Panamanian "revolution" of 1903 remained strong in Colombia: in 1909 President Rafael Reyes Prieto had been forced to resign after negotiating a treaty that recognized the independence of Panama. In 1914 the Woodrow Wilson administration in Washington negotiated a new treaty (the Urrutia-Thomson Treaty) that provided $25 million (USD) in compensation for Colombia's loss of Panama; but this had been held up by the US Senate because of opposition by the Republicans. The passage of the oil regulatory law in Colombia reinforced the reluctance of the US Congress to ratify the treaty. Although Colombia's President Marco Fidel Suarez sought to placate the Americans in order to get the treaty approved, he was assailed for proposing to suspend the petroleum law. So the issue continued to influence the political environment in Bogota. An openly American venture, particularly by the notorious Standard Oil company, would encounter resistance. In these circumstances the Canadian identity of IPC could provide cover, however threadbare.[15]

To help him achieve his goals in Colombia, Teagle relied on a "secret agent:" "Captain" James W. Flanagan, who combined the skills of an entrepreneur and those of a lobbyist, and whose connections to Jersey Standard were often concealed even from other company officials. In 1914 Flanagan had gone to Mexico to scout out potential oil concessions and gather information on events in that revolutionary country. Shortly thereafter he turned up in Peru, posing as a potential railway contractor while "lavishly entertaining" political figures in Lima and reporting (privately) to Teagle on the tumultuous events there.[16] In Bogota in 1919 Flanagan presented himself as the representative of a Canadian company, the Andian National Corporation,[17] interested in constructing either a railway or pipeline to connect the Infantas oil field to Cartagena on the Caribbean coast.

Andian was indeed a Canadian company, whose president and board chairman was Sir Herbert Holt, the chief executive of a range of prominent Canadian enterprises, including Montreal Heat, Light & Power, the largest electric utility in Quebec, and the Royal Bank of Canada. Teagle and Hanna had devoted a good deal of energy to bringing Holt into the orbit of Imperial, as a shareholder and financial adviser, and his position with Andian was to provide a degree of legitimacy that was less apparent with Flanagan, who was vice president. Flanagan, however, was the main figure in this undertaking, in terms of both its business and its political machinations. Flanagan brought Carlos Urrutia, the Colombian ambassador in Washington, onto the Andian board, which helped smooth the way

FIGURE 4.1. "Captain" James Flanagan, with daughter Diva, 1936. Glenbow Archive IP-26-8b-Flanagan, J.W.-1, Imperial Oil Collection.

for land concessions for the proposed pipeline. He also lobbied behind the scenes with Republican Senators such as Albert B. Fall and Henry Cabot Lodge, chairman of the Senate Foreign Relations Committee, to ensure ratification of the Urrutia-Thomson Treaty, which was finally approved in 1921.[18]

In due course these various operations came together: Tropical Oil became part of IPC in August 1920 in exchange for 1.8 million shares of the Canadian company; Joe Trees remained as president of Tropical, but G.H. Smith of IPC became the vice president and effectively the managing director. IPC's capital was increased to $100 million (CAD), with the

Tropical shareholders retaining 33 per cent. Andian did not become part of IPC until 1925, when it issued $15 million (CAD) in bonds to finance the pipeline. Meanwhile, the terms of the transferred De Mares concession were worked out with the Colombian government. In many respects they resembled the 1919 legislation: the concession was limited to a thirty-year period; there would be a 10 per cent royalty on production; and IPC/Tropical was to establish a refinery within two years to supply the domestic oil needs of Colombia. In addition IPC agreed to ensure that 25 per cent of the workforce was hired locally, and to establish supervisory positions in the company for Colombians.[19]

By all accounts, the conditions in which the Infanta oil fields and the Cartagena pipeline were developed were extraordinarily challenging. Despite these initial problems, crude oil production increased sixfold in the first two years of operation under IPC. A small refinery was completed at Barranca by the end of 1922. Barges and steamers were detailed to carry fuel oil and other products to the local Colombian market. Housing for employees, commissaries, and hospitals (malaria and related diseases were endemic) were set up—the latter with help from the Rockefeller Foundation. In his report to Imperial Oil shareholders in 1923, board chairman Charles Stillman offered the optimistic observation that "the Colonies [sic] which they [IPC employees] constitute are happy, prosperous and contented, despite the disabilities of residence so far from home."[20]

Transportation was the major issue. In 1924 a narrow gauge railway was built from the refinery to the Magdalena River, but the pipeline was not completed until 1927. At that point, Andian had invested $26.8 million (CAD) in the 360-mile system, one of the largest outside North America. Almost immediately, however, De Mares production increased from 18,000 to 36,000 bbl./day and annual exports rose from 4 million to 13.7 million barrels. Within two years output from Colombia doubled that of Peru. Meanwhile a new producing field was under development. Although oil prices had stagnated through the mid-1920s due to overproduction globally, the addition of this huge influx of Colombian oil provided a stable production base for Imperial Oil—and for Jersey Standard.

1927 was a benchmark year for IPC. Within two years oil production leaped from 58,000 to 79,000 bbl./day. "For the first time," Imperial Oil's Charles Stillman exulted, "the Republic of Colombia became a contributor to the world's supply of petroleum."[21] It also marked a high point for IPC in terms of its capital investments in the region. Although the company sustained its existing operations in Peru and Colombia through the 1930s, there were few new initiatives in terms of expanding or intensifying the business. In 1937 IPC played a role in a complicated scenario involving Mene Grande oil field in Venezuela: Jersey Standard (through IPC) and Shell (through a Dutch subsidiary) acquired a half interest in the Mene Grande Oil Company. Gulf Oil Corporation had developed the field. IPC as a junior partner played no operational role in Mene Grande, but as Jersey Standard's surrogate "obtained the right to inspect Mene Grande's books and to approve or veto its exploration and development plans."[22] This proved to be a valuable investment: by 1947 Mene Grande was producing 40 per cent of IPC's crude oil. In the meantime Jersey Standard acquired other oil holdings in Venezuela, notably the Creole Syndicate with production on Lake Maracaibo in 1928, which would eventually eclipse IPC's output from Colombia and Peru.[23]

There were several factors at work in this situation. In 1928–30, IPC was exploiting the benefits of its substantial investment (via Andian) on pipeline development. After 1931, the combined impact of the Great Depression on markets and overproduction (particularly in the new East Texas fields) depressed export prices. After 1934, IPC increased its output for the domestic markets in Colombia (which was legally required) and Peru. But there were other, political, considerations. In Peru another military coup toppled Augusto Leguia in 1930, followed by new nationalist efforts to reverse the 1922 settlement. These were thwarted; but looming in the background was a populist movement, APRA, which threatened to revisit the tax issue and perhaps take even stronger measures against foreign companies.[24]

In Colombia, IPC was the target of a premature effort led by the Minister of Development José Antonio Montalvo to extend government authority over the petroleum industry in 1927–28. A more foreign investment-friendly regime came to power in the early 1930s under the Liberal president Enrique Herrera but the issues resurfaced after Mexico nationalized its oil fields in 1938. In 1941 the Colombian government demanded that the De Mares concession terminate within five years. Although Colombia's Supreme Court reaffirmed the original concession date to 1951,

Jersey Standard was on notice that IPC's days were numbered. In both Peru and Colombia, then, the Depression, plus continuing political unrest, discouraged interest in bold new initiatives to expand IPC's operations.[25]

International Petroleum, Imperial Oil, and Jersey Standard

In most accounts of the oil industry in this period, International Petroleum Co.—if it is mentioned at all—appears as a surrogate for Jersey Standard, a view obviously shared by contemporaries in the host countries, Peru and Colombia. This is not surprising: in the early stages of its entry into South America IPC was clearly carrying out strategies worked out at 26 Broadway. Walter Teagle, the dominant figure at Jersey Standard from 1917 through 1941, was a person of immense energy, determination, and breadth of vision. These are all entrepreneurial qualities, but Teagle was a quintessential "company man" and the company he served was Jersey Standard. IPC was conceived and developed as a means of establishing a Jersey Standard presence in an unfamiliar, even hostile environment; if it served the needs of Imperial Oil, this was incidental to the purpose. Even after his departure into the upper echelons of Jersey Standard, Teagle took a great interest in the activities of IPC, seeking "intimate attention to details," according to Jersey Standard's historians, and leaving "little independence of action" to the local managers.[26]

But both Imperial Oil and International Petroleum were more than "paper" organizations on a chart: they were real entities, and as IPC's operations matured in the mid-1920s, these characteristics became clearer. G. Harrison Smith, who was the leading figure at IPC in the 1920s and later became president of Imperial Oil, was a protégé of Teagle's. He had joined Imperial just after the 1899 takeover and worked his way up through the Standard system. Smith was a loyal company man but also capable of standing up to Teagle, who opposed his decision to shut down production in Peru in 1918. R.V. LeSueur was a Canadian lawyer who handled IPC's legal cases in Peru in the early years and became president of IPC in the 1930s and then president of Imperial Oil in the 1940s; fluent in Spanish, LeSueur had a Peruvian wife and a relatively good reputation with the business and political elite in Lima. Alex McQueen, who became

FIGURE 4.2. G. Harrison Smith, president IOL, 1944. Glenbow Archive IP 26-8b-Smith, G.H.-3, Imperial Oil Collection.

vice president of IPC in 1921, was an "old Petrolia hand," whose roots went back to the early days of the Canadian industry. He was also a key figure with both IPC in the 1920s and Imperial's Alberta subsidiary in the Turner Valley, Royalite.[27]

In its first years of operation in Peru, IPC had relied substantially on American drillers to develop the fields. By the mid-1920s, Imperial's President could claim that "the Company's organization of both Peru and Colombia are manned very largely by Canadians," and although this may have been hyperbole, the list of Imperial managers who worked with IPC runs into the hundreds, and many of them assumed major managerial roles with Imperial in the 1950s–60s.[28]

In 1926–27 International Petroleum became more visible in the Canadian press. The business journal, *The Financial Post*, published a series of articles lauding Tropical's (IPC's) development of the oil fields and pipelines in Colombia, and emphasizing the role of "Canadian courage, Canadian ability and Canadian patriotism."[29] The *Imperial Oil Review* featured articles on IPC's work in Peru and Colombia, emphasizing the company's efforts to address health and housing needs for their employees. The company also hired locally as promised: by 1926 there were over 2,000 employees in the Infanta oil fields and the Barranca refinery, only 7 per cent of whom were non-Colombians.[30] There were, however, complaints that management positions were principally occupied by Canadians; and there was growing labour militancy, culminating in a strike in 1927 that was put down by government intervention. Wages were better than those offered by many other employers in the country, but the labour movement was growing stronger and a Standard Oil subsidiary was an obvious target—particularly at a time when even some Conservative politicians were clamouring to revisit the country's petroleum policy and revise royalty agreements.[31]

The rationale for Imperial's investment in South America, to the Canadian public and minority investors, was to augment declining domestic supplies, with Peruvian oil going to Vancouver and Colombian oil to Montreal. The arrival of the first tanker from Colombia in 1927 received much publicity in Montreal, with Sir Herbert Holt ceremoniously turning on the tap.[32] But Imperial's largest refinery in Sarnia was supplied by the Cygnet pipeline from Ohio, and Imperial invested in the Cygnet's supply line from Oklahoma—Ajax Pipeline—in 1930. In 1941 Jersey Standard built a pipeline from Portland, Maine to Montreal, which it sold to Imperial in 1948. Meanwhile, Jersey Standard received a substantial volume of oil from both Peru and Colombia at its Bayonne, New Jersey refinery, as the South American light crude was deemed highly desirable for motor fuel, which had a much larger market in the US than in Canada: the Colombian Ministry of Mines and Resources in 1944 estimated that over 80 per cent of exported crude went to the US refineries.[33]

From the perspective of Imperial's managers, the destination of various sources of crude was not a particular issue as long as Imperial's own needs were served: as Imperial's Charles Stillman emphasized in his 1927 report, Colombia had become "a contributor to the world's supply of petroleum," not just for Canada. Equally important was the issue of over-production, which was a recurring feature of the oil markets throughout this period. In 1922, when Peruvian oil production was just beginning to exceed local market requirements, Stillman lamented "the demoralization of markets in the United States," as a result of overproduction. This overproduction depressed oil prices and left refiners with surplus gasoline, which they were dumping "on the Canadian and Eastern American markets." The situation persisted over the next several years so that even as he welcomed the arrival of Colombian exports, he expressed concern over "the condition of over-production and low prices of crude" that Imperial experienced "indirectly through its association with the International Petroleum Company."[34]

Conditions improved toward the end of the decade, but as the Depression deepened prices declined—in part because of diminished market demand and also because of overproduction, particularly in the Texas fields. By 1931–33 IPC was cutting back production; output increased in the latter part of the decade, reaching a high point in 1937, but then fell again during the recession. Even during the Second World War, the volume of production and exports remained lower than it had been in the late thirties, in part because of the hazards of tanker shipping in the North Atlantic and the diversion of Imperial tankers to convoy duty.[35]

Imperial Oil, and through it Jersey Standard, did very well financially from the International Petroleum investments. During the 1920s dividends from IPC represented an average of 22 per cent of Imperial's net income. But this figure rose dramatically during the Depression due to increased earnings by IPC and declining returns to Imperial from its domestic operations: between 1931 and 1941, IPC dividends rose from 50 per cent to over 80 per cent of net income; the income from the South American investments was almost eight times larger than Imperial's profits from its Canadian manufacturing and marketing. During this same period, the dividends paid by Imperial to its shareholders (with almost 80 per cent going to Jersey Standard) exceeded net income. From 1921 to 1947 income from subsidiaries accounted for more than half of Imperial's net income (with IPC contributing more than 80 per cent through most of this time); and dividends paid to Jersey Standard represented more than two-thirds of Imperial's net earnings.[36]

For both Imperial Oil and International Petroleum, the dividend policies that followed in the 1930s left their respective companies with relatively little income available for new capital investment. As John Ewing, Imperial Oil's historian, observed: "over the 20 years from 1926 to 1945 Imperial Oil had returned to its shareholders about 100 per cent of its earnings;" and its capacity to do so relied on "the income that the company received from its investment in other companies, conspicuously in the International Petroleum Company."[37] After 1940, Imperial stabilized its dividend draw-down from IPC to $8.7 million (CAD) per year and its own payments to shareholders stabilized at $13.5 million (CAD) per year.[38] Consequently, both companies had increased retained earnings for reinvestment. Nevertheless, both Imperial and IPC emerged from the Second World War with inadequate reserves to sustain major new investments.

For Imperial Oil this problem became particularly acute when (after almost thirty years) the company struck oil at Leduc in Alberta in 1947. In the following year new discoveries substantially transformed the future domestic prospects for the Canadian company. But it faced immediate capital needs to exploit these finds, not only in developing production and refining capabilities but also to establish pipelines to carry the oil from the remote reaches of Alberta to Canadian and US markets. By 1948 Imperial's board decided to sell most of its subsidiaries, notably International Petroleum.[39]

There was another factor that influenced this decision: in 1947 the Colombian government had announced its intention not to renew the De Mares concession when it matured in 1951, but to take it over and operate it as a national company. Of course, much could change in four years, and the Colombians would probably need to contract with an established company to develop its own capabilities in this field. Nevertheless, this was a Damocles sword hovering over IPC, and the company had substantially expanded its Venezuelan commitments while allowing Colombian output to stabilize in the years following the end of the war.[40]

Jersey Standard took over control of International Petroleum in 1948, paying Imperial $80 million (CAD). In light of Colombia's apparent intention to nationalize IPC's assets there, this might appear to be a curious decision. But at this point Jersey Standard believed that by 1951 some kind of contractual arrangement could be worked out, and in any case it acquired direct control of IPC's investments in Peru and Venezuela. Since

Imperial remained as a subsidiary of Jersey Standard, in some respects this amounted to an internal transaction. But Imperial may have come out ahead in this deal: in 1951 Colombia did proceed to take over the oil fields of the Tropical Oil Company, which was renamed Ecopetrol, although IPC remained as a partner in running the domestic refining and distribution system for several years. In the 1960s the military government of Peru seized IPC's properties there in far more contentious circumstances, which led to years of bickering over compensation; meanwhile the government used the IPC assets as the base for a national company, Petro Peru.[41]

International Petroleum, Peru, and Colombia

International Petroleum was established for the purpose of opening up the oil fields of Peru and Colombia for exploitation and exports and augmenting the reserves of Jersey Standard and its Canadian affiliate. This was a supply-driven strategy, and serving the markets of the host countries was not initially a major consideration. In 1914, neither was in the forefront of the demographic and economic growth that characterized larger South American countries such as Argentina, Brazil, and Chile. Peru's exports expanded significantly after 1907, but it was still recovering from the loss of the nitrate beds of Tacna and Arica to Chile two decades earlier. Colombia was in the early stages of expansion of its coffee production, challenging the domination of Brazil, but civil wars at the turn of the century had disrupted its economic growth. These circumstances were to change dramatically in the years after the First World War, when GDP growth in Colombia and particularly in Peru substantially exceeded those of their larger neighbours and South America as a whole.[42]

Although in both countries wealth was concentrated in the hands of a small elite of landowners and merchants, the sheer growth of the economy expanded consumer markets. Urbanization also played a role in fostering demand: Colombia in particular experienced significant urban growth, with the cities of Bogota, Medellin, and Cali increasing from 3 per cent to more than one-third of the nation's population between 1918 and 1951.[43]

International Petroleum was attentive to the demands of domestic markets in Peru and Colombia during this period. In Colombia, the requirement to serve local needs was built into the 1920 agreement. There was no parallel for Peru, but the repercussions that IPC encountered after kerosene supplies to Lima were curtailed in 1918 led the company to ensure that the Peruvian market was not stinted. During the early 1930s—the worst years of the Depression—production for internal consumption in Peru rose from 1.9 million bbl. to 3 million bbl./year; and this figure doubled over the next decade.[44] Although the onerous conditions attached to new concessions had driven out most of the large companies in production and refining, IPC still faced competition in imports in the Peruvian and Colombian markets (except for kerosene, which was protected), particularly during periods of global overproduction and always from large integrated companies such as Shell and Gulf. So IPC followed a policy of low prices for these local markets through much of this period.[45]

During the 1930s International Petroleum was clearly treated as a "cash cow" by its owners and there was little new investment in the plant or in equipment. In 1939 IPC acquired a concession in Ecuador and began exploratory work, but little came of this venture at the time. In 1945, a joint Jersey Standard/Imperial team sent to investigate La Brea concluded that it "lagged behind other affiliates" in maintaining working and housing conditions.[46] In light of its obvious financial status within the Jersey Standard system, this situation may not seem too surprising. The company had begun as the favoured project of Walter Teagle, and had embarked on an ambitious and costly development program in the 1920s. As other regions became the focus of growth in the 1940s—particularly Venezuela and the Middle East—IPC's Colombian and Peruvian operations became a backwater, facing growing nationalist pressures and diminishing production runs. Had Imperial not discovered oil in Alberta in 1947, the Canadian company might have been induced to put more capital into reviving IPC. But of course Leduc altered Imperial's course, and IPC became something of a problem child for Jersey Standard.

The Legacy

Today Exxon Mobil is not only the world's largest petroleum company; it is also well versed in the complexities of global oil diplomacy. This was not the case in 1914: although Standard Oil was a sophisticated organization that sold its products in global markets, it had relatively limited experience dealing with foreign governments, particularly those driven by economic nationalism. As in Mexico, Jersey Standard learned through its experiences in Peru and Colombia in the post-1918 era.

In this context, the link to the British Empire through Imperial Oil proved useful. It helped facilitate the acquisition of the London & Pacific properties in Peru, and later enabled Jersey Standard to enlist British aid in resolving IPC's tax problems with Peru as well. In Colombia the Imperial/IPC cloak may have served a different purpose, given the degree of anti-American sentiment in that country. Nevertheless, the greatest benefit of the Imperial connection to IPC in the longer run was the generous tax breaks available to Imperial from the Canadian government, which were duly passed on to Jersey Standard as dividends. For its part, Imperial Oil may have been little more than a loyal follower and cash cow; but by the 1930s the Canadians were playing a larger role in running IPC and it was a valuable training ground for geologists, engineers, drillers, and pipeline layers who could apply their knowledge to the Canadian scene after Leduc.

At that point, Jersey Standard had to make some critical choices: the Canadians had finally discovered significant oil reserves but lacked the capital to exploit them. IPC faced the prospect of dissolution, at least in Colombia, by 1951. In the end, Jersey Standard determined that the future of Imperial Oil was more important to its own corporate needs, and that there was at least the prospect of a negotiated agreement with Colombia over the IPC oil fields. The trade-off worked for at least a decade in Colombia, and Imperial continued to be an important part of Jersey Standard's global profile through the present.

5

COGS IN THE WHEEL

Teagle's Shadow

On February 28, 1918 Walter Teagle resigned as president of Imperial Oil to take up the more august position of president of Standard Oil of New Jersey. Teagle had in fact departed from Toronto for 26 Broadway in New York in November 1917 when Standard's board hurriedly reorganized its top management to enable the incumbent president, A. Cotton Bedford, to serve as the head of the Petroleum Committee of the US Council on National Defense that was coordinating industrial mobilization for the country's war effort.[1] Teagle's presidency of Imperial had only begun officially in January 1914, so he had occupied the position for a little more than four years; and even in that period his activities were divided between Toronto, New York, and London as he continued to hold a directorship at Standard Oil and in effect managed all of Standard's foreign operations throughout the First World War.

Nevertheless, during that brief tenure Teagle had a lasting impact on the Canadian company. Imperial became the parent entity for Standard's oil ventures in Peru and Colombia. The tanker fleet, which in 1910 consisted of two steamers that hauled oil across the Great Lakes from US sources, increased to ten ships and began bringing South American oil to Canada's west coast by 1918. Refinery capacity also expanded dramatically: in 1912 the company had a single refinery at Sarnia processing a little over 3,000 barrels daily. By 1919 new refineries were in operation in Halifax, Montreal, and Vancouver, and production had quadrupled. Distribution and sales networks had been reorganized and extended to cover the national market. Imperial's capitalization was vastly expanded, pensions and benefits were given permanence, and an employee share purchase plan introduced.

Teagle's influence on Imperial continued long after his physical departure from Toronto. He remained as a director until 1919, and in the ensuing years directors and managers who had been closely associated with him sustained his initiatives—including W.J. Hanna, the long-term legal counsel for Imperial and a prominent Tory political figure in Ontario, who succeeded Teagle as president briefly until his untimely death in 1919; G.W. Mayer, who had carried out the reorganization of Imperial's sales force; Victor Ross, a financial journalist with the Toronto *Globe* who set up the *Imperial Oil Review*, the first "in-house" publication in the Standard Oil system in 1915 (at Teagle's instigation, he later established *The Lamp* for Jersey Standard); and G.H. Smith and R.V. LeSueur, both of whom rose to the presidency of Imperial Oil after holding similar positions with International Petroleum.[2]

More significantly Teagle's position as chief executive of Jersey Standard for more than twenty years, as well as the strategies and policies he pursued at the parent firm, would have both an indirect and a direct impact on the evolution of Imperial Oil during this era. Jersey Standard faced a range of substantial and continuing challenges in these years, and while Imperial was no longer the potential flagship of Jersey's international operations by the 1920s, Teagle's experience in Canada made him more aware than most of his colleagues at 26 Broadway of the role that Imperial played in the Standard system. On a more personal level, Teagle retained a connection to Canada as a result of his interest in hunting and fishing, with an annual visit to Kedgwick Lodge in a remote area of New Brunswick for salmon fishing.

When Teagle was chosen "to fill John D.'s shoes"[3] in 1918, Jersey Standard was still the largest oil company in the world—despite the effects of the post-1911 breakup of the trust. The onset of the First World War and US entry in 1917 increased demand for petroleum and silenced the trustbusters as government and public attention focused on the war effort; in 1918 the Webb-Pomerene Act allowed US oil companies to "cooperate" in seeking overseas markets. Meanwhile, the Russian Revolution and civil war in 1918–20 disrupted the operations of one of Jersey Standard's major international rivals, the Nobel group, and even for a time seemed to open opportunities for the American company to get a foothold in the Caspian Sea region. Nevertheless, the new president of Jersey Standard had to cope with an array of interconnected dangers and vulnerabilities.

As in 1912–14, Jersey Standard's formidable refining capacity required a constant supply of crude, which for the most part was under the control of other survivors of the breakup. These survivors, who could still be regarded as "friendly concerns," were now able to sell on more advantageous terms to both Jersey Standard and potential rivals, including some of the larger remnants, Standard of New York (the future Mobil) and Standard of California (the future Chevron). These vulnerabilities had led Teagle to promote the search for foreign sources, in Peru and Colombia, as well as a vigorous effort to find domestic crude—although Jersey Standard was politically barred from access to the most promising fields in Texas until it acquired a local company there, Humble Oil, in 1919. These efforts had increased in-house sources from 8 per cent to 17 per cent of Jersey Standard's refining capacity by the time Teagle took over.

The First World War had demonstrated the military importance of oil as a fuel source for naval ships, airplanes, and mobile vehicles on land, leading governments to take an unprecedented interest in finding reserves for future wars. At the same time warnings of an approaching, perhaps irreversible age of scarcity—a recurring nightmare among oil producers— pervaded the industry. So for Teagle and Jersey Standard, a renewed quest for new sources of crude shaped strategic thinking in the early 1920s. The Americans faced a formidable rival in this race with the emergence of Royal Dutch Shell as an international power.

In 1907 Marcus Samuels' Shell Transport and Trading Company had merged with the Royal Dutch Petroleum Company, which was developing oil fields in Sumatra and Borneo in the Dutch East Indies. Within a few years Samuel had been ousted by the ambitious chief executive of Royal Dutch, Henri Deterding, who spent the next two decades seeking to surpass Jersey Standard in the global oil markets. Mexico provided an early site for competition, and by the mid-1920s the focus had shifted to the Persian Gulf region. Teagle, fearing a possible amalgamation of Royal Dutch Shell with the Anglo-Persian Petroleum Company, both with close ties to the British government, importuned the US State Department to help Jersey Standard get a foot in the door of the prospectively large oil fields of Iraq. The contest also featured rivalry in markets across the world as Teagle probed for oil concessions in the Dutch East Indies.[4]

Canada had been the scene of an early skirmish between Jersey Standard and Royal Dutch Shell. In 1915 Teagle learned of a scheme presented by the Shell group to the Canadian government that would give it a virtual monopoly over oil exploration and development in the western provinces. Although ultimately little came of this proposal, it stimulated Teagle to initiate Imperial's first ventures into Alberta in 1917–19, representing its entry into the western oil patch (to be discussed in the next chapter).

Jersey Standard's concerns over the diminishing prospects of new oil reserves, along with a growing interest in the use of petrochemical by-products of thermal cracking, led the company to enter into negotiations with the German chemical giant, I.G. Farben, over patent exchanges covering the development of synthetic fuel oil from coal, discussions which led to a much broader range of patent agreements in the late 1920s–30s. These agreements, particularly on the subject of synthetic rubber, would lead to an unprecedented collaboration between Imperial Oil and the Canadian government during the Second World War, and the establishment of what became Canadian Polysar. By this time, however, controversies in the United States over the "conspiracy" between Jersey Standard and the German company marred the final years of Teagle's presidency.

By the late 1920s, however, the issue was not scarcity of oil supplies but surplus (also a recurring feature for the industry). New oil fields in the Middle East, South America, and the Dutch East Indies were coming on stream. The main contributors were the huge fields in Oklahoma and East Texas, the largest to be discovered until the Saudi Arabian "elephant" of the 1940s. In addition, improvements in refining enabled the oil companies to double the recovery from each barrel of oil, which exacerbated the glut.

Teagle and other industry leaders in the US recognized the need to impose some kind of control on new production through cooperation, but even a pro-business Republican administration in Washington was reluctant to reopen the doors to the antitrust battles of the past. Controls eventually came about in the Depression through quotas imposed by the Texas Railroad Commission, which had regulatory authority over the largest fields in the country.

There were fewer constraints on agreements among international companies, and by this time Royal Dutch Shell was as eager as Jersey Standard to stop the slide in oil prices that excess production and competition had generated. In 1928 Teagle, Deterding, and representatives from Anglo-Persian, Gulf Oil, and Standard of Indiana got together at Achnacarry castle in Scotland ostensibly for a hunting weekend (which stretched into several weeks). The result was what became known as the "As Is" Agreement, in which the parties promised to allocate foreign business on the basis of current market shares, to close down some wells and limit the number of new production facilities based on market conditions.

A quarter of a century later, the As Is Agreement was portrayed by the US Justice Department in a new antitrust suit against Jersey Standard and other oil majors as marking the moment of creation of an international oil cartel, a characterization echoed by many histories of the industry (and embraced as well by the founders of the Organization of Petroleum Exporting Countries in the 1960s). In the immediate years following the Achnacarry meeting, however, the agreement had little impact as oil surpluses continued to flow and prices stagnated. Market discipline, such as it was, came about through the quota allocations set by the Texas Railroad Commission, which effectively determined the world price. As with its parent, Imperial Oil's fortunes were shaped by this context of global boom and bust.[5]

One other feature of the Teagle era at Jersey Standard would have at least an indirect impact on Imperial Oil. The vast expansion of production during and after the war, the quest for overseas supplies and markets, the shift in refining from kerosene to fuel oils and more variegated by-products, and the imposition of government taxation and regulation all contributed to increasing strains on the corporate structure erected by Jersey Standard after the 1911 dissolution decree. The business historian Alfred Chandler Jr. characterized the organization that had evolved as a "partly federated and partly consolidated enterprise." Integrated operations such as Imperial Oil and Standard Oil of Louisiana functioned with a good deal of autonomy while other units were subject to varying degrees of direction by departments at 26 Broadway. As the company expanded and developed new product lines, new divisions sprang up with functions that overlapped those of the existing units and blurred lines of responsibility.

Some departments—such as Export Trade and Development—that were regarded as essential to the future of the company received close attention and support from the board, while others—such as Domestic Marketing and Manufacturing—floundered.

Organizational weaknesses were less apparent during the period of overseas expansion and general growth after the First World War—but by the mid-1920s, with a glutted inventory and falling oil prices, the costs of management inefficiencies became clear. In 1925–26 Teagle undertook a first round of changes. The domestic departments were consolidated into a single division, and export and foreign operations were similarly reorganized—with Imperial Oil remaining as a separate entity. The old system of management by committee—inherited from pre-1911 Standard Oil—was replaced by single executives with staffs and full responsibility for divisional performance. In 1927 a second round of restructuring followed with the aim of reducing the involvement of board directors in the minutiae of routine administration, so that they could focus instead on long-term planning. Although the reorganization emerged from Jersey Standard's own experiences, it paralleled in many respects the changes being introduced in this same era by large companies such as DuPont and General Motors.[6]

Within this new structure, however, there were outliers whose special status was reflected in the retained autonomy. Humble Oil, by now one of the largest production units in the company, was one exception—possibly in deference to the sensibilities of the ever-suspicious Texans. Imperial Oil was the other. While major financial commitments had to be cleared through Jersey Standard's executive committee, most operations were under the control of Imperial's own Board. The main point of contact was a representative of Jersey Standard on Imperial's Board. Over the years similar arrangements were extended to other Jersey Standard affiliates, and members of the Imperial Board would also serve on the board of the parent company, beginning with Smith and LeSueur in the 1940s. This special status for Imperial may have reflected an appreciation on the part of Jersey Standard for Canadian sensitivities, and perhaps a recognition of its unusual role as the official parent of International Petroleum. But it may also have been an outgrowth, at least in this era, of the continuation of a special relationship between Imperial and its benefactor, Walter Teagle.

The Automobile Revolution

For almost half a century the most commercially significant by-product of petroleum—in Canada and elsewhere—was kerosene, used primarily for illumination. On the eve of the First World War, kerosene accounted for close to 50 per cent of the output of the refineries of Imperial and Jersey Standard. By this time, however, electric lighting was emerging as a competitor with oil and gas lamps, particularly in urban areas served by grids fuelled by coal and hydro power. Providentially for the oil industry, a new and even larger potential market was taking shape with the arrival of an automobile based on the internal combustion engine. The earliest automobiles had been developed in Germany in the 1880s but the key event was the introduction of the mass-produced motorcar by Henry Ford in the United States in 1908–12, using gasoline refined from petroleum.

Although Canada had a much smaller and more rural population than the United States, the impact of the automobile was delayed but eventually just as substantial: in 1906 the number of registered motor vehicles in Canada was 565, increasing to 28,000 five years later. By 1914 this number had risen to 75,000 and in the early 1920s to more than 500,000, doubling again by the end of the decade. In 1904 the Ford Motor Company had established a beachhead in Canada through an agreement with Duncan McGregor in Windsor, Ontario, and four years later Robert McLaughlin of Ottawa had formed a partnership with the company that would become General Motors of Canada. By the 1920s the Canadian automotive industry was the tenth largest in the world, and gasoline sales accounted for more than 25 per cent of the country's petroleum refining output. In addition, the Canadian prairies provided a strong market for gas-powered farm vehicles, including the Fordson Tractor as well as the established Massey-Harris and other producers of combines converting from steam to gas.[7]

Gasoline had been a by-product of petroleum refining since the 1860s, but in the early years of the industry it had been discarded as waste. As demand grew in the early 1900s, not only for gasoline but also for related by-products including fuel oil and lubricants, Standard Oil and other major companies in the industry began exploring ways of improving refining processes. In 1913 William M. Burton and R.E. Humphreys, chemists at Standard of Indiana's Whiting refinery—where Frasch had developed his sulphur reduction process a quarter century earlier—patented a new pet-roleum "cracking" technique that would extract substantially more gaso-line and other by-products from each barrel of petroleum and reduce the cost of motor fuel by 80 per cent per gallon. The process involved separat-ing hydrocarbons into wet gas and distillate that resulted in the splitting or "thermal cracking" of heavy molecules into lighter products.[8]

Teagle, who was on the verge of taking on the presidency of Imperial Oil, determined that the Canadian company should reap the benefits of the Burton-Humphreys process as part of his strategy for expanding its refinery operations. Negotiations dragged on as Standard of Indiana con-templated setting up its own refineries in Canada; but in January 1914 Imperial purchased a license to the process for $15,000 (USD) for the first 50,000 barrels per year and 30 cents per barrel for amounts above that level. It was a coup, as Jersey Standard did not acquire access to the process until 1915 (on the basis of much tougher terms).[9]

Imperial continued to benefit from its technological ties to Jersey Standard over the next decade, in part because Charles Stillman, presi-dent of the company from 1919 to 1932, had been in charge of the Sarnia refinery and retained an interest in improving the efficiency as well as the output of Imperial's production. In 1924 Imperial acquired a license to the "tube and tank" cracking process developed by Jersey Standard as an improvement to the Burton process (and incidentally to circum-vent Standard of Indiana's patents). Stillman also established a technical department under R.K. Stratford, initially as an inspection division for new products, but it evolved into a more broad-ranging research and de-velopment unit with links to the Standard Development Company, Jersey Standard's research affiliate. During the 1920s this was a fairly modest operation that focused on improvements to motor oil refining, leading to the introduction of a higher-octane product branded as "Three Star Gasoline" in the early 1930s.[10]

While Stillman focused on improving and expanding refinery pro-duction and expansion, Imperial faced equally significant challenges in the marketing and distribution of gasoline to the Canadian market. One issue was the abundance and low price of gasoline. The 1920s witnessed the dramatic growth of petroleum output including the expansion of oil fields in the US, particularly Texas, as well as gas production in the Turner

Valley in Alberta. In response to pressures from auto manufacturers and dealers, and the emerging mass market for motorcars, import duties on gasoline were held below 1 cent per gallon up to the onset of the Depression and the Bennett tariff of 1930, which raised them to 2.5 cents.

Surplus inventory posed a continuing problem for Imperial throughout the interwar period, which the company tried to offset through sales to independent distributors. As had been the case for Imperial in the 1880s, however, there was a recurring concern that these jobbers might become large enough to establish their own refineries or threaten to take their business to Imperial's equally desperate competitors. Imperial sought to avoid this situation by buying shares in the distributing companies—in effect subsidizing their own customers.[11]

Imperial also proved reluctant to adapt to the emerging environment of the market for gasoline. The company had marketed kerosene and related products through bulk sales to wholesalers, and this continued to be the practice in selling gasoline, particularly in central Canada where associations of garage owners were the major customers. Imperial had experimented with retail gas stations as early as 1908 in Saskatchewan; and during the Teagle era it had set up a subsidiary, Consumer Gas Supply Agency, to retail gas bought directly from the United States. But the logical move to establishing a national service station chain was slow to take hold.

Jersey Standard had been similarly backward in anticipating the new era of gasoline marketing. In 1919 it had only eleven service stations in the United States, and although Jersey Standard increased this number between then and 1924, it share of the country's gasoline business declined from 56 per cent to 47 per cent. The Texas Company (Texaco) had been particularly aggressive in this field. In part this conservatism reflected the influence of the legal department, which was still worried about antitrust implications; the intervention of the legal department may have been involved in the closing of Imperial's retailer, the Consumer Gas Supply Agency, in 1920. The major issue involved the application of exclusive agency contracts with local service stations. By 1925, however, challenges from Texaco and the Sinclair Company galvanized a shift in Jersey Standard's approach, which now focused on establishing stations that could offer full-service maintenance including mechanical and tire

THE FIRST GASOLINE SERVICE STATION IN CANADA
OPENED IN JUNE 1907 - SMYTHE STREET, VANCOUVER

FIGURE 5.1. First gas station, Vancouver, 1914. Glenbow Archive IP-12-1-1, Imperial Oil Collection.

installations. In 1927 Jersey Standard introduced its "Esso" service stations, which were extended into Canada in the 1930s.

Imperial delayed its embrace of the full-service stations in the 1920s in part because of the capital commitments involved, which became an issue between the two companies. Imperial's managers later claimed they wanted to expand into service stations but were deterred because Jersey Standard vetoed the capital commitment involved. Teagle, now wearing his Jersey Standard hat, believed that the benefits of such a move were limited because the Canadian market was already saturated with low-cost gasoline distributors and the US had too many service stations. Imperial did move to a full-service system in the 1930s, using the "Esso" brand (which continues to the present time). The company, however, was careful to limit its capital commitment to a relatively small proportion of the stations involved, with a much larger number of semi-independent garage contractors selling Esso gasoline. This complicated system would later pose public relations problems for Imperial in its never-ending battles with regulators over gas prices.[12]

Competition, Boom, and Bust

The advent of the gasoline era and the petroleum glut in the 1920s contributed to the growth of competition with Imperial in Canada. In 1921 it held 80 per cent of the gasoline market in the country, but this had dwindled to a little over 60 per cent by the end of that decade. The competitors included both large US and other foreign companies and also smaller homegrown enterprises.

Imperial faced its greatest challenge on the west coast with competition from both Shell, which set up a bunker storage plant for fuel oil in Vancouver in 1919, and Union Oil Company, a long-time rival of Standard Oil in California, which established a refinery in British Columbia two years later. Victor Ross of Imperial's board became so incensed over this threat that he suggested Imperial denounce their competitors as "foreign companies." The company dispatched their best sales manager, A.E. Halvorsen, to stem the challengers, and by 1928 Imperial had regained much of its market share in the region, in part through arrangements with independent jobbers and distributors. [13]

In central Canada, Imperial faced some older rivals and a new one in the 1920s, but limited their inroads. Canadian Oil Companies, which had been set up by dissident refiners in Petrolia in 1906 was, ironically, taken over by a US company—National Refining of Cleveland—two years later. During the 1920s its ability to exploit the gasoline market in Ontario was hampered by a lack of capital investment from the American parent company (curiously similar to Imperial's experience). In 1938 it returned to Canadian ownership, but remained a relatively smaller player; in 1962 it was acquired by Shell for $6 million (CAD).

Shell itself, which had loomed so menacingly over Imperial during the Teagle era, also proved to be less of a threat in the years after the First World War, as Europe and East Asia became the focus of Standard-Shell rivalry. In 1911 Royal Dutch Shell had set up a Canadian subsidiary that established a foothold in Quebec, while manoeuvring to control the exploration

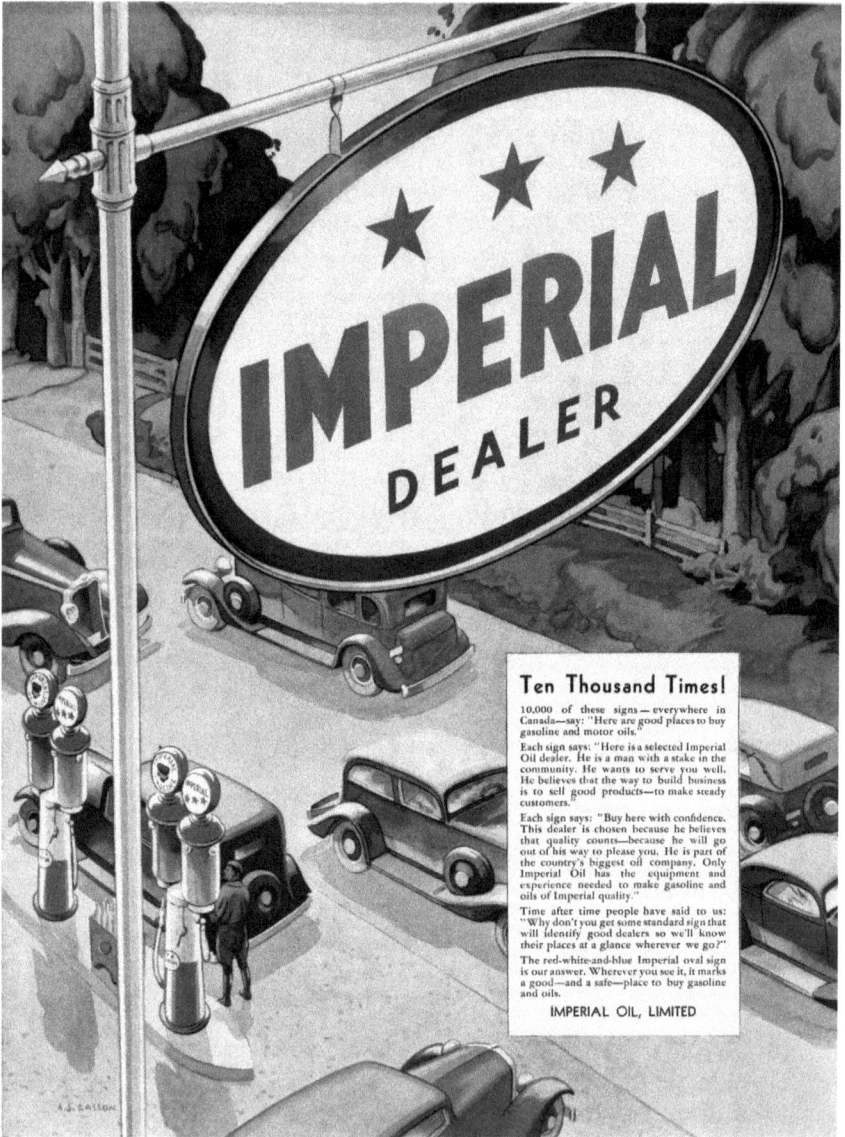

FIGURE 5.2. Imperial Oil advertisement, 1934. Glenbow Archive IP-13f-2-a, Imperial Oil Collection.

for oil in the West. Although it competed with Imperial for the British Columbia market, expansion was limited elsewhere—refineries were only set up in Vancouver and Montreal in the late 1930s. Shell did not become a player in the post-Leduc boom in Alberta until the 1960s when it began buying up existing operations such as Canadian Oil Companies.[14]

Another small-time Ontario refiner became a much bigger challenge to Imperial's ascendency in the interwar period. British American Oil Company was originally neither British nor American; it was the creation of Albert L. Ellsworth, who had been an accountant for Standard Oil of New York at the Buffalo refinery and relocated to Ontario in 1906. Ellsworth joined forces with Silas Parsons, of the Canadian Manufacturers Association, plus a handful of other investors to set up a refinery in Toronto. Focusing on the declining kerosene market, British American struggled—but by the 1920s it had shifted to gasoline refining, established pipelines connected to cheap US suppliers, supplemented by exploration and drilling by its own subsidiaries, and expanded refinery operations into western Canada. Ellsworth backed the wildcat oil drillers Robert Brown and George Bell in setting up Turner Valley Royalties in 1936, which was Canada's largest twentieth-century oil find before Leduc. By the end of that decade, British American was the second largest integrated oil company in Canada.[15]

One other company emerged in the late 1920s as a potentially formidable rival to Imperial. In 1926 the Montreal financial firm Nesbitt Thomson cobbled together an amalgamation of refiners and distributors that included Frontenac Oil of Montreal, Three Rivers Oil & Gas in Quebec, and McColl Brothers Ltd., a Toronto refiner, along with some smaller enterprises. Capitalized at $17 million (CAD) in 1928–29 at the height of the Bull Market, McColl-Frontenac sold at $45 per share. Within a year that boom had collapsed, and shares fell to $24.50. By 1937 share prices were down to $8.50, aggravated by a disastrous investment in oil production in Trinidad. In 1938 the US company Texaco took it over and restructured its financing just in time to benefit from increased demand generated by Canada's involvement in the Second World War.[16]

The crash of 1929 and its aftermath hit all the companies in the industry, and Imperial was not unscathed. During the 1920s Imperial had undergone two rounds of recapitalization, and the general rise in stock market prices boosted the company value, to the delight of the minority shareholders—Jersey Standard retained control of more than two-thirds of the stock, but the numbers of smaller investors swelled from fewer than 1,000 to over 5,000 by the end of the decade, abetted in part by the employee stock purchase plan Teagle initiated.

In 1915 Imperial's authorized capital had been increased from $15 million to $50 million (CAD) to provide resources for Teagle's expansion program, with 2 million shares offered at $25 par value. By 1925 the company's actual asset value had risen to close to $240 million (CAD), and Imperial, with Jersey Standard's approval, issued 8 million new shares at no par value. This allowed for the conversion of the old shares, with a book value of $30 per share. A second recapitalization came in April 1929 with 32 million shares issued at no par value. In the midst of the stock market boom, Imperial's shares quickly rose above $100 and peaked at $119 per share shortly before the crash. By 1930 share values had gone below $30, and there was no further change in the capital structure until 1947.[17]

Throughout the 1930s Imperial was essentially in a holding pattern. Sales remained virtually flat from 1931 to 1937, although earnings rose from $14 million to $25 million (CAD) after 1934, thanks in part to the effects of the Bennett tariff and slowly rising prices of oil by the middle of the decade. Imperial regained some ground from its smaller competitors, particularly in British Columbia, and it retained a dominant role in the Maritimes and Quebec. But overall, the markets were shrinking. Although production and sales had also flattened in South America, the contributions of International Petroleum gave Imperial's balance sheet a more solid appearance than might otherwise have been the case.[18]

One episode highlights the exceptional conditions that Imperial faced during the Great Depression. Newfoundland, not yet part of Canada, had become a self-governing Dominion in 1907. Standard Oil had acquired a foothold there in 1902, establishing storage facilities supplied by tankers, and Imperial assumed this role after 1918. The company had a virtual lock on the market, primarily for kerosene—a small market, to be sure, as the Dominion had a population of fewer than 300,000 people in 1930.

The Depression had a devastating impact on an economy based principally on fish processing for export, and was aggravated by the burden of debts incurred by the government for constructing a railway and other investments intended to boost industrial growth in the 1920s. Critics of the government in power under Sir Richard Squires charged that these costs were exacerbated by widespread public corruption. By 1932 public debt exceeded $98 million (CAD) and interest on the debt amounted to 64 per cent of public revenues. Squires had desperately sought to stave off disaster, seeking, unsuccessfully, to sell Labrador to Canada and arranging a series of short-term loans at increasingly onerous rates.

With a $2.5 million payment looming, and unemployed constituents laying siege to the legislature, the Squires government proposed to take over the importation and sales of all petroleum products in the Dominion. This came as an unwelcome surprise for Imperial Oil. Although Newfoundland was a relatively small market, Victor Ross warned that this experiment in "government oil monopoly" would likely tempt the premiers of provinces in Canada facing similar financial problems—particularly in Quebec and western Canada—to follow its lead.

The Squires government responded to Imperial's protests with an alternative (and probably preconceived) arrangement: Imperial could be awarded "exclusive rights" in Newfoundland until 1947 in return for a subscription of $1.75 million of a new bond issue of $2.5 million (CAD) called a "Prosperity Loan." The company would also guarantee a payment of $300,000 in royalties annually into a "petroleum fund." Imperial's board was reluctant to enter into an agreement that could resurrect its image as a "monopoly" but Ross's fears about the alternative situation seem to have been persuasive: G.H. Smith, who was due to take over the presidency of Imperial when Stillman retired in 1933, certainly had experience from South America in dealing with politicians threatening nationalization.

In the first year of operating under the new dispensation, Imperial's earnings from Newfoundland were less than $300,000 and the company had to make up the shortfall. But the era of monopoly proved to be short-lived. Later in 1932 Squires was driven from office by a Conservative coalition under Frederick Alderdice. When Alderdice in turn proposed to allow Newfoundland to default on its debts, the British government—with support from Canada—intervened, dispatching a Royal Commission under Lord Amulree to find a solution to Newfoundland's problems. The Amulree Commission recommended a suspension of Dominion status, placing Newfoundland into what amounted to receivership. With regard to Imperial's "exclusive rights," the commission arranged for its cancellation, and for the redemption of the bonds within two years. Imperial no longer had a monopoly, but it continued to play a dominant role in the market for many years.[19]

Imperial Oil's ties to Jersey Standard proved to be a mixed blessing during the Great Depression. Throughout the early 1930s Jersey Standard pressured Imperial to buy its crude oil exclusively from its major supplier, Carter Oil, but both Stillman and Smith resisted, arguing that "from a political standpoint" the Canadian company needed to meet its needs from a variety of sources and to increase refining operations to capacity before importing. More seriously, Jersey Standard's relentless demand for dividends from both Imperial and International Petroleum throughout the decade significantly limited the Canadian company's ability to reinvest for future development. Imperial's fixed assets barely changed between 1929 and 1939, and with depreciation its total asset value diminished from $209 million to $164 million (CAD). Some of Imperial's managers grumbled that Jersey Standard was "eager to keep its own shareholders happy" by drawing "even more from its subsidiaries than their own earnings." But in this dimension Smith was a loyal adherent to the parent company and dissent was discouraged.[20]

On the other hand, the Jersey Standard connection was valuable— and not only because of the access it provided Imperial to technological improvements in refining and product development. Imperial was also integrated with Jersey Standard's transportation network, and received assistance in developing sales operations—the Esso brand itself proved significantly beneficial by the 1940s. Although Jersey Standard limited Imperial's access to long-term capital investment, short-term financing was available for "everyday needs." In the context of the desperate circumstances of the Depression this was an important factor. Imperial was by no means the best managed nor the most entrepreneurial company in the industry; but its sheer size, coupled with its links to Jersey Standard, ensured that it would remain the largest integrated oil company in Canada throughout this era. Even British-American Oil Company, the second ranked company in 1939, was only one-tenth the size of Imperial Oil in terms of assets, sales, and employees.

The Joint Industrial Committees

In 1913 Imperial had only one operating refinery, at Sarnia with a 3000 bbl./day processing capacity, serving slightly more than one-third of the country's market demand (another 40 per cent was covered by imports, primarily from Standard Oil and its US affiliates). Five years later the company had more than doubled Sarnia's capacity and had built new refineries in British Columbia, Saskatchewan, Quebec, and Nova Scotia, extending its reach across the entire country and increasing its market share to more than 60 per cent.

The transformation of Imperial was more than an expansion in its scale of operations. Refining had become much more complex, no longer a matter of distilling crude oil into a relatively limited line of products. Thermal cracking processes, thanks to the improvements introduced by Burton-Humphreys and related patents, enabled continuous flow operations that reduced the costs of producing not only motor fuels for the growing automobile market but also a range of other hydrocarbon derivatives. It furthermore facilitated constant improvement of the quality of gasoline, heating oil, and other by-products.[21]

Imperial Oil, like its American parent, emerged from the First World War as a company with an enlarged manufacturing base and a larger work force concentrated in its refining operations. The establishment of new refineries across the country required a coordinated approach to labour relations. This need was exacerbated by tensions between workers and employers across a range of industries—tensions produced in part by the traumatic experience of wartime mobilization and demobilization and the growth of a militant trade union movement that culminated in the Winnipeg General Strike and a host of other confrontations in 1918–20.

Teagle, who in other respects seemed a relatively enlightened representative of the emerging managerial elite, appears to have been singularly blind to these challenges, at least during his tenure as president of Imperial Oil. On the other hand, Standard Oil, which was experiencing similar tensions at its large US refineries, took the lead in developing labour policies that would hold the unions at bay for many years, and prodded Imperial to follow its example. In the accounts of these events, the rotund Canadian figure of W.L. Mackenzie King is often cited as a key player, although his direct influence on Standard Oil may have been exaggerated.

By 1912 the Rockefeller investment interests extended well beyond the oil business. John D. Sr. was more or less in retirement but his son John D. Jr. played a more active role in managing the family fortune as well as the Rockefeller Foundation. One of these far-flung investments was a mining company, Colorado Fuel & Iron, which in 1913 was embroiled in a bitter labour dispute. The strike culminated in the "Ludlow Massacre" when state militia assisted by company guards attacked a camp of locked-out strikers and their families, killing more than a dozen people, including women and children. Coming in the wake of the Standard Oil monopoly battles, the Ludlow Massacre was a black eye for the Rockefellers, and John D. Jr. cast about for a resolution of the strike. To that end he recruited Mackenzie King, the former Labour minister in the Laurier government in Canada, who was temporarily unemployed when the Liberal party went down to defeat over the issue of Reciprocity with the United States. King had devoted a great deal of time and effort to finding peaceful resolutions to labour disputes and promoted a range of measures that employers could adopt to reduce these tensions.

Rockefeller invited King to join him in Colorado to address the problems of Colorado Fuel & Iron, and King accommodated him with a series of ideas: arbitration of labour disputes, compensation for injured miners, establishment of pensions, and consultation between workers and managers that could alleviate workers' hostility and distrust. To assist King, Rockefeller brought in Clarence Hicks, who had worked for the Young Men's Christian Association and then advised International Harvester on ways to improve its labour relations. Later King, who returned to Canada to resume his (very successful) political career, wrote *Industry and Humanity*, a book that detailed his views lugubriously.

Meanwhile Jersey Standard was encountering its own labour problems. In July 1915 a protracted and violent strike erupted at the company's largest refinery in Bayonne, New Jersey. President Cotton Bedford rejected proposals from the state governor that the issues be subject to arbitration, denouncing the strike as the work of "professional agitators" and "alien" influences. But the US Commission on Industrial Relations, which had already focused its attention on the Ludlow Massacre, criticized Jersey

Standard for the way the Bayonne strike was handled, leading Bedford, prodded by Rockefeller, to change his tune. Hicks was brought in from Colorado in 1917, and he proposed extending the industrial relations plan that he and King had developed to Jersey Standard. It was unveiled with fanfare early in 1918; by this time Teagle had arrived at 26 Broadway, where he belatedly embraced the plan and directed its adoption by Imperial Oil.[22]

Many of the elements in the King-Hicks program were featured in other "welfare capitalist" initiatives of the early twentieth century: an employee stock purchase plan, along the lines championed by Teagle, which proved to be among the most successful aspects of the program as it evolved at Imperial; retirement benefits that included contributions from the company with additional voluntary contributions from employees up to 3 per cent a year; sickness and disability benefits (accompanied by a vigorous "safety" program promoted in the *Imperial Oil Review*); and an array of social activities including athletic clubs, company picnics, and related "morale-boosting" events. An "Employment Department" was established whose role, as in other large-scale industries, was to limit the arbitrary power of shop foremen through very detailed manuals that covered the criteria for hiring and the grounds for dismissal of workers.

The most important components of the program, at least from the standpoint of its designers, were the "joint industrial councils" that would provide a forum in which representatives of managers and workers would meet monthly to discuss a range of issues including (in theory) wages and hours as well as working conditions, the airing of grievances, and related matters. There would be an equal number of worker representatives (one representative per forty employees) and management-appointed delegates, chaired by the senior supervisor—in most cases the head of a refinery.

In introducing this system, the *Imperial Oil Review* maintained that it was not undertaken in a "spirit of patronizing philanthropy," but rather intended to encourage "an *esprit de corps*" that would result in "efficiency, harmony, and mutual profit." Needless to say, trade union leaders and some employees regarded it as "a scheme to break unions," and certainly Imperial's managers were alarmed at the progress of the craft union organizations at the Sarnia refinery. More than half of the workers had joined one or another local, although the company refused to negotiate with any of them. In British Columbia the Ioco refinery experienced a

FIGURE 5.3. Joint Industrial Council, Sarnia refinery, 1919. Glenbow Archive IP-23-6a-1, Imperial Oil Collection.

twelve-day strike in early 1918, and President Stillman raised pay rates across the company as well as reducing work times to eight hours per day and a six-day week at the same time that the new Industrial Councils were getting underway.[23]

Joint councils were to be set up across the company, but the largest and most significant ones were formed at the refineries: in 1920 refinery employees accounted for more than half the workforce, and it was on these sites that workers were concentrated and considered most susceptible to the appeals for unionization. The first council was set up at Sarnia, the largest refinery with 1,600 workers. By 1920 there were councils in all five refineries, and another one was established at Calgary in 1924. For the first months of organization, the *Imperial Oil Review* dwelt at length on the numbers of workers participating in councils and their various achievements. By the middle of the decade the dangers of unionization had receded and the *Review* would cover council events in less detail. In the meantime, however, the councils were providing a range of opportunities for managers to facilitate the stock purchase plans and encourage charitable contributions to local communities, as well as other "morale-building" activities. The councils also served as an early warning system for potential problems in the plants.

A better sense of how the Councils functioned in practice can be provided through the contrasting experiences at the Montreal East refinery and the Ioco refinery in Burnaby, British Columbia. The Montreal oil business had been handled by Edward Hewitt, an agent for Samuel Rogers, until the amalgamation in 1899. By 1912 Imperial had two bulk plants in Montreal, which served the Quebec market. The threat of competition from Shell may have prompted Teagle to build a refinery in Montreal that began operating in 1916 with a 4000 bbl./day capacity, which more than doubled by 1920, by which time it had a work force of over 400. The Montreal refinery was unusual in that for many years its most important product was asphalt refined from crude oil, supplemented by bunker fuel oil for ships and later a variety of gasoline products and base stocks. The refinery was built in an area that had been intended as a "garden city" suburb for Montreal but by the end of the First World War had become a diversified industrial site.[24]

A refinery workforce comprised a complex array of skilled specialists as well as yard labourers. The distilling process required stillmen, gaugers to control the flow of oil, firemen to feed the boilers, and cleaners to remove the coke residue from the stills. Machinists, boilermakers, and pipefitters were required to maintain the equipment. Each of these groups could command a different pay rate and had to be carefully tended to by managers: boilermakers had staged a strike for better pay at the Montreal refinery shortly after it began operations; the still cleaners, who performed some of the most dangerous work, had been behind the strike in Bayonne, New Jersey in 1916.[25]

Refinery supervisors had to ensure that all the different groups were represented adequately on the councils, and sometimes also adjudicate their varying demands. For example, the council elected at Montreal East in 1924 had three representatives from the "Refinery [distilling] department," two representatives from "Mechanical," two from "Still Cleaning," and one each from the "Boiler and Power House" and "Asphalt" departments.

A good deal of time was spent on working through and reviewing the pay differentials. In Montreal, still cleaners maintained that they should receive extra pay for having to wear gas masks, a demand that other representatives did not agree with, and the chairman (refinery superintendent G.C. Mechin) pointed out that the gas masks were a safety measure. At another point process (distillery) workers, who had been detailed to yard duties in the winter months when the distillery was operating at a lower level, demanded higher pay; Mechin responded that "all employees are paid in accordance with the work they are doing," and a differential with other yard workers would be "unfair."

Mechin, however, was willing to provide a range of benefits requested by council members. Residual coke was given to workers for home fuel during winters, and for a time those who had their own automobiles were allowed to refuel their vehicles from a plant pump at a discount rate when market prices were high (although when prices declined, the company backed out of this commitment). During the worst years of the Depression, Mechin worked with the council in scheduling reduced working hours to avoid layoffs, and those who were laid off temporarily retained their seniority. The Montreal council also arranged for refinery workers to contribute to a fund providing aid to the city's unemployed.

Both the refinery superintendents and company officials found the councils to be handy conduits for promoting programs they wished to encourage. The employee stock purchase programs were particularly successful. Unveiled as the "Cooperative Investment Trust," the plan allowed employees to purchase—on instalment—shares in Imperial Oil with the company contributing one-third of the amount, with the stipulation that the stock be held for five years. The first plan introduced in 1920 was subscribed completely at Montreal and elsewhere, and council representatives eagerly called for a second issue in 1925. In that round the Royal Bank in Montreal agreed to hold the stock certificates as collateral for loans at 5.5 per cent interest. After the 1929 stock market crash, the company undertook to assist employees who might be forced out of the program to meet their loan obligations.

In 1941 the company used the councils to help sell Victory bonds, and also agreed to enable employees in Montreal to participate in the Hospital Service Plan set up in Quebec, although this was not a company subsidized health program. A company life insurance benefit program was negotiated with Sun Life, and the Montreal council arranged for those who were laid off to continue participating in the plan, although they were still required to contribute. Employees who were obliged to enter military service after 1942 (a contentious issue in Quebec) were guaranteed seniority when they returned to the company.

Mechin proved adept at dealing with recurrent calls from council members for wage and salary increases. When the issue surfaced in 1922, he produced a detailed analysis of cost of living changes both nationally and in Quebec to demonstrate that Imperial wages were competitive. Later, he argued that wage rates were being set at the company level. When council members proposed that the minutes of their meetings should be shared with other refinery councils (and vice versa) he maintained that the issues were very different in different jurisdictions so comparisons were unhelpful. When prices began to spike after war broke out in 1939, the company arranged for bonuses rather than permanent wage increases (unfortunately, the bonuses were later made taxable) and then took refuge in the wage controls established by the Canadian government. The councils, it should be noted, were willing to accept most of these arguments without protest.[26]

By contrast, the Ioco Council proved to be obstreperous from the outset. The Ioco refinery, which opened in December 1914, was the first step in Teagle's expansion plans. It was set up in part to head off the anticipated foray by Union Oil & Gas of California into the western Canadian market, but also to receive oil imports from International Petroleum in Peru. It was in a remote setting, far from the city of Vancouver (there was no road connection until 1918). In the early years workers lived in bunkhouses like lumberjacks. Later the company decided to build a model town with prefabricated housing and social centres. As seems to often be the case, the utopian community did not evolve as planned. Instead it became a hotbed for labour militancy.[27]

In 1922, when the superintendent presented the same cost-of-living figures that Mechin unveiled in Montreal, Ioco workers protested against the costs imposed by the "townsite" and argued that the labour rates in Vancouver were higher. This particular complaint settled down, but issues continued to simmer. In 1927, when the refinery was contemplating layoffs, the superintendent complained that there was "propaganda" that "we have waited until men were in a few months of being retired" to fire them "so as to save their pensions." He maintained the company followed a policy of layoffs that would not affect qualified pensioners, but this argument was not persuasive with skeptical workers. This issue continued to cause complaints for the next twenty years.

These problems acquired more saliency in the 1940s as wartime expansion replaced the cutbacks and restrictions of the Depression era. As the cost of living rose, the council became the focal point for demands for a bonus, which was finally granted by the company in November 1941. Two years later the provincial legislature in effect ensured that a union could bargain with an employer. Although no particular company was identified, it was clear that the law was intended to apply to companies like Imperial Oil.

By 1946 council representatives were warning that "some . . . employees were contemplating joining an outside organization," and there were calls for a "conference" of all the company's industrial councils, a prospect that managers found even more alarming than the possibility of an independent union emerging at Ioco refinery. The company had consistently discouraged councils from sharing information (except on issues raised by management), arguing that circumstances were very different across the country and councils should find "local" solutions to their concerns. Not surprisingly, Ioco employees eventually joined the Oil Chemical and Atomic Workers union, although the contagion of unionization was contained.[28]

There were many factors accounting for the variations between councils in this comparison. To some extent it may reflect the managers' approach to the situation: Mechin exhibited some diplomatic skills in contrast to other refinery managers, such as the superintendent at Sarnia (who was frequently at odds with his council). Montreal East had a relatively stable work force—described in the *Imperial Oil Review* as almost "dynastic" with numerous relatives and generations populating the refinery; in contrast there was more turnover in the Ioco refinery, and less homogeneity. The social context may also have played a role—in Quebec, labour strife was relatively rare, in part because of the anti-union practices of political leaders such as Premier Maurice Duplessis. In any case, Imperial employees had more job stability and higher wages than many other industrial workers in that province. In contrast, British Columbia had a much stronger tradition of labour militancy.

During the Second World War, the Canadian Congress of Labour set out to organize workers in the petroleum industry, but met with limited success. At this point the American Oil Workers International Union, an affiliate of the militant Congress of Industrial Organizations, entered the scene—possibly at the invitation of the CCL—and took over several locals, including one at Ioco (the only one established with Imperial Oil), where 65 per cent of the workers voted to affiliate with it in 1946; 26 per cent declined to participate in the vote. In 1955 the OWIU merged with workers in the chemical industry to form the Oil, Chemical and Atomic Workers Union (OCAW).

Two years later, Ioco was the site of Imperial's first major labour confrontation since the First World War. The issues were familiar: disputes over pay rates for different job classifications, overtime work, and vacation time. The strike began in late September and dragged on for more than two months. Although negotiations were left to management in British Columbia, at one point two members of Imperial's Executive Committee visited the refinery to see if it could be reopened on a limited scale. Shortly thereafter a tentative settlement was made, but one of the Executive Committee members observed that the company "should have better knowledge of [OCAW] organization," and its relationship with the Canadian Labour Congress.[29]

Another, larger strike erupted in Vancouver in May 1969. In this case it was not restricted to Ioco, as OCAW also confronted the Shell Canada and Texaco Canada refineries in Vancouver. The issues focused on wages during a period of high inflation. More alarming to Imperial's Executive Committee was the entrance of the powerful Teamsters union, which proposed to organize workers at the newly established Lougheed Terminal in Vancouver. One Executive Committee member warned that "if the Company found it necessary to resist strong Union demands to the point of a [Teamsters] strike, the repercussions could be great." The committee put up a brave front and the strike was prolonged, but in the end a settlement was reached that provided for a 15 per cent wage increase over two years with no reduction in benefits and more liberal vacation policies.[30]

Despite the upheavals at Ioco, Imperial Oil had far fewer labour problems than many other companies in Canada, and could maintain that the industrial councils played an important part in maintaining this stability. In the United States the Wagner Act of 1935 undermined Jersey Standard's industrial councils as "company unions," but there was no parallel in Canada. In 1977 an Imperial Oil official maintained that "Joint Councils . . . function efficiently and have employee acceptance even though they may not [resemble] unions in a power sense. Joint Councils do not have the right to strike but they are in the possession of the members who elect them, control them and look upon them as a means of service."[31]

6

THE WINNING OF THE WEST

The Northwest Company

In 1917 Imperial Oil and Jersey Standard established a company tasked with the mission of finding oil in the Athabasca region north of Edmonton and stretching into the Northwest Territories. It was named the Northwest Company, in part as tribute to an exploratory enterprise more than a century before which had opened the way to the development of western Canada.

The North West Company, a Montreal-based fur trader consortium, sent its agents ranging from James Bay to the Rocky Mountains in the late 1700s, circumventing the remote posts of its rival, the Hudson's Bay Company, penetrating deep into the wilderness of what is now northern Alberta and British Columbia. Peter Pond, a Connecticut-born trader with the North West Company, observed "quaking bogs" of bitumen in the Athabasca region, which he explored in the early 1780s; and his better known successor, Alexander Mackenzie, who mapped the great northern river that bears his name, wrote of "bituminous fountains" that "emitted a smell like sea coal" during his travels in the same area.[1]

After the Hudson's Bay Company acquired its rival in 1821, the region became virtually terra incognita to all but the company's employees and their aboriginal trading partners. When "Rupert's Land" passed into the hands of the Dominion of Canada in 1869, the country's geological survey sent several expeditions into northern Alberta, and in 1882 Robert Bell of the survey projected the existence of petroleum in large quantities there. Meanwhile the Dominion had provided land grants to the

Canadian Pacific Railway to foster the rapid completion of a transportation link to the west coast, and in 1883–84 CPR builders encountered natural gas deposits adjacent to its line in the vicinity of Medicine Hat in southeastern Alberta. Six years later the CPR drilled a gas well of about 650 feet, and by 1904 residents of Medicine Hat had set up a municipal utility to provide natural gas to the community. Drilling for oil was undertaken in 1905 in the Pincher Creek area near Waterton Lake, on the Alberta-Montana border.

The CPR mounted a more ambitious project a year later, recruiting Eugene Coste, who had worked with the Geological Survey of Canada, to head an effort to find both oil and gas on company lands in southern Alberta. In 1909 Coste reported a natural gas strike at Bow Island near Medicine Hat. At the same time, however, CPR also learned of another gas venture in the Calgary area under the auspices of a local group who had formed the Calgary Natural Gas Company with A.W. Dingman as their general manager, and it invested in this enterprise as well. Coste responded by recapitalizing his operation with new investors and making an agreement with CPR in 1911 to lay a pipeline to Lethbridge, and ultimately Calgary, to carry gas from the wells he was drilling; his company was organized as Canadian Western Natural Gas, Light, Heat & Power Company and by the summer of 1912 the pipelines were pumping gas from the Bow Island wells.[2]

All of this activity indicated the presence of natural gas in Alberta, although in quantities sufficient only for local consumption and with little evidence of oil. Nevertheless, Alberta was attracting the interest of a wider audience, which included Imperial Oil with its declining production in Ontario but also the British Admiralty, which was converting its fleet from coal to oil and combing the empire for potential reserves. The largest landowner (and owner of the subsurface mineral rights) in Alberta, and the western provinces generally, was the Dominion of Canada. Since 1898 the Crown had authorized the sale of mining rights in 640-acre parcels on its lands. In 1910, however, the Dominion changed from selling to leasing mineral rights (for twenty-one years), and in an obvious concession to the Admiralty allowed the pre-emption of petroleum production on any leased lands to meet the needs of the Royal Navy. With war clouds gathering in Europe in 1913, the Admiralty increased its pressure on the

Dominion of Canada (and its other colonies) to protect potential oil reserves. Under new regulations of Crown-owned mineral rights adopted in 1914, certain areas could be set aside for what would now be called a "strategic reserve." In addition, leasing of mining and petroleum drilling rights would be restricted to individuals and companies of "British" nationality; and the company that would most clearly be excluded was Imperial Oil with its Standard Oil (American) owners.[3]

Although Walter Teagle was on the lookout for possible oil reserves for Imperial Oil, in 1914 his focus was primarily on prospects in South America. Nevertheless events in Alberta at this point did indicate potential future resources closer to home. In 1913 William S. Herron, an entrepreneur from Ontario who had settled near the Turner Valley south of Calgary, sent samples for analysis in Toronto of gas collected near a coal mining area called Sheep Creek. With the results in hand, he persuaded Archibald W. Dingman, who had managed the drilling activities of the short-lived Calgary Gas Company, along with two rising Calgary lawyers, James Lougheed and Richard B. Bennett, and a prominent rancher and businessman, A.E. Cross, among others, to join him in setting up Calgary Petroleum Products Company.

After a year and a half of drilling with promising if not spectacular results, on May 21, 1914, Calgary Petroleum struck oil at 2,718 feet. The naptha was described as "of such light gravity it could be pumped directly" into automobiles. The "Dingman well," as it came to be called, also stimulated the province's first oil rush with more than 500 companies suddenly emerging, many of them fraudulent. Other wells that sprang up produced mostly natural gas, and the boom collapsed within a few months. But Calgary Petroleum Products continued to operate and would eventually play a role in Imperial Oil's westward expansion.[4]

After the Dingman strike, Jersey Standard sent two geologists, Malcolm Thompson and Raymond Yost, to the Turner Valley to survey the prospects. Their report was mostly negative with regard to oil, and so Imperial did not pursue the subject further. By 1916, however, Teagle was once again thinking about Alberta. Excluded from Crown lands, Teagle approached CPR about leases in the Viking-Wainwright area near the Alberta-Saskatchewan border where Coste had earlier done some drilling. Imperial proposed to spend up to $100,000 (CAD) on exploration over the next two years, but negotiations with CPR moved sluggishly when the railway company had wanted the project to move forward on a faster schedule.

At this point Imperial had to face a far more formidable challenge. Royal Dutch Shell, under the vigorous leadership of Henri Deterding, proposed in April 1917 to lease mineral rights on a huge swath of Crown lands in northern Alberta, encompassing the Athabascan region, the Peace River, and Grand Prairie. Alluding to the scandals of stock jobbery in the Turner Valley, Shell promised to provide opportunities for profit sharing with the government (Crown regulations did not require royalties before 1930). The timing was also well considered as the Dominion at the time faced the greatest crisis of the First World War. Furthermore Shell could present itself as a genuinely "British" enterprise (even though half the company was owned by the "neutral" Dutch).

Imperial had its resources as well, particularly W.J. Hanna, the Conservative politician who succeeded Teagle as president of the company in 1918. Relying on his contacts with the Borden government in Ottawa, Hanna was able to offset the tantalizing promises of Shell by highlighting Imperial's new commitments to exploration in the west. In addition, politicians in Alberta (including Lougheed and Bennett) were adamantly opposed to the Shell proposal. As the 1918 armistice ended the war in Europe, pressures for rapid oil development faded, and the "yellow peril" of Shell was turned back. But Imperial now had to demonstrate that its commitment to finding oil in the west went beyond mere promises.

To meet the challenge from Royal Dutch Shell, in 1917 Imperial and Jersey Standard had organized the Northwest Company. It was capitalized at $500,000 (CAD) with Jersey Standard initially holding more than three-quarters of the shares. By 1919, it was almost wholly owned by Imperial. The company relied on two men with experience in wildcat drilling: Alexander McQueen, who had begun his career working for Fairbank in Petrolia, carried out oil explorations for Imperial in Wyoming, and now became president of the Northwest Company; and Charles Taylor, an "old timer in western affairs" who had his own enterprise, Grattan Oil, that had been searching for oil in the Edmonton area since 1914. Taylor brought a crucial qualification to the task: he had leases in both the Viking fields (where Imperial was negotiating for access through CPR) and in the Fort McMurray area far to the north. With Taylor's leases, the Northwest

FIGURE 6.1. Charles Taylor, Norman Wells, 1920. Glenbow Archive IP-6b-1-9, Imperial Oil Collection.

Company could circumvent the 1914 restrictions on leasing mineral rights on Crown lands.

With the threat of Shell's entry into Alberta looming in 1918, and Teagle moving to 26 Broadway, Jersey Standard and Imperial agreed to mount a major expedition into the wilds of Athabasca. To that end the Northwest Company retained T.O. Bosworth, regarded as one of the leading petroleum geologists in the United States (like Herbert Hoover, he ran his own mining and petroleum company in addition to providing service to large oil companies, including Shell). Bosworth had conducted surveys for International Petroleum in Peru; he had also led an expedition in 1914 that investigated oil prospects in northern Alberta, including the Fort Norman area and the Athabasca region. Joining in this venture into the wilderness were O.B. Hopkins, another geologist exploring petroleum prospects in Colombia for the IPC, and Theodore Link, who had recently acquired a PhD in geology at the University of Chicago.[5]

Bosworth had an ambitious program encompassing fourteen expeditions ranging from the Great Slave Lake and Mackenzie River area to Calgary. But relations among the company managers were rocky from the start: Bosworth had his own ideas about where to search, and he feuded constantly with Taylor. Most of the drilling proved fruitless. In the summer of 1920, Taylor and Link found oil in an area south of Fort Norman in the Northwest Territories (at "Bosworth Creek" named after the geologist). Output was limited—by 1923 it was yielding at best 100 bbl./day. But Link, in particular, was optimistic: an article in the *Edmonton Journal* in October 1920 quoted him saying "this is the biggest oil field in the world — stretching to the Arctic coast," although the journalist may have provided a hyperbolic interpretation of what Link actually said.[6] Charles Stillman, the president of Imperial, was more skeptical of the commercial potential of the site, pointing out that it was 900 miles from the nearest port on the Mackenzie River. Nevertheless, the Northwest Company staked fifteen more claims in the area. More positively, in 1920 the Dominion reversed its policy excluding "non-British" companies from leasing mineral rights on Crown lands, and Stillman set out to acquire extensive leases across Alberta and the Northwest Territories to forestall future forays by other oil majors like Shell.[7]

In 1921 Bosworth resigned from the Northwest Company and Taylor died under mysterious circumstances a year later (allegedly he shot himself by accident but there were rumours of suicide). By this time the company had spent $3 million (CAD) on what seemed to be a fruitless venture. Meanwhile, however, Hopkins and Link had emerged as key players in the search for oil in the remote reaches of northern and western Canada; and later both spent time exploring for oil in Colombia. In the winter of 1921 Link participated in a hazardous but historic flight from Peace River to Fort Norman. These were the pioneer days of what became known as "bush flying," and the airplane—a German Junkers leased by Imperial Oil—encountered numerous dangers, including a near-crash landing and jury-rigged repairs to the propeller *en route*. But from Link's point of view the trip was a success: he discovered the benefits of aerial geological mapping, which were particularly useful in the remote wilderness of northern Canada.[8]

Romance, danger, adventure—but not much oil. By this point, Imperial had decided to turn its attention back to prospects in southern Alberta, particularly in the Turner Valley. The Fort Norman site continued to be worked until 1925 and then the wells were capped. Seven years later, however, they were reopened in part to supply anticipated needs of uranium miners in the Great Bear Lake region. By the end of the 1930s a small refinery was in operation, producing about 400,000 gallons per year of various motor and fuel oils from the wells near Fort Norman.

Turner Valley and Royalite

Although in 1914 Jersey Standard geological reports expressed skepticism about the potential for oil in the Turner Valley, Stillman's policy of pre-empting rival companies indicated that Imperial needed to establish a presence there. The Calgary Petroleum Products Company, which was the largest remaining producer with its own gas plant, was an obvious target for acquisition. And since it was producing a small amount of naptha as well as natural gas, there was at least the possibility of finding oil by drilling more deeply. Dingman had approached Teagle in 1915 about selling CPPL to Imperial, but nothing came of that initiative and some of the shareholders, especially Herron, opposed a sale to the Canadian subsidiary of the Standard octopus. But the company needed more capital to pursue expansion plans, including drilling a fourth well. When a fire destroyed the gas extraction plant in October 1920, CPPL shareholders, represented by R.B. Bennett, were ready to negotiate.

The existing shareholders retained 25 per cent of the reorganized company, which was renamed Royalite Oil Co. Ltd. (the brand name used for Imperial products sold in Toronto in the 1890s). The capital stock was set at $1 million (CAD), although only $615,000 was issued initially. Imperial Oil agreed to spend $400,000 to rebuild the plant and continue the planned drilling program. Alexander McQueen became president of Royalite from 1922 to 1926, when he went back to Imperial and was succeeded by Bennett. Another Imperial veteran from Petrolia and International Petroleum, John H. McLeod, became vice president of Royalite in 1928 and then president in 1930 when R.B. Bennett left the company to become prime minister of Canada.[9]

Imperial also intended to establish a pipeline to supply gas to Calgary from the Turner Valley. But this plan was derailed when a bill to approve it came before the Alberta legislature early in 1921. A reform party—the United Farmers of Alberta—had emerged, advocating public ownership of utilities and demanding that any pipeline should be designated a "common carrier" along the lines practiced in US states such as Oklahoma and Texas. Shortly thereafter the UFA formed the new government in Alberta. Imperial withdrew the proposal, and a year later Royalite built a small 4-inch pipeline to provide gas to consumers in Calgary.

Imperial had more success in its dealings with the Dominion government, perhaps in part because the Minister of the Interior, whose responsibilities included the administration of federal regulations around petroleum and natural gas, was James Lougheed—a shareholder in Royalite. After 1920 Imperial could lease mineral rights on Crown lands, but the company chafed under the leasing rules, which allowed 25 per cent of the costs of exploration and drilling to be applied against the lease; Imperial argued that 40 per cent was a more realistic figure, and at one point McQueen threatened that the company was "seriously considering abandoning further operations in western Canada," unless there was such a change. Given the commitments Imperial was making in Alberta, this was something of a bluff, but in any case the concession was made in December 1921. Subsequently Lougheed's successor as Minister of the Interior, Charles Stewart (who had been premier of Alberta), allowed an expansion of the maximum area for "group" leases from 2,560 acres to 20,000 acres. Stewart also reconfirmed delaying the collection of royalties on production from Crown leases to 1930.[10]

By the end of 1923 the crew on what was called Royalite Number 4 well had drilled down more than 2,800 feet, yielding 7 million cubic feet of gas per day. But the company still hoped to find oil, and drilling continued into limestone rock. In October 1924, the well experienced a huge blowout of gas, followed by an explosion and runaway flaring that could be seen in Calgary. The site became known as "Hell's Half Acre." Royalite had to bring in "wild well" experts from Oklahoma and Wyoming to quell the blaze by December 1924. Royalite Number 4, however, then became a major producer of naptha as well as natural gas. By 1925 Royalite was producing more than 160,000 bbl./day, more than half the total petroleum output of Canada. The blowout also stimulated the second Turner Valley oil boom, attracting hundreds of wildcatters to try their luck. Meanwhile Royalite stock soared from $25 (CAD) to over $200 per share. Imperial Oil built a refinery in Calgary in 1924, perhaps anticipating further discoveries

FIGURE 6.2. Oil rig workers, Turner Valley, 1930s. Glenbow Archive IP-6c-12, Imperial Oil Collection.

in Turner Valley, but also eyeing the Kevin-Sunburst oilfield across the border in Montana.

There was a downside to Royalite's unanticipated good fortune. The gas produced in Turner Valley from the initial drilling was light and sweet, requiring a limited amount of processing. The gas from Royalite Number 4 and other deeper wells was "sour," imbued with hydrogen sulphide. Royalite was in the midst of negotiating with Coste's company, Canadian Western, to build a larger 10-inch pipeline to Calgary when the new gas discovery came on stream, and the transportation company demanded that Royalite install a scrubber in its new gas plant to remove the toxic emissions. Royalite was particularly anxious to complete the deal since Imperial was building a refinery in Calgary to serve the western market. When this was finally accomplished in 1925, the pipeline was built, and Royalite joined Canadian Western as the "big businesses" in the oil industry in Alberta, suitable targets for both the UFA and independent producers in Turner Valley. The "sour gas," however, continued to be a health and safety issue for workers in the Royalite gas plant.[11]

In 1926 Royalite issued 400,000 shares at no par value, distributed on the basis of the current shareholders' percentages. Imperial's stake in Royalite rose to over $1 million (CAD). The Calgary company then began to expand, partly by drilling two new wells (one proved unproductive and was abandoned) and more significantly by acquiring other Turner Valley companies or establishing new ones that took out more leases. In 1925 Royalite set up the Dalhousie Oil Co. Ltd., which in turn acquired Alberta Southern Oils Ltd. and Midwest Petroleums Ltd. In 1926 Royalite took over London Union Oils Ltd., Mayland Oil Co., Southern Lowery Oils, Calgary Development & Producers Ltd., and Sterling Pacific Co. (all of which were liquidated during the Depression). Meanwhile, Imperial Oil was setting up and/or acquiring Turner Valley companies directly, including Foothills Oil & Gas Ltd. in 1927, Lowery Petroleum Ltd., Southwest Petroleum, and Dolomite Oils Ltd. By the end of this expansion spree, IOL and Royalite effectively controlled an estimated 75 per cent of the producing companies in the Turner Valley.[12]

All of these activities were (supposedly) carried out surreptitiously. The architect of this strategy was Richard B. Bennett. By the mid-1920s Bennett was one of the most prosperous and influential corporate lawyers in Alberta. He was on numerous boards, including Calgary Power, Alberta Pacific Grain Co., Royalite and, from 1924 to 1929, Imperial Oil. From 1926 to 1930, he was president of Royalite. He was also a rising star in national politics, becoming the leader of the Conservative party in 1927 and the prime minister of Canada three years later (just in time for the Depression). Bennett was an eccentric figure, particularly in the "wild west" atmosphere of Alberta. He lived with his sister in a suite in the Palliser Hotel in Calgary, always dressed in formal attire with top hat and spats, and ate huge meals—apparently in order to literally become the virtual caricature of the "bloated plutocrat." But despite these hyperbolic behaviours, business leaders nevertheless took Bennett's advice seriously, and Imperial followed his recommendation to "buy up small companies and keep them separate to avoid 'radical' legislation."[13] It is hard to believe that these *sub rosa* measures were really successful in remaining secret in the small and tightly knit community of oil producers in Turner Valley.

The "radical" politicians who preoccupied Bennett's thoughts were the United Farmers of Alberta who were in power in Edmonton from 1921 to 1935. By the middle of the 1920s, however, the responsibilities of governing had muted their ambitions for progressive reforms to some extent. One of the major issues in the petroleum industry in Alberta was the wastage of natural gas through flaring, a common problem in gas fields. As the largest producer in Turner Valley, Royalite was a contributor to this problem, which had an unforeseen consequence: gas flaring reduced underground pressure, making it more difficult for drillers to find the oil deposits below the gas. McQueen, now a vice president of Imperial Oil, maintained that since 1924 Royalite had equipped its wells to shut down when required to conserve gas. But he pointed out that since other drillers in the field were allowing their wells to run "unimpeded," any restraint on that company's part would not have much effect.[14]

The solutions seemed to be either to find export markets for the gas or to impose substantial restrictions on output, which would require capping wells and closing some operations entirely. Imperial Oil had raised the issue of exporting, proposing to sell gas from a well it co-owned in Lethbridge to Montana residents. The premier, Herbert Greenfield, blocked the proposal, arguing that "all the requirements of Alberta [must be] fully protected" first. This view was shared by some of the business community in Calgary and other municipalities who believed that the availability of cheap gas could attract industry to Alberta.

In 1926 Greenfield's successor, premier John Brownlee, proclaimed an Oil and Gas Wells Act that was patterned on the conservation regulations established by the Dominion in 1910. These regulations, which only applied to Crown lands, provided for the closure of wells when necessary to reduce flaring and measures to protect water supplies from gas intrusion. Brownlee's dilemma, however, was to find a way to impose these regulations on the ornery oilmen of Alberta. A.A. Carpenter, the chairman of the provincial Board of Public Utility Commissioners, pointed to the example of California, which had achieved conservation goals "as a result of agreement among the operators themselves." This view was endorsed by the director of Alberta Lands and Mines, William Calder, who was assigned the responsibility of finding ways to enforce the law, which was simply being ignored by the industry. Inevitably, this approach would require acceptance by Royalite, whose managers (much like Rockefeller and Standard Oil in the US in the nineteenth century) were interested in stability so long as it could be achieved through "cooperation" rather than government fiat.

In 1932 the larger producers agreed to allocate gas production in order to reduce wastage. This measure was adamantly opposed by the "independents" whose spokesman, William S. Herron, denounced the plan as "bolshevism" and "communism" and at the same time as a scheme to benefit "big business" in the Alberta oil fields. Herron, who was one of the founders of CPPL in 1914, was a feisty and combative embodiment of the western entrepreneurial spirit. After Royalite took over CPPL in 1921, he retained his shares in the company but also set up his own drilling operation in Turner Valley. In 1928 his company, Okalta Oils Ltd. made a strike almost as large as Royalite Number 4, and after years of feuding with banks and the federal government, he became a rich man. He remained an outspoken defender of the small business, focusing particularly on the sins of Imperial Oil, but also became a member of the board of directors of Royalite in 1933, where he lobbied for bigger dividends. Like many other independents, Herron lost most of his fortune in the Depression before he died in 1939 "with his boots on" while working on one of the derricks of his beloved Okalta company.[15]

The convoluted relationship between Herron and Royalite reflected the dynamic business environment of the Alberta oil industry at the time, where large and small enterprises alternately battled and cooperated with one another. The oil glut and the Depression of the 1930s bankrupted many small companies and communities as well, and even Royalite had to lay off workers. The company spread work out to keep people at least partially employed, and provided direct aid to people in Turner Valley in an era when governments could not or would not address the problems of unemployment and literal starvation. Meanwhile many wildcatters continued to try to emulate Herron and strike it rich.

In 1934 Robert Brown, superintendent of Calgary Light and Power, joined with George Bell, publisher of the *Calgary Albertan* newspaper and John Moyer, a lawyer, in one such effort, hoping to strike oil by drilling much deeper than the gas wells in Turner Valley. Within a year they had exhausted their own financial resources and could find no investors in the midst of the Depression. They set up a company called Turner Valley Royalties, which offered royalties of 70 per cent of the value of any oil produced to those willing to provide financing. Imperial Oil provided $22,500 (CAD) worth of equipment in return for royalties, and other companies—including British American Oil—participated as well. On June 16, 1936, with drills going more than 8000 feet deep, the company struck oil, producing 850 bbl./day as well as 60,000 cubic metres of gas per day. The discovery, touted as Alberta's first real "crude oil gusher," set off the third petroleum boom in the Turner Valley, but also exacerbated ongoing controversies over the control of production.[16]

In 1930 premier Brownlee had achieved a long-term goal of western Canadians when the federal government agreed to transfer control of Crown lands from the Dominion to the Prairies. This outcome may be attributed principally to the new prime minister, R.B. Bennett, who had been a long-time advocate of provincial ownership of resources, but Brownlee and the UFA could take credit for it, which helped preserve the party in power for five more years. But Brownlee's efforts to impose conservation on the gas fields continued to be frustrated. When voluntary agreements failed to take shape, the UFA government set up a Turner Valley Gas Conservation Board to set limits on production and reduce wastage, but this measure was challenged in court successfully by an Alberta company on the grounds that no such constraints could be placed on producers who held leases before the 1930 transfer. After that debacle, the UFA government virtually gave up on enforcing its conservation laws and was swept from office in 1935 by a new militant agrarian party, Social Credit, under the leadership of William Aberhart.[17]

Focused initially on its monetary experiments, the new regime did not assign much priority to the imposition of environmental and production controls on the petroleum industry in Alberta. By September 1937, however, the boom set off by Turner Valley Royalties was forcing these issues to the forefront. The Imperial Oil and the British American refineries in Calgary both announced reductions in the amount they would pay producers for naptha and crude oil, citing the local "oil glut" as the reason. In January 1938 John McLeod, president of Royalite maintained that his company would be obliged to cut its prices even further. In less than six months the price of crude oil fell from an average of $1.60 to $1.26/bbl. (CAD).

The new Minister of Lands and Mines, Nathan Tanner, sought to negotiate a voluntary agreement to reduce production, called "prorationing." As in 1932, this proposal divided the industry, with Imperial and British American accepting it, while the independent producers resisted. They demanded that the Dominion government impose higher tariffs on imported oil and gas, and dispatched a delegation to Ottawa to lobby the tariff board and the federal Minister of Mines and Resources, Thomas Crerar, a western progressive who had joined the ruling Liberal party in 1935. Crerar's advisers, however, pointed out that the major problem for Alberta oil was the cost of transportation to central Canada, and in any case the Liberal party was not in favour of raising oil import duties when it was trying to negotiate a reciprocity agreement with the United States.

Fortunately for Tanner, divisions surfaced among the independents, as oil producers recognized that continuing depletion of natural gas would force them to drill even deeper to find oil, and so they became advocates of conservation measures. Tanner, a Mormon schoolteacher with no business experience, also benefited from his association with Ernest Manning, Aberhart's second in command in the Social Credit party who would become premier of Alberta for more than twenty years. Thus reinforced, Tanner introduced a new Oil and Gas Conservation Act in 1938. He brought in an American, William Knode, from the Texas Railroad Commission (which had brought effective prorationing to the anarchic world of East Texas oil), to enforce the law. But Knode also fell afoul of the Alberta oilmen, and in 1940 Tanner replaced him with Robert Allen from California to try to bring peace to the oilfields.[18]

The latest iteration of petroleum conservation legislation survived a court challenge, but independents continued to defy efforts to enforce prorationing, which was becoming unpopular as oil prices continued to stagnate. Ultimately it was necessary to arrange for a compensation scheme for those producers who were negatively affected by prorationing. Meanwhile the government announced the formation of a provincial royal commission to be chaired by Justice A.A. McGillvray of the Alberta Supreme Court. The McGillvray Commission was directed to conduct a "thorough investigation" of conditions in the industry and to recommend "the fair and equitable price ... of petroleum products sold to consumers."[19]

Much of the McGillvray Commission hearings was devoted to the ongoing debates about prorationing, the powers (and limits) to be given the new Conservation board, and instances where compensation was not provided. Since Royalite was the largest producing company with twenty-eight wells, and Imperial Oil had the largest refinery in the province, it was perhaps inevitable that they became the focus of attention also. They were variously charged with arbitrarily setting low prices for producers and high gas prices for consumers, receiving preferential treatment from the conservation board, and (inconsistently) for refusing to drill new wells because they were opposed to government regulation of the oil fields.

The commission report did not come out until 1940, by which time wartime production and related issues preoccupied the public. Many of the recommendations of the commission involved the conservation board, only some of which were embraced by the government. The commission rejected charges that Imperial (or Royalite) had set prices "arbitrarily or whimsically," but rather acted "in accordance with its best judgment" based on prices "fixed by world competition." It also dismissed proposals that a government agency should be set up to regulate consumer prices and asserted that the conservation board's power should be restricted to "proration and conservation." On this subject the commission closed with an encomium to the free enterprise system: "no case has been made for government intervention in Alberta ... the public in Alberta is adequately protected by the play of contending forces prompted by the desire for gain."[20] Ironically, this statement of faith was made in the context of a report that sustained government intervention in the oil and gas industry.

Canol

The Second World War, to a much greater extent than its predecessor, was a conflict in which oil played a predominant role, fuelling mobile ground forces—tanks and armoured personnel carriers—as well as ships, landing craft, trucks, and earth-moving equipment, and of course the vast air armadas of bombers, fighters, and supply carriers deployed by all the forces involved. Control of oil was central to the strategies of the warring powers: Nazi Germany invaded Russia with the aim of seizing the Caspian Sea fields; Japan gambled on war with the United States to capture the oil wells of the Dutch East Indies. The sheer scale of organization of the world's major oil companies, particularly Jersey Standard, and their technological achievements were major factors in the ultimate success of the Allies during the war.

US neutrality in 1939–41 produced some awkward moments for Imperial Oil because of its connection to Jersey Standard, as had been the case in the early period of the First World War. In the context of the hysteria that engulfed the US after Pearl Harbor, congressional investigators pursued Jersey Standard over its prewar patent agreements with the German chemical behemoth, I.G. Farben, and some of this criticism percolated north to Canada. But by the end of 1942 it was clear that Jersey Standard was a crucial player in American industrial mobilization, and through its connection to Standard Imperial Oil had much to offer the Canadian war effort.

Imperial Oil contributed significantly to the survival of Britain in 1940–41, in part through its ties to the American oil industry. The Canadian company built a large oil storage facility in Halifax that received shipments from US suppliers during the period of American neutrality, and trans-shipped them to Britain using not only Imperial's own tankers but also seventeen Panamanian-registered carriers, leased from US owners. Imperial lost four of its own tankers to U-boat attacks in 1941–42.[21]

During this same period, Canada became the major site for the British Commonwealth Air Training Program, to train pilots for service with the Royal Air Force as well as the Commonwealth countries—over 130,000 pilots went through the program, more than half of them Canadian. Imperial Oil provided two substantial components to this program. The

BCATP had to set up a large number of airfields on an emergency basis in 1939–41, and Imperial was able to provide huge quantities of an asphalt that was both low cost and durable, based on research carried out during the interwar era in its own labs: by the end of 1940 more than 10 million square yards of asphalt were laid on fifty-one training fields. Imperial also developed a system of "portable runways," which combined asphalt and burlap so that mats could be rolled and unrolled to provide short-term landing strips for fighter planes.

The other major requirement for the program was aviation fuel. During the 1920s–30s, Ethyl Gasoline Corporation, a joint venture between Jersey Standard and General Motors that had developed the tetraethyl lead "no knock" gasoline for automobiles, also addressed the question of providing more efficient fuel for airplanes. In 1926 Ethyl produced a gasoline using iso-octane (hydrogenated di-isobutylene) that became the standard for aviation use: four years later the US Army Air Force made 87-octane gasoline the accepted grade for combat planes.

Work continued on the processes for refining high-octane gasoline for airplanes, and by the eve of the Second World War Jersey Standard, using a process called sulphuric acid alkylation, could produce 100-octane fuel. The problem was that production of this highly efficient gasoline required a huge capital investment in catalytic cracking units, which only a company operating on Jersey Standard's scale could afford.[22] Imperial did not have the capabilities to set up these sophisticated refining operations, but it could produce 87-octane by modifying its distilling equipment using the processes developed by Ethyl and Jersey Standard; and the BCATP agreed to use this lower grade gasoline for training purposes. Once the US entered the war, a much greater degree of technology sharing was possible, not only between Jersey Standard and Imperial but also among the Canadian oil companies. Imperial Oil at its Calgary refinery and Shell Oil in Montreal used the alkylation process to develop 100-octane fuel; Imperial's Sarnia refinery produced cumene, used in the alkylation process and British-American provided isobutene to the refineries. In 1944 Imperial estimated it had spent $2 million (CAD) on war-related operations, more than 60 per cent on improving aviation fuels.

Imperial Oil was also involved in one of the most ambitious technological ventures in Canada during the war. After the Japanese conquest of Malaya in 1942, supplies of natural rubber in North America were restricted. One of the controversial patents Jersey Standard had acquired through its agreements with I.G. Farben involved the production of synthetic rubber, and the American company made its patents in this field available to the US government for the duration of the war. It also built plants to produce polymerized rubber through butylene dehydrogenation in Baton Rouge and Bayway. When the Canadian government decided to set up its own synthetic rubber production, it turned to Imperial Oil which created a subsidiary, Saint Clair Processing Corporation, using petroleum from its new "Suspensoid" catalytic unit at the Sarnia refinery, initially set up to develop high octane gasoline. The Imperial operation was eventually absorbed into the crown corporation, Canadian Polymer/Polysar—which was, ironically, sold to Bayer A.G., formerly part of I.G. Farben, in 1990.[23]

But the most bizarre and controversial episode in the history of Imperial Oil's activities in the Second World War focused on the remote wilderness of northern Canada and the long neglected refinery at Norman Wells. The "Canol Project" originated in the crisis months following the attack on Pearl Harbor, when fears were widespread that Japan might invade the west coast of the United States and Canada. This was the same atmosphere of hysteria that also led to the forcible "relocation" of people of Japanese ancestry from California and British Columbia. Later the project produced intense controversy involving ambitious congressional investigators and rival military and civilian bureaucrats in Washington.

Japanese military strategy did indeed contemplate the seizure of the Aleutian Islands off Alaska to protect the northern Pacific flank of its fast-expanding empire, and in the summer of 1942 Japanese forces captured the islands of Attu and Kiska, before finally being expelled a year later. In the meantime, the US War Department mounted an ambitious and expensive program to build a highway and a set of airfields that would link the northwestern US to Alaska. The aim was not only to enable American military forces to repel a Japanese attack, but also to facilitate the supply of Lend-Lease aid to the Soviet Union via Alaska and Siberia.[24]

One of the many challenges facing a project of this magnitude was the provision of oil and gas to fuel the airplanes and trucks that would run the long supply lines. Standard Oil of California proposed using tankers and barges from its refineries to Skagway, Alaska, but the US War Department

FIGURE 6.3. Ted Link, Norman Wells area, 1920. Glenbow Archive PD-132-30-149, Imperial Oil Collection.

feared that Japanese submarines could prey upon them, and many of the tankers were needed for Atlantic convoy service. An alternative proposal came forward from an unlikely source: Vilhjalmur Stefansson, a prominent Arctic explorer and ethnologist.

Born in Manitoba, Stefansson was raised in the United States, and received a degree in anthropology from Harvard. Even before the First World War, he had achieved fame as an intrepid and accomplished explorer of the Arctic region, particularly on the Alaskan shelf and Beaufort Sea and in Siberia. He had campaigned for the construction of an Alaskan highway even before the outbreak of the Second World War and was a consultant with the US Army Air Forces in the 1930s.

Stefansson shared Ted Link's conviction that there were huge deposits of oil in the Mackenzie River region north to the Beaufort Sea. In early 1942 he began buttonholing officials in Washington advocating expanding the oil fields at Norman Wells and building a pipeline to the Yukon River to supply the needs of the US army and air force in Alaska. These overtures were apparently rebuffed by General George Marshall, the chairman of the US Chiefs of Staff, as well as the Petroleum Coordinator for War Harold Ickes, but Stefansson found a more sympathetic listener in Frederic Delano, chairman of the US National Resources Board, and, more crucially, the uncle of President Franklin Roosevelt.

Stefansson also met with Eugene Holman, a member of Jersey Standard's Board, who served as an industry liaison with the Office of the US Petroleum Coordinator, and Ronald MacKinnon, who was the superintendent of the Norman Wells refinery for Imperial Oil. The refinery had reopened in 1933 to supply the petroleum needs of El Dorado and Yellowknife gold mining operations, but the output never exceeded 840 bbl./day. Between 1929 and 1941 the total production of the three operating fields was 128,000 barrels. MacKinnon indicated that the refinery could increase output to 3,000 bbl./day but would require significant capital investment, which Jersey Standard was not in a position to provide.

Stefansson finally found a champion in the formidable figure of General Brehon Somervell, who was appointed Commanding General of the US Army Service Forces in March 1942. This position put him in charge of what one observer described as "everything except the actual fighting."[25] Within a month Somervell, a man of action, had one of his advisers, James

Graham, dean of Engineering at the University of Kentucky, meet with Jersey Standard's Holman and two Imperial Oil engineers. The Imperial men were cautious, saying "no assurances could be made" about raising output to 3000 bbl./day. But nevertheless, Graham was apparently satisfied and recommended to Somervell that they proceed with a plan to increase production at Norman Wells, and build a pipeline to Whitehorse where a refinery could be constructed to handle the expansion.

On the same day—April 29, 1942—Somervell approved the proposal and summoned R.V. LeSueur, president of Imperial Oil, to come to Washington and sign a contract. As an afterthought, the Canadian government was notified "through an informal note." The cabinet of Prime Minister Mackenzie King was initially divided, but the forceful (and American-born) Minister of Munitions and Supply, C.D. Howe, enthusiastically endorsed the proposal and saw to it that information was leaked to Parliament to bolster support for the project as a wartime measure. On May 19 the cabinet approved the "Canol Project" as it came to be known and the US and Canada agreed to it on June 29, less than two months after Somervell's recommendation.[26]

The contract Lesueur negotiated for Imperial with the US War Department was complex, and modified by agreements involving the Canadian government. But on the whole it could be considered a good deal for the company, which was provided with "the means of enlarging the Norman Wells field and their production . . . without having to invest any risk capital."[27] War Department negotiators were in a hurry but they were also mindful that future Congressional committees might scrutinize their work in search of wasteful spending—as indeed came to pass.

Imperial agreed to drill at least nine new wells as well as increasing the production of its existing wells at Norman to reach the 3,000 bbl./day target by October 1942. Any royalties due to the Canadian government under the 1921 federal regulations would be waived for both the new and existing wells, backdated to 1939 "to ensure that Imperial could offer a reduced price to the War Department for its output." Imperial would own all the wells; the cost of development, estimated at $2 million (USD) would be covered by the US War Department, and the Canadian government would waive import duties on the equipment brought in to develop the project. Imperial would be paid $1.75 (USD) per bbl. for oil produced in existing wells, and $1.25 (USD) for oil from new wells, whose cost would have been covered by the War Department. After the US government had bought 1.5 million bbl. of crude oil, the price would be set at 0.50 (USD) per bbl. until the $2 million was paid off.[28]

This complicated process all but ensured that Imperial would seek to cover as much of its required output as possible by expanding the existing field at Norman Wells rather than developing new fields whose output would have to be sold at a discount. Not surprisingly, more than 80 per cent of the oil from Norman Wells that was sold through the Canol Project came from existing wells. On the other hand, Imperial was under considerable pressure from their War Department "partners" to explore and drill for oil anywhere they could go. By one account, by 1943 General Somervell and his associates had acquired "wildcat fever," anticipating strikes the size of the East Texas fields in the remote wilds of northern Canada. In 1943 Somervell boasted that the Norman oil fields could produce up to 100 million barrels of crude oil, and projected output of the (as yet uncompleted) refinery in Whitehorse up to 20,000 bbl./day. The Canadian government by now had pinned its hopes on the great white whale, since three quarters of the oil it was using had to be imported.[29]

To facilitate this grand quest, in November 1942 the US government persuaded Canada to expand the original leasing area for Norman Wells from 3,400 acres to 5 million acres, and to limit the prospecting and drilling rights to the nominee of the War Department, Imperial Oil, at least for the duration of the war. New regulations were imposed to keep out "nuisance staking" by wildcatters not associated with the project. Imperial dutifully expanded its exploration operations in 1943: Ted Link "swept out the senior class of the University of Alberta's Department of Geology" to fill the ranks of those needed to cover this wider territory.[30] Surveys by the US Army Air Force initially intended to identify the best route for the pipeline from Norman Wells to Whitehorse were expanded to provide aerial coverage of the enlarged domain of the Canol Project. But all these activities did not lead to an increase in actual production output. Imperial reported in 1945 that it had drilled sixty-three wells, with a potential capacity of thirty-six million barrels—little more than one third of the figure Somervell had projected in 1943. The company capped most of the wells at the end of the war.[31]

FIGURE 6.4. Means of transportation, Canol, 1944. Glenbow Archive IP-17a-3712, Imperial Oil Collection.

Meanwhile, the rest of the project was foundering amid scandals and investigations. The Whitehorse refinery, which was supposed to be in place by October 1942, was not completed until the following year by which time the Japanese threat to Alaska had receded. The pipeline from Norman Wells to Whitehorse, undertaken through unexplored territory, was not completed until early 1944 and was plagued with problems—oil leaks, wildfires, and damage to the permafrost. This was truly a "pioneer" undertaking, with no environmental considerations. Fortunately for Imperial Oil none of these debacles could be attributed to their company, which had done its job of producing the oil. In 1942 LeSueur had advised General Somervell that aviation gasoline could probably be provided more cheaply to the US bases in Alaska by flying supplies in by air rather than by building pipelines from Norman Wells.[32]

Meanwhile, American Congressional watchdogs were circling the fetid carcass of Canol. Harold Ickes, the US Petroleum Coordinator, had long opposed the project as an intrusion on his turf (even though it was in Canada) and useless in any case; he was joined by the Secretary of the Navy Frank Knox and assorted other bureaucratic rivals to the War Department. Senator Harry Truman's Special Committee to Investigate the National Defense Program honed in on Canol in the autumn of 1943. It concluded that the project, estimated to cost $25 million (USD), came in at more than $125 million (USD), much of it wasted. In its final report on Canol in 1944 the committee "cited the great benefits Canada and Imperial Oil got out of the contracts drawn up by the War Department. The United States paid for the exploration and development of the oilfield but retained no rights to the oil after the war."[33]

As might be expected, the demise of Canol was accompanied by much backbiting and finger pointing. Amazingly, the US War Department tried to keep a foothold in the Norman Wells operation after the war, demanding that the US should retain a 60 million barrel "strategic reserve" in return for turning over all the equipment provided to Imperial to expand its operations. LeSueur objected to this proposal, as did the Canadian government; in the end a bizarre, face-saving agreement was reached— Imperial would agree to hold a 60 million barrel reserve for the US Army, but only if the company discovered enough oil to export beyond covering its local market. Imperial was already in the process of capping its wells and had no plans to export any output from Norman Wells—its production fell to 200,000 bbl. in 1946.

When the project was under negotiation, much attention was paid to the disposition of properties after the war. As the war wound down, however, the US government embarked on a policy of systematic liquidation of the assets in which it had invested for wartime purposes, both at home and abroad. The Canadian government was offered a first option on taking over the pipeline from Norman Wells to Whitehorse, which it declined, and the poorly constructed system was allowed to deteriorate until it was largely dismantled in the 1960s. In 1947 Imperial Oil purchased the Whitehorse refinery, which had cost $22.5 million (USD) to build for $1 million; it then dismantled the refinery and shipped it to Edmonton at a cost of $9 million to be rebuilt as the refinery for the Leduc oil field. A very good bargain. During the war the company had produced 1,675,132 barrels of crude oil at Norman Wells, processing more than one-fifth of the output at its own refinery there and earning a $1.16 million (CAD) profit from its operations. On the other hand, explorations in the region by Imperial in 1946 did not indicate the presence of the large-scale oil field the company needed to find as output from its other domestic operations, including Turner Valley, declined.[34]

Leduc

Imperial Oil emerged from the Second World War as still the largest petroleum company in Canada. In terms of assets, it was larger than all the other oil companies in the country put together. It had the only nationwide refinery and distribution system. Despite inroads on its sales in the 1930s, Imperial still held 50 per cent of the Canadian market. It had been the major contributor to wartime production of essential materials, including synthetic rubber and aviation fuels. Yet the company faced an internal crisis on several levels.

First, there was the issue of leadership. In 1945 G.H. Smith, who had presided over International Petroleum in the 1920s and Imperial Oil in the following decade, retired. His successor, R.V. LeSueur, another International Petroleum veteran, retired and died that same year. Both men owed their rise in part to their association with Walter Teagle, and they reflected his view of Imperial Oil as a loyal player in Jersey Standard's global game with Shell, Anglo-Persian, and American-based international competitors. Jersey Standard was going through its own changing of the guard, as Teagle, Farish, and others of that generation departed.

Jersey Standard's executives were aware of the management problems and the succession issues at Imperial even before the Second World War. After Imperial's share of the Canadian gasoline market fell from two-thirds to one half, Teagle had ordered a sweeping critique of Imperial's marketing policies in 1936 that found many failings despite Smith's (accurate) protests that Jersey Standard's depletion of the Canadian company's capital investment funds had contributed to these problems. In 1938, Jersey Standard sent in a new man to run the show.

Henry Hewetson had been born in the United States, but had many Canadian ties: he had served with the Canadian forces in the First World War and was married to a cousin of Victor Ross. But his work experience was with Jersey Standard, first at Bayway refinery and then as vice president of Standard Oil of Louisiana, one of the largest of the American subsidiaries. He was very much in the Walter Teagle mode—a big man with a square jaw and an-around-the-clock manager. At Imperial, he reported directly to Smith and then LeSueur. Among his other achievements, he could boast of establishing thirty-eight new service stations to boost Imperial's sales. Since the war improved Imperial's business, it is hard to know whether he was the primary contributor to the company's turnaround, but Jersey Standard's executives were obviously impressed.[35]

Hewetson was indeed a breath of fresh air in the halls of Imperial's headquarters in Toronto. Given his background in marketing, a great deal of attention was given to improving performance in this area: product sales doubled between 1939 and 1947, although net income only rose by 10 per cent, in part because of wartime taxes, and the imposition of rations on gasoline from 1942–45. During the war, he held prices down for "large industrial accounts" while allowing them to rise elsewhere, in order to retain these clients. Hewetson also opposed federal government proposals to allow lower priced oil imports for the civilian market, on the grounds that Canadian refining capacity needed protection. He lobbied successfully to force co-operatives in Saskatchewan to be subjected to federal taxes, to the delight of colleagues in the private (profit) sector.

Hewetson was also mindful of the issues of supply and supported the construction of the Portland to Montreal pipeline in 1941, which was intended in part to protect eastern Canada from the submarine attacks on tankers that peaked in that year. When he became president in 1945, Hewetson authorized the establishment of catalytic cracking plants and set up a separate division to that end. In addition he set up an Economics and Supply Department to encourage new innovations. At the senior level, he established an executive committee, modelled on Jersey Standard, to provide an overall strategic review and guidance for the company's operations—a major change in a company that had largely been run by the chief executive, with occasional prodding from Jersey Standard.[36]

Despite these energetic achievements, Hewetson faced the same challenge that had bedevilled his predecessors, all the way back to Teagle. The Petrolia fields were all but defunct, the Turner Valley output was declining, and for all its sound and fury Canol had produced no elephants. The Colombians were threatening to nationalize International Petroleum's holdings there by 1951, and Imperial Oil faced the prospect of becoming a refining and distributing company with no secure source of crude oil—not very different from the situation in 1914. Meanwhile, Imperial's familiar competitor in Canada, British American, took over Union Oil of Canada, and there was a potentially formidable American entrant, Sun Oil of Philadelphia, which focused initially on the eastern Canadian market but also acquired a half-million acre block for exploration in Alberta in 1945. Also in the west, Shell and Standard of California showed renewed interest in Alberta, joined by another American company, Husky Oil of Wyoming. The field was becoming more crowded.[37]

The government of Canada was also concerned about the declining domestic reserves, and the need to import more oil from the US during the war exacerbated dollar exchange problems. Since 1921, the federal government had allowed oil companies to offset exploration costs against their taxes. In 1941 the Dominion War Exchange Conservation Act allowed oil companies special depreciation and depletion allowances to encourage domestic production, and two years later duties were removed on equipment imported for use in oil and gas exploration.[38]

The lure of government tax breaks may have attracted some of the new entrants into the exploration game during the Second World War, but Imperial Oil remained the company most committed to finding new oil and gas in Canada. In 1946 Imperial reported that it had spent more than $18.7 million (CAD) on exploration and $6 million (CAD) on leases since 1919, representing 40 per cent of all the exploration costs recorded for the country; almost half of its expenses since 1942 had been offset by tax relief, but the record indicated the degree of engagement—or desperation—the company placed on finding new reserves.[39]

As exploration expenses—and frustrations—grew, Imperial's managers began looking at alternative ways of rebuilding reserves. One of the patents that Jersey Standard had acquired in the 1930s from German sources (not, in this case, from I.G. Farben, but from a coal-based company called Ruhrchemie) involved the conversion of coal into synthetic fuels, which the Germans had used during the Second World War. Research at Jersey Standard indicated that a similar process could be deployed to convert natural gas into various forms of high-octane fuel. Since Alberta appeared to have abundant supplies of natural gas, Imperial began drilling for gas at the Viking-Kinsella field near Edmonton in late 1945. Although the synthetic fuel conversion process would be an expensive proposition—50 million cubic feet of natural gas per day would be required to produce 5,000 barrels of synthetic fuel—it was still deemed better than relying entirely on imported oil.

But Hewetson was not yet prepared to give up the quest for oil in Alberta, and he was supported by not only the ever-optimistic Ted Link but also O.B. Hopkins, now vice president of Imperial, who—like Link—had been involved in the early explorations of the North West Company. They persuaded Jersey Standard's top managers in the exploration area, including Lewis Weeks, the chief geologist, to send Michael Haider to help coordinate a final attempt to find the holy grail: Haider was a petroleum engineer from Stanford who had been involved with Carter Oil, Jersey Standard's major exploration arm, before coming to headquarters. Haider would later join the Imperial board and go on to become president and board chairman of Jersey Standard.[40]

A crucial meeting in this process took place on April 19, 1946, attended by the major geologists from both companies including Link, Hopkins, Haider, and Weeks. They mapped out an ambitious strategy that would cover a range of potential western Canadian sites, but focused on an area in Alberta around Edmonton that they regarded as most likely to yield good results. Seismic studies of the 25,000 square mile area were ordered for the search, a novelty for Alberta at that time—seismographic research had been pioneered by Carter Oil for Jersey Standard in the 1930s and was now being applied to their other affiliates.

Imperial's accounts of the steps that led to the Leduc discovery imply that it was carefully planned and executed; some historians have maintained that although the reasoning behind the strategy was well developed, there was still more than a bit of luck involved: the initial drilling was intended to penetrate to "Mesozoic" depths (formations dating back 225 million years) at about 4,000 feet; the promising but limited results led the

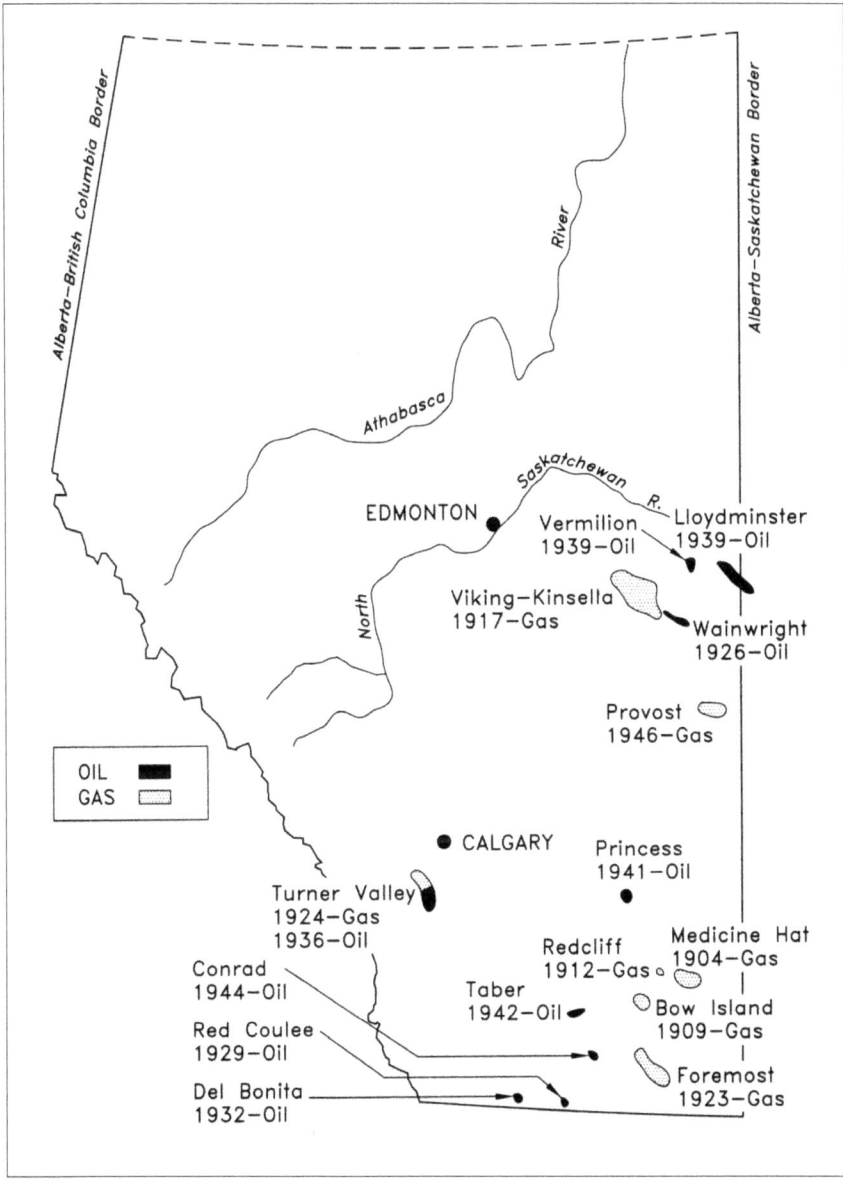

MAP 6.1. Alberta Oil and Gas Fields 1946. David Breen, *The Alberta Petroleum Industry and the Conservation Board*, Edmonton: University of Alberta Press, 1992, p. 237. Courtesy of David Breen.

drillers to go further into "Paleozoic" levels (formations going back 600 million years) at more than 5,000 feet—and most of the big oil discoveries to follow in Alberta went to these depths. In any case, by early February 1947, after three months of drilling at Leduc, Imperial managers felt confident that a strike was imminent and set the date for the public unveiling of their success for February 13, 1947.[41]

At the same time, Imperial was drilling more wells in the Leduc area—a second well proved disappointing, but Leduc #3 at 5,380 feet also proved to be a gusher. In the following year Imperial discovered another field, larger than Leduc, at Redwater. By this time, the other oil companies had joined enthusiastically in the search.

Imperial's managers could not bask in success. There were a number of issues to be resolved: where would this oil be refined? How would it get to market, and particularly to the central Canadian markets? Where would the capital come from to finance this major increase in the infrastructure required to ensure that Alberta's oil would provide the basis for Imperial's long-term growth? These were challenges that the company would face and overcome during the next several years, ensuring its predominant role in the Canadian oil industry for at least two decades.

PART THREE

AFTER LEDUC 1947–1980

7

GOLDEN AGE

After Leduc Number One, Imperial Oil was on a roll, with major new discoveries every few months. The initial well ran through 1974, producing over 300,000 barrels. At first a second well in the Leduc area brought up only gas, but after drilling probed past 5000 feet it struck oil, in May 1947. Less than a year later a new well came in at Woodbend, adjacent to the Leduc field. In July 1948 Imperial discovered the largest producer yet at Redwater, which ultimately held 800 million barrels of recoverable oil. Within six months another well—designated Golden Spike—came in, with a 200 million barrel reserve. Other discoveries included Excelsior and Bon Accord northeast of Edmonton, as well as the Acheson field with an estimated reserve of 75 million barrels, developed by Imperial with Standard of California (Socal). By 1951 Imperial's wells were producing 64,000 bbl./day, more than four times its output on the eve of the Leduc discovery.[1]

Imperial was attentive to the impact of these rapid developments on the communities affected. After a generation of dealing with powerful local organizations like the United Farmers of Alberta, Imperial officials were careful to keep people in the Leduc area informed about their activities. In October and November 1947 public relations people from Toronto, accompanied by Vernon Taylor, held meetings with groups of farmers to ascertain their concerns over the impact of drilling operations while presenting themselves as having "no knowledge of mineral rights, surface rights or land rental rates."

Many farmers in the Leduc area were "of Central European extraction" and spoke little English but had a strong sense of community according to the Imperial observers. They also detected the influence of

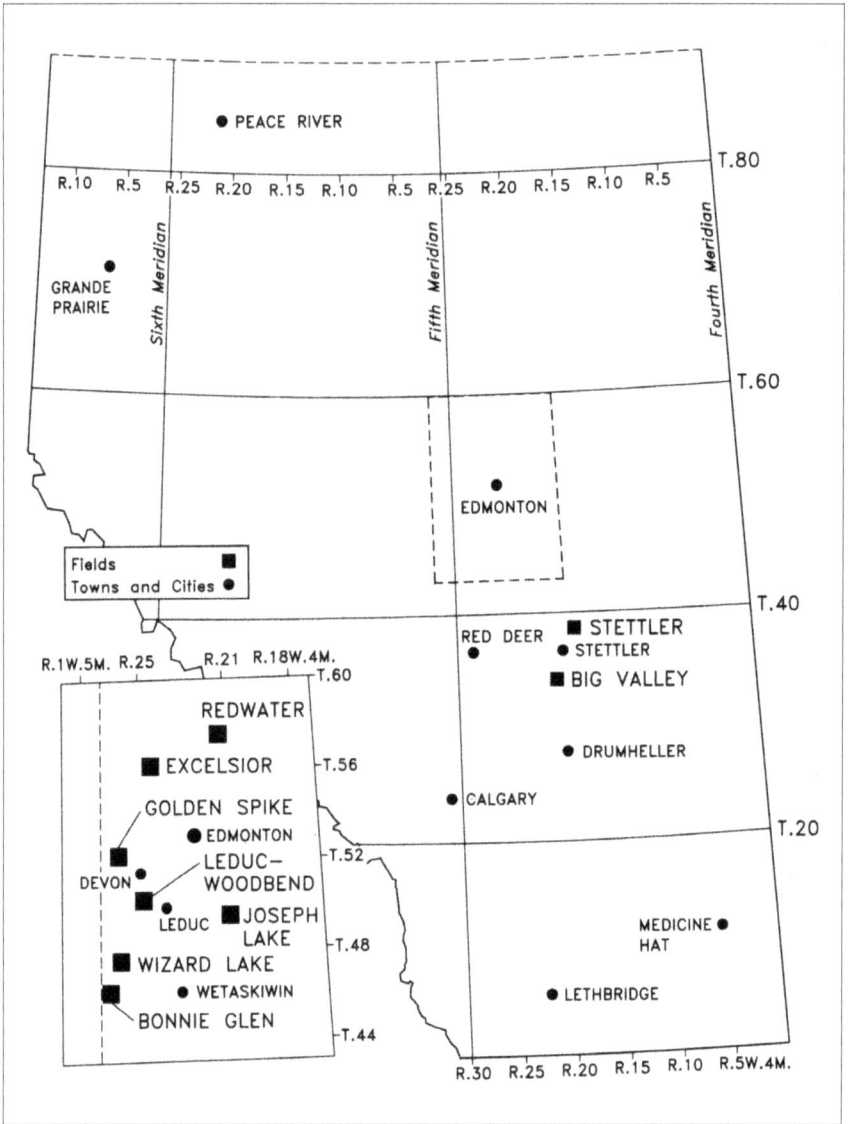

MAP 7.1. Alberta Oil Discoveries, 1947-51. David Breen, *The Alberta Petroleum Industry and the Conservation Board*, Edmonton: University of Alberta Press, 1992, p. 291. Courtesy of David Breen.

a "Surface Rights Association," which was demanding that leasing rates should be standardized. This would become a major source of acrimony over the next few years. The Social Credit government passed a Right of Arbitration Entry Act in 1947 that set up a process for adjudicating these concerns, but after several years many landowners became disillusioned about the lack of results.[2]

The farmers also expressed concern over the effects of oil drilling on soil fertility. Imperial brought in an agriculturist from the University of Alberta to advise them on how to re-fertilize the soil. There was less concern over the pipelines that the company was installing to gather oil from various sites, since they would "clean up" the spills from initial drilling.[3]

As the size and scale of operations in the Leduc field expanded, Imperial took steps to provide more stable accommodations for their production workers, in place of the trailer camps usually found near drilling sites. The company obtained a quarter section of land close to Leduc Number One and a planned gas conservation plant, and worked with the Department of Municipal Affairs to establish a town called Devon, with water, sewer, and gas supplies. Imperial set up a real estate subsidiary to handle financing with the Central Mortgage and Housing Corporation. Services were also provided to the other less developed communities near the drilling sites. The company had experience in developing "planned communities" near worksites at the Ioco refinery in British Columbia and the Imperial refinery in Dartmouth, Nova Scotia as well as in Peru and Colombia. In this case, however, Imperial sought to encourage employees to take up home ownership.[4]

Imperial also paid close attention to the measures undertaken by the Alberta Conservation Board to regulate access and development of the booming new oil fields. The success of Leduc Number Two lured oil seekers, large and small, to the Edmonton region. Among the big players were McColl-Frontenac, now owned by Texaco, which struck oil at Wizard Lake and Bonnie Glen in 1951–52, just south of Leduc-Woodbend. The Canadian Atlantic Oil Company controlled by Frank McMahon, who had been active in British Columbia and Turner Valley since 1938, had the dubious distinction of experiencing one of the largest and longest-lasting blowouts in Alberta's oil history in 1948, the Atlantic Number 3, which was located close to the Leduc field and forced Imperial to temporarily close its own production. The Atlantic No. 3 disaster was finally brought under control by a Standard-Imperial engineer, Tip Moroney, after burning for six months—incredibly there was still an ample amount of oil recovered.[5] In 1953 Standard of New York (Socony Vacuum—later Mobil) and a Delaware-based company, Seaboard Oil, discovered an even larger oil field on the Pembina River west of Edmonton that ultimately was found to hold 1.7 billion recoverable barrels. More than 5,000 wells were drilled in the Pembina area over the next few years.[6]

The conservation board scrambled to head off renewed criticism in mid-1947 when it realized that Imperial had carefully acquired rights to much of the subsurface oil and gas around Leduc. New regulations stipulated that when the holder of a reservation converted it to a lease, 50 per cent would revert to a "crown reserve"—some of which would then be auctioned off. The intent of the policy was to create a "checkerboard" of lease holdings that would presumably prevent large companies (like Imperial) from amassing consolidated units that could drain entire fields. Inevitably these measures drew attacks from those like C.J. Nickle, publisher of an influential oil newsletter, who saw it as "strangling Alberta's oil industry," but this did not temper criticism from the left-wing CCF that the government was in effect turning over "these great pools of wealth" to Imperial Oil.

A related issue involved royalty rates tied to leaseholds. Imperial and other large companies wanted a specific royalty rate so they could budget their operations on a stable basis. In 1948 the Alberta government ignored these demands and allowed a "royalty bonus" in addition to a "cash bonus" for bidders on highly desirable parcels such as those in the Leduc fields. The companies mounted a new lobbying campaign opposing royalty rates that exceeded 15 per cent. Fortunately for the lobbyists the Social Credit party faced what it regarded as a serious challenge from the CCF, which was promising to take over half of the province's oil production and impose 25 per cent royalties on private producers (with emphasis on Imperial as the largest of them). With backing from the oil industry, Social Credit swept the election, ensuring that Ernest Manning would remain premier, a position he held until 1968.[7]

Financial Restructuring

Even before the Leduc discovery, Imperial confronted challenging demands for new capital investment. Many of the refineries had been built more than a quarter century earlier and except for Sarnia there had not been much in the way of renovation through the Depression and war years. Marketing and service facilities also needed updating—during the war the Canadian government barred any spending on upgrading service stations, so in 1945–46 they were clamouring for new investment.

Dependence on imported US oil had become more costly as the exchange rate for the Canadian dollar fell precipitously after the end of the Second World War, an additional impetus to developing new domestic sources. Expenditures on exploration and wildcat drilling more than doubled between 1944 and 1946: more than half of the $18.7 million (CAD) spent on exploration since 1917 was accounted for in these three years. Had the Leduc gamble failed, Imperial would have faced huge new capital investments to build synthetic fuel plants.

Wartime production expansion had increased domestic profits from $7 million in 1940 to $14.9 million (CAD) in 1946 although taxes levelled net income through the war period. More critically, the dividend policy constrained Imperial's capacity to expand its net working capital. Although Jersey Standard as chief shareholder had adjusted its demands for dividends after 1940, Imperial was still paying out an average of 70 per cent of net income in dividends through the war and postwar period. While Imperial's president Hewetson recognized the need for renovation and inventory expansion to meet the pent-up civilian demand for oil products as the war ended, beyond the obvious need to beef up exploratory operations the board adhered to a cautious policy with regard to investments.[8]

The good news from Leduc in February 1947 brought with it, of course, a new set of investment demands. As competitors flocked to the Alberta oil fields, Imperial had to continue and expand its exploratory efforts. Even more challenging were the issues of getting the oil to markets, particularly in central Canada. Huge increases in crude oil production would overwhelm the capacity of existing refineries in Calgary and Winnipeg, and

FIGURE 7.1. Henry Hewetson, 1950. Glenbow Archive IP-26-8b-Hewetson, H.H.-2, Imperial Oil Collection.

the transportation of both crude oil to refineries and refined oil to markets posed thorny problems involving politics and logistics as well as financing.

The last time Imperial Oil had significantly increased its capital base, in 1917, it had issued new equity shares. Walter Teagle had been president of Imperial, and Jersey Standard had picked up a significant proportion of the issue in order to maintain its ownership stake. In 1947, however, Jersey Standard was dealing with a variety of financial demands: the government of Venezuela was pushing for "fifty-fifty" profit sharing, and Jersey Standard was on the verge of joining Aramco, the Saudi Arabian consortium. Imperial had no champion with the heft of a Teagle at 30 Rockefeller Plaza (Jersey Standard's headquarters after 1933). The parent company had no intention of diluting its position with Imperial, however, and currency constraints on both sides of the border limited Imperial's access to US lenders.

On the other hand, Jersey Standard was receptive to proposals that Imperial explore the possibility of raising funds from Canadian sources. The parent company authorized Imperial to look into borrowing up to $35 million (CAD) although it set a three-year limit on terms for financing. In September 1947 the Imperial board settled on an alternative approach that would give them greater flexibility—and a novel one for the company: a bond issue. A special meeting of shareholders on September 22 approved issuing debentures up to $60 million (CAD). The board immediately authorized a $24 million (CAD) bond issue at 2.25 per cent, maturing between 1950 and 1955. The Royal Bank of Canada subscribed for the entire amount and it was successfully marketed within days, reflecting the post-Leduc aura that surrounded Imperial with the Canadian investing public.[9]

By early 1948 it was apparent that the costs of expansion were greater than initially anticipated, and in particular a pipeline to central Canada was vitally necessary to meet demand and reduce the growing inventory of crude oil emanating from Leduc, Woodbend, and Redwater fields. A new debenture issue of $6 million (CAD) was authorized, but the company needed to look for a longer-term solution to its capital needs. This was the context within which the sale of its largest subsidiary, International Petroleum, emerged as a move that would serve a range of goals for the company not just in terms of augmenting its capital budget.

Imperial's initial investments in Peru and Colombia had been largely orchestrated by Jersey Standard for its own strategic purposes. Even in the 1920s–30s, most of the crude oil brought into Canada came from the US, not from International Petroleum, and the establishment of a pipeline from Portland to Montreal in 1941–42 had reduced Imperial's eastern Canadian reliance on South American oil even more. Neither Imperial nor Jersey Standard had put new investment into International Petroleum after the mid-1920s, and Imperial was not likely to put its limited resources into the renovations that the fields in Peru and Colombia required after the Second World War. The most salient consideration was that the government of Colombia had made it clear that it intended to nationalize the de Mares concession and other IPC properties in 1951.

Imperial's board proposed to sell its holdings in International Petroleum early in 1948. This move obviously required the agreement of Jersey Standard, the largest shareholder, which apparently was obtained as it offered all its investors the opportunity to purchase shares in IPC at $9.20 (USD) per share, including an exchange of Imperial for International Petroleum shares on a three-for-one basis. The Canadian Foreign Exchange Control Board facilitated sales for the minority shareholders. In September 1948 the transaction was completed: Imperial had divested itself of IPC for $80 million (CAD), a little more than half in cash and the balance in 2 per cent interest bearing notes (principally from Jersey Standard).

Why did Jersey Standard buy IPC, given the imminent crisis that company faced with the Colombian government? There is no clearly articulated rationale from any of the parties involved. By the mid-1940s, IPC's largest source of revenue came from its partnership with other oil companies in Venezuela. Jersey Standard already had a significant stake in Venezuela through its investment in Creole Petroleum. In 1948, demands from the Venezuelan government for a greater share in oil profits were at least temporarily forestalled by a military coup that promised a relatively more hospitable environment for multinational oil companies. Jersey Standard was of course well aware of the nationalist pressures in Colombia, but hoped to at least maintain a foothold there by providing management services for the nascent government enterprise that would own the oil fields, and it was able to continue providing such services for several years. Nevertheless, the willingness of Jersey Standard to provide support for Imperial Oil by accepting its divestment of International Petroleum was surprising, in view of its more hard-line views when the Canadian company was seeking financial support in 1947.[10]

The financial moves in 1947–48, along with the growth of its working capital, provided Imperial with a net infusion of $180 million (CAD) in capital resources, although of course it was offset by increased debt obligations and the loss of dividend revenue from International Petroleum. But the capital enabled the investments in infrastructure essential for exploiting the benefits of new and continuing oil discoveries that would yield significant growth after 1949–50. There was one other restructuring move made in this period that, while it was not as lucrative as the sale of International Petroleum, marked an important break with its past.

Royalite had been the second largest and second most profitable subsidiary for Imperial Oil through the 1920s–40s. But as opportunities for development in Turner Valley dwindled, Royalite had begun exploring for oil and gas in new areas, placing it at least potentially in a competitive position with Imperial in Alberta. Although obstreperous figures like William Herron were gone from the scene, Imperial still found the minority shareholders in Royalite a troublesome presence, and in June 1948 the Imperial board offered them an opportunity to share in Imperial's promising future through a generous share exchange (1.25 shares in Imperial for 1 share in Royalite). In October Imperial's new president, George B. Stewart (Hewetson was now chairman of the board), could report that Imperial's shareholdings in Royalite had increased from 68.5 per cent to 80 per cent.

Relations with Royalite's board appeared to have soured, however. When Imperial proposed to buy out the remaining shares in Royalite for $17 million (CAD) the Royalite board balked, and produced a counter-offer of $20 million (CAD), which Imperial rejected. There was an internal struggle within the board and ultimately president S.F. Heard plus Imperial's representatives were outvoted. In January 1949 Heard advised his fellow directors that Imperial had sold all of its shares in Royalite through Dominion Securities. Imperial's motives are not clear, but it seems the board determined that a clean break with Royalite was preferable to further negotiations. In any case, Imperial ended up with a net return of $20 million (CAD), which included selling Foothills Oil & Gas and Lowery Petroleum as well as its shares in Royalite.[11]

There was one other transaction carried out in this period that was not related to post-Leduc financing, but also marked a significant break with the past and had a lasting impact on the oil industry in eastern Canada. For many years Imperial had relied on independent distributors to supplement sales of the company's products to retailers. During the late 1920s Imperial had begun a process of establishing closer control over these distributors through direct investment, or holding bearer bonds or stock options as collateral for loans. The Imperial board was advised about what were referred to as "marketing organizations," but they were not formally identified as affiliates—although in most cases Imperial owned virtually all the shares in the companies.

By 1946 there were "marketing organizations" in each part of the country: Irving Oil in the Maritimes, Champlain Oil in Quebec, Supertest Petroleum in central Canada, Maple Leaf Petroleum in Alberta and Ronerk Company Ltd., which controlled three distributing companies in western Canada. For the most part their book value was small, the largest being Champlain at $1.8 million (CAD), Supertest at $2.3 million (CAD), and Imperial's share of Irving at $2 million (CAD). But they supplemented the company's direct sales to ensure a retail market share ranging from 24 to 36 per cent across the country.[12]

At this point Imperial's board became uneasy about the legality of these arrangements. While Canada's Combines legislation was far less onerous than the panoply of antitrust and state and federal regulatory bodies that confronted would-be monopolists in the United States, in the postwar years Jersey Standard was once more facing antitrust investigations, and the anxiety at 30 Rockefeller Plaza may have percolated down to the Imperial executives in Toronto. In any case, in September 1946 they consulted D.L. McCarthy, a prominent Toronto lawyer who had been involved in a Combines case against Imperial Tobacco. McCarthy's response to president Hewetson in January 1947 was reassuring: Imperial Oil's commitments with the "marketing companies" was unlikely to arouse the investigative ire of the Combines Commission, with one exception: the arrangements with Irving Oil in the Maritimes, which should be dissolved.[13]

This recommendation was likely greeted with relief by at least some members of the board, as Imperial's relationship with Irving had been exasperating for both parties for some time. Kenneth C. Irving had begun his career running his father's general store in rural New Brunswick in the early 1900s. During the 1920s he became interested in the emerging auto industry, acquiring a Ford dealership but also branching into the service station market. Although Imperial was a major supplier, Irving was a thorny partner who also marketed his own brand of "Primrose" gas. For a time he was buying his products from Cities Service in the US—until the Bennett government imposed protective duties on imported oil and gas in 1930.

Irving returned to the Imperial fold, but continued to sell his products using the "Irving Oil" logo. By the late 1930s, Irving was the second largest retailer of automotive products in New Brunswick and had expanded his service stations into Nova Scotia and New England. Irving was also ambitious, moving into tire retailing, manufacturing wood veneers, and setting up a steamship company during the 1930s. This expansion was backed by Imperial Oil, which underwrote bank loans of more than $400,000 (CAD). In 1945 Irving announced his intention to set up a refinery in Saint John (New Brunswick) if he could obtain the financing—which, among other consequences, would compete with Imperial's Halifax refinery.

This was the context within which Imperial set out to consolidate its arrangements with the marketing companies. In Irving's case, Imperial proposed to convert loans into bearer shares. This would mean that, should Imperial exercise its options, it would own 70 per cent of Irving Oil. At the same time, Irving would be retained as manager of the company, holding power of attorney over the shares held by Imperial. Nevertheless, as McCarthy pointed out, Imperial—with its somewhat clandestine ownership of Irving—would effectively control more than half the oil and gas market for the Maritimes, a situation that could lead to a Combines investigation. Since Irving was continuing to campaign for his own refinery, the Imperial board appears to have withdrawn from further moves to take over the New Brunswick company, eventually selling its bearer shares in Irving Oil.[14]

Irving had used earnings from wartime production of the wood products of Canada Veneers to the RCAF to help finance expansion into shipyards, railroads, and the pulp and paper industry in the Maritimes. By the 1950s he was competing with Imperial in the Quebec market and tried to persuade Jersey Standard to underwrite his refinery. When that proposal fell through, Irving entered a partnership with the Canadian subsidiary of Standard of California (Chevron) to finance his dream. Irving Oil continued to be an important player in the eastern Canada oil and gas market over the next half century, and the Irving dynasty was among the richest families in the country.[15]

Building Infrastructure

Even as it was assembling the financial resources to exploit the opportunities presented by Leduc, Imperial was seeking to create the infrastructure required to bring their newfound oil to markets. One of the first steps was to establish refining capacity in Edmonton, in part because the city itself provided the most immediate market for their growing output, but also because it would provide the base for expansion beyond Alberta. In this undertaking Imperial benefitted from its earlier involvement in the Canol debacle.

Although the US Army had hoped to retain a foothold in its ill-fated venture into Canada's Northwest Territories, the Truman administration in Washington was committed to sloughing off this costly white elephant, not least because President Truman himself had been directly involved as a senator in investigating the Canol follies. When the questioned about holding onto Norman Wells and its pipeline to Skagway, the president dismissed Canol as a "dead cat." After Imperial completed its last operations in April 1945, the government of Canada declined to take it over and the Canol properties were assigned to the US Foreign Asset Liquidation Commission.

Responsibility for its operations, such as they were, was assigned to the US-Canadian Permanent Joint Defence Board. In September 1946 Canada's Air Vice Marshall Curtis, a member of the PJBD, approached Imperial Oil about the possibility of re-opening the Whitehorse refinery and pipeline to provide aviation fuel for military aircraft operating in Fairbanks, Alaska. Even though the Cold War had yet to become a preoccupation of the US government, military officers were girding for potential threats. The Imperial executives, who included soon-to-be board chairman Hewetson and incoming president George Stewart, reacted cautiously to this overture: the company was obviously wary of further entanglements with the American military bureaucracy and their congressional watchdogs. In the end, nothing apparently came out of these discussions, but in certain respects the episode confirmed that Imperial was regarded as a trustworthy partner in the management of North America's oil resources.[16]

After Leduc, the Imperial board took another look at Canol's Whitehorse refinery. It had limited capacity but it was newer than many of Imperial's existing refineries and included catalytic cracking and crude distillation units from Texas. Even more enticing was the fact that the US government was anxious to get rid of it. In May 1947 Imperial purchased the refinery for $1 million (USD); the estimated cost of construction had been $22.5 million (USD).

Imperial contracted with a Los Angeles company, W.W. Barnes, to dismantle the refinery and ship it, by truck and rail, to a 360-acre site the company had purchased just east of Edmonton. This was not a simple or easy operation in the Canadian winter, but it was accomplished, and the company reopened on July 17, 1948, with an initial capacity of 6,000 bbl./day. The cost of the project was $8.7 million (CAD), so the total cost of the refinery was around $10 million (CAD). C.E. Carson, the Imperial board member who was also head of the company's manufacturing department, commented that "a complete new refinery could have been built for this amount," but the acquisition of the Whitehorse property "save[d] about eighteen months' time," and would "conserve foreign exchange."[17]

Fuel prices in Alberta and Saskatchewan were significantly reduced over the next six months, and by 1949, with the installation of a second distillation unit, output was increased to 25,000 bbl./day. As new discoveries expanded the prospective output of the fields around Edmonton, in 1951, Imperial negotiated an agreement to provide crude oil supplies to a new Edmonton refinery built by McColl-Frontenac/Texaco with a 5,500 bbl./day capacity, which was later increased to 11,000 bbl./day. British-American Oil also built a refinery in Edmonton in 1951, with an eventual capacity of 7,000 bbl./day. In 1975 Imperial built a new and much larger refinery, the Strathcona, in Edmonton. The Strathcona replaced older refineries in Calgary, Regina, and Winnipeg that were now supplied by pipelines from Edmonton. During the cutbacks in production in the 1990s, Strathcona was the only refinery operated by Imperial in western Canada.[18]

Building a pipeline to link Leduc and other emerging Alberta oilfields to markets was a more complex task, involving a number of difficult decisions; indeed given the magnitude of the project as it evolved, the actual construction time of 150 days was astonishing. Imperial Oil had limited experience in pipeline development: the most significant effort was the construction of a six-inch line from Cygnet, Ohio to the Saint Clair River in 1913 to supply the Sarnia refinery. Five years later, the addition of loops and intermediate pumping stations increased capacity from 3000 to 10,000 bbl./day. Imperial established a US affiliate, Transit & Storage Company, to manage the American part of the 454-mile Cygnet line; another company, Imperial Pipe Line, ran the Canadian side. Initially the Cygnet line drew crude supplies from the Lima, Ohio fields; by the 1930s Imperial joined with Jersey Standard and Carter Oil to invest in the Ajax Pipe Line, which drew on the large Oklahoma fields.

Of course the International Petroleum Company had experience constructing pipelines in Peru and particularly in Colombia in the 1920s. A number of the managers who were seconded to Interprovincial Pipeline from Imperial Oil had been involved in these projects. In addition, shorter oil and gas lines had been constructed in Alberta and, if nothing else, the problems of the Canol pipeline provided examples of the pitfalls of construction in a difficult environment.

During the Second World War, Jersey Standard, concerned over the vulnerability of tankers in the Atlantic to U-boat attacks and the seasonal closing of the Saint Lawrence to large ships, built a line from Portland to Montreal with an 80,000 bbl./day capacity. Humble Oil—a Texas-based affiliate of Jersey Standard—built the 489-mile line in six months; it opened shortly before the US entry into the war in December 1941. After the war Jersey Standard doubled the capacity of the line and then sold it for $50,000 (USD) to a consortium of Canadian companies, with Imperial acquiring a 40 per cent share of the line.[19]

After Leduc, the characteristically cautious Imperial board initially contemplated building a 16-inch pipeline from Edmonton to Regina, a distance of 450 miles over prairie, which would serve the Saskatchewan and Manitoba markets. But even this modest proposal involved unprecedented action. A pipeline that crossed provincial boundaries required federal approval. Fortunately, Imperial was not the only company contemplating building an inter-provincial pipeline, and the Liberal government in Ottawa was receptive to projects that would promote Canada's economic growth in the postwar era.

In April 1949, a Pipe Line Act was hastily pushed through Parliament on the eve of an election, which the Liberals won. Days after the bill passed, a number of pipeline companies were chartered under the Act, including Imperial's Interprovincial Pipeline Company—and also a British-American Oil Company pipeline and a natural gas pipeline to British Columbia, undertaken by Frank McMahon among others.

In the meantime the Redwater discoveries in late 1948 had widened horizons for Imperial—with potential reserves exceeding 500 million barrels, the prospects of serving markets in central Canada, or the United States, became more viable. Imperial vice president John R. (Jack) White maintained that the company contemplated moving at least 75,000 bbl./day for 25 years. In February 1949 Imperial Oil had recognized the need for a separate organization to manage this more ambitious project and set up the Interprovincial Pipeline Company, capitalized at $200 million (CAD). Imperial Oil held 40 per cent of the shares, and the balance was issued to the public; but the management was clearly determined by Imperial: Interprovincial's president was O.B. Hopkins, the Imperial geologist who had played an important role in Imperial's quest for oil in Alberta since the 1920s. Other Imperial figures on Interprovincial's board included Jack White, who would become Imperial's president in the 1950s, Frank G. Hall, and A.E. Halvorsen.[20]

Once the construction was agreed upon, supply issues came to the fore. A special steel plate was needed for the pipeline, but it was not available in Canada. The federal government, via the Minister of Trade and Commerce C.D. Howe (also known as the "Minister of Everything"), arranged for the waiving of special duties on importing 40,000 tons of steel plate from Britain. This actually proved to be unhelpful, as the steel did not meet the requirements for the tubing required by Imperial; but Stelco agreed to use the imported steel for other customers while Page Hersey Tubes Ltd. could draw on Stelco for steel needed for Imperial's pipes. The government proved to be very patient with the particular requirements of Interprovincial Pipeline.[21]

More contentious was the internal debate at Imperial Oil (and Interprovincial Pipeline) over the next steps in expansion. Everyone agreed that the goal should be supplying a market with a refining capacity of at least 100,000 bbl./day. But there were many different potential clients and each of them had advocates on the company board. Shipping to Imperial's refinery in Sarnia was an obvious destination: the refiner only had 55,500 bbl./day production, but this could be supplemented by those of other companies, including British American Oil and Canadian Oil Companies. A pipeline to Sarnia would cost less than one-twentieth the amount of rail shipments from Alberta. But there were other alluring markets, including Chicago, which would enable Interprovincial to tap into the huge "Mid-Continent" market; Minneapolis, which had at least a 100,000 bbl./day prospect; and the coast of British Columbia, which had inadequate refinery capacity and a high cost for construction but could give Imperial a foothold in a potential (albeit distant) California market. Each of these options had vigorous supporters.

Perhaps not surprisingly the Imperial/Interprovincial preference was for the established central Canadian market. In June 1949 the federal Board of Transport Commissioners approved Interprovincial's application to build a line from Edmonton to Regina. Interprovincial dispatched representatives to communities along the proposed route to persuade landowners to sign right-of-way options, and to assure the public (particularly in Saskatchewan) that the company would operate as a "common carrier," just as the Imperial Pipe Line Company in Alberta provided access to all producers in the Leduc-Redwater fields.[22]

To finance the project, Intercolonial raised $90 million (CAD) by issuing twenty-year bonds at 3.5 per cent, twenty-one-year convertible debentures at 4 per cent, and the sale of 20,000 shares of common stock at $50 (CAD) per share. An important component of the financing arrangement was a "Throughput Agreement" signed by Imperial Oil, under which Imperial, in the event Interprovincial's revenues fell below a certain level, would cover the shortfall to enable the pipeline company to meet its bond and debenture obligations through 1970.[23]

Interprovincial's next move proved the source of much public controversy. Imperial had retained the consulting services of a Tulsa, Oklahoma pipeline operator, Transit Company Ltd. By the summer of 1949 cost comparisons indicated that the most efficient route from Regina to the Ontario refineries would be to build the pipeline to Gretna, Manitoba on the Canadian-US border, then extend a line to Superior, Wisconsin near Duluth on Lake Superior; tankers would then carry the crude oil to

Sarnia. Interprovincial would set up a US subsidiary, Lakehead Pipeline Inc., to manage the line from Gretna to Lake Superior. The extended pipeline would now stretch 1,150 miles from Edmonton to Superior, more than double the distance of the initial project.

Even before Interprovincial presented its application to the Board of Transport Commissioners for an extension to Gretna, opposition was growing. Interprovincial and the other pipelines had been represented as a kind of twentieth-century version of the transcontinental railway lines—not just a harbinger of economic development but also symbols of nationhood. This implied on the one hand that the federal government should play a supportive role in its development, as indeed was the case; but it could also be interpreted as a national project that required an "all Canadian" route, "in defiance of geography" if necessary. The communities that stood to benefit from an "all Canadian" route were naturally among the strongest advocates of this view.

In June 1949 the manager of the Fort William chamber of commerce urged Imperial Oil to consider his city and its twin, Port Arthur, as the logical terminus for an Alberta pipeline to the Lakehead. These communities had been the entrepot for the Canadian fur trade in the nineteenth century, and Imperial had an agency there. The chamber manager did not need to point out that it was also in the Parliamentary riding of C.D. Howe, the most powerful member of the Liberal cabinet. An article in the *Port Arthur News Chronicle* in May implied that the choice had already been made to use the route. Similarly, the city of Winnipeg anticipated a return to its era of prosperity that had slipped away in the Depression and Imperial's board chair Henry Hewetson had indicated the possibility of a new refinery there, as an adjunct to the pipeline project.[24]

Needless to say, the tone of the discussion took a turn for the worse after Interprovincial revealed its plans. O.B. Hopkins, president of Interprovincial, in testimony before the Board of Transport Commissioners, pointed out that constructing a pipeline across northern Ontario would add $10 million (CAD) to the cost of the project, involving construction of an additional pumping station and blasting through the Canadian Shield. The company's counsel, J.W. Hamilton, noted that no special permission was required by the US government to build the Gretna to Superior section of the line. The Board of Transport Commissioners approved Interprovincial's application for the Gretna extension on September 12, 1949.[25]

The Port Arthur city council made a last-ditch effort to derail Interprovincial's application, resolving that "every possible effort should be made to keep our Canadian resources and their transportation in Canada." When this plea was ignored by the Board of Transport Commissioners, the Port Arthur city fathers urged Parliament to reverse the decision, appealing to familiar themes: "American capital has played a part in development and progress in Canada, but at a price . . . Surely we are not so shortsighted that we will sell our birthright for a few million dollars."[26] Interprovincial representatives protested that there was a good deal of Canadian investment in the pipeline, although acknowledging that they could not provide percentages. In any case the real target was Imperial Oil and, looming behind it, Jersey Standard.

In Parliament the Progressive Conservatives and CCF both lambasted the government for not supporting an "all Canadian" line "regardless of cost." C.D. Howe, however, rejected these criticisms, arguing that the "all Canadian" route would hurt Alberta's oil producers by increasing the costs of transporting oil to central Canada. He also asserted that the government would not subsidize the pipeline in any case, thus reaffirming his image as a "business minded" politician.[27]

Over the years Imperial's executives had learned the value of public relations—a field pioneered by John D. Rockefeller Jr. with Ivy Lee and Mackenzie King in the aftermath of the "Ludlow Massacre." Although the government of Canada had essentially vindicated Interprovincial's proposal for a pipeline partly through the US, the company engaged in fence mending with the aggrieved parties at the Lakehead. On September 21, Hopkins wrote to Mayor C.O. Robinson of Port Arthur, a leading figure in the opposition to the Gretna-Superior route, reiterating the economic arguments underlying Interprovincial's decision, but insisting that "our relations with the people of Port Arthur and Fort William have always been excellent," and offering to send representatives from the company to meet with city leaders to discuss the matter. A week later Intercolonial and Imperial executives—including Hopkins, White, Hewetson, and Stewart—showed up at Port Arthur to explain their position to the local business community. Imperial Oil also followed up with an assurance to

Winnipeg that a spur pipeline would be built from Gretna and a new refinery built there within the next few years.[28]

There were other, technical issues that confronted Interprovincial as it moved toward the construction phase. The original plan for a pipeline to Regina contemplated a 16-inch pipeline. With the extension of the project and the influx of more crude oil from Redwater, the Tulsa consultants recommended a 20-inch pipeline; but Interprovincial already had on order the 16-inch pipe, and its Canadian supplier, Page-Hersey, did not have the capacity to produce a 20-inch pipe. The upshot of the complex negotiations surrounding this issue was that Interprovincial built a line that combined sizes: 20-inch pipe for the Edmonton to Regina component, 16-inch from Regina to Gretna, and 18-inch from Gretna to Superior. The larger pipes were provided by American suppliers; once again, duties and taxes were waived by the federal government to hasten the completion of the project. Eventually, in the 1950s, a 30-inch pipeline was built from Superior to Sarnia, replacing the tankers.[29]

After the complexities of the preliminaries, the actual construction of the pipeline moved rapidly, although by the time the project got underway the estimated cost had risen to $100 million (CAD) due in part to the price of larger tubes. The Tulsa consulting company had conducted aerial and ground surveys along the entire route during the summer of 1949, and in October Interprovincial reviewed construction bids from ten contractors. Here again, the ticklish issue of Canadian content had to be addressed. Few of the Canadian companies had much experience in pipeline projects of the scale contemplated in this case, but there would be another uproar if American contractors were to be chosen, particularly for the Canadian phases of the line.

Interprovincial (and Imperial Oil) managers had consulted with the large US contractor, Bechtel, in an earlier phase of planning. Bechtel had built a pipeline for the Mene Grande oil fields in Venezuela, in which International Petroleum was a player, in the early 1940s; and it was a major contractor for the large Trans-Arab Pipeline (Tapline) being built for a consortium of oil majors that included Jersey Standard. Bechtel's Canadian subsidiary had the foresight to partner with Fred Mannix of Calgary, whose family firm was well established in construction projects in Alberta.

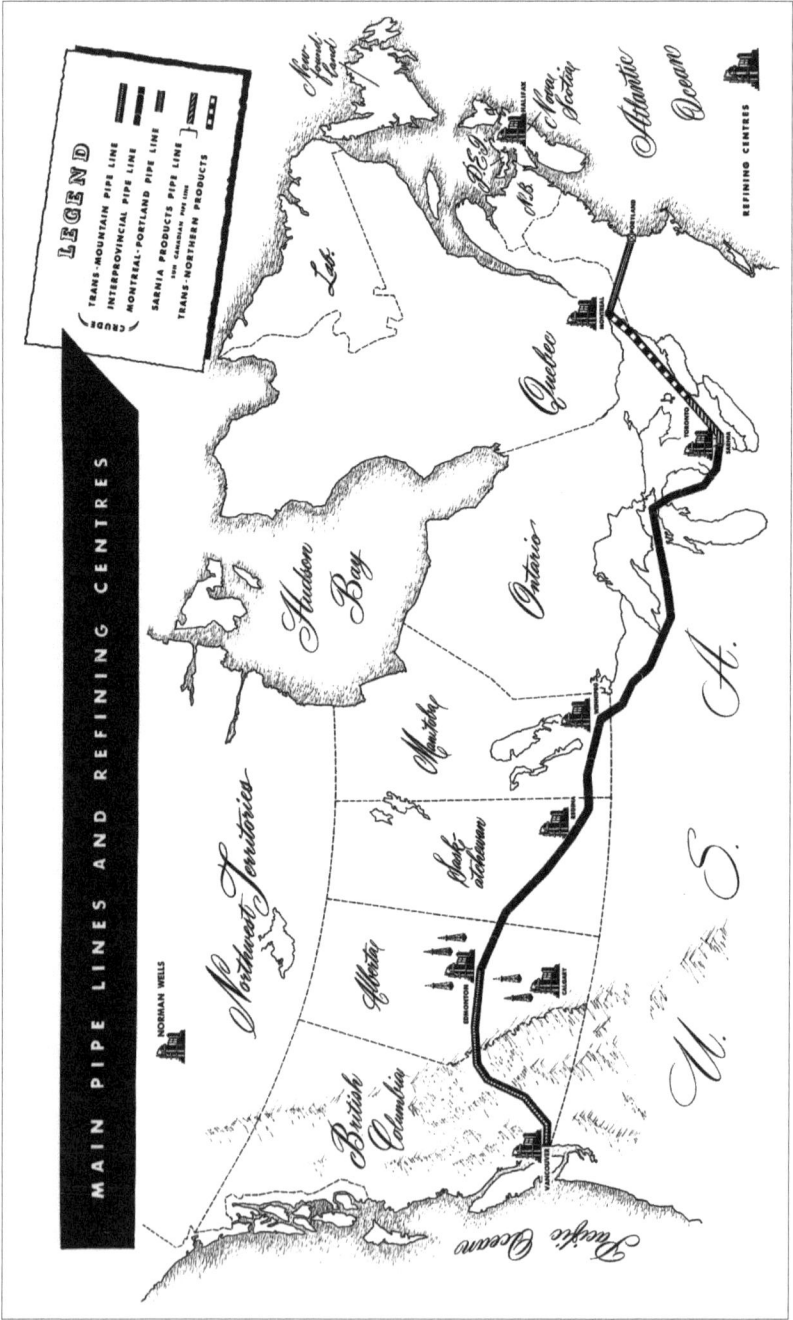

MAP 7.2. Main Pipe Lines and Refining Centres in Canada, 1956. Imperial Oil. Glenbow Archives IP-9B-4-1, Imperial Oil Collection.

In the end, Interprovincial chose Canadian Bechtel to construct the largest part of the project from Edmonton to Regina. The Regina to Gretna phase was awarded to Williams Brothers, a Canadian company that had been involved in the Portland to Montreal pipeline project. The American phase from Gretna to Superior went to Anderson Brothers, a US company that had extensive experience with Texaco, Shell Pipe Line Co., and Ohio Oil. In a meeting with the federal Deputy Minister of Mines and the Deputy Minister of Industries and Labour, Interprovincial spokesmen took pains to highlight the Mannix connection with Canadian Bechtel and the fact that most of the supply contracts, except for the 20-inch tube, would be procured from Canadian sources.[30]

Once these impediments were overcome, construction moved along quickly—until the project met a delay in March 1950 when the South Saskatchewan River began to flood early, before the pipe had been laid. Nevertheless, on October 4, 1950, Alberta premier Ernest Manning was present to turn the valve to start Edmonton's oil flowing eastward. On April 24, 1951 Ontario premier Leslie Frost was on hand at Sarnia to greet the first tanker carrying Alberta crude oil to Imperial's refinery. It was a major achievement in record time, and a benchmark in the history of Canadian oil.[31]

Over the next three years the capacity of the pipeline was steadily expanded with the addition to loop-lines, enlarged pipeline capacity, and ultimately the construction of a pipeline from Superior to Sarnia, replacing the tankers. Meanwhile pressure increased for a pipeline to British Columbia, hastened by the Korean War, which seemed to justify the need for more oil capacity on the Pacific coast. In March 1951 the Canadian government approved the creation of a Trans Mountain Oil Pipe Line from Alberta to Vancouver. Imperial was part of a consortium set up to build Trans Mountain, which proved to be a major engineering challenge but was completed in 1953. Imperial increased the capacity of its Vancouver refinery from 12,000 to 22,500 bbl./day. Goals that would have seemed quixotic a few years earlier had now been achieved.

The decade after the Leduc discovery had truly been a "golden age" for Imperial Oil. The company had invested more than $1 billion (CAD) in its expansion between 1950 and 1959, but the returns had been substantial. The book value of shareholders' investment rose from $257 million to $630 million (CAD) in that period; dividends amounted to $283 million (CAD), representing 55 per cent of earnings after taxes.[32] It had also been a "golden age" for Alberta's "oil patch:" $2.4 billion (CAD) in new capital investment had flowed into the province between 1947 and 1957, and the economic activity generated by the development of the industry had contributed an estimated $3 billion to income growth for Albertans; petroleum accounted for 45 per cent of the income gains to Alberta households by the end of the post-Leduc decade.[33] For the Canadian public, it was a period of rapid growth with low inflation, as oil prices remained low and stable, and new consumer products—many of them tied to the petrochemical industry—raised standards of living to unprecedented levels. In that era the growth of the oil industry seemed to be a win-win proposition for all parties.

8

DIVERSIFICATION

Research

Technology had always played an important role in the relationship between Imperial Oil and Jersey Standard. Losing the services of Herman Frasch to Standard Oil in 1887 crucially weakened Imperial's competitive position after Frasch perfected his desulphurization process several years later. In 1914, Walter Teagle, as president of Imperial (and Jersey Standard's director in charge of foreign production and marketing) negotiated with Standard of Indiana for access to the Burton-Humphreys thermal cracking process in Imperial's expanded Sarnia refinery. In 1923, Imperial also acquired rights to Jersey Standard's "tank and tube" process that enabled continuous cracking for its new Calgary refinery. Two developments in the mid-1920s were to have an even more substantial impact on the direction of technological development at Imperial Oil.

In 1918 Edgar M. Clark, who had worked with Dr. William Burton at Standard of Indiana, was lured to Jersey Standard to head up a new research effort. The initial focus was to be on further improvements to the Burton thermal cracking technology, but this soon expanded into a plan developed by Clark and Frank Howard, a patent lawyer and engineer, to control research activities throughout the Jersey Standard organization. In 1922 a new subsidiary, Standard Oil Development Co., was established to manage all the patents generated by Jersey Standard's various departments. In the larger reorganization of the corporation in 1926–27, this entity was assigned the task of coordinating research not only for Jersey Standard but for all its domestic and foreign affiliates.[1]

At this point there were only two affiliates with substantial research operations: Humble Oil and Imperial Oil. Humble Oil, which Jersey Standard acquired slightly more than 50 per cent ownership of in 1919, had its own development department working with that company's large refinery at Baytown in Texas. Imperial's research was centered at Sarnia and was in large part produced by the efforts of one man: Dr. Richard K. Stratford.

Born in Brantford, Ontario, Stratford studied agricultural chemistry at the Ontario Agricultural College (Guelph) and Amherst, and earned a doctorate at Université de Lyon in France, where he wrote a thesis on hydrocarbon cracking. In 1924 he was hired by Imperial as Sarnia's first research chemist, working with engineers at the refinery, where his earliest work was on use of clay and phenol in treating lubricating oils, a subject that would become a hallmark for research at Imperial.[2]

The initial plan of the Standard Oil Development Co. in 1927 proposed an arrangement in which affiliates would conduct research on "routine problems," while Standard would provide engineering and research services and would function as a data centre for all research, with the operating companies paying a fee for services. Both Humble and Imperial countered with a proposal in which affiliates would pay a fee to Standard Development for shared patent access, but would also conduct research in selected fields, exchange licenses for patents, and share in the income generated for Standard Development Co. proportional to their investment in the research. This led to the establishment of "mutualization agreements" between Jersey Standard and the two companies in 1929.[3]

Imperial set up a Technical and Research Department in 1928, in part to coordinate work done under the mutualization agreement; Stratford was chief research chemist and then head of the department in 1929. By that point the organization had twenty-five scientists and support staff. The department conducted a wide range of research activities: among the most significant involved examination of asphalt production methods and the treatment of lubricating oils with a hydrocarbon derivative called phenol to reduce the sulphur compounds found in oil being shipped from South America. Both of these areas of research would prove valuable for Imperial's contributions to industrial mobilization during the Second World War. At the same time, the Imperial research department

Graham D. Taylor

FIGURE 8.1. Richard K. Stratford, R.V. LeSueur, 1945. Glenbow Archive IP-14a-282, Imperial Oil Collection.

developed a process of treating US imported oil with ketone to reduce wax content in lubricating oils.

During the 1930s, however, friction emerged between Imperial and Jersey Standard over the costs of patent sharing and development related to agreements that Standard Oil Development Co. made with the German chemical colossus, I.G. Farben, in 1927–29. In 1926 Frank Howard and Teagle had toured the impressive research labs of the I.G. affiliate, Badisdche Anilin und Soda Fabrik (BASF) in Ludwigshafen, Germany. They were particularly taken with the work being done on the conversion of coal into oil through a process called hydrogenation, involving the treatment of coal with hydrogen under high pressure and high temperatures. Teagle, as always, was interested in securing potential new sources of oil, and Howard was anxious to demonstrate the value of the Standard Development Company to Jersey Standard. After convoluted negotiations between Jersey Standard and I.G., several agreements were completed in 1929–30, involving patent exchanges relating to synthetic oil research through the establishment of a Standard-IG Company, and a follow-up agreement dealing with products that fell on the borderline between the oil and chemical industries. This included research on synthetic rubber through another joint venture entitled the Joint American Study Committee (Jasco).[4]

These agreements, and others related to synthetic fuels, would become significant during the Second World War. In the immediate situation, however, their value was more controversial. With the discovery of the East Texas oil fields and with Middle East oil coming on stream at the end of the 1920s, the usefulness of high cost synthetic oil was questionable. Imperial Oil, which was paying 14 per cent of the shared expenses of Standard Development Co. in 1929–32, bridled at the cost of the hydrogenation patents. Unlike the US, with rich coal fields in the Midwest, Canada's coal reserves were far from markets (and refineries) and in any case imported oil was abundant and cheap. Nevertheless, Imperial supported the overall aim of the mutualization agreements and sent Charles Leaver, a former superintendent of the Sarnia refinery, to represent Imperial with the Standard Development Company's coordinating committee in New York.[5]

Meanwhile Stratford's department continued its research into lubricating oils. In 1937 Eugene Houdry, a French engineer supported by Sun Oil of Marcus Hook (Pennsylvania) and Standard of New York (Socony-Vacuum), discovered a process that would accelerate the conversion of crude oil into gasoline fuel, including high octane gas used for aviation fuel, through the introduction of an external "catalytic agent." Jersey Standard researchers had been working on these processes from the early 1930s drawing on feedstock from hydrogenation plants in Louisiana. Stratford and his associates had also begun exploring cracking improvements through the introduction of powdered clay as a catalyst. In 1940 Imperial announced plans to move to commercial operation of a process it designated "suspensoid" cracking.[6]

After Pearl Harbor, the technological agreements between Jersey Standard and the Germans became more salient. Nazi Germany threatened the Russian oilfields on the Caspian Sea. The Japanese Imperial forces overran South East Asia, seizing oil fields in the Dutch East Indies and the rubber plantations in Malaya. Thurman Arnold, the US Assistant Attorney General for Antitrust, asserted that the rubber shortage the US faced in 1942 was the result of the Jersey Standard-I.G. Farben patent agreements that had delayed the development of synthetic rubber. A US Senate committee summoned Jersey Standard executives, including president William Farish, before it, and some senators including the committee chairman, Harry Truman, suggested that this could be considered "treason." Jersey Standard's spokesmen responded that these patent exchanges provided them with technical knowledge that was essential to a successful program in that field. The company also announced, pursuant to an agreement with the US Justice Department, that it would make available all patents received from I.G. Farben relating to synthetic rubber without requiring licensing royalties.[7]

During the 1930s both I.G. Farben and the American chemical company DuPont had experimented with techniques to produce synthetic rubber for specific uses, but the costs involved limited its commercialization. These uses could most readily be derived from by-products of petroleum refining, such as butadiene, combined with polymers—large chain-like molecules formed from chemical reactions in a range of raw materials. The by-products could be derived from other "feedstock" sources, including ethyl alcohol made from grains, but improvements in petroleum refining through catalytic cracking processes made large-scale production of synthetic rubber (and other polymerized products) more feasible. Shortly before the war broke out, I.G. Farben had developed a general-purpose synthetic rubber called Buna-S, which was made available to Jersey Standard through the Jasco agreements.

Even before the US entered the war, Jersey Standard had begun production of petroleum feedstock for synthetic rubber. In 1940 the company proposed to set up a company with other petroleum and rubber makers that would have access to all the Jasco patents in the field; but this plan was abandoned as possibly running afoul of US antitrust laws. A year later the US Reconstruction Finance Corporation authorized Jersey Standard to set up a pilot plant to produce butadiene and styrene that could be used by chemical companies to produce synthetic rubber. But production targets were much smaller than the country would require, in part because the RFC head, Jesse Jones, believed a synthetic rubber program would only be needed if the US went to war. In the wake of the controversies in early 1942, a US Office of Rubber Production took over a crash program to develop synthetic rubber. Jersey Standard's affiliates, Standard of Louisiana and Humble, produced over 190,000 tons of butadiene as feedstock for the program between 1943–45—slightly less than one-third of the butadiene used by the US government for that purpose during the war. The company also established experimental plants in Louisiana and Texas to develop an alternative form of synthetic rubber, called Butyl, which produced about 48,000 tons by 1945.[8]

Polymer Canada

In Canada the synthetic rubber industry was very much the creation of one strong-willed figure: C.D. Howe. As the federal Minister of Munitions and Supply during the Second World War, Howe had sweeping authority to expand Canada's military production and he used these powers extensively, creating a range of crown corporations to boost output of aircraft, ships, ordnance, and much else. In 1941 Howe had set up an organization to stockpile natural rubber from scrap materials—everything from auto tires to garden hoses, erasers, and rubber bands. But, as had happened in the United States, it soon became clear that supplies from these sources could not keep up with the country's military requirements. In January 1942 Howe set out to establish synthetic rubber production from scratch.

Sarnia would be the site of Polymer, the crown corporation Howe set up on February 13, 1942 for this purpose. A number of reasons were cited to justify this decision: Sarnia was of course the location of Imperial Oil's largest refinery, with secure pipeline supplies of crude oil from Ohio. The Saint Clair River and the confluence of the Great Lakes enhanced the shipment of coke from Hamilton, to be used to produce styrene, which was vital to synthetic rubber. US rubber companies had also located their major Canadian operations in southern Ontario. But certainly a major factor was that Imperial Oil had immediate access to Jersey Standard's patents for Buna-S and Butyl, and could bring in technical people from the US already familiar with the processes required. Although Howe was pressured to look at alternative feedstocks from grain alcohol, Imperial's Sarnia refinery already had the capabilities of producing butadiene using the "suspensoid" cracking technologies that Stratford's research team had been developing there.[9]

Imperial also donated land for the site of the Polymer plants adjacent to its refinery. Construction began in August 1942 and was completed a little over a year later, employing more than 5,500 workers at a cost of $50 million (CAD). Meanwhile, Polymer was able to bring in the Michigan-based Dow Chemical Company to operate a styrene conversion plant. Imperial Oil agreed to operate two plants connected to the Polymer project: one to produce sufficient butadiene to fuel the production of 30,000 tons of Buna-S rubber; and a second smaller plant that would produce 7,000 tons of Butyl rubber, using the Jersey Standard process. The two operations were managed during the war by an Imperial subsidiary, Saint Clair Processing Corporation. Both plants were located on the Polymer site, as was the Dow styrene processing operation.[10]

The president of Saint Clair Corporation was Leo McCloskey, who had headed Imperial's manufacturing department, and the general manager was F.C. Lantz from the Sarnia refinery; C.E. Carson was the superintendent of Sarnia; Stratford was also a director. In later years consortia of this type became more common in the Canadian petroleum industry, but this one was particularly complex, requiring coordination of the work of a Canadian crown corporation, an American chemical company, and Jersey Standard's research operation with the Imperial refinery and a subsidiary. A plethora of coordinating committees emerged, while Imperial tried to keep its own structure simple by setting up a technical committee comprising the managers of the Sarnia refinery and the Saint Clair Corporation, and developing a fee for service arrangement with the other companies.[11]

By the end of the war in 1945, Polymer had produced 80,000 tons of Buna-S rubber and 15,000 tons of Butyl rubber. Many of the crown corporations created for wartime purposes were scheduled for closure and, in some cases, sales to private enterprise. Polymer was presumed to be among them, particularly as there was an expectation that natural rubber would once again be flowing in from Southeast Asia. Imperial Oil might have seemed to be an obvious interested party, but that company's postwar strategy was focused on securing new crude oil in Alberta. In April 1946, the assets of the Saint Clair Processing Corporation (but not its charter) were turned over to Polymer.

In any case, C.D. Howe had a different perspective. Re-elected to Parliament with the Liberals in 1945, he was appointed Minister of Reconstruction with a broad mandate to use government powers to develop a postwar economic development strategy for Canada. Polymer figured prominently in those plans as the catalyst of a petrochemical industry in central Canada, and was retained as a crown corporation. To that end it was empowered to expropriate more land in the Sarnia area to attract chemical companies, and was provided with a research department to look beyond the diminishing market for synthetic rubber. Dow Chemical was one of the early entrants, building an ethylene glycol plant near the Polymer plants, followed by Fiberglass Canada, Standard Chemical, Ethyl Corporation, and Sun Oil, which built a refinery in Sarnia in 1950. By this time the St. Clair region was being called "Chemical Valley" and held out as an example of economic development through public-private partnership.[12]

After the war Imperial's Research department resumed development work on the "suspensoid" cracking process, but this was terminated abruptly in 1951. During the war Standard Oil Development Co. had introduced a new process called fluid catalytic cracking, developed by

W.K. Lewis and E.R. Gilliland, two MIT scientists, which became the prevailing method used by Jersey Standard. In this process a powdered catalyst would be treated so that it functioned as a liquid that could be moved more efficiently through pipes. In 1948 Imperial set up a fluid-cracking unit at its Montreal refinery, and it soon became the industry standard.

After the initial mutualization agreements on research expired in 1948, Jersey Standard began moving toward a more consolidated global approach under "Standard Research Agreements" in which affiliates would establish areas of research specialization, relying on Standard Oil Development Co. to provide access to technical knowhow in other areas. This was an approach that led eventually to the concept of "research mandates" adopted by other multinational companies in the 1970s–80s.

In the immediate situation, Imperial's Research department continued its earlier work on phenol extraction in treating lubricating oils and waxes, processes adopted by other Jersey Standard refineries. In 1951, Stratford retired and was succeeded by his assistant director, George Gurd. During the 1950s research focused on improving fuel applications in cold weather conditions—an obvious Canadian issue. As Imperial's orientation shifted to heavy oil recovery in northern Canada in the 1960s, the research focus moved in that direction as well, although the company continued to be involved in the more mundane issues of building materials and petroleum by-products, particularly polyvinyl chloride plastics. One of the department's achievements in this period was a process called DILCHILL that replaced earlier work with ketone dewaxing of lubricating oils developed under Stratford. Jersey Standard awarded Imperial a corporate-wide mandate in this field. Among the researchers on DILCHILL was Jim Livingstone, who later became president of Imperial Oil, as well as John Tiedje, who took over the research department, which had grown to over 650 staff with operations in Montreal and Calgary as well as Sarnia.[13]

Esso Chemical Canada

Despite the dramatic growth of the petrochemical industry in Sarnia and in Alberta—where a number of companies including Royalite used natural gas to produce ammonia after the Second World War—Imperial did not enter the field until 1955. To some extent this may have resulted from the company's strategic preoccupation with, and capital investment in, expanding crude oil production in Alberta and developing infrastructure to support that part of the industry. But the delay may also have reflected the cautious perspective toward petrochemicals adopted by Jersey Standard in this period.

Jersey Standard had always pursued a strategy that focused on the oil industry rather than expanding its scope of operations into ancillary businesses. As technology prodded the oil and chemical fields closer, Jersey Standard opted for partnerships and agreements—with General Motors for Ethyl Gasoline, for example, and the patent exchanges with I.G. Farben rather than seeking to incorporate what was seen as an external field into its organizational fold. A subsidiary called the Enjay Co. marketed chemical products that emerged from refining operations in the US, and of course Standard Oil Development Co. was keen to put chemical patents they had acquired to wider use. But even advocates of greater diversification in the parent company "never dreamed that some day we would wear shirts of petrochemical origin."[14]

After the Second World War Jersey Standard faced impediments to building on its achievements in developing synthetic rubber. The US Alien Property Custodian held the Jasco patents, and the federal government owned the properties, showing no sign of disposing of them in the immediate future. In any case, the company needed to attend to rebuilding its European refineries, and, like Imperial, expanding its commitments to developing large crude oil fields in Venezuela and the Middle East. In 1945 Frank Howard, the president of Standard Oil Development, presented a strong case for expansion of the "oil chemical business." But Howard stepped down as vice president of Jersey Standard soon thereafter, although he continued to press the board to give greater priority to petrochemicals.

In 1952 the Jersey Standard board undertook a review of the company's policy in the field. By this time other US oil majors had advanced into chemicals: Texaco had set up a joint venture with American Cyanamid, and both Socal and Standard of Indiana had established chemical affiliates. The review acknowledged that Royal Dutch Shell "threatened its leadership in the oil-chemical field." Finally, in 1955 a second review identified petrochemicals as a "rapidly growing and profitable business throughout the world" and urged affiliates to "move aggressively to make the most of investment opportunities."[15]

By this time Imperial Oil had a powerful in-house advocate for moving in this direction. J. Kenneth Jamieson was an Imperial vice president, but more significantly, he was already on the fast track to a leading position in Jersey Standard. Born in 1910 in Medicine Hat, Alberta, son of a veteran of the North-West Mounted Police, Jamieson studied engineering at University of Alberta and MIT, but also worked for a time as a labourer at Imperial's Calgary refinery. During the Second World War Jamieson liaised between the US and Canada on oil issues, then resumed a career with Imperial Oil. On Imperial's board in 1952, he pushed for investment in petrochemicals, and was assigned the task of setting up a program to that end a year later. Jamieson would go on to become head of International Petroleum, and then president of Humble, Jersey Standard's largest affiliate, in 1961. Four years later he was president of the parent company, and became chairman of the board in 1969, steering it through the difficult shoals in the Middle East in the early 1970s.[16]

Jamieson brought in Clay Beamer, who was assistant general manager for chemical products for Jersey Standard's principal US affiliate, Esso Standard Oil Co., and had been sales manager for the chemical division of Enjay Company to head a new Chemical Products department. In 1956, Imperial's president, Jack White, announced with great fanfare that the company would build a $28.5 million (CAD) plant to produce ethylene, propylene, butylene, and butadiene as feedstocks for petrochemicals—"the first big venture of any oil company in the Canadian petrochemical field." At the same time, however, White was meeting with C.D. Howe—attempting, unsuccessfully, to persuade him to sell Polymer Corporation to Imperial in order to kick-start their company's entry into the field. Polymer Corporation subsequently announced its intention to build a butadiene plant in Alberta, which Imperial regarded as an unfair move "in competition with private enterprise."[17]

Despite an ambitious startup, Imperial's Chemical Products Department floundered for some time while seeking a role beyond supplying intermediaries for other companies in the chemical industry. In 1959, Humble Oil began producing polypropylene for plastics, and Imperial was offered the opportunity to develop production capacity in Canada, but the

Board felt this was beyond the capabilities of its in-house organization, and arranged to purchase the product from Enjay.[18]

In 1961, Beamer provided a laundry list of potential areas for expansion, including plastics, resins, oil additives, and "agricultural products." A year later, Chemical Products joined with the producing department in exploring the potential for development of potash production in Saskatchewan. Meanwhile, Jersey Standard, encouraged by reports on the potential "green revolution" in agriculture in Latin America, was supporting diversification into fertilizers and related agricultural chemicals. This also appeared to be a promising market in Canada where demand for fertilizer was predicted to grow from 460,000 tons in 1965 to over 1.4 million tons by 1970, with "higher enlarged nitrogen fertilizer" leading the way. Imperial already had more than 500 agents supplying petroleum needs to farmers in the Prairies, and fertilizer sales could be handled through these agents. The project would soak up extra Redwater capacity; production and marketing costs would total $110 million (CAD) over fifteen years, with a 14 per cent return on investment.[19]

As with many such projections, this one proved to be premature. Prairie grain exports faltered in the late 1960s; by 1970 retail sales from the Redwater fertilizer operation were running at little more than one-third the forecast levels. Furthermore, because of the low cost of oil in North America, Imperial faced stiff competition from US fertilizer importers. Nevertheless, in 1969 Imperial had transformed the Chemical Products Department into a new division, Esso Chemical Canada, optimistically anticipating a growth in synthetic fertilizer market share from 15 per cent in 1971 to close to 20 per cent by the middle of the decade. Providentially, the 1973 energy crisis boosted oil costs for all competitors, enabling Imperial to draw on its lower-cost feedstock supplies and its well-organized network of dealers. Recovery in the fertilizer market provided a more stable base for Esso Chemical's overall operations, which by now embraced a wide range of basic chemicals, intermediates, and retail products, ranging from alkylates in detergents to polyvinyl chlorides to plastic moulds. Sales grew dramatically from $107 million in 1972 to over $314 million by 1975, and earnings before taxes rose from a loss position to $16 million in that period.[20]

The emergence of Esso Chemical reflected another significant trend that affected many large businesses in this era: the urge to "diversify." Fuelled in part by the largest sustained stock market boom since the 1920s, companies were lured beyond their comfort zones. At the extreme end were the "conglomerates" of the 1960s to early 1970s such as Gulf + Western and Ling-Temco-Vought in the US (and Argus Corporation in Canada) that cobbled together disparate business ventures marketed to the investing public as examples of "synergy." But even staid and well-established enterprises in fields such as telecommunications and petroleum were setting up "New Product Lines" and exploring unfamiliar terrain. The petrochemical market with its porous boundaries provided an attractive arena for these adventures.

Jersey Standard had begun exploring the prospects for diversification in 1960; moving in its characteristically cautious and deliberative manner, the company did not get around to unveiling its plans to affiliates until 1963, at which time it set up a new subsidiary, Jersey Enterprises, to undertake "New Investments." Imperial Oil would play an important role in the early development of this new strategy. One of the areas of new applications that had been reviewed by Esso Research involved a process called Fluid Iron Ore Reduction (FIOR), for heavy fuel injection in blast furnaces. The Canadian steel manufacturer, Dofasco, was interested in the process, and in 1961–62 Imperial's sale of heavy fuels for this purpose accounted for one-sixth of the total output for Jersey Standard companies. The new entity, Jersey Enterprises, funded construction of a FIOR pilot plant at Imperial's Halifax/Dartmouth refinery, and later pursued large-scale projects in Venezuela and India.[21]

Imperial followed up on this initiative in 1964 with the acquisition of Building Products Ltd., which was well positioned in the construction materials market, and whose projected move into plastic laminates and extrusions would provide an outlet for Imperial's chemical intermediates as well as asphalt from the company's refineries. Over the next two years this new subsidiary acquired a resilient flooring manufacturer and a Quebec company that specialized in making precast concrete panels for commercial building siding. Although Building Products was tied to the business cycles in the construction industry, which slumped in the late

1960s, it provided an in-house buyer for PVC products generated by Esso Chemical Canada.[22]

Imperial's quest for diversification was not always as successful as these early ventures. In 1965 Industrial Estates Ltd., a Nova Scotia crown corporation set up to promote industrialization in that province, approached Imperial with a proposal to take over the construction and operation of a heavy water project at Glace Bay, that would supply Atomic Energy of Canada with nuclear fuel. Imperial had no experience in this field, and the projections of costs were suspect: the projection of a $46 million cost for a 400-ton capacity plant seemed low. The company's Executive Committee was reluctant to respond to pressure for a quick commitment, which proved to be a good decision: the Deuterium Ltd. project overran its projected cost and was eventually taken over by A.E.C.L. in 1968; the entire operation was closed down in 1985.[23]

Imperial Oil also investigated the possibility of investing in the pulp and paper industry in Quebec, a notoriously risky market with many larger players on the field. This particular initiative may have been prompted by Jersey Enterprises, which was also looking into forestry products, despite the fact that there was little to connect it to the petroleum industry. In the end Imperial decided not to proceed, in part because the capital investment required to upgrade the processing technology exceeded the benefits in terms of competitive advantage.[24] But a company of Imperial's size could afford some missteps. By 1975 the chemical and building products divisions were contributing close to $20 million to the company's net earnings, about half as much as the refining and marketing operations.

9

A MORE COMPLEX WORLD

Competition

Leduc attracted a wide range of entrepreneurs and companies, large and small, to explore and exploit the western Canadian oil fields, and some evolved into integrated firms that challenged—on a regional or even national scale—the Big Four that had dominated the industry before the Second World War. Among them was the Belgian-based Petrofina, which had started in the Romanian oil fields: it was intended from the outset to integrate into refining and marketing, and expanded through the 1950s through mergers and takeovers of smaller companies. Another was Ultramar, a British company that had holdings in Venezuela. Initially it set up an exploration venture in Alberta, but came to focus more on eastern Canada and Newfoundland where it established a large refinery and a strong presence in distribution of petroleum products. A much larger British enterprise, Anglo-Iranian—later to become British Petroleum (BP)—invested in a western exploring company, Triad, in 1953, and then established itself in marketing gasoline in Ontario and Quebec; in 1964 it acquired the Cities Service refinery, and later took over the Supertest Petroleum Corporation that had been one of Imperial's quasi-autonomous retail agencies until the early 1960s.

Other companies entered from the opposite direction. Sun Oil, a major US independent, had formed a Canadian subsidiary in 1919 to market its products. It built a refinery at Sarnia in 1935, and in 1953 extended a pipeline to Toronto from Sarnia, giving it access to one of the country's largest consumer markets. A decade later Sun began taking steps to enter the Athabasca oil sands—where now, as Suncor, it is the dominant player. Standard Oil of California (Chevron) also came into Canada through refining and marketing, setting up Standard of British Columbia in 1935, and by the 1960s was one of the largest oil and gas distributors on Canada's west coast. On the other side of the country, as recounted earlier, Irving Oil built a refinery in New Brunswick in 1957, in partnership with Standard of British Columbia, which held 51 per cent of the refinery's shares. The Irving Oil company extended its distributorships across the Maritimes and into Quebec and New England. Glenn Nielson's Husky Refining Company was started in Wyoming in the 1930s and established a refinery in Alberta in 1946, moving later into exploration and a national distribution network.[1]

For at least two decades after Leduc, however, the "Big Four"—Imperial Oil, Shell Canada, Texaco Canada (McColl-Frontenac), and British-American Oil—retained their dominant positions in virtually every phase of the Canadian oil industry, with Imperial playing the leading role. (In 1969 the American major Gulf Oil acquired British American, which then became Gulf Canada). In the middle of the 1960s the four companies controlled 80 per cent of the country's refining capacity and sales of petroleum products, 75 per cent of the service stations across Canada, and slightly less than one-third of crude oil production.

Imperial continued to tower over its main competitors in many respects: the company's net sales in 1963 were equal to the combined total of the other three companies, and exceeded them all in terms of net earnings. It held one-third of the shares of the two largest pipeline companies, Interprovincial and Montreal Pipeline, and more than one-third of the country's refining capacity. The only area where it lagged was in production of natural gas—Imperial entered the field late in the 1950s—where it ran second to Shell Canada, but still accounted for one-third of the output of the "Big Four;" the natural gas sector was more competitive than other parts of the petroleum industry, with a large number of smaller producers in Alberta and British Columbia.[2]

Imperial's greatest vulnerability was in the retail auto gasoline market. According to one reckoning, Imperial had been losing market share in this sector since 1935 when other oil companies began building service stations; but conditions worsened in the 1950s–60s. Imperial's sales of petroleum products grew by 18.5 per cent between 1958–63, but lagged well behind the other three majors, particularly Shell (although arguably that company's biggest spurt of growth came in 1962 after it took over Canadian Oil Companies Ltd.). Even taking Shell out of the equation, the average growth rate for the other companies exceeded 32 per cent. Imperial's market share declined in every region except Atlantic Canada and the Prairies during this time: in Quebec it fell behind both Shell and Texaco, although sales by Imperial's affiliates—specifically Champlain and Supertest—offset these losses. In Ontario Imperial held its position as leading retailer, but it had lost 5 per cent market share, due in part to new entrants, Sunoco, BP, and Petrofina. On the west coast, it also held a lead, but was challenged by Standard of British Columbia as well as Shell and Texaco.[3]

In 1955 Bill Twaits, who would become Imperial's chief executive in 1960, examined the company's ongoing issues with marketing. Twaits had begun his career with Imperial working at the Sarnia refinery, then held a wide range of positions, which provided a broader perspective on the company than others who had worked exclusively in one area. From his point of view Imperial's top management was focused primarily on the supply side, with little interest in marketing; Twaits furthermore observed that the conditions of limited supply and a stable competitive environment left the company unprepared for a "period of ample supplies and a buyer's market." He urged Imperial to integrate sales more closely with overall company strategy, and to create "an atmosphere of responsibility within the organization toward the sales effort." He insisted: "Everyone must contribute to sales objectives."[4]

As president and chairman of the board through the 1960s and early 1970s, Twaits pursued this approach to marketing, but finding solutions to the market challenges of the era proved elusive. Not surprisingly, the company looked first to improving product quality: in 1956 Imperial introduced a new motor oil christened "Multilube Uniflow," and two years later another higher grade "Esso Extra'" motor oil. The most effective sales campaign originated with Humble Oil in Texas, which marketed a premium gasoline product in the early 1960s also called "Esso Extra"—and featured the slogan "Put a Tiger in Your Tank," festooned with a cartoon "friendly tiger." The promotional campaign was also popular in Canada,

FIGURE 9.1. William O. Twaits, 1962. Glenbow Archive IP-26-8b-Twaits, W.O. 1961-1-16, Imperial Oil Collection.

and welcomed by Esso dealers because it was accompanied by measures to upgrade service stations' facilities. A subsequent analysis, however, observed that the effort boosted sales temporarily but did not stem the longer-term market share decline.[5]

Over the years the marketing department (and later the auto division) undertook a variety of experiments to improve sales performance, and in many cases the other major companies emulated them. One approach was to try to find ancillary businesses that could attract motorists. For a time carwash services were seen as a panacea, and the department produced an ambitious plan to couple service stations with carwashes; but by 1975 Imperial was divesting itself of more than a dozen locations. Another idea was to attach restaurants with fixed menus to service stations, which led to the establishment of Voyageur restaurants on the Trans-Canada Highway during the 1960s; Shell and Texaco also ventured into this ancillary market. By the late 1970s, however, these experiments were being scaled back; some outlets were also sold to third parties.

FIGURE 9.2. "Put a Tiger in Your Tank," 1965. Glenbow Archive IP-13d-1-38, Imperial Oil Collection.

The 1950s–60s were golden years for advertising and Imperial was a beneficiary of the substantial investment Jersey Standard made in establishing the "Esso" brand throughout North America. In the early 1960s Imperial began quietly replacing its own name on service station signs, replacing it with the Esso oval logo; the name Imperial Oil only appeared on the buildings.[6] As demonstrated in the "Tiger" campaign, the Esso brand could boost sales—but in the more nationalist period of the 1970s the association could also be counterproductive with some Canadians. Similarly, Imperial's sponsorship of the popular "Hockey Night in Canada" had both positive features for the company and also some drawbacks.

Imperial's involvement with professional hockey in Canada dated back to the 1930s. Canadian General Motors had begun sponsoring hockey broadcasts on radio in 1931, but by 1934 they dropped the sponsorship—at which point Imperial Oil took over. This decision reflected more of a commitment to institutional sponsorship than a specific attempt to boost gasoline sales, where the company was already the dominant player at the time. In 1952, when the Canadian Broadcasting Corporation (CBC) proposed to televise professional hockey, Imperial extended its sponsorship. The story presented in the *Imperial Oil Review* was that the head of the Canadian Hockey Association expressed reservations about approving televised broadcasting, fearing loss of revenue as fans would no longer flock to the arenas. But Conn Smythe, head of Maple Leaf Gardens, approached Imperial with a proposed contract of $100 (CAD) in the first year to test the waters.[7]

In 1953, Smythe raised the ante to $150,000 (CAD) per year for a three-year contract. This demand exceeded the figure budgeted by Imperial's advertising department. At the same time, CBC expressed its desire to take over the franchise if Imperial dropped it. In the end Imperial's executive committee agreed to undertake a partnership with McLaren Advertising to retain the franchise. This was just the beginning of regular debates at the senior level of Imperial over the wisdom of the increasingly costly sponsorship. In 1961 Twaits mused about "a possible alternative medium for public contact," noting that much of the company's advertising budget was tied to Hockey Night. Molson took over co-sponsorship in Quebec, and later Imperial secured a partnership with Ford of Canada, but each time the contract came up for renewal the cost-benefit issue was revisited. In 1976 Imperial relinquished the franchise to its partners.[8]

On a more substantive level, the debate over gasoline marketing focused on the relationship between the company and service station dealers, swinging between centralization and decentralization. In the early years of service station development, the company had relied on wholly owned dealerships, except for the autonomous affiliates like Irving and Supertest, who had their own dealer organizations. By 1948, though, Imperial was exploring a more decentralized model: they offered to support dealers who wanted to be autonomous by underwriting mortgages and providing direct financing with up to ten years' repayment. Dealers were expected to market Esso products and maintain standards of operation but were no longer under Imperial's direction.[9] By the end of the decade, however, the marketing department was touting a different approach.

To some extent, this alternative was based on an accurate analysis of the gasoline market. All of the major companies (and some of the newcomers as well) had pursued similar strategies, locating stations in areas of substantial traffic, but the result was overbuilding and diminishing returns for all the competitors. With full service stations on virtually every corner and crossroads, consumers could pick and choose: ancillary incentives like carwashes and free drinking glasses had at best limited returns.

In this context, Imperial's marketing department took another look at centralization. In 1963 they introduced the concept of market pattern programming, which would treat "a local urban market as one complete integral unit," and would result in "fewer and more strategically located units." Almost inevitably this led to the idea of "automotive service centres" first introduced in Windsor (Ontario) in 1963, that would require higher initial investments to cover the range of services covered, but would allow for the closure of many smaller service stations in "uneconomic" locations.[10]

Predictably, this initiative did not work out as expected. The Windsor project itself exceeded its original estimated cost by more than $100,000 (CAD), and the initial plan for ninety-five service centres was substantially modified. By 1973 Twaits was musing about "whether increasing the number of salaried outlets was the correct response to present conditions." Franchising was raised as the model of the future. Furthermore, the concept of "full service" stations was being called into question.

Inspired by the "self-service gas market" that had originated in Europe in the 1960s Imperial planned to triple the number of stations between 1973 and 1975, and at least half of the future stations were to be "dealer operated." By the end of the decade only 21 per cent of gasoline sales were accounted for by stations under direct company ownership, with dealers contributing one-third of the total, and the remainder covered by the independent agencies.[11]

In fairness, all of the major oil companies in Canada were facing similar challenges. The common threat was from "unbranded" discounters, who thrived from the late 1950s through 1971 as new oil sources came on stream, independent producers and refiners flourished, and crude oil prices fell. In some cases the discounters were companies like Canadian Tire, marketing lower-priced gasoline to attract customers to their chain stores; in other cases they were simply small operators offering a stripped-down model of service: no carwashes, no repair bays, no free glassware, just cheap gas.

In the days of John D. Rockefeller, the appropriate response would have been a ruthless price war until the interlopers had capitulated or been driven out of business. Although Canada's Combines laws were less onerous than the antitrust measures periodically invoked in the United States, large companies had to avoid charges of predatory pricing, and, even trickier, collusion with others to suppress competition. Both provincial and federal authorities were apt to show up when a "price war" broke out.

One strategy pursued by Imperial and the other oil majors was to temporarily drop prices in a local or regional market against discounters. The aim was not to drive them out of business but to "discipline" them (not a term used by Imperial) to accept what the majors regarded as a "normal" range within which all competitors could operate with reasonable margins. Of course the larger companies had the resources to outlast small discounters if necessary. To ensure that their dealers followed the strategy, the majors would subsidize them on a short-term basis to ensure their profit margins. An alternative to temporary subsidies was the practice of longer-term supply consignments to dealers; but although the practice gave the company more flexibility in changing price levels when required, Imperial was not happy with the fact that consignments tied them to a fixed rate of supply.[12]

Price wars were not entirely random: they were apt to erupt in the wake of a significant reduction in crude oil prices, strengthening the leverage of discounters, as for example in 1957 when companies accumulated large inventories in response to the closure of the Suez Canal, and again in the late 1960s when new oil came onto world markets because of discoveries in the North Sea and Libya. They would surface in urban markets such as Toronto and Vancouver and could last a long time: a Toronto price war ran from April to August 1958, and spread to southern Ontario, eventually diminishing when Combines authorities began investigating—only to emerge again the following spring.[13]

In 1961, Imperial's Marketing department reported that the discount sector, which accounted for less than 4 per cent of the Ontario market, was projected to grow to 17 per cent by 1965. This was the context in which the ill-fated service centres strategy was unveiled, but other options were also raised that proved more viable. One proposal was to emulate the Canadian Tire model by partnering with chain stores such as Eaton's and Simpsons-Sears, offering retail gasoline and other auto products. This idea was pursued off and on over the next decade: the most ambitious venture was a program to lease equipment and provide gasoline to Eaton's Horizon stores in the early 1970s, but the undertaking was not successful and Horizon stores were phased out by 1978.[14]

The other proposal made in 1961 envisioned the creation of a "second brand" of low-priced retail gasoline that could challenge the discounters on a sustained basis; and this proved to be the most enduring legacy of the era of "price wars." Over the next ten years Imperial established a three-tiered gasoline marketing strategy. The first tier embraced higher priced gas sold at full service stations; a second tier was set up to compete with Canadian Tire discounts, carrying an "Econo" brand in Ontario and "Relais" in Quebec. A third deep discount tier carried a brand named "Gain" and was aimed at the small-scale discounter, with a similarly streamlined operation. This structure converged with the move toward "self serve" gas bars later in the 1970s.[15]

Once in a while, the marketing department would take a look at the service station dealers, those who had to endure these frequent shifts in direction. They were a disparate group—some were Imperial employees, others quasi-independent business people with varying degrees of reliance on the company as a supplier. There were also those who held loan guarantees from Imperial, and dealers in a completely arms-length relationship. Consequently, many surveys of their views were not particularly revealing: dealers wanted to be treated with respect, or wanted a say in the local implementation of company policies, and so forth. But one report, from a survey conducted at the end of the 1950s, in the midst of the price wars, provided interesting insights. The survey also reflected the end point of a period of decentralization of Imperial's relationship with its dealers.

One feature that stood out was that the dealers, at that time, placed greater emphasis on their auto repair and service activities, and resented efforts by the company to promote gasoline sales—particularly when extra hours were imposed or frequent price changes were required. They recognized that there were too many service stations in certain locales and insufficient services elsewhere, for which they tended to blame—rightly or wrongly—company policies rather than municipal restrictions or other factors. Surveys tend to bring out the critics but the dealers also appreciated the fact that the Esso brand and the size of the company provided stability even in volatile markets. Imperial was always wary of allowing their dealers to join wider dealers' associations, in part because this would bring them into contact with discounters. But on the whole the Esso dealers were loyal to the company, if not necessarily to the company emissaries they encountered.[16]

Red Tape

From its earliest years, Imperial Oil had been interacting with governments at virtually every level: refiners in London (Ontario) contended with municipal authorities concerned over the fire hazards and pollution emitted by their activities. The company's leaders lobbied politicians in Ottawa for protective duties under the National Policy. Imperial's managers in South America confronted unfamiliar legal systems and, sometimes, hostile political regimes. In western Canada, the company had to adapt to changing regulations imposed by the federal, and then by the provincial governments. In the years following the Second World War, however, these interactions were magnified, both in scope and detail, as public authorities assumed a wider range of responsibilities and powers—while also feuding with one another over issues of jurisdiction. At the provincial level, for Imperial, Alberta remained the most critical player, as so much of the company's newly found resource base was located there, and the province's government laboured to master unfamiliar tasks of regulation, balancing a belief in free enterprise with the demands of a jostling new cohort of multinational businesses and local entrepreneurs. By 1949, with the development of the Redwater oil field, it was clear that a regulatory system developed primarily for a limited number of natural gas producers in the Turner Valley needed to be revised. The Social Credit regime under Ernest Manning, with Nathan Tanner continuing as the government's point man on energy matters, was pro-business and pro-development but also wanted to protect the province's natural resources and provide opportunities for Albertans to reap the greatest benefit from their carbon riches.[17]

A first step in this direction was the "checkerboarding" of leases on the Woodbend and Redwater fields. Despite this measure, by 1949, with the federal Pipe Line Act opening the way to the exporting of oil (and eventually gas) out of the province, and the appearance of new major players including Socony-Vacuum, Socal (Chevron), and Shell, the smaller independents once again feared displacement from the New Golconda. The revised Oil and Gas Resources Conservation Act expanded the goals of the legislation beyond "conservation . . . to prevent waste," and to encompass the aim of giving "each owner [of a lease] the opportunity of obtaining his [sic] just and equitable share of any pool [reservoir]."[18]

The devil was in the details. The Imperial position as presented to the Alberta Oil and Gas Conservation Board (newly rechristened as the Petroleum and Natural Gas Conservation Board) embraced the standard praise for the free enterprise system: "In undertaking a drilling operation, an experienced operator knows he may either find no oil at all, or . . . marginal production, or . . . prolific production. If the operator . . . finds prolific production he [sic] should be afforded the opportunity to produce the prolific wells at much higher rates than other less productive areas," subject to limits on "wasteful" rates.[19]

In practice, Imperial's negotiators, led by Tip Moroney, the conqueror of the Atlantic Number 3 fire, recognized that the overwhelming majority of producers supported some form of prorationing of oil field production along the lines sought by the government, and undertook to get the best deal that they could from the outcome, which set up an elaborate procedure where the board set calculated rates at which oil could be produced from each "pool" or reservoir without impairing the total amount of oil that could be recovered with secondary recovery methods, such as water flooding, called the Maximum Permissible Rate of Recovery (MPR). Refiners (including Imperial) would provide "nominations" each month, indicating the amount of oil ordered per refinery and determining the actual output of the pools (which up to the 1970s was significantly less than the available supply).

In the first rendition of this process, in December 1950, the Board set a market demand order of 81,855 bbl./day for all participants. Even taking into account checkerboarding and the input of independents, Imperial's share exceeded more than half that total. Nevertheless, Imperial's executive committee lamented the unfairness of the formula and tried to limit the allowable production rate accorded to the Pembina field (in which the company had no investments), fearing the reduction of its own allowables from Leduc and Redwater.[20]

Conditions for Imperial improved in the 1960s: a revised prorationing formula permitted production in fields determined to have good potential development to be increased beyond the basic cost recovery with a fixed return on investment, opening the way for a significant expansion of the company's production allocation. In addition, a new well-spacing arrangement was introduced that reduced the number of wells that could be drilled in a given field, thus enhancing the potential output of the remaining operators. By 1969 Imperial's crude oil and natural gas production from the Alberta fields was running at 179,000 bbl./day, double the amount ten years earlier and quadrupling the 1950 figure.[21]

The gasoline "price wars" that roiled the industry through the late 1950s and 1960s invited scrutiny not only by the federal Combines Act Branch, but also a number of provincial governments. The most serious episode, from the viewpoint of Imperial and the other majors, was the British Columbia "gas probe" in the mid-1960s, instigated by the province's premier, W.A.C. Bennett. Bennett, who ruled—and the term is apt—British Columbia from 1952 to 1972, was committed to the rapid economic development of the hinterland of his province, which was populated by his supporters. Although Bennett was a businessman and propounded a pro-business agenda, he was fully prepared to use governmental authority to accomplish his aims, including a public takeover of British Columbia's electric power industry in 1961.

Shortly before that dramatic event, Bennett had met with Bill Twaits, at that point the incoming chief executive of Imperial Oil. Imperial of course had a number of assets in the province—including the Ioco refinery, which it had enlarged in 1953, a planned expansion of capacity in Vancouver, and a 50 per cent interest in the Trans Mountain Pipe Line. On this occasion, Bennett indulged in a rant against the export of oil produced in British Columbia "where it is beyond his control," and threatened "discriminatory taxation" and other measures against companies that did not accede to his demands. Although British American Oil rather than Imperial appeared to be the target of his ire, the message was directed at all the big producers and refiners.[22]

Twaits was very different from his predecessors: as chief executives at Imperial, Jack White and George Stewart tended to be low-key in public, preferring behind-the-scenes conflict resolution. Twaits by contrast was outspoken and opinionated, in public and private, traits that seem to have prepared him for the contentious years of the 1960s and 70s. In this situation, however, he appears to have been bemused, and a few weeks later he and the heads of Shell, British American, and Standard of British Columbia met with Bennett to reassure him that BC oil would be processed in the province and the prices would be held at $2.00/bbl. Imperial also took up a 25 per cent participation in the Gas Trunk Line of British Columbia.[23]

If Bennett was placated, it didn't last long. In September 1962, in the midst of a re-election campaign, Bennett announced his intention to set up a Royal Commission to look into "the whole retail gasoline business." Imperial's legal department advised the Executive Committee that Bennett had the authority to take over the gas distribution system in British Columbia just as he had "provincialized" hydro power a few years earlier.[24] Subsequently, the premier of New Brunswick indicated that his government might undertake a "gasoline inquiry," and even Alberta raised the issue of prices at the pump. By the middle of 1963 Imperial's senior management was feeling beleaguered on all sides.[25]

As was often the case with these events, the public hearings of the British Columbia Royal Commission sometimes took on the aura of a circus. A representative of the BC Federation of Labour brought in an Esso "tiger tail" to illustrate his argument that the large oil companies preferred to rely on advertising gimmicks rather than lowering gasoline prices for consumers. Imperial retained the services of a team of economists from the Stanford Research Institute, and the press had a field day contrasting the buttoned-down presentation of the academics with the testimony of "regular folks" from the BC hinterland—notably Cyril Shelford, a rancher from northern British Columbia who purportedly had initiated the entire inquiry by complaining to the premier about the price differentials between his community and consumers in Vancouver. The Stanford group maintained there was no evidence that Imperial and the other oil majors had engaged in "predatory pricing" and that price fluctuations around the province reflected situations of oversupply in some areas, particularly urban areas, and scarcity elsewhere. Ronald Ritchie of Imperial went into detail about the complexities of gasoline pricing, but was dismissed by another witness with the statement "if you can't convince them, confuse them."[26]

Judge Charles W. Morrow, the Royal Commissioner appointed by Bennett, was hampered to some extent by limited funding and staffing: the report did not come out until the spring of 1966. Twaits, who had been increasingly critical of the time and expense Imperial incurred dealing with the inquiry, welcomed the final product. Although Morrow recommended that wholesale and resale operations in the gasoline industry should be separated, he rejected the idea of a single province-wide price for gasoline and opposed the idea of establishing price controls based exclusively on costs—an issue that would roil government relations with the industry over the next decade.[27]

Imperial Oil was a federally chartered corporation, and over the years it had maintained a generally positive relationship with the government in Ottawa—in part because the company had endeavoured to keep on good terms with political leaders of the major parties, as well as key figures in the bureaucracy, but also because officials, particularly during and after the Second World War, regarded Imperial as a valuable contributor to the economic (and military) strength of the country. This relationship began to deteriorate in the 1960s and 1970s, not because the company had changed, but because politicians and bureaucrats reinterpreted their range of responsibilities to embrace social and environmental agendas that extended beyond the traditional goals of economic development and balancing regional interests and antagonisms. The days when an Imperial executive could arrange to have some obstacle removed by placing a call to C.D. Howe were (almost) over.

Howe himself was an early victim of the changing political environment. By 1956 there were divisions, even within the governing Liberal party, over Howe's policies. In particular there were skirmishes related to the issue of direct US investment in Canada, with the oil and gas industry once again featured: a Liberal Toronto businessman, Walter Gordon, chaired a Royal Commission on Canada's Economic Prospects that lamented foreign control of Canada's petroleum and proposed that the government require a 25 per cent equity share for Canadians in all companies operating in the country. The opposition parties were even more vocal on the subject, and exploited a controversy over a proposed natural gas pipeline from Alberta to Ontario to fan the flames in advance of an anticipated federal election.

The Trans Canada Pipeline Co. had been set up in 1954 by a consortium of Canadian and US investors, including Clint Murchison, a prominent Texas independent oilman, after the Alberta Oil and Gas Conservation Board approved the export of surplus gas from the province. Unlike the Interprovincial Pipe Line, however, Canada's Board of Trade Commissioners (and Howe) insisted that the line follow an "all Canadian" route through Port Arthur to Toronto. There were technical and political factors involved: oil from the west could be trans-shipped to northern Ontario by lake tankers, whereas natural gas had to be carried to its final destination by pipeline. And Howe was anxious not to disappoint his constituents this time around. Since Trans-Canada needed exports to meet its financial goals, however, the company would be allowed to build a separate line to export gas to Minnesota.[28]

For a variety of reasons, including the reluctance of financial institutions to support the project as well as opposition by US-based gas providers to this new competitor, Trans Canada turned to the federal government to underwrite an $80 million (CAD) loan. When Howe presented the proposal in Parliament, however, opposition parties engaged in a filibuster to delay approval. The government invoked closure, which exacerbated political tensions as Prime Minister Saint Laurent and Howe were charged with seeking to undermine parliamentary rule and selling out the country to foreign interests. In the ensuing election in 1957, the Liberals were defeated for the first time in more than twenty years; Howe lost his own seat in the debacle.[29]

The new prime minister, John Diefenbaker, was a Progressive Conservative from Saskatchewan, regarded as a kind of populist in contrast to the Bay Street businessmen and lawyers who traditionally had dominated the party. As a western Canadian, he was expected to support the interests of the region's oil and gas entrepreneurs as well as Prairie farmers. One of Diefenbaker's first initiatives was to establish a Royal Commission on Energy; it would look into potential wrongdoing by the former government in promoting the Trans-Canada Pipeline, but was also mandated to take a broader view of the longer-term prospects for development of Canada's petroleum industry. The chairman of the Commission was not, however, a westerner, but Henry Borden, a full-fledged member of the Tory establishment. He was also a nephew of former prime minister Robert Borden, Toronto corporate lawyer, and head of Brazilian Light & Traction, one of Canada's largest overseas companies.

Two big issues loomed over the proceedings of the Royal Commission. First was the demand, by western independent oil producers, for an oil pipeline from Edmonton to Montreal, which had the backing of Alberta's premier, Ernest Manning. The second, and related, issue was more vexing: the establishment by the US government of oil import quotas, responding to pressure from that country's own independent petroleum producers. The Borden Commission and the Canadian government had to devote much of its attention to trying to resolve these interconnected matters over the next four years.

1957 was not a propitious year for Alberta's oil producers. During the Suez Crisis the previous year, allowable production had increased by 15 per cent but then subsided to pre-crisis levels. Refiners had large inventories and the North American economy was lurching into its first major recession since the Second World War. The independent drilling companies in particular were operating well below capacity and were seeking new markets; an Edmonton-to-Montreal oil pipeline seemed an obvious solution, as it would parallel the Trans Canada gas pipeline to eastern Canada and reduce the need for prorationing. A leading figure in this movement was Robert A. Brown Jr., head of Home Oil: his father had been co-producer of the pre-war Turner Valley Royalties, and "Bobby" Brown had parlayed the acquisition of Imperial's (and Royalite's) Turner Valley wells after Leduc into a large and diverse empire of wildcat drilling operations. These drilling operations were heavily leveraged, so Brown was anxious to find markets outside the province. The proposed 30-inch pipeline would have an initial capacity of 200,000 bbl./day upon completion in 1960, rising to over 300,000 bbl./day by the middle of the decade.[30]

Premier Manning initially supported the Montreal pipeline idea, although his main goal was to promote production and exports regardless of the destination. Imperial and the other oil majors, however, were resolutely opposed. As executive vice president of Imperial, Twaits—meeting with Manning in December 1957—argued that the problems for Alberta's oil producers related to international factors: the general economic downturn, excess inventories, and the advent of oil supertankers that could carry large cargoes of oil from overseas to North America. A pipeline from Edmonton to Montreal would cost more than $200 million (CAD) and would require firm long-term commitments from refiners in eastern Canada (which of course included Imperial). He took the view that the best solution for Alberta lay in enlarged refinery capacity in Ontario, already served by Interprovincial, and lobbying for export markets in the United States.

These were arguments that would be reiterated by Imperial's president Jack White before the Borden Commission several months later. But Imperial Oil was not the only critic of the Montreal pipeline: the final report of the Gordon Commission, released in December 1957, noted that Canadian consumers were paying "up to 50 per cent more for their energy than consumers in the United States," and covering the capital and transportation costs of the proposed pipeline would require even higher prices, exacerbating the difference. A report prepared by Walter Levy, an economic consultant retained by the Canadian Petroleum Association, concluded that constructing a Montreal pipeline would require government subsidies for the project and the imposition of restrictions on oil imports to eastern Canada.[31]

The alternative was to increase exports of Alberta's oil to the United States, particularly to the American west coast and the Midwestern states, where transportation costs would be lower. Imperial argued that, although currently US refinery inventories were at or near capacity, in the longer term the country was becoming a net importer of oil and the US government would recognize that Canadian crude was a "safe" source in terms of national security, in contrast to imports from the turbulent regions of the Middle East and South America.[32]

At this point, however, there was a significant impediment to expanding Canadian oil exports to the US Since the early 1950s independent oil producers in the American Southwest had been lobbying for protection against cheap oil imports from Venezuela, the Middle East, and elsewhere, and had secured support from the powerful Southern Democrats in the US Congress. President Eisenhower, a Republican, had resisted these pressures for a time, but in 1955 he had agreed to establish a Voluntary Oil Import Program. Canada and Venezuela had initially been exempted, but this exemption was removed when the program acquired a more formal structure in 1957.

In March 1959, the US government moved on to establish a Mandatory Oil Import Program, which initially provided no exemptions, and was applied most forcefully to regions east of the Rocky Mountains, with imports limited to 8 per cent of demand. On the west coast, the limits were less onerous and Canada retained one-third of the quota. Nevertheless, the measure was a serious setback for advocates of Alberta exports to the US, and strengthened the arguments for the Montreal pipeline. Inevitably the issue became entangled in the deliberations of the Borden Commission and Canadian-US diplomacy.[33]

As a western Canadian Prime Minister Diefenbaker might have been expected to support the Montreal pipeline, but his attitude appears to have been ambivalent—in part because of the cost of the project, which was likely to require government loan guarantees if not equity participation. These were precisely the features that Conservatives had criticized in the Trans-Canada Pipeline case. In addition, it was clear that the major refiners in Montreal, with ties to the oil majors, were reluctant to buy western Canadian crude, which would be more expensive than imported oil, unless compelled to do so through government regulation, which Conservatives also opposed. There was also no indication that the Montreal pipeline was supported in Quebec: none of the members of Parliament from that province had even raised the subject.[34]

On the other hand, Diefenbaker wanted to help the Alberta oil producers, and the best way to do so was to use diplomatic influence to open up the US markets by getting the exemption reinstated. After the initial exemption was cancelled he had devoted time in personal meetings with President Eisenhower to press this case, citing national security reasons in particular. These efforts appear to have been effective: less than two months after the announcement of the Mandatory Oil Import Program, an "exception" was made for "overland" oil shipped by pipeline or rail. This exception would apply to Mexico as well, but it was primarily intended to benefit Canada. Canadian oil exports doubled in volume between 1959 and 1961.[35]

In its first report in October 1958 the Borden Commission dodged the Montreal Pipeline issue, but recommended the establishment of a National Energy Board to provide a coordinated approach to the regulation of all energy matters as well as oil and gas transportation, imports and exports. The second report was issued in July 1959, by which time the Canadian exemption to the US import control program had gone into effect. Not surprisingly, the commission recommended an export push and the shelving of the Montreal pipeline unless Canadian production and exports continued to stagnate.

In February 1961 the federal government unveiled its National Oil Policy and the Montreal Pipeline was indefinitely postponed. Canada east of the Ottawa Valley would be supplied by imported oil. The rest of Canada, including most of Ontario, would be supplied by oil from western Canada, whose producers would also be encouraged to export to its "natural" market in the Midwestern United States. This policy remained more or less in effect until 1973. On the whole, all interested parties appeared satisfied: consumers in eastern Canada continued to have access to less costly oil; western producers had access to the Ontario market as well as the US export market—Manning's Social Credit party continued in power for another twelve years. The oil majors retained their hold on eastern Canadian markets.[36]

During the energy crises of the 1970s, when oil prices spiked for consumers in eastern and central Canada, and tankers bound for the Canadian east coast were rerouted to meet surging demands in the US market, the issues that loomed during debates in the 1950s over national oil pipelines and "continental" energy policies regained saliency. Imperial Oil and other affiliates of the petroleum multinationals were assailed for blocking the Montreal pipeline at the behest of their corporate masters; the parent companies, particularly Jersey Standard, were accused of exercising influence over US and Canadian foreign policies to foster a "continentalist" approach to energy resource development—to the detriment of Canadian national interests.[37]

Imperial Oil did indeed have a long-term supply contract in the 1950s with another Jersey Standard affiliate, Creole Petroleum in Venezuela, and the Canadian market absorbed 10 per cent of that company's production in 1958. The company and the country both had a turbulent history. In the aftermath of the Second World War, a civilian regime under Romulo Betancourt had negotiated the first fifty-fifty profit-sharing agreement with Jersey Standard, a pattern followed by other concessionary countries including Saudi Arabia. In 1948, the government had fallen to a military coup, which dominated the country for ten years until another revolution toppled the regime of Marcos Perez-Jiminez. Betancourt and his energy minister, Juan Perez Alfonso, returned to power and the multinationals feared increased taxes on foreign oil concessions, and potentially the nationalization of the industry. Both the US government and Jersey Standard hoped to head off this outcome by providing stability for Venezuela's exports. Since Venezuela also lost its exemption from the US Mandatory Oil Import Program, both parties sought to ensure that the Canadian market remained accessible.[38]

This was not, of course, the argument Imperial presented to the Borden Commission, but in any case the cost of Venezuelan crude was lower than that of western Canadian oil shipped to Montreal. In the lead-up to the National Oil Policy, however, there were diplomatic trade-offs that reflected what might be called converging corporate and national interests. By the time the National Oil Policy was under consideration in Ottawa, there was a new Democratic administration in Washington that was less likely than its predecessor to respond to pressures from

Jersey Standard and the oil majors. But throughout 1959 and 1960, US State Department representatives—in conversations with their Canadian counterparts—had made it clear that their government was unlikely to extend an exemption to the Mandatory Oil Import quotas for Venezuela, but nevertheless hoped to maintain stable relations with that country. This was not exactly an outright demand that Canada shelve its commitment to the Montreal pipeline as a *quid pro quo* for retaining its exemption, thus ensuring Venezuelan access to eastern Canada—but the underlying message was clear enough.[39]

Through a judicious mix of public presentations and behind-the-scenes manoeuvring, Imperial and the other oil majors in Canada had been able to contain the threat of a Montreal pipeline in 1957–61—although the issue would resurface repeatedly: in 1969, again during the energy crises of the 1970s, and as late as 2015, in the form of debates over extending an oil pipeline through Quebec to Atlantic Canada. During the next decade, however, the entire industry—oil majors and independents—faced a new challenge to a much-treasured tax benefit: the depletion allowance. During the 1920s when the federal government controlled most of the subsoil leases in western Canada, provision had been made for a 25 per cent tax deduction for costs associated with exploration for oil and gas. An additional and even better benefit was introduced by the federal government during the Second World War.

In the United States unwarranted fears of the imminent disappearance of new oil fields had led to the establishment of a "depletion allowance" that would permit oil producers to deduct up to 27.5 per cent of earnings from sales of oil from their taxable income: this was a kind of "depreciation in advance," since the actual decline in value of the resource being exploited was hard to calculate at the time of discovery. This deduction first appeared in American tax laws during the First World War, but was enshrined in semi-permanent (to 1975) form by the US Congress in 1926. In Canada an even more generous rate of 33.3 per cent was put into effect in 1944 by the Dominion War Exchange Conservation Act, which was applied to mining as well as petroleum enterprises, and was supplementary to the exploration tax credits already in effect. Imperial Oil's vigorous oil drilling efforts from 1942, culminating in the Leduc discovery, were stimulated at least in part by these benefits. Imperial reported that it had spent $8.4 million (CAD) on drilling in the period between 1942 and 1947, offset by $4 million (CAD) in tax relief from a combination of exploration and depletion allowance credits.[40] The 1949 Income Tax Law retained these provisions, which applied to all Canadian petroleum (and mining) companies and contributed to dramatic growth in these sectors in the 1950s.

By the middle of the decade oil producers were adopting a somewhat more jaundiced view of the tax benefits provided by the Canadian government. In 1953 Twaits urged the Finance Department in Ottawa to look at US tax incentives, arguing that "oil and gas industries receive more generous treatment under the US than under Canadian law." A few years later the Canadian Petroleum Association, which represented independents as well as the oil majors, recommended a revision of the depletion rules in place to replace what Carl Nickle, an influential Alberta spokesman for the industry, described as "a largely ineffective and unobtainable depletion allowance."[41]

In 1955 Home Oil filed an appeal to the Supreme Court of Canada for recovery of income taxes paid in 1949–50, which the company argued was based on a misapplication of the depletion allowance formula. Bobby Brown had acquired Home Oil in 1953 and was looking for any possible revenue source to offset the company's debt. Lawyers for Home Oil maintained that the depletion calculation should be applied against the profits of individual wells, including those operating at a loss, which the Revenue Department had set aside. The Exchequer Court had upheld the government position, but the Supreme Court overruled that decision, awarding not only Home Oil but also other oil producers an additional allowance that returned $2 million (CAD) to the companies.[42]

Imperial Oil decided to try extending the tax windfall to the years 1951–53, when it was operating a large number of wells, productive and otherwise, that could net a rebate of up to $13 million (CAD). Needless to say, other companies followed the proceedings, which could award the industry more than $60 million (CAD). In the course of their presentation, Imperial's lawyers reiterated the argument that "present regulations discriminate against producers engaged in extensive exploration and gives an advantage to US companies exploring in Canada," an interesting perspective from the largest US-owned enterprise in the Canadian oil industry—of course Imperial as a Canadian chartered company operated under the tax laws of that country.

The Supreme Court in this case, however, did not accept Home Oil as a precedent. The ruling read by Chief Justice Kerwin asserted that a change in tax regulations in 1951 required companies to offset losses from non-productive wells against profits from its aggregate production in calculating the depletion allowance, so the circumstances were different. Three of the seven justices dissented from this interpretation, arguing that computations should still be based on the performance of individual wells. Nevertheless the court reduced the anticipated windfall to $790,067 (CAD).[43]

Imperial did not give up its quest for tax reductions. In 1962 the company, acting on the advice of Lazarus Phillips, Canada's leading tax lawyer, undertook a major internal reorganization. A new company, Imperial Oil Enterprises Ltd., would be established to take over the assets of the manufacturing department (refineries), chemical products, and exploration operations, while Imperial Oil Ltd. would continue to include production (operating wells), marketing, transportation, and other activities. In addition to exploration, the new entity processed crude oil on a fee-for-service basis. Imperial Oil Enterprises was incorporated under the federal charter that had been given to the Saint Clair Processing Corporation during the Second World War and headquartered in Sarnia. Phillips maintained that this change in structure would reduce Imperial Oil's tax liability by $4.5 million (CAD) per year.[44]

In a manner reminiscent of the good old days when Victor Ross and William Hanna would go to Ottawa to cut deals with this or that cabinet minister, Phillips and other representatives of Imperial met with the Deputy Minister of National Revenue and the Deputy Minister of Finance to ensure that they accepted the proposed reorganization. The Deputy Minister of Finance was quoted as saying, "Why would [we] discriminate against one taxpayer who was endeavouring to get itself into the same competitive position as others in the industry?"[45] This kind of reorganization that separated "upstream" and "downstream" operations would be followed by other oil companies in the coming years, sometimes leading to results that may not have been originally intended, including the closure of less profitable refineries. In 1968, Imperial decided to consolidate its western refineries into a large new one, Strathcona, located in Edmonton, selling or closing its operations in Winnipeg, Regina, and Calgary.[46]

By 1962 Diefenbaker's Progressive Conservative regime was on its last legs. In an effort to rekindle the spirit of change that the party had promised five years earlier, the government unveiled a platform that included establishing a Royal Commission on Taxation that would make the system more efficient and address inequities. This was a fairly esoteric subject to the public generally, but business interests had been clamouring for an overhaul of the tax code: in the United States tax cuts for business had boosted a recovery while the Canadian economy remained in the doldrums. Kenneth Carter, who was appointed to head the commission, was a Toronto accountant of impeccable credentials, a former head of the Canadian Tax Foundation, acceptable to the major political parties. When Diefenbaker went down to defeat in 1963, the Royal Commission continued its arcane deliberations with the approval of the Liberals.

The oil and gas industry in Canada demonstrated unusual unity in its presentations to the Carter Commission in 1963. British-American Oil Co. president Ed Loughney argued for more liberal depletion allowances to "spur future exploration." A group of independent oil producers echoed this call, urging that the depletion allowance be applied to gross rather than net profits, to bring it into line with the US tax laws. Twaits, speaking for Imperial Oil, urged Canada to become a "tax haven," by reducing or eliminating corporate taxes and moving away from the concept of progressive income taxes, which discouraged "capital generation and retention of skills." He also pointed out that the oil and gas industry paid hefty royalties and other taxes to provincial governments that should be taken into account in assessing federal tax levels.[47]

Like Saint Paul on the road to Damascus, Kenneth Carter and two of his five other colleagues on the commission were converted to the gospel of tax reform during the four-year process of completing the report. When it was released in February 1967 in six volumes, it recommended (among many other things) that Canada should introduce a capital gains tax, and that the multitude of special tax arrangements should be winnowed away, including the depletion allowance.

The Carter report rejected the argument that companies in the extractive industries needed the allowance to offset the reluctance of Canadian

Graham D. Taylor

investors to support these "high risk" undertakings: this was particularly the case for the large companies that could "raise capital in the market at costs that are no higher than those incurred by corporations of comparable size in other industries," although the report acknowledged that smaller mining and petroleum companies encountered more obstacles in raising necessary capital. Similarly, the report dismissed the argument that Canadian companies in these industries were at a disadvantage in competition with US companies that benefited from the American depletion allowances. It pointed out that those foreign-owned corporations would have to pay the 15 per cent non-resident withholding tax. The alternative the commission proposed, which involved a rapid write-off of initial costs for all corporations, would—the report maintained—improve the after-tax cash flow for smaller petroleum companies. Nevertheless it acknowledged that this would not offset the loss of benefits the larger firms enjoyed under the existing depletion allowance.[48]

Predictably, the Carter Commission report aroused the ire of the large mining and petroleum companies that, according to that report, accounted for 85 per cent of the benefits provided under the depletion allowances. The Mining Association of Canada denounced the proposals, arguing that the depletion allowances "have been devised over many years by consultation between industry and taxing authorities." Twaits, speaking at the Imperial Oil annual general meeting on April 19, 1967, castigated the members of the commission for their ignorance of the way companies had to operate in the extractive industries and maintained that the commission's alternative "would drive Canadian investment funds into the purchase of mature, dividend-paying stocks and away from growth enterprises." He asserted that "the petroleum industry is probably the most heavily taxed in this country . . . Yet, in the public eye, as a result of the commission's report, we are represented as not paying our share of taxes."[49]

The federal government, now again under the Liberals, quailed before this onslaught. In May 1967, Finance Minister Mitchell Sharp assured the mining industry that the three-year tax holiday for new mines, which the Carter Commission recommended eliminating, would be maintained for at least seven years. Subsequently he promised to provide a "White Paper" that would deal with the Royal Commission's recommendations, but this was delayed throughout the year on the grounds that the government needed to assess all the briefs submitted by critics of the report. Even Carter backed off somewhat, saying that not every proposal needed to be enacted, although he insisted that certain features, including the capital gains tax, were essential to the reform program the commission had presented. In December Sharp indicated that he was "opting for reform of the existing system rather than adoption of a completely different system," citing "uncertainty" about the impact of the Carter proposals on "international capital flows . . . and regional development."[50]

In 1968, the Liberal leadership changed hands and Pierre Trudeau led the rejuvenated party to victory. Tax reform was not a major issue in the election. But Edgar Benson, Sharp's successor as Finance Minister, promised to produce the long-awaited White Paper on the subject. It was finally released in November 1969. Business leaders, particularly in the extractive industries, were inclined to be suspicious of Benson who, as Minister of National Revenue, had been a zealous enforcer of regulations on tax avoidance.

In his first budget, in December 1968, Benson vowed to close "loopholes" in the depletion allowance rules, in particular where "companies can obtain greater benefits than were intended by having one subsidiary carry on production activities and another exploration and development activities. This allows the production company to obtain greater depletion allowances . . . by not having to subtract exploration and development expenses," which "can then be deducted from the profits in another part of the parent company's operations." This proposal targeted the kind of reorganization Lazarus Phillips had orchestrated with Imperial six years earlier. In 1969 Twaits complained that this measure would reduce Imperial Oil's profits by $2 million (CAD).[51]

Despite this inauspicious inaugural event, the White Paper proposals in 1969 were less onerous than the industry expected. In the overture to the White Paper, the government compared exploration and development in the mining and petroleum industry with scientific research in other fields and thus "warrant[ed] some special public support," although not as "generous" as in the past. Specifically, the proposals would retain the depletion allowance "if firms 'earned' the rights to the allowance by capital expenditures of $3 for every $1 of depletion allowance claimed. In addition, sales of properties that had benefitted from the depletion allowance would be subject to the new capital gains tax.[52]

Although the outcry was somewhat less strident than the response to the Carter Commission, the industry was only partially mollified. Imperial Oil's presentation to the Canadian Senate banking committee reiterated the call for a "depletion allowance . . . competitive with the United States rate;" Imperial also objected that the $3 capital expenditure for $1 of depletion allowance would "penalize all those who spent less than 150 per cent of their net profits on exploration." In particular Twaits concluded that if the new formula came into effect, it would have to suspend ongoing projects in the Athabasca and Cold Lake oil sands.[53]

Despite the arguments presented by Imperial and others, many of the features of the White Paper appeared in legislation brought forward by the government in 1971, but the implementation was to be delayed until 1976. By that time, however, the climate had changed—in the wake of the energy crisis of 1973–74, the search for "frontier oil" and the development of "unconventional" sources in the oil sands and elsewhere became a preoccupation of governments at both the federal and provincial levels, even as they fought one another over sharing the royalties from the new oil boom. In place of the Carter Commission-era proposals to eliminate or limit the depletion allowances, by the mid-1970s a new era of "superdepletion" incentives had dawned—at least for a time.

10

NORTHERN VISIONS

During his successful campaign for prime minister in 1957, John Diefenbaker sought a theme that would distinguish his leadership not only from the Liberals but also from the "old guard" Tories he had displaced. He turned to Merrill Menzies, a young economist from Manitoba who persuaded Diefenbaker to embrace a "Northern vision" that would open a "New Frontier" for economic development and exploitation of natural resources in the remote areas of northern Canada, a twentieth century renewal of the National Policy, counterposed to the "continentalist" orientation of the Liberal regime.[1]

As was often the case in politics, the "Northern Vision" was easier to articulate than to translate into effective policies. Even before its final defeat in 1962, Diefenbaker's Progressive Conservative government was in disarray and none of Menzies's ambitious ideas had come to fruition. But the concept of the "North" as the next frontier for development resonated with the business leaders in Canada's natural resource industries, not least those in the oil and gas field. By the end of the next decade the prospects for new finds in the Arctic region and the possibilities of exploiting the potentially huge reserves in the oil sands of northern Alberta were receiving more than perfunctory attention from the industry. Lack of infrastructure, the limits of technology, and persistently low oil prices were impediments to action through this period. Some of those conditions changed in the 1970s, but resource developers then confronted challenges from First Nations communities and from environmentalists, who had very different versions of the "Northern Vision"—not to mention challenges from a federal government with its own agenda for the region and the industry.

As early as 1963, Imperial Oil was looking ahead to future prospects beyond its maturing fields in southern Alberta. In a report submitted to the company's executive committee, the producing department concluded that "the Southern basin does not appear to have a significant potential as a source of new cheap conventional oil in the 1970s," and it recommended that the company consider alternative sources including "the Athabasca Tar Sands and other heavy hydrocarbon deposits," and "areas of the north including the Arctic Islands, and possibly reserves which might exist on the Atlantic Continental Shelf." Jack Armstrong, then a vice president and the chief executive of Imperial a decade later, asked if the producing department "was in effect 'walking off' the Southern basin." The representatives of the producing department responded that "this was not the case" but reiterated that "the Company was limited to some extent by its current . . . position."[2]

Imperial's parent, Jersey Standard, and other American oil majors were also looking to future sources of supply in this period, even as the country seemed awash in cheap oil and gasoline. In 1956 M. King Hubbert, a geologist with Shell, had presented a paper to the American Petroleum Institute estimating that established fields in North America would reach a production peak between 1965 and 1970, and draw down on diminishing reserves thereafter. Although this warning had little resonance with the industry at the time, and the oil majors could rely on global sources to sustain their operations, by the middle of the 1960s, with growing tensions in overseas regions including the Middle East and Latin America, prudent oil executives were looking at options closer to home. In 1968, two years after the Alaskan coast had been opened by the US Interior Department for oil exploration, the Atlantic Richfield company, backed by Humble Oil of Texas and Jersey Standard (soon to be renamed Exxon), announced a huge discovery at Prudhoe Bay on Alaska's North Slope, with potential reserves exceeding 10 billion barrels. Shortly thereafter, British Petroleum made a strike nearby and a new "oil rush" was on.[3]

This was the context in which Imperial Oil undertook its adventures into the geographic and technological frontiers in the 1970s. In retrospect, the virtual abandonment of development in southern Alberta proved

Graham D. Taylor

premature, and the company had to buy its way back into the burgeoning Elmworth field later in the decade. Arctic exploration yielded disappointment, and the oil sands and heavy oil investments were both frustrating and a continuing expense. Imperial was not alone in its difficulties with northern initiatives, which ultimately swallowed up some even bolder ventures and roiled Canadian politics into the 1980s.

The Oil Sands

During the summer of 1914, the eminent British geologist Dr. T.O. Bosworth, who would head the Imperial Oil expedition to Fort Norman five years later, traveled to the Athabasca River region at the instance of two Calgary businessmen, to survey the prospects for oil extraction from the "Tar Sand District." Surprisingly, Dr. Bosworth offered the view that the oil-infused bitumen of that area offered a better opportunity for profitable development than did the possible underground deposits in the Turner Valley. "This remarkable series of Bituminous Shales and Limestones . . . is an admirable oil generating formation," he proclaimed. Bosworth went on to recommend that his clients form "a controlling company or syndicate" of all the oil seekers in Alberta to exploit "the oilfields of the north."[4]

The outbreak of the First World War interrupted further developments until 1918, by which time Bosworth appears to have shifted his focus to finding more conventional oil sources in the Northwest Territories. At the time he extolled the merits of oil extraction from the tar sands, no viable commercial process had been developed for this purpose. The oil discovered in the Turner Valley and later at Leduc and other fields in southern Alberta was light and largely free of the sulphurous content that had troubled the Ontario product. By contrast, the oil embedded in the bitumen around Fort McMurray had to be laboriously separated and even then its sulphur-laden content required more refining than the standard product pulled directly from underground sources. Based on exploratory work by American geologists Ralph Arnold and J.L. Tapley in 1917, Imperial Oil took out seventeen leases in the Fort McMurray area, but further investigation indicated that "if there was oil in the Athabasca region, it was not going to yield to traditional methods of drilling."[5]

During the late 1700s Peter Pond and Alexander Mackenzie, fur traders with the North West Company, encountered what Mackenzie described as "bituminous fountains" near the forks of the Athabasca and Clearwater rivers in what is now northeastern Alberta: "A pole of twenty feet long may be inserted without the least resistance" into the bitumen along the river banks.[6] Mackenzie observed that the Cree, the aboriginal people in the region, mixed the bitumen with spruce resin to provide caulking for their canoes. Over the following century other English and Canadian explorers filled in more details of the region and its resources. In the early 1880s Dr. Robert Bell of the Geologic Survey of Canada investigated what he called the "asphaltic sands," which he maintained could contain "abundant" quantities of petroleum.[7]

In 1913, a year before Bosworth's expedition, the engineer Dr. Sidney Ells was commissioned by the federal Department of Mines to look into the commercial potential of the oil-embedded bitumen near the former Hudson's Bay Co. trading post, Fort McMurray. Ells concluded that it could be used as a base for asphalt paving, and was so enthusiastic about the prospects that he formed a company two years later to pave roads and sidewalks in Edmonton. During the mid-1920s, following completion of a railway line to Fort McMurray, Ells joined with an American businessman, Thomas Draper, to form McMurray Oil & Asphaltum Co. It operated for about ten years producing paving materials primarily for the Alberta market. Meanwhile, the Alberta government established a Scientific and Industrial Research Council that employed Dr. Karl Clark, an associate of Ells, to develop a process to separate bitumen from the tarry sands. In 1924 Clark experimented with suspension of bitumen solids in hot water and caustic soda in a rotating drum, producing a liquid that could be converted into synthetic crude oil. Although it did not entirely overcome the problem of impurities in the bitumen, the "hot water extraction process" became the basis for the oil sands industry.[8]

For more than twenty years the oil sands attracted a variety of entrepreneurs, some of them little more than con artists, others with more serious intentions but meeting with limited success. In 1922 Robert Fitzsimmons acquired a federal lease north of Fort McMurray and set up International Bitumen Co., which used a crude variant on the hot water extraction process but relied primarily on the production of asphalt paving and roofing materials and some fuel oils. Although Fitzsimmons improved the hot water process and built a small refinery, the plant at Bitumount had to be shuttered during the Depression. In 1942 Fitzsimmons sold the company to Lloyd Champion, who reorganized it as Oil Sands Ltd. and sought to resurrect it—with help from the Alberta government—as a prototype for Karl Clark's extraction process.

Meanwhile, Sidney Ells, who now saw Clark as a rival, was approached by an entrepreneur from Denver named Max Ball, whose partner James McClave had developed an alternative bitumen extraction process. Shortly before the Canadian government transferred its mineral leasing rights to Alberta in 1930, Ball, with help from Ells, acquired a federal lease near Fort McMurray to set up a "demonstration plant" that would not only extract bitumen from the sands but also refine it into gasoline and fuel oil on a small scale. The company, Abasand Oils Ltd., was set up in 1936 and went into operation several years later—in time to contribute to wartime production—but burned down in 1941. It was taken over by the federal government under the War Measures Act and the plant was rebuilt under direction of Claude Humphreys, a refinery engineer seconded from Imperial Oil; but it was destroyed by fire again in 1945. The Canadian government refused to contribute to another rebuilding effort.[9]

By this time Ernest Manning had become premier of Alberta; with Turner Valley output in decline and no new large conventional oil finds on the horizon, he supported the proposal to rebuild Bitumount as a demonstration plant for Clark's extraction process. The province put up $500,000 (CAD) to back Champion's undertaking. But circumstances changed by 1948. The discovery of Leduc opened the door to a renewed oil industry in southern Alberta. The reconstruction of Bitumount encountered increasing costs of close to $1 million (CAD), and Champion bailed out of the project. Even Karl Clark was frustrated by the disorganization on the ground. Both the Abasand and Bitumount ventures were in limbo.[10]

Up to this point none of the oil majors—or for that matter, medium-level oil companies in North America—had exhibited much interest in the oil sands: the resource was in a remote location, far from any prospective markets, the technology had yet to be tested on a large scale operation, and there was plenty of conventional oil available. Nevertheless, Premier Manning still hoped to stimulate investment in the region: in 1951 Alberta sponsored an "international" conference of oil companies to hear about the potential benefits of the oil sands. Sidney Blair, an associate of Karl Clark and head of Canadian Bechtel, provided an optimistic analysis of projected oil sands production costs and Nathan Tanner promised generous leasing and royalties policies to prospective investors. But many of these participants were put off by the expectation that those seeking leases must undertake development of an operating plant within two to five years.[11]

An exception was J. Howard Pew, chief executive of Sun Oil Co. of Pennsylvania. Sun Oil had entered the Canadian market several years earlier, and was seeking sources of crude oil for its Marcus Hook refinery. But in the context of the Cold War Pew also was committed to the belief that the US, for national security, should rely primarily on North American oil. Pew and Alberta's Premier Manning were both stalwart political and religious conservatives, and they formed a close personal relationship over the next two decades that would have a significant impact on the development of the oil sands. Sun Oil was one of the few companies to take up Alberta's appeals for investment in its northern frontier region.

Lloyd Champion embarked on a new oil sands venture in 1953, cobbling together the remnants of previous ventures at Bitmount and Abasand into Great Canadian Oil Sands Ltd. As with previous forays into the field, this one soon began to founder, but Sun Oil stepped into the breach, taking over 75 per cent of the lease and supporting mining and processing of the oil extracted from bitumen in return for exclusive rights to sell the company's output. Development work commenced at Ruth Lake north of Fort McMurray. The Manning government helpfully arranged in 1955 to exempt oil sands production from Alberta's prorationing process.[12]

Imperial Oil's entry into the field came through a side door and in the wake of one of the more bizarre episodes in the history of the oil sands. In the mid-1950s, as part of President Eisenhower's "Atoms for Peace" concept, the US Atomic Energy Commission initiated "Project Plowshare," a review of proposals to use nuclear weapons for economic development ends. These included ideas such as creating a new interoceanic canal in Nicaragua, vastly enlarging harbours on the Alaskan coast, and blasting through mountains in California to expand highway and railway lines. During the Suez crisis of 1956–57, attention turned to the development of oil resources in North America.

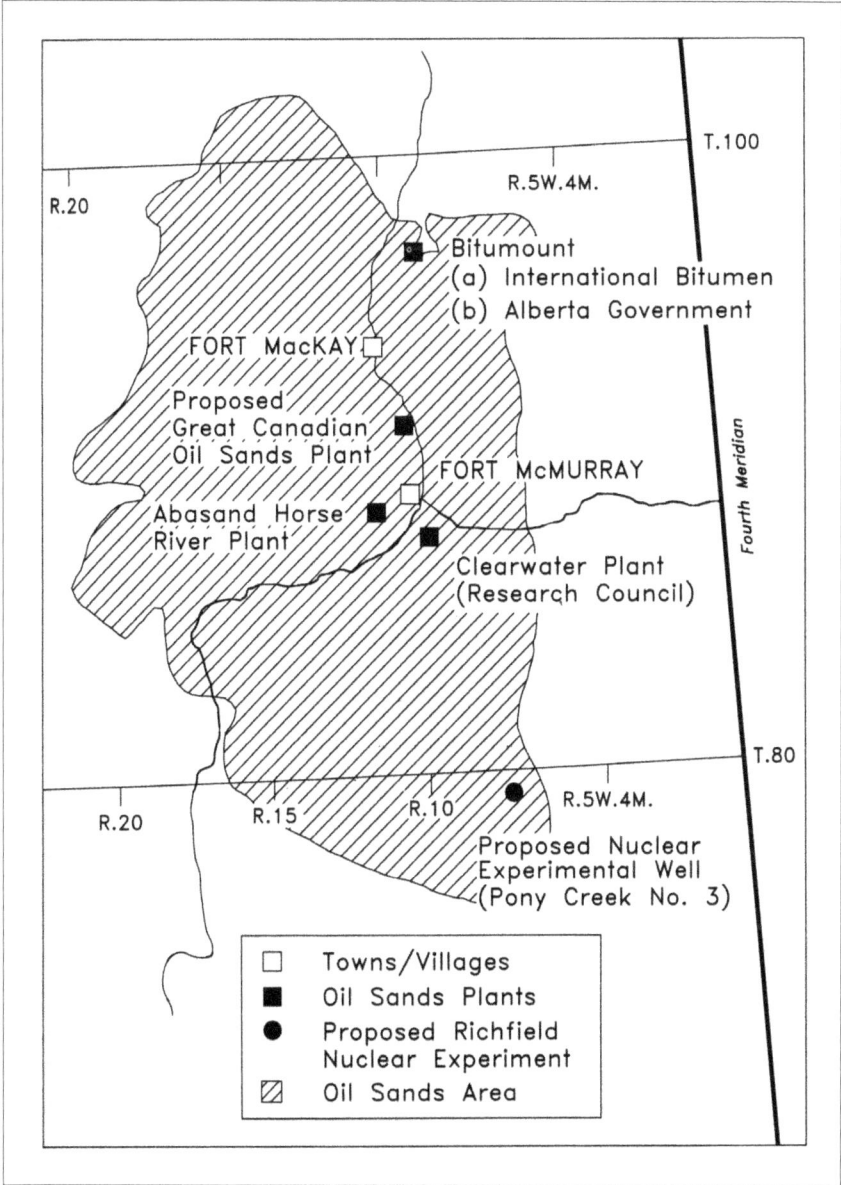

MAP 10.1. Alberta Oil Sands, 1960. David Breen, *The Alberta Petroleum Industry and the Conservation Board*, Edmonton: University of Alberta Press, 1992, p. 441. Courtesy of David Breen.

Manfred Natland, a petroleum geologist employed by Richfield Oil, a medium-sized California company, proposed to address this need. Natland was familiar with the basic problem of the oil sands, the viscous intermixture of bitumen and tarry sand that made the costs of extraction prohibitive even before the residue could be refined. As Karl Clark had noted, recovery of the bitumen from underground would reduce the costs of mining the surface, and also its environmental effects. After witnessing a vivid sunset in Saudi Arabia Natland claimed it occurred to him that using an underground nuclear explosion in the oil sands would "reduce the viscosity" of the bitumen and "permit its recovery by conventional oil field methods."[13]

The Richfield company had limited involvement in the Alberta oil fields, but it entered a partnership with Cities Service, a long-time operator in western Canada that, with Royalite, was engaged in a venture in the Mildred Lake area north of Fort McMurray. Cities Service Athabasca was experimenting with a German-designed bucketwheel dredge to mine the bitumen at Mildred Lake, and a hydrogenation process to extract the oil. Imperial Oil had also been approached as it held leases in the Fort McMurray area, including Pony Creek. Richfield's proposal "to test underground combustion in the oil sands" appeared to be "less costly" than the Cities Service mining venture.[14]

In 1958 Richfield, joined by Cities Service and Imperial Oil, approached the US Atomic Energy Commission with a proposal to test a 9-kiloton nuclear bomb at a depth of 1250 feet at Pony Creek. If successful, the project could be expanded to up to 100 underground explosions, freeing up much of the oil sands for exploitation. At the same time, in June 1958, Richfield presented its proposal to the Atomic Energy Board of Canada, the federal Department of Mines, and the Alberta Conservation Board. The inclusion of Imperial Oil in the proposal may have helped buttress the case presented by the smaller companies, given Imperial's connections with Canadian defence officials. Imperial also took the precaution of having Richfield present the plan to the Jersey Standard executive committee.[15]

In February 1959 the Alberta government hosted a press conference—attended by representatives of the Canadian government and the US Atomic Energy Commission—that outlined the proposal. Its original title—"Operation Cauldron"—had been modified, for public relations purposes, to "Operation Oil Sands." The *Calgary Herald* enthused that the project "will give the Western world a measure of independence from huge Middle East oil deposits," and quoted the federal Department of Mines minister that it would "double the world's petroleum reserves."[16] In outlining Imperial's involvement to the company's executive committee, Vernon Taylor—who now had responsibility for the oil sands as well as conventional production—noted that Richfield hoped to bring in "five or six more companies" to spread the costs of the project, which was now estimated to climb to $10 million (CAD) over a five-year period.[17]

The enthusiasm of government officials for "Operation Oil Sands" was not universally shared. Robert Fitzsimmons, the founder of Bitumount, warned: "if it does not turn the whole deposit into a burning inferno, it is absolutely sure to fuse it into a solid mass of semi-glass or coke." The president of a nuclear engineering company in Utah predicted that an underground blast would lead to "a second hydrogen explosion above ground" and spread radioactive dust for more than 200 square miles.[18] More critical for the project were the shifting views of Canada's prime minister, John Diefenbaker, plus Howard Green, who became Diefenbaker's Minister of Foreign Affairs in April 1959. Green was skeptical of the plans for the placement of US nuclear weapons in Canada. As early as the autumn of 1959 the oil sands bomb test had been "indefinitely postponed." By April 1962, when Green spoke out against all nuclear testing, "Operation Oil Sands" was virtually moribund.[19]

Despite the uncertain status of "Operation Oil Sands," in September 1959 Imperial's executive committee decided to proceed with a partnership with Cities Service Athabasca and Richfield in developing the Mildred Lake mine site, with Imperial assuming a $4 million (CAD) commitment in return for a 30 per cent interest. Royalite, which had acquired Bitumount, was also included with a 10 per cent participation, and the other partners each held 30 per cent. The arrangement was restricted to research and development costs, with a planned 3,000 bbl./day distillation unit in addition to the mining and extraction operations. A Cities Service executive, A.P. Frame, was in charge of the as-yet-unnamed project.[20]

The partnership was not without friction. By 1961 Cities Service, backed by Royalite and Richfield, was anxious to move on to the next stage of development: building a plant capable of processing up to 100,000 bbl./

FIGURE 10.1. Oil sands pilot plant. Mildred Lake, 1960. Glenbow Archive IP-6s-1-1-1, Imperial Oil Collection.

day and filing an application with the Alberta Conservation Board for a commercial operation. Imperial's representatives, including Taylor, Jack Armstrong, and D.S. Simmons were less sanguine. A consulting firm, C.F. Braun, projected the costs of the full-scale plant at $246 million (CAD)—much higher than Cities Service's original estimate—with a potential return of 10 per cent (later adjusted to 13.5 per cent) and a probable time frame of five to six years for completion, which far exceeded the two to three year requirement of the Alberta government.[21]

Graham D. Taylor

There were other factors influencing Imperial's hesitation. One concern involved the mining technology. After a visit to Mildred Lake, Vernon Taylor reported "disappointing" progress—in part because the German-designed bucket wheel excavator could not function in the harsh winter conditions of northern Alberta. Eventually the consortium would move toward a process that used scrapers operating on drag lines to remove the overburden, and bucket wheel reclaimers to feed the bitumen onto a conveyor belt—rather than mobile dredgers with giant bucket wheels (which were featured in the operation under development by Great Canadian Oil Sands). In the 1980s Syncrude would replace its draglines and dredgers with gigantic shovels and computerized trucks. But Imperial's engineers remained interested in the concept of some form of underground injection process to loosen the bitumen, which could then be drawn up to the surface. The technology, which would emerge as a steam-driven injection process, would be applied to Imperial's Cold Lake venture.[22]

Another impediment was the shifting perspective of the Alberta Conservation Board. In 1960 the government, under pressure from independent conventional oil producers in the province, had extended the board's reviewing authority to cover oil sands development. By this time, the Cities Service consortium and Great Canadian Oil Sands (GCOS) were actively pursuing large projects, and other big companies, including Shell and Canadian Pacific Oil and Gas, were considering entering the field. Declining market demand for oil in 1958–59 heightened the anxiety of Alberta's conventional producers. Although Premier Manning continued to support GCOS, the conservation board, in reviewing its initial application, was only prepared to consider a project limited to 31,500 bbl./day; and the Alberta government introduced a new royalty scheme that raised the province's take to 20 per cent of production above 900,000 barrels of oil and required advance royalties on the first 8 million barrels. Even though GCOS was willing to proceed under these rigorous terms, the Board delayed reconsideration until 1962. In this context, Imperial's caution was understandable.[23]

The Alberta Conservation Board gave GCOS preliminary approval of its application in October 1962, but the company was now in financial difficulties because of cost overruns in its initial preparations, a common theme in the story of oil sands ventures. Sun Oil, i.e., J. Howard Pew, bailed the company out in exchange for 80 per cent of its shares, and prevailed on the Alberta government to accept a 45,000 bbl./day operation, which would enable GCOS to meet its financial obligations more rapidly—at least in theory. In early 1963 Shell announced plans to enter the oil sands by constructing a 100,000 bbl./day operation at Cold Lake, south of the Athabascan fields. The oil sands market was becoming more crowded.[24]

Despite Imperial's reluctance, the Cities Service consortium proceeded with the 100,000 bbl./day Mildred Lake proposal, which—predictably—was rejected by the conservation board, along with Shell's initiative. Shortly thereafter, the Mildred Lake facility was closed. But the partnership was not dead: in 1964 it was revived, and christened Syncrude Canada Ltd. Once again, Imperial, Cities Service, and Richfield held 30 per cent of the shares, with Royalite receiving the 10 per cent residue. Frank Spragins of Imperial Oil was designated general manager, with Vernon Taylor as the President: Spragins had worked for Carter Oil, Jersey Standard's exploration branch, before joining Imperial in 1949, and was involved in the Mildred Lake project from its outset. For the next decade he would be a key figure in Syncrude; unfortunately, Spragins died shortly after Syncrude opened.[25]

On September 30, 1967, the GCOS plant was officially opened, attended by the usual retinue of politicians, journalists, and business leaders. J. Howard Pew was the featured speaker, emphasizing as usual that "no nation can long be secure in this atomic age unless it be amply supplied with petroleum," and that "oil from the Athabascan area must of necessity play an important role."[26] Behind the congratulatory speeches were some troubling developments. A project initially estimated to cost $59 million (CAD) had exceeded $260 million (CAD) and required several infusions of new financing from Sun Oil. Bad weather delayed the move to full production, and the company had yet to find a satisfactory way of disposing of mine tailings. Sun had to come up with more funding and GCOS ran up losses of more than $90 million (CAD) between 1967 and 1974. Only rising conventional oil prices from $2.55/bbl. to over $10/bbl. in 1973–74 provided GCOS with some respite.[27]

Chastened by the conservation board's rejection of its 1962 application, the Syncrude consortium proceeded more slowly, and benefitted from observing the problems GCOS had encountered: more conventional excavation equipment used in strip mining, for example, replaced the bucket wheel technology, and a fluid coking process developed by Esso Research & Engineering was licensed to Syncrude. In 1966, following a meeting with Premier Manning, the consortium was advised that it could apply for a 50,000 bbl./day plant. A more realistic cost estimate of $350 million (CAD) was projected. The conservation board approved an 80,000 bbl./day operation in 1969, and Syncrude successfully pushed for an amended figure of 125,000 bbl./day in 1971.[28]

But divisions continued within the consortium. In 1968 Imperial expressed concern over the growing cost estimates of the enlarged Syncrude proposal, which had risen to over $800 million (CAD), and also noted the "uncertain market picture" for oil sands crude in light of the Prudhoe Bay discoveries in Alaska. The other consortium members insisted that there should be no further delays in construction plans once the conservation board approval was assured. That approval was forthcoming but the board demanded that production should commence by the beginning of 1977, which increased cost pressures as construction of the plant would have to begin by 1974, at a time when contractors would be in demand for the Alaskan pipeline project and other northern operations—including ventures being undertaken by Imperial itself in the Arctic and the Cold Lake project.[29]

Ironically, it was another member of the consortium that pulled out in order to pursue other opportunities. Richfield had merged with Atlantic Refining in 1966, and under the leadership of Robert Anderson, the company embarked on an aggressive exploration program, playing a lead role in the Prudhoe Bay discovery in 1968 and the development of the Trans Alaska Pipeline in the mid-1970s. In 1974, after the US Export Import Bank turned down a loan application for its Canadian affiliate to cover growing expenditures for Syncrude construction, Atlantic Richfield left the consortium; the Canadian company would be swallowed by Petro Canada two years later.

There were other factors at work. In 1968 Manning retired, and three years later the Social Credit party was defeated by resurgent Conservatives led by Peter Lougheed—grandson of Sir James Lougheed. The new regime was eager to make its mark; ironically, much like the federal government under Pierre Trudeau, Alberta's Conservatives wanted the province to play a more active role in shaping the direction of the oil and gas industry and in particular the future of the oil sands. In the summer of 1973 Lougheed and his Energy minister, Don Getty, met with Syncrude representatives, including Spragins and Jack Armstrong, soon to take over as Imperial's president. Lougheed laid out major new terms: the province wanted a 50 per cent share of the net profits over twenty-five years of Syncrude's operations, a majority share of the pipeline to handle oil shipments from Fort McMurray to Edmonton, plus the option to acquire a 20 per cent ownership of Syncrude once it had become a profitable venture. For two days the talks deadlocked, but an agreement was finally reached when Lougheed accepted Syncrude's demand for a revised royalty formula, which would be based on net rather than gross earnings—the prevailing policy with regard to conventional oil production in the province. As a fillip to the agreement, Syncrude would give hiring preferences to Alberta workers on the project.[30]

This episode took place on the eve of the first major energy crisis of the 1970s and the spike in oil prices, which may have eased the concerns of parties on both sides but also aroused the suspicions of critics of the long-term connections between the oil industry and governments, particularly in Alberta.[31] The outcome may have precipitated Atlantic Richfield's departure from Syncrude. In any case, it gave the Syncrude negotiators more leverage when the parties met again in February 1974 to address the future of the consortium. With inflation, the estimated costs of the project had risen above $2 billion (CAD), and the remaining partners could realistically threaten to close it down. Anxious to retain the gains extracted the previous year, Lougheed and Getty were prepared to deal, joined by the premier of Ontario and the federal energy minister, Donald MacDonald, worried about the escalating price of imported oil for central Canada. Armstrong in particular made the case for refinancing Syncrude, and in the end the federal government accepted a 15 per cent ownership position, with Alberta picking up 10 per cent and Ontario 5 per cent, leaving the private sector partners still in a majority. The government of Alberta also agreed to extend a $200 million (CAD) loan to Cities Service of Gulf Canada to keep them in play. Later the province converted the loan into an additional 20 per cent equity in Syncrude.[32]

The Syncrude plant officially opened on September 15, 1978. After its long period of gestation, the undertaking avoided some of the growing pains that had affected GCOS. With investment from both federal and provincial governments, regulatory issues were less irksome and capital more readily available—which was fortunate, since an explosion and fire in 1984 halted production and legal disputes drove up reconstruction costs. The extended period of low conventional oil prices from the mid-1980s had the paradoxical effect of deterring other companies from embarking on rival projects on the Syncrude scale for more than twenty years. In the late 1970s Shell Canada led a consortium planning an oil sands project to compete with Syncrude, but suspended it as oil prices began to slide, although it did complete a bitumen upgrader and refinery at Stopford near Edmonton. During the 1990s the Alberta government, now under Premier Ralph Klein, sold its stake in Syncrude and reduced its royalty charge to one per cent on gross income and decreased its draw on net profits from 50 per cent to 25 per cent. The company increased capital investment by $10 billion (CAD) between 1996 and 2006. After this second round of expansion, Syncrude was producing over 300,000 bbl./day, running the largest oil mine in the world.[33]

As conventional oil prices began to rise again after 2003, there were new entrants into the oil sands. There was Royal Dutch Shell (which effectively bought out minority shareholders in Shell Canada to secure control of the Albian Sands consortium), and five other companies—including Imperial Oil Resources Ventures Ltd., which held 70 per cent ownership of the Kearl Oil Sands mine, with an estimated 5.5 billion barrel reserve. Exxon Mobil held the remaining 30 per cent. Imperial Oil also maintained a 25 per cent interest in Syncrude. The majority owner (53.7 per cent) of Syncrude is Suncor, the successor company to Sun Oil of Canada, which also took over GCOS in 1979. In 2009 Suncor acquired Petro Canada, the former government-owned corporation, and in 2015 it carried out a hostile takeover of Canadian Oil Sands, making Suncor not only the largest company in the oil and gas industry, but the largest company in Canada, ranked by revenues—a position that Imperial Oil had occupied through most of the twentieth century. It also inherited Imperial's reputation as the most reviled corporate entity in the country—the behemoth of the tar sands.

At the same time that Imperial was joining in the Syncrude venture, it began pursuing a different route toward exploiting the petroleum potential in the oil sands. During the late 1950s the company began assembling leases in the vicinity of Cold Lake, about 160 miles south of the Athabasca region, near the Saskatchewan border. The Alberta Conservation Board reckoned the field could yield up to 164 billion barrels of oil, about a quarter the size of the Athabasca fields. Preliminary work by Imperial indicated that 44 billion barrels were potentially recoverable from Cold Lake, but in contrast to Athabasca the deposits of sediment-laden petroleum was around 1,600 feet underground—the surface mining techniques pursued by GCOS and Syncrude could not be applied here. The efforts to recover oil from these underground sources was referred to as *in situ* production.

There had been efforts since the early 1900s to penetrate this reservoir and separate the bitumen and sand sufficiently to permit the use of conventional drilling techniques. Two approaches were used: one based on underground blasting and the other on the application of steam pressure to reduce the viscosity of the oil and sand mixture. One of the most persistent of the early entrepreneurs in this field was Jacob Owen Absher. In 1926 Absher set up the Bituminous Sand Extraction Company—backed by William Fisher, a Turner Valley oil producer. Absher used both techniques, initially experimenting with steam pumping, but when that proved to be expensive, he tried pouring burning kerosene underground, with disastrous results. Although Absher was undeterred by these setbacks, and his work attracted the attention of both Sidney Ells and Karl Clark, the company failed to produce adequate commercial grade oil and collapsed during the Depression.[34]

Imperial Oil may have been interested in the Richfield idea of using nuclear explosives in part because of possible application to the Cold Lake reservoir, but it was exploring alternatives. Pan American Petroleum, a subsidiary of Standard Oil of Indiana, was experimenting with a process called waterflooding that involved the application of hydraulic pressure to create underground fractures through which steam could be applied directly to the bitumen, pumping it to the surface. At the same time, Imperial's researchers at Sarnia developed a process called cyclic steam stimulation (CSS) and more commonly known as "huff and puff." After drilling down into the viscous bitumen level, steam was pumped through

FIGURE 10.2. Roger Butler. Glenbow Archive IP-26-8b-Butler, R.M., Imperial Oil Collection.

the pipe for several weeks or months. After a period of "soaking," the heated oil was drawn up to the surface. The cycle would then be repeated until the cost of steam pressure exceeded the value of the oil produced, at which point the well would be closed down. The process was developed by Roger Butler, a British-born researcher with Imperial Oil.[35]

In contrast to the friction-filled progress of the Syncrude consortium, at Cold Lake Imperial Oil proceeded at its preferred pace: cautious, methodical, and attentive to costs. In 1964 it drilled four wells and experimented with the cyclic steam process, using a portable generator. Three years later came a more substantive commitment: additional wells were brought in along with a steam plant drawing water from a nearby lake. Meanwhile a bid by Royalite for a share in the Cold Lake venture was deflected, and the Alberta Conservation Board approved a pilot project of 1,500 bbl./day. At this point, Imperial suspended work in order to assess results, in particular relating to the steam process that was now patented.

In 1971 a pilot program got underway with twenty-three wells, an enlarged stem plant linked to an oil separation operation. The processed oil was shipped to Lloydminster in Saskatchewan where Husky Oil had established a heavy oil market for its own production. A larger plant of fifty-six wells went into operation in 1975, with a 5,000 bbl./day output, most of which was used for asphalt in Edmonton. One innovation that opened the way for larger scale production involved setting up platforms that could handle a number of connected wells simultaneously. Between 1964 and 1979 Imperial spent $85 million on the Cold Lake project, a miniscule figure compared to the Syncrude costs.[36]

In 1979, however, this stately procession was accelerated, at least temporarily. In the wake of the second energy crisis of the decade, and the federal government's ambitious National Energy Policy, "megaprojects" were fashionable: massive oil plays in the Beaufort Sea and Shell's giant Alsands venture provided examples. Imperial Oil brought forward a dramatic expansion of Cold Lake, proposing to drill 8,000 wells at a cost of more than $4 billion (CAD) and production targets of 140,000 bbl./day with an enlarged steam plant and a separation upgrader and refinery. The construction project alone would employ 10,000 workers, doubling the local population and creating scenes reminiscent of Fort McMurray.[37]

Sliding international oil prices plus cutbacks in the Alberta government's support for megaprojects brought a halt to these plans in 1981 when Imperial suspended the expansion. Two years later it unveiled a more modest initiative, phasing in further development keyed to shifts in oil prices. The provincial government, now under Premier Don Getty, agreed to scale back royalty payments until the company had recouped its investment costs. By this time, Shell was developing a project at Peace River and a Japanese group (JACOS) initiated a project in 1978, although it did not move forward to production until the 1990s. By 2015 Imperial had the capability to produce 154,000 bbl./day at Cold Lake, awaiting a break in the drought in oil prices.

Meanwhile, Roger Butler, who had pioneered oil sands technology for Imperial, moved to Calgary to join the government-sponsored Alberta

Graham D. Taylor

Oil Sands Technology Research Agency. At Sarnia, Butler had developed an improved version of the cyclic steam stimulation process, which he had applied to recovery of potash ore in Saskatchewan. Along with other researchers, including veterans of Imperial, Butler experimented with a process called steam assisted gravity drainage (SAGD) initially developed in the 1960s by Standard Oil of California (Chevron) for deep heavy oil pools in southern California. This process involved drilling two parallel horizontal wells into a reservoir: steam would be pumped into the upper well, and the bitumen mix would be heated in a "steam chamber" in the lower well until it could be drawn up to the surface.

The SAGD process enabled drillers to exploit deeper reservoirs and also to operate on a continuous basis, reducing costs to the point where oil sands wells could compete with more conventional drilling when oil prices rose to $30 (CAD) per barrel. Although Imperial continued to rely on the CSS process in its established Cold Lake site, SAGD was used in most of the newer *in situ* wells, and Imperial held patents to both processes. Roger Butler was named to the Canadian Petroleum Hall of Fame for his achievements.[38]

Arctic Adventures

Imperial Oil was the first major company to undertake exploration of the Northwest Territories and the Yukon, through its affiliate the Northwest Company, beginning with the Bosworth expedition in 1918–19 and the establishment of Norman Wells, 125 miles south of the Arctic Circle, in 1920–21. During the Second World War, Norman Wells was resuscitated and expanded as part of the ill-fated Canol Project. Even as that wartime program was being phased down, Imperial geologists conducted surveys in the Yukon in 1947. With the Leduc discovery, the company's attention shifted to the southern Alberta oil fields.

Not surprisingly, the Arctic region remained largely "undeveloped" by the petroleum industry for more than a decade. Exploration and drilling had to be carried out primarily in the winter months, supplied by airplanes that had to battle through whiteouts, or more primitive transportation: the Imperial survey in 1947 was conducted with dogsleds. Roads and drilling rigs disappeared into the thawed permafrost in the spring, and the Canol experience demonstrated the hazards of building pipelines even in sub-Arctic conditions. There were, however, wildcat drillers willing to take risks in the hopes of getting a foothold in a region that the Canadian government had touted as "the most extensive petroleum field in America, if not the world." In the 1950s John C. "Cam" Sproule, a geologist who had worked for Imperial Oil in Saskatchewan and International Petroleum in Colombia and Peru, set up shop in Calgary as a consultant for those entrepreneurs. By the end of the decade, small-scale drillers were exploring the Mackenzie River north of Norman Wells all the way to the Beaufort Sea.[39]

Although little of substance came out of Prime Minister Diefenbaker's "Northern Vision," the federal government eased leasing regulations for 94 million acres in the Arctic that had been mapped by the Canadian Geological Survey's "Operation Franklin." Permits to explore Crown reserve lands could be converted to leases without payment of a "cash bonus," subject to royalty fees based on production of 5 per cent for the first three years and 10 per cent thereafter. Anticipation of the new regulations led to a flurry of interest among larger oil companies, including British American (Gulf Canada), Texaco, and Shell Canada, accounting for about 15 per cent of the area available for leasing, much of it on the Peel Plateau in northern Yukon and along Canada's Arctic coast.

In 1959 acreage in the Arctic Islands was opened for leasing: here again, some oil majors took an interest, including Texaco, Sun Oil, and Amoco, but a large proportion was taken up by smaller drillers, some associated with Sproule. Two years later, initial drilling in the Arctic Islands began, dubbed "Operation Santa Claus," with a leading role played by Dome Petroleum, an offshoot of the US-owned Dome Mines. Jack Gallagher, who led Dome Petroleum, was another Imperial Oil veteran who left that company in the early 1950s after a confrontation with Tip Moroney. He would figure prominently in the history of oil in the Canadian Arctic for the next two decades.[40]

Drillers in the Arctic Islands discovered some lead and zinc deposits and a small amount of natural gas, but the search for oil proved fruitless. Dome's operations closed down less than a year after its much-touted startup, although Gallagher and Dome would be heard from again. Enthusiasm, particularly among the big companies, noticeably cooled. Imperial Oil kept tracking developments, but adopted its usual cautious course, carrying out seismic surveys to identify potentially valuable acreage, but limiting itself to a "minimum position." When the production department proposed bidding on a new round of leases in the Arctic region in early 1964, President Twaits warned that "the amount of effort being applied to long term plays"—a reference to the Arctic—must be considered "in relation to the Company's total exploration program."[41]

On the other hand, smaller exploration-minded companies were looking at pooling resources to continue their costly ventures. In 1966 Sproule and the heads of some mining and oil companies persuaded the Toronto investment house Nesbitt, Thomson and Co. to underwrite Panarctic Oils Ltd., which would provide a platform for operations by up to seventy-five companies of varying sizes on a "farm-in" basis. Investor interest was boosted by the announcement of the Northern Minerals Exploration Program, funded by the federal government and promising to cover up to 40 per cent of exploration ventures in the Arctic, with generous repayment terms.

Within a year the government stepped in to help the floundering enterprise, taking 45 per cent ownership of Panarctic Oils. Gallagher occupied the chief management position, even though Dome Petroleum held only 5 per cent of the shares—a tribute to his capability as a politically minded entrepreneur and salesman. With government involvement, some larger companies joined up, including Canadian Pacific Oil and Gas and Cominco. Even Imperial took up a "farm-in" position on Immerk Island in the Beaufort Sea, although its preferred exploration area was in the familiar terrain of the Mackenzie River Delta.[42]

The biggest impetus for Canadian exploration in the Arctic, however, came from across the border in Alaska. American oil companies had been aware of the region's potential for many decades: in 1923 US President Harding had proclaimed a large part of Alaska's North Slope to be part of the country's strategic petroleum reserve, for exclusive development by the US Navy. There had been test drilling in the area during the Second World War, and in 1944 Wallace Pratt, geologist and vice president of Jersey Standard's affiliate Humble Oil, identified the Arctic as "marked by conspicuous seepages of oil . . . the last of our [petroleum] frontiers."[43] The Navy resumed surveys after the war, but there was little interest on the part of the oil industry in the region until the late 1950s. The renewed

Figure 10.3. Aerial view, Esso Resources Rig #3, Beaufort Sea (1983). Glenbow Archive
IP-7f-9, Imperial Oil Collection.

interest was triggered by two developments: the Suez crisis of 1956 and
the imposition of mandatory oil import controls by the US government
three years later. As Alaska moved toward statehood, the prospect of oil
leases outside of the federal reserve proved hard to resist: in 1964 the state
opened up areas near Prudhoe Bay for exploration.

The two largest players were Humble and the ubiquitous Richfield
Oil Company (which merged with Atlantic Refining Company in 1966),
but there were others lurking nearby, including Sinclair Oil and British
Petroleum (BP). Early work proved to be as frustrating to the Americans
as the Arctic Islands were for the Canadians; BP and Sinclair cut operations in 1967. But a year later, after an investment of $1 billion (USD),
Humble and Atlantic Richfield discovered an "elephant," estimated to be
larger than the fabled East Texas fields: 16 billion barrels of recoverable oil
and 35 trillion cubic feet of natural gas.[44]

Graham D. Taylor

In January 1970, after five years of drilling "dry holes," Imperial reported a "discovery well" at Atkinson Point, about 50 miles from Tuktoyaktuk. When drilled to 5700 feet it produced a "medium gravity low sulfur crude." The company continued to work in the Delta, with additional discoveries over the next three years. But President Jack Armstrong observed that "the oil found so far is insufficient to warrant commercial development," although the natural gas finds were "significant," and potential reserves could be 55 trillion cubic feet. Between 1965 and 1975, Imperial spent over $150 million (CAD) in the area, with six discoveries out of forty-six wells drilled—a better record for Imperial than its 133 dry holes before Leduc, as one wag suggested. Armstrong estimated that over the following decade Imperial could spend between $2.5 and $3 billion (CAD) on "exploration and development in the frontier areas," including the Arctic and the offshore Atlantic.[45]

The North Atlantic was another "frontier area" for oil companies in the 1960s–70s. Imperial had begun looking into this opportunity in 1966 when the premier of Newfoundland, Joey Smallwood, began offering permits for exploration. By 1971 the company had accumulated permits for 46 million acres, mostly off of Labrador. Using submersible rigs, Imperial drilled ten wells, but the results were so unpromising that it reduced its interests in the Grand Banks. The company also conducted test drillings off Sable Island in Nova Scotia, but, as in the Arctic islands, it mostly found gas deposits. Although there were large offshore finds on the other side of the Atlantic, in the North Sea during the 1970s, Imperial found the offshore prospects more frustrating than those it encountered in the Arctic.[46]

To accommodate the challenging conditions of drilling in the Mackenzie delta and the Beaufort Sea, Imperial built artificial islands constructed from silt dredged from the river bottom, then packed them with sand bags, rock, and other materials—including clamshells and even anti-submarine torpedo netting—to hold the soil in place, and gave them sloping surfaces to break incoming waves. The islands functioned only during the winter when the ice locked the "island" in place. Imperial constructed twenty of these islands that could operate in depths up to 60 feet. These makeshift rigs were eventually superseded by platforms resting on caisson-retained islands with ice-resistant walls that could operate in greater depths and for longer periods during the drilling season. These rigs could also be reused where their more primitive precursors were abandoned at the end of each winter. Gulf Canada pioneered with this design, which was adopted on a larger or modified scale by Imperial Oil and Dome Petroleum: the *Esso Glomar Beaufort Sea* was one of the largest of these specialized vessels in the 1980s.[47]

As in the case of the oil sands, transportation was a key requirement for the exploitation of Arctic oil and gas. To that end Humble Oil retrofitted a 115,000 ton supertanker, the SS *Manhattan*, as an icebreaker and launched it from Philadelphia in the summer of 1969 to go through the Northwest Passage to Prudhoe Bay. Although it successfully completed a round trip, the voyage was not without hazards. At one point, the *Manhattan* had to be aided by a Canadian coast guard icebreaker when it was stuck for thirty-four hours. The Canadian government protested that the route followed violated its sovereignty, and also expressed concerns over the potential pollution of Arctic waters by tanker traffic. The *Manhattan* took one more trip in 1970, but then suspended operations.[48]

Meanwhile, oil companies on both sides of the border were organizing consortia to develop plans for pipelines from the Arctic. In Alaska, Humble, Atlantic Richfield, and BP proposed to construct an 800 mile Trans Alaska Pipeline to carry crude oil from Prudhoe Bay to the port of Valdez. On the Canadian side, things were more complicated. In late 1969 Imperial Oil—together with Interprovincial Pipeline, Trans-Mountain Pipeline, and Canadian Bechtel—formed Mackenzie Valley Pipe Line Research Ltd. Eventually the undertaking brought in Hudson Bay Oil and Gas, Texaco Canada, Gulf Canada, and Shell Canada, and developed an alternative to the Trans Alaska consortium that would piggy-back Mackenzie Delta crude onto oil from Prudhoe Bay to Alberta where it could feed into the established pipelines to the United States. Not surprisingly, the Canadian government supported the consortium's argument that it would be environmentally safer than relying on tankers from Valdez to the US west coast. This was not persuasive with the oil majors who wanted to circumvent the US oil import quotas—although the *Exxon Valdez* disaster later demonstrated the merits of the argument.[49]

In 1973, pressured by public fears about rising foreign oil prices, the US Congress passed the Trans Alaska Pipeline Act, and the pipeline was completed in 1977. The amount of oil available in Arctic Canada was insufficient to justify another oil pipeline, but natural gas finds were ample, and the US market was growing. In 1972 Imperial joined another consortium, the Gas-Arctic Northwest Project Study Group, initiated by Trans Canada Pipe Lines with several gas utilities in the American Midwest: the objective was to build a gas pipeline from the Mackenzie Delta to southern Alberta where it would hook up with TCPL's lines, and would supply both the US and central Canada. Ultimately the consortium embraced more than twenty-five companies, including Atlantic Richfield, Standard Oil of Ohio, and Humble Oil, whose participation introduced the prospect of bringing in natural gas production from Prudhoe Bay. The plan that emerged, the Canadian Arctic Gas Pipeline, would run a 48-inch pipe 1600 miles, making it the largest pipeline in North America.

Before long the consortium faced rivals with different pipeline plans. One of the early participants had been Alberta Gas Pipeline Ltd., the trunk line set up in the 1950s by the government of Alberta to handle intraprovincial gas shipments. Bob Blair, who took charge of Alberta Gas Pipeline in 1969, had larger ambitions, including connecting Prudhoe Bay gas to his system. In 1974 he broke ranks with the Trans Canada group, forming an alliance with Frank McMahon's Westcoast Transmission in British Columbia and coming forward with a plan in which an Alberta Gas subsidiary, Foothills, would build a shorter pipeline from the Mackenzie Delta to the northern border. Here it would hook up with Westcoast to run a pipeline to the US border. This morphed into a more elaborate proposal with another partner, Utah-based Northwest Pipeline Corporation, which would build a gas line through Alaska, paralleling the Alaska Highway, hooking up with a Foothills pipeline built through the Yukon rather than along the Mackenzie River. To make things even more complicated, another US company, El Paso Gas, proposed to carry natural gas in tankers from Valdez to Los Angeles, bypassing Canada altogether.[50]

Each of these proposals would have to run the gamut of regulatory approvals in both the US and Canada; but they also faced unfamiliar technical, political, and environmental challenges. On the technical side, the land through which a pipeline would run presented a complex problem. Permafrost conditions characterized the terrain across the Northwest Territories, the Yukon, and northern Alaska, with depths ranging from 40 feet near the Alberta border up to 300 feet at Inuvik on the Mackenzie

Delta. Damage to permafrost would magnify the impact of frost heave and flooding in thaws. The standard practice of burying a pipeline or running it along the surface could result in permafrost destruction due to the heat generated by the passing fuel, which undermined structures and created potential pollution from pipeline breaks.

The builders of the Trans Alaska Pipe Line addressed this problem by running pipe well above the ground surface, although this aroused the ire of Native people, environmentalists, and others because of its effect on caribou migration. The Canadian Arctic Gas Pipe Line designers came up with an alternative approach: "chilling" the gas into packets that would be delivered through a pipeline seated in a trench with berms to offset possible frost heaves. During hearings on the Mackenzie Valley pipeline, critics raised the problems of maintaining the "chilling" through areas of discontinuous permafrost. Arctic Gas developers came up with more elaborate plans for insulating the pipes and maintaining heat probes to monitor the packets. All these plans of course would drive up the construction costs of the line, which were already substantial as the actual building of the line was restricted to winter months.[51]

By 1974 the Canadian Arctic Gas project had cost over $100 million (CAD) in preliminary research and development and Imperial's executive committee reckoned the ultimate cost would exceed $8.6 billion (CAD), which was more than $2 billion (CAD) over the 1972 estimates. Even with cost sharing in the consortium, "many participants were unwilling to sign a financial support agreement . . . in the event of upset conditions." Even the large backers—Exxon, BP, and Sohio—"vowed they would never undertake such a project again." Meanwhile, Blair and the Foothills group had wrapped themselves in the Canadian flag, exploiting the involvement of US majors in the Arctic Gas project, and adding that their plan to run the pipeline through the Yukon would have less potential impact on the permafrost. But the challenges confronting all the would-be pipeline builders extended well beyond technical issues.[52]

As they advanced to the frontiers in the Athabasca region and the Mackenzie River and Beaufort Sea, the oil companies encountered First Nations peoples to a much greater extent than they had before: the Cree in northern Alberta, and the Dene and Inuit in the Northwest Territories and the Yukon. As the numbers of Indigenous employees grew, Imperial

Oil addressed questions relating to both hiring for short-term construction jobs and longer-term commitments. At its peak, the company anticipated needing about 15,000 workers on pipeline construction, which would more than absorb the relatively small population of "employable northerners," estimated at about 2,000 in the Inuvik region. But the report also maintained that "flooding employment pools with requisitions for labourers" could be "a long-term catastrophe for northern residents." For the longer term, the executive committee discussed "educating young people to take 'permanent' jobs in drilling, production, pipeline operation and maintenance" through seasonal hiring and on the job training (in cooperation with the local Indigenous governments) for "students with good potential."[53]

But the issues relating to land use and project development would shape the more immediate relationship between First Nations leaders and the companies. This was a period of uncertainty and growing self-consciousness among the Indigenous people across northern Canada. In Alaska, the Alaska Federation of Natives was able to hold up progress on plans for the Trans Alaska Pipeline until their land claims were settled in 1971. In Canada, tensions were higher: the Cree people were confronting the Quebec government over the province's plans to take over and flood their lands as part of the James Bay Hydro Project. In 1969 the Canadian government of Pierre Trudeau had released a "Statement on Indian Policy" that proposed to eliminate the special status of First Nations.

In the Mackenzie River the Dene had a particular concern: in 1921, after the discovery of oil at Norman Wells, the federal government had imposed treaties that effectively deprived Indigenous people of full land rights although little had happened since then to carry out the implications of the agreements. In 1970 Bob Blair had orchestrated meetings with Indigenous groups in the Mackenzie River and maintained they had no clear understanding of the implications of a pipeline for their traditional hunting and fishing rights.[54]

At the same time, the pipeline advocates faced opposition from another quarter. The 1970s witnessed the dramatic growth of an environmental movement that ultimately challenged basic precepts of industrial development that undergirded the foundations of the oil and gas industry. In contrast to the conservationists of the early 1900s, the new environmentalists opposed not just pollution and waste but the degradation of the natural world by economic growth: in this context the threat to the "pristine" wilderness of the Arctic represented a clear and present danger to the planet, and certainly to Canada. The oil spills offshore Santa Barbara in 1969 and the *Arrow* disaster in Nova Scotia in 1970 dramatized the threats posed particularly by the oil and gas industry. In 1972 the Club of Rome's report, *The Limits to Growth*, magnified this argument, arguing that the uncontrolled exploitation of the world's fossil fuels and other resources would destroy the global economy over the next century.

In the United States there were well-established environmental organizations, including the Sierra Club, which had lobbied against the potential polluting effects of the Trans Alaska Pipe Line. In Canada the opposition to the Mackenzie Valley pipeline projects was more diffuse, featuring a largely intellectual group—the Canadian Arctic Resources Committee (CARC)—who were supported, providentially, by nationalist organizations such as the Council of Canadians. That council opposed the Canadian Arctic Gas consortium because of the role of multinational corporations like Exxon and BP. But the most important player in the unravelling of the Mackenzie Valley pipeline was an outlier, Thomas Berger.

Between 1972 and 1974, the federal Liberals under Pierre Trudeau clung to power through a tacit alliance with the New Democratic Party that led, among other things, to the establishment of Petro Canada during the first energy crisis in 1973. This arrangement fell apart the following year, but in the meantime, the Liberal government established a one-person Royal Commission to address the Mackenzie Valley pipeline issue, even though it would also be subject to review by the National Energy Board. Berger had served as leader of the NDP in British Columbia and as a provincial judge had demonstrated a commitment to aboriginal rights, attributes that led to his appointment as the commissioner. Aware of his proclivities, lawyers for the Canadian Arctic Gas consortium sought in vain to narrow the focus of the commission's investigation. For the next two years Berger conducted a wide-ranging review, meeting with community groups in the Mackenzie Valley as well as holding more formal hearings in Yellowknife where environmental groups like CARC were provided opportunities to testify along with oil industry representatives and technical experts.[55]

Meanwhile the National Energy Board started its own hearings in October 1975, but proceedings were delayed when environmentalists objected to the presence of a former Arctic Gas adviser on the board. Six months later the review resumed, meeting with hundreds of witnesses in Yellowknife, Inuvik, and Whitehorse as well as Ottawa. In the US, the Federal Power Commission undertook its review of the Mackenzie Valley Pipeline in 1976. As the proceedings dragged along, W.G. Charlton of Imperial Oil vented the frustration shared by many oil industry observers. "Interprovincial Pipe Line Limited was incorporated on April 30, 1949. Eighteen months later it began operations," he observed. In contrast, "the Gas Arctic Study Group was formed in mid-1972. At this time—42 months later—the movement of Arctic gas was still being studied by government agencies."[56]

On May 2, 1977, the US Federal Power Commission submitted its recommendations, with the members divided between the Arctic Gas and Foothills proposals. Seven days later, in his report *Northern Frontier, Northern Homeland*, Berger issued his far less equivocal conclusions: the Arctic Gas route was rejected outright because it would intrude on the Arctic Wildlife Range, and all pipeline construction should be suspended for ten years, pending the settlement of First Nations land claims in the region. The National Energy Board report also rejected the Arctic Gas proposal as "environmentally unacceptable" while giving a cautious recommendation for the Foothills project, with revisions.

This was by no means the end of the Mackenzie Valley Pipeline saga. Prime Minister Trudeau gave tentative approval to the Foothills project, and the US and Canada negotiated a Northern Border Pipeline Agreement to coordinate the Alaskan portion of the plan. But in 1979 the National Energy Board reported that Canada's gas supply needs could be satisfied without the Arctic component. By this time the estimated costs had risen to almost $15 billion (CAD) and the huge projects emerging from the National Energy Program absorbed the attention and financial resources of the government and the oil industry. A "pre-build" section covered under the Northern Border Pipeline Agreement was completed in 1982, but the Mackenzie Valley Pipeline was on hold, seemingly indefinitely.[57]

The events of 1977 put an end to the Arctic Gas consortium, but Imperial vowed to continue its exploration program in the north. At the same time, the company was forced to reassess its strategy: the "frontier" investments had yet to produce big payoffs, and Imperial had allowed leases in southern Alberta to expire just before a renewed round of new finds in the West Pembina and Elmworth fields. In 1978 the company reorganized its exploration and production operations into a new entity, Esso Resources Canada Ltd., with a budget of $139 million (CAD) for conventional oil exploration, while sustaining its one-third investment in Syncrude and continuing development of Cold Lake. In that same year, Imperial struck a deal with Canadian Hunter to invest another $150 million (CAD) for a 17.5 per cent share of that company's acreage in the Elmworth field. The timing was good as a new spike in oil and gas prices boosted its earnings, and the company began planning a return to the Mackenzie Valley through a resuscitation of its original foothold there at Norman Wells.[58]

Norman Wells was still producing oil for local needs, at a rate of about 2,000 bbl./day in the 1970s. Based on the tenfold rise in oil prices in 1979, Imperial contemplated an increase to 25,000 bbl./day with gross revenues of $250 million per year. The federal government would retain one-third ownership and 16 per cent of the revenues. Of course expanding production required the resuscitation of the pipeline. In 1981 Imperial and Interprovincial Pipeline [Enbridge] proposed the construction of a 12-inch line to run to Zama Lake on the northern Alberta border, ultimately to be tied into the Enbridge line from Edmonton. The project fit in with the Trudeau government's ambitious plans for northern oil and gas development, but the Dene and Metis organizations objected to the disruptions that would affect local communities and continuing land claims litigation, supported by the public interest group that had fought the Mackenzie Pipeline, the Committee for Justice and Liberty.[59]

In the summer of 1981, with oil prices still at high levels, the federal cabinet came up with a plan that would delay the project for two years to settle outstanding claims and sweetened the deal with an offer of a $10 million (CAD) job training program and an equity position for the Dene in a $9 million (CAD) joint venture with Esso Resources to expand drilling and servicing the Norman Wells fields. The National Energy Board gave conditional approval to the project, and a legal challenge by the Committee for Justice and Liberty was turned back. With the agreement of the First Nations' groups the project moved forward and the pipeline was officially opened in May 1985. By that time oil prices were plunging, but Esso Resources expressed confidence that improvements in drilling and refining technologies would enhance the recovery rate, and planned an expansion of the field by 150 new wells.[60]

Oil prices continued in the doldrums in the 1990s, and in 1996 Imperial, as part of a general retrenchment, closed the refinery at Norman Wells, although it continued to send crude oil through the pipeline until 2016, at a reduced rate of about 11,000 bbl./day by that point. Meanwhile, however, there was renewed interest in a gas pipeline from the Mackenzie Valley, intended for both Canadian and export markets, which were predicted to grow by 17 per cent between 2002–10. By the mid-1990s most of the major First Nations land claims were settled and the Mackenzie Valley highway was completed, easing some of the logistical challenges to earlier pipeline projects. Trans Canada Pipe Line had acquired the right of way permits held by Foothills for the original route. New gas field discoveries in the region had raised estimated supply rates to 800 million cubic feet/ day. The major companies involved in developing the fields were Exxon (now Exxon/Mobil) with Imperial, Conoco-Phillips, and Shell Canada. Imperial played a lead role in bringing a new consortium together, the Mackenzie Gas Project, in 2003–04.[61]

There was an additional participant. In 2000 representatives of thirty First Nations communities in the region formed the Aboriginal Pipeline Group (APG) specifically intended to be involved in the project. A key figure in the organization was Fred Carmichael, who began his career as the first aboriginal bush pilot in the Northwest Territories and was president of the Gwich'in Tribal Council as well as the chair of the APG. Through Trans Canada Pipe Line, the APG secured $80 million (CAD) towards financing its participation in the Mackenzie Gas Project, with Imperial holding 34 per cent, Exxon 5 per cent, and the balance by Conoco Phillips and Shell Canada. The estimated cost of the 800-mile gas pipeline was $7.5 billion (CAD). Imperial Oil and Exxon took a 40 per cent share of the project, with Conoco Phillips Canada holding 16 per cent and Shell Canada 11 per cent. The balance, one third of the total, was to go to APG, although the issue of its financing was not clear.

The consortium filed a formal application with the National Energy Board in 2004. But, as in the case of the original Mackenzie Valley Pipeline, the federal government set up a separate panel to review environmental and social issues. Once again, the process got bogged down. Environmental critics, including the Sierra Club of Canada and the Pembina Institute, again raised the issue of damage to the permafrost, and expressed concern over the role of the pipeline in the increasingly controversial development of the oil sands, as the gas could be diverted in part to service the energy needs of those projects. The financing of the APG participation remained a matter of contention: at one point Imperial threatened to pull out of the project. The federal government sought to paper over divisions by pledging $500 million (CAD) to underwrite APG's involvement plus another $40 million (CAD) to support an aboriginal training fund. Although the government declined to take an equity position in the project, it eventually agreed to absorb a "portion of the risk" in return for future royalty sharing. In 2011 when the National Energy Board gave its final approval, tied to over 200 "conditions," the project's cost had swelled to $16 billion (CAD). By this point Exxon had joined with Trans Canada in an even larger Alaska gas pipeline project that could compete with the Mackenzie Valley project.[62]

This was not the end of the tribulations of the Mackenzie Valley Gas Project. When the proposal went to the National Energy Board in 2004, natural gas was priced at over $15/mm BTUs, but by the time the approval had gone through, it had slumped to $4.57/mmBTUs, in part because of the "shale gas revolution" in the United States. Imperial hoped to resuscitate the venture by transforming its focus to developing a liquefied natural gas (LGN) dimension. LGN technology had been around for almost a century but came into more general use in the 1970s–80s. Exxon was a latecomer to this field but became more interested in it after the 1999 merger with Mobil, which had developed LGN operations in Qatar—the Alaska gas pipeline was under consideration for conversion to an LGN operation. If Imperial followed suit, the pipeline from the Mackenzie Valley would be shortened and tied to an LGN terminal to be established in northern British Columbia. In 2015 the Mackenzie Gas Project backers requested an extension of the "sunset clause" for completion of the line from 2018 to 2022. A year later the National Energy Board agreed to the extension, but with gas prices remaining in the doldrums, the project was in limbo.[63]

Meanwhile, in January 2017, Imperial announced that it was suspending operations on its Norman Wells fields for an indefinite period. Enbridge had shut down the pipeline to Zama in the autumn of 2016 because of problems with ground stability around the line. The line had experienced more than seventy reports of spills, leaks, and fires over the preceding decade, some of them leading to contamination of the town's water supply. The federal government had reported a decline in its revenue share from the operation, from $102 million (CAD) in 2010 to $75 million (CAD) in 2014. Imperial estimated the continued life span of the field at ten years, and was seeking a buyer. According to one report, "this development is further proof that the industry's majors are staging a quiet retreat from Canada's Arctic, ending the . . . prospects in the Central Mackenzie Valley."[64] Forty years after Thomas Berger's report, the Mackenzie Valley Pipeline remained on hold, and after almost a century of operations at Norman Wells, Imperial Oil was pulling out of its first venture on Canada's "northern frontier."

• EPILOGUE •

SINCE 1980

11

THE ROLLER COASTER

From Stability to Chaos

From its earliest days the oil industry in both the United States and Canada had been plagued by boom and bust cycles, with crude prices escalating from $1 to $10 per barrel and back again within a matter of months. Rockefeller made price stability a major objective for his strategy of integration and amalgamation, which was attained by the 1880s, but the challenges persisted through more than half a century. The discovery of large oil fields in the early twentieth century in Texas, Mexico, Russia, Persia, and the Dutch East Indies brought new competitors onto the scene, and the forced breakup of the Standard Oil Trust exacerbated the situation. Each new discovery attracted hordes of enterprising wildcatters, reproducing the cycles that had roiled the oil fields of Pennsylvania and Petrolia.

The 1920s–30s witnessed the biggest finds yet in Oklahoma and Texas. The effort of the large international companies to impose price stability through the "As Is" cartel arrangement in 1928 was undermined by these developments. The Texas Railroad Commission, backed up by the US federal government in the depths of the Great Depression, established some degree of price stability. Because the oil output of the Texas fields was so large, accounting for almost half the world's crude production, the system imposed by the state regulatory commission in effect achieved a degree of predictability in oil prices that Rockefeller would have appreciated. After the Second World War, the measures of the "As Is" cartel (dubbed the "Seven Sisters") and the Texas Railroad Commission resulted in an

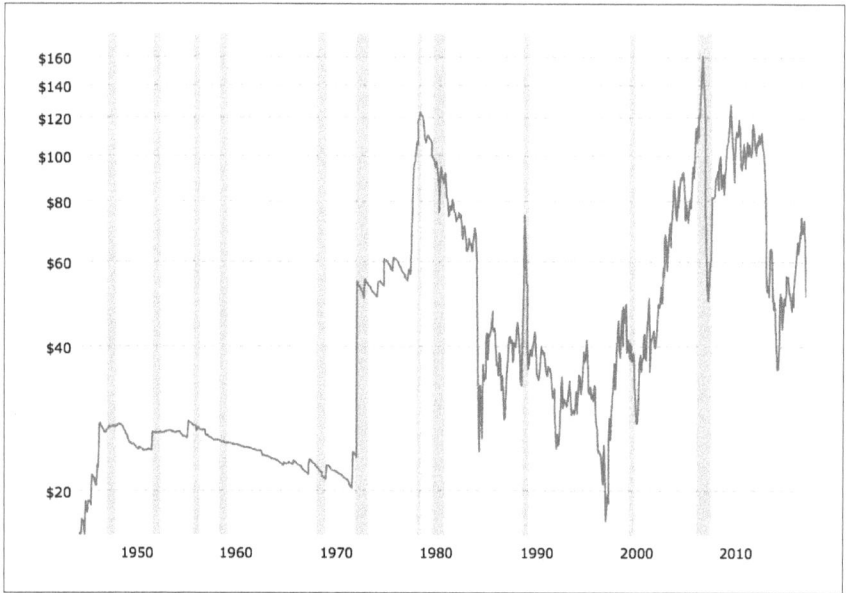

FIGURE 11.1. WTI Crude Oil Prices from 1946 (in USD). Courtesy of Macro Trends LLC, 2018.

unprecedented period of price stability that lasted until the early 1970s, absorbing and coordinating the growth of large new producers in the Middle East, Venezuela, and Canada.[1]

This period also saw the dramatic growth of petroleum consumption, with the vast expansion of the auto industry, accompanied by increased use of oil for residential heating, electrical power generation, and as a feedstock for petrochemicals. Escalating market demand also lured more entrepreneurs into the industry, not just into the search for new sources but also into refining and marketing. The appearance of new would-be players on the scene provided bargaining leverage to political leaders in the countries graced with the resource base, particularly those in the "concession states" of the Middle East who controlled access to these oil riches and increasingly felt that the big companies were retaining the lion's share of the revenues.[2]

Graham D. Taylor

Tensions between the producing countries and the international oil companies grew in the 1960s. The "official" crude oil prices, which determined tax sharing and royalty payments to the producing states, hovered around $1.00/bbl. (USD). But the entry of oil from the Soviet Union affected actual market costs for refiners. The oil majors, particularly Jersey Standard, believed that the gap between the official and market costs of crude placed them at a disadvantage with independent refiners, particularly the Italian company ENI. To offset that problem, the big oil companies unilaterally reduced the official crude oil price in 1959. This move led to the creation of an alliance of the producer states, led by Venezuela and Saudi Arabia and called the Organization of Petroleum Exporting Countries (OPEC), a year later.

For much of the following decade the oil majors regarded OPEC as a "paper tiger." A test of this view came during the Arab-Israeli war of 1967 when the Arab member states of OPEC sought to embargo the shipment of oil to countries such as the US that were perceived as supporting Israel. The failure of that effort appeared to demonstrate that OPEC was an inherently unstable cartel of countries with wildly different objectives. But by 1970–71 the situation was changing dramatically. Despite the Prudhoe Bay discoveries the United States had become a net importer of petroleum, while demand in Western Europe and Japan provided increasing leverage to the OPEC states. In 1971 Jersey Standard found itself in an awkward position in Libya, where it had made substantial investments, forced to accept concessions to the new ruler of that country—Muammar Qadaffi— that resulted in a wider price rise from $1 to $2/bbl. (USD).

Two years later emboldened members of OPEC met in Vienna and proposed to more than double the posted price of their oil exports, based on the value of Saudi Arabian light crude, to $5/bbl. (USD). In the midst of their deliberations another Arab-Israeli war erupted, and the Arab oil states once again agreed to cut production and mount an embargo against countries supporting Israel. In this situation, the US did not have the excess capacity to offset the Middle East supplies, and other OPEC members including Iran chose to stand on the sidelines. By the end of the year the OPEC posted price had spiked to $11.65/bbl. (USD) while "spot prices" rose even higher, as traders from non-OPEC countries exploited panic buying. The embargo was lifted in March 1974 but posted prices remained above $10/bbl. (USD) and the producing states extracted further conces-sions from the large refining companies, including nationalizing the fields and refineries in their own countries. The era of price stability in world oil markets had unravelled.[3] Another round of price spikes came in 1979–80 when the Iranian revolution and Iran-Iraq war disrupted exports from the Middle East. Even before the fall of the Shah of Iran, spot oil prices surged from $12.80 to $21.80/bbl. (USD) and then on to $40/bbl. (USD) by the end of 1979. OPEC, which had not created this chaotic situation, nevertheless exploited the crisis. By 1981 the OPEC posted price was $34/bbl. (USD). Just as significantly, the major consuming countries, including the United States and Canada, began to frame energy policies based on the assumption that high oil prices were here to stay.[4]

But OPEC, much like the early producer cartels, was inherently un-stable. Many member countries habitually exceeded their quotas, selling advantageously on the spot market. Fundamentally the organization was divided between countries like Iran and Venezuela with diminishing re-serves and large politically volatile populations, and the oil-rich, thinly populated Arab nations of the Persian Gulf, particularly Saudi Arabia. Wary of the expansionist inclinations of their bellicose neighbours, Iran and Iraq, and with ties to the United States going back to the Second World War, the Saudis sought stability in the market, with prices set at a level that would sustain the consuming countries. The disruptive circumstances of the 1970s favoured the views of OPEC hardliners.

In 1981, however, market conditions began to change. Oil demand fell, due in part to a hard recession in the industrialized nations and con-servation measures that were particularly effective in Japan and Western Europe. North Sea oil began to come on-stream and new discoveries in Africa offered the prospect of larger non-OPEC reserves. For several years Saudi Arabia tried to sustain a benchmark price of $29/bbl. (USD) but by 1985, with its OPEC partners cheating by sales on the spot markets, the Saudis deliberately lifted production limits, although it tried to maintain prices that would ensure marginal profits to the big refining companies. By the middle of 1986 Arab light crude prices fell from $28/bbl. (USD) to $11/bbl. (USD).[5]

After this triumph, Saudi Arabia exercised leadership of OPEC, with tacit support from the United States, through its potential capability to discipline the other members by increasing or reducing production. Cheating continued to be a problem for the cartel, and prices could spike up when unforeseen events intruded, as happened in 1990–91with the collapse of the Soviet Union and the Gulf War. But markets achieved relative stability between 1991 and 2003, with price ranges fluctuating between $18/bbl. (USD) and $30/bbl. (USD), and OPEC retained a 35 to 40 per cent market share.[6]

This happy equilibrium began to unravel after 2003. The Iraq War temporarily removed a major producer from the field, and the expansion of Russian production stalled in the context of power struggles within the post-Soviet elite. More significantly, the rapid industrial development of "emerging economies," particularly China (as well as India and Brazil), boosted demand. By 2005 Saudi Arabia indicated that its production capacity was being strained, although it subsequently announced plans to develop hitherto untapped fields. By this time "peak oil" warnings resurfaced for the first time since the 1970s, feeding speculation in oil futures. During 2004–05, posted prices rose from $28/bbl. (USD) to $42/bbl. (USD), and continued to surge, climbing to $140/bbl. (USD) in 2008.

By this time both producers and governments were returning to the mindset, which prevailed in 1980, that high oil prices would be a permanent feature. The oil sands once again attracted new entrants, Arctic dreams resurfaced, and projects involving exploitation of higher-cost sources in places like Kazakhstan and Chad looked more feasible. But as before, the market began to shift. The collapse of the US real-estate bubble in 2008 spread to Europe, leading to the worst recession in the industrialized nations since the 1930s. Although continuing economic growth in China propped up demand, by 2016 crude prices were plummeting from over $115/bbl. (USD) to less than $30/bbl. (USD), reminiscent of the early days of the industry in North America. By 2017 prices seemed to have firmed up to over $40/bbl. (USD) but the underlying uncertainties remained.

Developments on the supply side played an important part in this downturn. After 2006 when Saudi Arabia embarked on a costly expansion into refining and natural gas production, the country had become reluctant to take on the task that it had pursued in the 1980s, using its own oil production rate to determine OPEC prices. None of the other cartel members had the capacity to play this role, and in any case they all wanted to continue to increase their production while the price was high. Inevitably this course led to saturation of a diminishing market.

But another element significantly affected this situation. The "shale revolution" began in the 1980s when the Houston oil and gas producer George Mitchell (and others) developed a hydraulic fracturing process to reach petroleum in shale rock areas that had defied conventional drilling. Initially expensive, by the year 2000 "fracking" techniques were yielding profitable quantities of gas from shale, enabling the dramatic growth of natural gas to replace both coal and oil in the heating and industrial fuel markets. By 2015 fracking had also expanded production of shale oil particularly in the United States. Since shale oil wells had a much shorter lifespan than conventional wells, producers were driven to exploit them as fast as possible and expand to new reservoirs constantly. Assumptions that shale production, like that in the oil sands, required oil prices in the $60+/bbl. (USD) range to be profitable proved wrong—at least in the short run—given the incentives to keep producing while trying to achieve cost efficiencies.[7]

The gyrations in oil prices from 1971 through 2016 (and likely beyond) affected the entire industry, but particularly the big oil companies that had exercised dominance in the preceding era, and Exxon perhaps most of all. For one thing Exxon had the misfortune of holding a stake in virtually all of the OPEC countries. It had been one of the first oil majors to move into Venezuela in the early 1900s, and gained a foothold in each of the Middle East oil consortia: Iraq in the 1920s, Aramco in the 1940s, and Iran after the 1953 coup. It had a large investment in the Libyan oil fields in the 1960s. Of course Exxon had many other commitments (including Canada), but upheavals in some of its largest supplier nations were bound to have serious consequences.

By the mid-1980s, Exxon found itself in a situation similar to the one that confronted Walter Teagle as head of Jersey Standard in 1918: a company with huge refining capacity, well-running transportation and distribution systems, strong research capabilities—but limited access, let alone control over crude oil reserves. One of the major goals of the company's chief executives, from Ken Jamieson in the 1970s to Rex Tillerson in the second decade of the twenty-first century, was to secure reasonably predictable supplies of oil and gas for its far-flung operations.

In the 1970s this quest led Exxon to expand offshore drilling, from California and the Gulf of Mexico to the North Sea and Malaysia. It also supported the development of Imperial's ventures in the oil sands and the Arctic, until the price collapse of 1985–86. By the 1990s post-Soviet Russia's newly privatized resources beckoned, leading to intricate and often frustrating "oil diplomacy" with that country's feuding power brokers. Exxon also sought footholds in undeveloped oil fields in the African states of Chad, Cameroon, and Angola, embroiling the company with dictators and revolutionaries reminiscent of its experiences in Mexico and Venezuela in the early twentieth century.[8]

Despite these difficulties and recurring controversies at home—US Congressional investigations of alleged profiteering by oil majors during the energy crises of the 1970s, environmental protests following the *Exxon Valdez* disaster in 1989—the company retained its powerful role in the industry, in part due to its organizational capabilities honed over more than a century, technological leadership, and the sheer size of its financial resources. As the twentieth century ended, a new struggle for power among the largest global oil companies ensued, culminating in a series of gigantic mergers in the industry that were themselves triggered by a price fall in the wake of the sudden financial collapse of the "Asian Tigers"—South Korea, Taiwan, Hong Kong, and Singapore, followed by other, larger East Asian economies—in 1998. BP [British Petroleum] pursued Mobil [Standard of New York] but eventually settled for a takeover of Amoco [formerly Standard of Indiana], and then Arco [Atlantic Richfield] with its large holdings in Alaska. These events precipitated more mergers, and Exxon's chief executive Lee Raymond—wary of the growing strength of BP and seeking to overtake the dominant player, Royal Dutch Shell— quickly orchestrated an agreement with Mobil. By the end of 1999 the world of oil had come resemble the one that existed before the breakup of the Standard Oil Trust in 1911, with four giant companies left standing: Shell, BP, Chevron [Standard of California], and Exxon Mobil.[9]

Canada was not immune to the wild gyrations in oil prices throughout this period, although the fluctuations were attenuated by the unusual circumstances of being both an exporter and importer of petroleum. Between 1974 and 1985, the Canadian government imposed controls on crude oil prices, which involved export taxes and import subsidies as well as regulations on the price of domestic production, leading to tense confrontations with the producing provinces, as discussed below. During that time period Canadian oil prices rose from less than $5/bbl. (CAD) to a peak of $37.50/bbl. (CAD) in 1984. Government regulation generated a gap with world oil prices that ranged as high as $10/bbl. (USD) in the "second energy crisis" of 1979–81.

In 1985 the "Western Accord" between the federal government and the western oil-producing provinces removed the regulatory regime. From that point, Canadian crude oil prices began to track two oil major global price benchmarks, West Texas Intermediate (WTI) light crude and Brent Crude, based on North Sea production. As these were valued in US dollars, fluctuations in the US-Canada exchange rate contributed to variations between Canadian and benchmark price ranges. From a low of $18/bbl. (CAD) in 1985, crude prices rose to $30/bbl. (CAD) in 1990 but fell back again by the end of the decade.

Canadian prices continued to track the benchmark indicators, but after 2004 a new marker was established by four of the largest oil sands producers—EnCana, Petro Canada, Canadian Natural Resources, and Talisman Oil—designated Western Select Crude (WSC). The pricing was applied to heavy crude oils with high acidic content with a limited range of refineries suited to process the product. As world oil prices began to rise again after 2005, WSC oil became more attractive, despite its high cost of production and processing and the continuing challenges of transportation to major consumer markets. But WSC prices trailed the other benchmarks throughout the ensuing boom and bust between 2008 and 2016. In 2013, WSC reached a peak of $82/bbl. (USD) while WTI and Brent ranged between $100–$110/bbl. (USD). WSC prices fell to $38/bbl. (USD) in 2016 with WTI and Brent hovering in the $60–$64/bbl. (USD) range. By this time heavy oil and upgraded bitumen comprised the preponderance of Canadian oil exports; conventional crude oil production had declined steadily since the 1980s to less than 1 million bbl./day while oil sands output had risen to 2.5 million bbl./day.[10]

The Energy Crises, 1973–1985

Even before the OPEC price hikes and the Arab oil embargo in the autumn of 1973, the conditions that shaped Canada's National Oil Policy were changing. In 1968–69 new political administrations took power in Washington and Ottawa, and both had agendas that embraced a more nationalist perspective than their predecessors. The Republican president Richard Nixon sought to straddle a political party populated by internationalist and protectionist factions. Although the Liberal party remained in power in Canada, the new leader, Pierre Trudeau, displayed a greater interest than had his predecessors in expanding the role of government in economic affairs.

In 1970 the US government unilaterally terminated Canada's exemption from the Mandatory Oil Import Control program. This was a preview of tough measures Nixon imposed on Japan and other US trading partners a year later, but it came as a shock to the Canadian government. During the 1960s continentalist trends had prevailed: the Lyndon Johnson administration had supported the extension of Canada's Interprovincial Pipeline system to Chicago, which opened the huge Midwest market to Imperial and other exporters—despite protests from some US producers.[11]

Meanwhile, in Canada, the new Department of Energy, Mines and Resources (EMR) was infiltrated by advocates of a "national" oil company to offset the influence of foreign-owned majors like Imperial Oil and Shell. Trudeau was not prepared to endorse such a venture at this point, but elevating the EMR fit into his efforts to centralize control of government policymaking in the prime minister's office.[12]

Nixon's move against Canadian exports backfired because of the growing US demand for oil and gas products. Oil exports surged through 1971–72, to the point where the Canadian government became alarmed: exports rose from 49 per cent of domestic production in 1969 to 63 per cent by 1973. In March 1973 the cabinet ruled that further exports would require approval by the National Energy Board, which imposed a restriction on exports to 1.25 million bbl./day, a relatively minor cut but symbolic of the changed circumstances. Six months later, the Trudeau government unveiled a more comprehensive plan—in advance of the OPEC crisis. A 15 per cent tax was imposed on oil exports, petroleum prices were to be "frozen" for five months, and a pipeline would be built between Toronto and Montreal, with government subsidies if necessary: the project would be completed by Interprovincial in 1976.[13]

The OPEC crisis dictated further actions. In November 1973 Prime Minister Trudeau announced that the price for Alberta crude oil would be regulated to prevent unsustainable price hikes for eastern Canada. The oil export tax, which had already been raised by 40 cents per barrel in September, was increased again by $1.90 per barrel. The rationale was that adequate reserves of heating fuel were needed for the ensuing winter months and that US refiners, clamouring for Canadian crude supplies, could deplete domestic oil sources. Soon the temporary restrictions on exports to the US were moving toward permanence: in November 1974 Donald MacDonald, the Energy Minister, unveiled a plan that would phase out oil exports completely within eight years.[14]

Meanwhile, the Trudeau government had to manoeuvre its way between the producing provinces, particularly Alberta, which wanted to see oil prices rise to "international" levels and the New Democratic Party, which opposed any increase in domestic prices. Since 1972 the Liberals, to buttress their minority government, had formed a tacit alliance with the NDP, but by early 1974 Trudeau hoped that the measures imposed during the energy crisis would boost his party's fortunes in an upcoming election. In March 1974 the federal government reached an agreement with Alberta that raised the domestic crude price from $3.80/bbl. (CAD) to $6.50/bbl. (CAD), roughly $4 per barrel less than the export price, while retaining the taxes on exports. An exception to the regulated price of domestic oil would be made for oil sands production. Two months later Trudeau led his party to a majority electoral victory.[15]

The combined impact of the imposition of regulated prices on western Canadian oil and the virtual ban on exports encountered pushback, from the oil industry as well as the producing provinces. The oil majors, including Imperial, were accustomed to being consulted by the National Energy Board about prospective policy changes, but the initiative had now shifted to the Department of Energy, Mines and Resources and new measures, often taken in haste, were made without consultation. In April 1974, Alberta increased its royalties, while Ottawa refused to allow the oil companies to apply them against federal taxes—a by-product of the continuing

FIGURE 11.2. Jack Armstrong, 1980. Glenbow Archive IP-26-8b – Armstrong, J.A. – 1980–81, Imperial Oil Collection.

feud between the federal and provincial governments. A report to Imperial Oil's Executive Committee noted that while federal tax revenues and provincial royalty revenues would both quadruple as a result of these arrangements, the oil producers' revenues would decline from \$1.18/bbl. to 0.71/bbl. (CAD)—a formula that would reduce "the viability of cash flows."[16]

Many conventional oil producers in Canada cancelled plans for exploration and development and "drilling rigs fled south." With its large long-term investments in the oil sands and Arctic exploration, Imperial Oil could not just pick up its marbles and leave the scene. Jack Armstrong, however, vented the company's frustrations in remarks to shareholders a year later: "Less than two weeks following the 1974 Annual Meeting we . . . faced . . . a situation where federal, as well as provincial policies . . . switched from being venture-oriented to revenue-oriented . . . No one anticipated an intensification of the federal/provincial struggle over resource revenue sharing with ensuing tax/royalty legislation that would jeopard-ize Canada's future supply of oil and natural gas."[17]

For all the grumbling, Imperial Oil did not come out too badly from the energy crisis of 1973–74. Total revenues doubled between 1972 and 1975, with petroleum products contributing over 50 per cent; earnings per share rose from $1.18 to $1.92 (CAD), and working capital increased from $375 million to $572 million (CAD). Royalties did indeed take a bite, rising from $81 million in 1972 to $273 million (CAD) in 1975, an increase of 237 per cent. As Armstrong implied, Imperial's conventional crude reserves declined in this period but exploration expenditures held steady and Imperial doubled its commitment to Syncrude, rising to over $100 million (CAD) by 1975—an acceleration occasioned in part by the reorganization of the consortium after Atlantic Richfield withdrawal and the exemption of the oil sands from price regulation.[18]

The first energy crisis left one more legacy in Canada. In October 1974, three months after a Liberal majority government was elected, a bill in Parliament was introduced establishing Petro Canada, which among a range of capabilities was given a mandate "for public intervention in the Canadian energy industries." The New Democratic Party had been agitat-ing for a "national oil company" for several years, but the genesis of Petro Canada probably owed more to the nationalist wing of the Liberals, going back to the days of Walter Gordon, the scourge of the multinationals in the 1960s. Trudeau was hardly a nationalist in the conventional sense, but he was willing to wield the full powers of the state when he chose, as dem-onstrated by the invocation of the War Measures Act during the October Crisis in 1970. The designers of Petro Canada—Joel Bell and Wilbert Hopper—had large ambitions for their creation, and Hopper would run the crown corporation until the 1990s.[19]

If Petro Canada was a stick to beat the oil industry, the federal govern-ment also offered carrots, beginning with a "super-depletion allowance" for a fast write-off of exploration and drilling costs, intended particularly to promote Arctic and offshore Newfoundland resource development. In 1977 Donald MacDonald, now Finance Minister, announced that certain "frontier" oil exploration costs could be written off within two years at a 66.67 per cent rate (which combined with a revised regular depletion al-lowance of 33.33 per cent amounted to a full write-off). In industry circles this was referred to as the "Gallagher allowance," as a major beneficiary was Jack Gallagher's Dome Petroleum, which he was positioning to be a "chosen instrument" for Canada's northern oil development. This was a precursor to the "Petroleum Incentive Program" (PIP) grants that were incorporated into the National Energy Program unveiled in 1980.[20]

In 1979 the Liberals were turned out of office in Ottawa for the first time since 1962. The Progressive Conservative government under Joe Clark proved to be short-lived for a variety of reasons, including the onset of a second international energy crisis precipitated by the revolution in Iran and the Iran-Iraq war. Once again the New Democratic Party joined forces with the Liberals to topple Clark. Trudeau led the Liberals to victory in an election in February 1980 promising lower energy prices, security of supply, and protection of "Canadian" oil. Trudeau personally was more interested in securing repatriation of the Canadian constitution, but a "strategy committee" under his close aide Marc Lalonde, who would become Minister of Energy, Mines and Resources, spent the Liberals' months in exile designing a comprehensive interventionist energy policy for the country.

The National Energy Program (NEP), unveiled on October 1980, was a complex array of subsidies, taxes, and regulatory measures that "turned the West against the East and manufacturers against natural energy suppliers while simultaneously enriching the coffers of the central government."[21] Consumers would continue to be subsidized, indirectly, by the establishment of a "blended" national price that would include imported oil, synthetic oil, and domestic conventional oil, to be administered through an Oil Import Compensation Program, that had already proven to be a disaster in the United States. Oil exports were (again) to be phased out, this time by 1990. "Frontier" oil exploration and development would be subsidized, emphasizing the role of the publicly owned Petro Canada and Pan Arctic Oils.

To pay for the projected $11 billion (CAD) cost, an 8 per cent Petroleum and Gas Revenue Tax (PGRT) would be imposed on net production revenues of oil and gas companies, with the provision that it could not be deducted from other taxes due. The most politically controversial measure was a new revenue-sharing formula between the federal government, the "producing provinces" (mainly Alberta), and the industry, so that the federal share would triple to 30 per cent—at the expense of the other two "partners."[22]

For the oil companies, and particularly for the multinationals like Imperial, there were some key irritants in addition to the tax and revenue-sharing components. The depletion and "super-depletion" allowances were terminated, to be replaced by federal grants under the Petroleum Incentives Program (PIP), which would give preferential treatment to companies with more than 50 per cent Canadian ownership. Dome Petroleum, which did not qualify, scrambled to set up an affiliate, Dome Canada, selling 52 per cent of the shares to Canadians. Imperial Oil did not have this opportunity, although it did farm out some of its holdings in the Beaufort Sea area to companies that met the "Canadian content" requirement. As a further aggravation of the private oil industry, another tax on oil products was included to enable Petro Canada to buy up other companies.[23]

In the meantime Alberta, in retaliation against the revenue sharing revisions of the NEP, vowed to cut its production by 15 per cent commencing in March 1981, and held up approval of Imperial's Cold Lake expansion project, as well as Alsands, another large oil sands undertaking by a consortium led by Shell. Once again the oil companies were caught in the middle of a constitutional struggle between the federal government and Alberta.

At this point, despite their preference for settling such issues behind the scenes, Imperial's executives mounted an unusual public counterattack. On November 19, Lalonde spoke to investment advisers in New York, cautioning them not to overreact to the NEP, and maintaining that the foreign-owned oil companies in Canada were on board. Later that day, Jack Armstrong, now the board chairman of Imperial, announced that his company was shelving further development of the Cold Lake oil sands project. This was a somewhat improbable move, since earlier in the year Imperial had issued $1 billion (CAD) in new stock, at below-market prices, to its shareholders, to help finance projects over the next decade, including a $7 billion (CAD) commitment to Cold Lake. Nevertheless, the very next day Lalonde met with Armstrong and offered Imperial at $40 million (CAD) loan to cover continuing development costs at Cold Lake, with no "Canadianization" strings attached, even though Petro Canada was exhibiting an interest in entering one of the oil sands consortia.

Cynical observers speculated that these were pre-rehearsed events intended to put pressure on Alberta to lift its restraints on oil sands development. But a few days later Armstrong indicated Imperial might halt a $300 million (CAD) "enhanced oil recovery" project at Judy Creek in Alberta. Imperial's president J.R. Livingstone argued that the $38/bbl. (CAD) "blended" price for synthetic crude was insufficient to justify expanding Cold Lake. In early January 1981 Armstrong asserted that if NEP passed, Imperial would cut capital spending by $2.5 billion (CAD) over the next four years, and in a presentation to the National Energy Board, Imperial warned it would reduce estimated production by 180,000 bbl./ day, a 14 per cent cut.[24]

Through the spring and summer of 1981, Alberta and the federal government bickered over the NEP, as Premier Peter Lougheed threatened more production cuts. In July Imperial announced that, despite the $40 million loan, it was suspending further work at Cold Lake, a move Lalonde denounced in Parliament as "blackmail." But by September, with the independents as well as multinational companies up in arms over NEP, Ottawa was prepared to cut a deal with Alberta, giving the province more control over PIP grants and agreeing to reduce its share of oil revenues to 25.5 per cent. The price of domestic oil was allowed to rise by revising the "blending" formula to recognize the higher costs of "new" oil from the Arctic and the oil sands.[25]

Even as Lougheed and Trudeau were (warily) toasting their agreement, the real world of oil prices was sliding out from under them. In May 1982 the Alsands "megaproject" dissolved; Dome Petroleum careened toward bankruptcy; the federal deficit had doubled to $20 billion (CAD). Although the decline in oil prices was less severe than the big drop to come in 1985–86, even a modest change was sufficient to puncture the speculative bubble in Canadian oil markets, aggravated by a deepening recession across the industrial world. The Liberal government in Ottawa tottered on until 1984 when a newly energized Progressive Conservative party led by Brian Mulroney displaced them. The NEP was rapidly dismantled by the new Energy Minister, Patricia Carney, rolling back many of the program's tax measures. The PIP was replaced with new tax incentives that were extended to foreign-owned companies, and in 1985 a new "Western Accord" was signed with Alberta and the other western oil-producing provinces.

In 1989 a Free Trade Agreement was signed between the US and Canada that was intended to prevent the recurrence of the kind of nationalist approach represented by the NEP.[26]

For Alberta, the confrontation with Ottawa during the NEP era was seared into political memory for the next generation. Imperial Oil too experienced turmoil through the NEP years, although the impact may have been less lingering. Between 1975 and 1980 the company's revenues more than doubled from $3 billion to $6.2 billion (CAD) and net earnings grew even more from $263 million to $682 million (CAD). Between 1981 and 1985 even as rising oil and gas prices pushed revenue upwards, the rate of growth slowed, going from $8 billion in 1981 to $8.8 billion in 1985 (CAD). But net earnings fell most sharply from $465 million in 1981 to $289 million (CAD) in the following year, and only recovered its pre-1980 level after 1985. Return on investment dipped from 8.9 per cent in 1981 to 5.3 per cent in 1983, rising to 9.2 per cent in 1985.[27]

Taxes and levies imposed through the NEP contributed to this slackening: the Petroleum and Gas Revenue tax alone took $91 million (CAD) of Imperial's earnings in 1981. But there were other factors at work. During the late 1970s exploration and development of conventional oil wells spiked in 1978 but then subsided. Proved reserves of natural gas fell steadily. Synthetic oil production at Syncrude and Cold Lake grew after 1977 but only accounted for 12 per cent of total output. The controversy between Alberta and Ottawa in 1980–81 led Imperial to shutter Cold Lake for several years. Drilling in the Arctic and Atlantic shelf produced mostly natural gas or dry holes. The restrictions on non-Canadian investment in frontier areas under the NEP limited Imperial's opportunities to expand although in 1982 the federal government contributed $600 million (CAD) to a Beaufort Sea venture with Imperial. Meanwhile, however, the company shelved a joint venture with Alberta Energy to build a new petrochemical plant, sold its interest in Trans Mountain Pipe Line and instituted staff cuts for the first time in many years.[28]

Imperial Oil's troubles occasioned some *schadenfreude* in industry circles during this time. Articles with titles such as "The Age of Imperialism Comes to an End" appeared. Liberal and NDP politicians proclaimed with ill-concealed satisfaction that Imperial would soon be eclipsed by Petro-Canada as the country's largest oil company. Even Peter Foster, a sympathetic journalist, expressed concern that Imperial had made misjudgments, not so much in its business strategy as in underestimating its public relations and the ability of political foes and business rivals to exploit its vulnerabilities.[29]

Nevertheless, Foster also argued, "rumours of Imperial's demise . . . have been greatly exaggerated." By 1984 Cold Lake was back in operation with plans for further expansion, and Syncrude increased output to 129,000 bbl./day. An enhanced recovery operation at Judy Creek and completion of Norman wells expansion increased conventional oil production by 8 per cent in 1986. Service stations were upgraded, featuring convenience stores and automated bank machines—another turn in the cyclic evolution of gas retailing. Exxon's agricultural chemicals division was assigned to Esso Chemical Co. in Redwater, Alberta. Although the company was to experience financial setbacks following the takeover of Texaco Canada and the recession of the early 1990s, it remained the industry leader in Canada in 1996, holding one third of the assets of the sector and accounting for 34 per cent of the sales of petroleum products ahead of Nova (22 per cent), Shell Canada (16 per cent), Amoco (16 per cent), and Petro Canada (15 per cent).[30]

EXXON AND IMPERIAL: TIES THAT BIND

In the midst of the controversies over the National Energy Program, Imperial and other Canadian oil multinationals faced a challenge on another front. In March 1981 Robert Bertrand, the Director of Investigation and Research for the Combines Investigation Act, issued a multivolume report entitled *The State of Competition in the Canadian Petroleum Industry.* Based on a study of gasoline and fuel oil prices in Canada between 1958 and 1973, the report charged that Canada's largest oil companies conspired to control retail prices, suppress competition from independent refiners and distributors, and overcharge consumers for imported oil. In the context of spiking international oil prices and fears of supply shortages in eastern and central Canada, the report appeared to give credence to suspicions that the big oil companies were, once again, earning windfall profits from an energy crisis.[1]

Imperial's Jack Armstrong indignantly rejected the report, which in his view represented opposition to the very concept of integrated oil companies, and he speculated that the timing of the release reflected the federal government's desire to put pressure on the oil companies to accept its ambitious energy plans. The company followed up with a public relations blitz, featuring full-page ads in newspapers across the country denying Bertrand's allegations with the headline: "Rip-off? Nonsense!"[2] Not surprisingly, what now was called the "Bertrand report" achieved a degree of popularity not usually accorded such bureaucratic tomes, and the Toronto publisher James Lorimer opportunistically produced a one-volume abridgement for public consumption.[3]

The architects of the NEP were perhaps not averse to putting their critics in the oil industry on the defensive, but the regime that was promoting Petro Canada and grand state-sponsored megaprojects in the Arctic was very different from the Texas trustbusters of the early 1900s. In addition, the Bertrand investigation had been underway for a long time, as Armstrong and other oil company executives were well aware: the Restrictive Trade Practices Commission had seized thousands of their records and haled them before hearings on retail price fixing in 1975. But the investigation, portrayed as the "longest, most expensive" undertaking by the Department of Consumer and Corporate Affairs, appeared to have lost momentum by 1979 as the public outcry over oil prices dwindled after the first energy crisis subsided. The fortunes of the Combines investigators were reinvigorated by the onset of the second energy crisis but once again the roller coaster of oil prices would influence the outcome of this effort to curb the multinationals.[4]

The Restrictive Trade Practices Commission commenced hearings in the autumn of 1981 with consumer organizations and independent petroleum distributors calling for oil majors to be divested of ownership ties with pipelines and prevented from charging higher prices for brand-name retail gasoline sales. Critics also claimed that the foreign owners of multinationals like Imperial and Shell had routinely marked up prices of oil imported into Canada to increase their earnings from the subsidiaries, an argument that had been featured in the Bertrand report. The hearings dragged on into 1982 with the multinationals continuing to argue that the investigation was being manipulated by the federal government to advance its controversial energy agenda. When Imperial's president Livingstone appeared before the commission, he maintained that Exxon supplied less than 40 per cent of the Canadian company's imports, and that much of the balance came from the state-owned Venezuelan oil company and from Petro Canada. Company spokesmen also pointed out that in 1973 Imperial's arrangements with Exxon benefited Canadian consumers because the parent company was obligated to supply Imperial despite the Arab oil embargo.[5]

Even before the 1984 federal election, the tide was turning in the battle between the oil multinationals and the Combines Act investigators. The Royal Commission on the Economic Union and Development

Prospects for Canada, chaired by the former Liberal cabinet minister Donald Macdonald, advocated reductions in trade barriers between the US and Canada, and recognized that mergers might reduce competition internally, but could strengthen Canadian companies competing in global markets. After the election, the Mulroney administration transformed the relationship between the federal government and multinational business: the Foreign Investment Review Agency was renamed Investment Canada and tasked with finding ways of attracting new foreign investors. Michel Cote, the new Minister of Consumer and Corporate Affairs, effectively terminated the Restrictive Trade Practices Commission's investigation of the petroleum industry, renaming the Combines Act as the Competition Act and setting up a new tribunal to review disputes and update regulations relating to mergers.[6]

Although the focus of both the Bertrand report and the commission investigation was ostensibly on issues involving domestic competition and collusion in restraint of trade, an underlying theme was the role of foreign-owned multinationals in the petroleum industry. Indeed the preamble to the Bertrand report asserted that "Canadian petroleum companies derived their power from their parents' domination in the world industry, which was itself characterized by less than full and open competition."[7] At the same time the dominant role of the multinationals worked to the disadvantage of the Canadian economy as well as consumers, constraining the growth of independent companies in production and refining as well as controlling the retail price of gas and oil. All these charges echoed the views of opponents of foreign ownership in Canadian industry going back to Walter Gordon's critique in the 1950s.

Events in the second energy crisis of 1979–80 reinforced the image of Imperial as the pawn of its American masters. Shortly after the Iranian revolution began, Exxon reduced shipments of oil from other sources to its affiliates to offset the unexpected shortage from Iran. The cutbacks included a reduction of shipments to eastern Canada from Venezuela. Although steps were taken to restore the shortfall in response to outcries from Canadian political leaders, the public relations damage was done, and the episode was cited later as the rationale for the federal government's demand to shift imports from Venezuela to Petro Canada in the NEP era.[8]

In 1980 the NDP leader in Parliament, Ed Broadbent, launched a broadside from a different angle: through its patent arrangements with Exxon, Imperial Oil was "bleeding the country dry," by transferring technology developed in Canada with "millions of Canadian tax dollars" to its US parent. This was a reference to the long-standing research agreement between Exxon and its subsidiaries for patent sharing, but the charge was made in the context of the Liberal government's $40 million (CAD) loan to Imperial to sustain its work at Cold Lake. At the same time the allegations reflected a view going back to the Gordon era, that Imperial and other multinationals were stifling innovation through their control of technology developed in Canada. Imperial's president Livingstone responded by making the point that through its agreements with Exxon, the company had access to the results of the parent company's $325 million (USD) a year research spending—ten times the amount that Imperial itself was able to commit to research.[9]

For the most part Imperial Oil's public relations department spent time rebutting charges of overcharging consumers or profiteering, but in the debates over the NEP and the Bertrand report in 1981, chairman Jack Armstrong presented a more expansive defense of his company and its relationship with Exxon. Rejecting claims by Energy Minister Marc Lalonde that the oil multinationals were responsible for net capital outflows of more than $3.7 billion (CAD) between 1970 and 1979, Armstrong argued: "access to a large international pool of research and technology, not just by Imperial, but all of the foreign majors, has helped build an oil industry in Canada which is among the best and most efficient in the world." What was remarkable about this address was that Armstrong acknowledged the ownership ties that Imperial and other oil majors had with foreign multinationals. In the 1960s, Imperial had insisted that "foreign control" was a "myth" and the company's president, Jack White, argued that "most of the control of a business comes from . . . its economic environment . . . by the customers it serves, by the competition, by the resources it is developing; by the laws, regulations and taxation under which it operates; by the quality of [its] employees; by changing technology."[10]

In certain respects, both Robert Bertrand and Jack Armstrong were right: Imperial Oil's long-lived domination of the Canadian oil scene was tied to its relationship with Exxon, the largest and most powerful

Graham D. Taylor

energy company in the world. While Imperial's connection with Exxon did not necessarily fit the stereotypes presented by critics as a satrap of Rockefeller's oil empire or an agent of American economic imperialism, the company's autonomy functioned within boundaries set by the strategic goals of Exxon. At the same time the parent company followed a pathway between centralization and decentralization in its relations with all its affiliates that provided the resiliency to survive major shifts in the global petroleum economy, in particular through the upheavals of the wars, revolutions, depressions, and nationalizations that characterized the twentieth century.

Over the years Jersey Standard/Exxon developed a variety of techniques to enable it to impose "indirect rule" over an increasingly complex and sprawling empire of subsidiaries, affiliates, and joint ventures. Among these the most significant involved budgeting, the establishment of "contacts" between Exxon's Board of Directors and the boards of its affiliates, and the promotion of lateral mobility for managers across the range of divisions within the company and in a variety of different geographic settings.

Budgeting was a key component of this process. In 1927 when Jersey Standard was reorganized as a holding company, coordination and control was to be exercised through the allocation of capital to achieve a common strategy. Each affiliate was to submit capital budget proposals to Jersey Standard's budget department, which would integrate them into a single capital budget for the entire system. In practice, however, this proved to be a challenge, as standard procedures had to be developed and adopted across hundreds of units with different tasks, requirements, and in some cases legal environments. Real budgeting coordination was not completed until the 1940s, and even then the dramatic expansion of the company's operations abroad—in Europe, the Middle East, and East Asia—required continuing reassessments of the procedures.[11]

The most significant development in this area came in 1959 when Exxon completed a merger with its largest affiliate, Humble Oil of Texas. As in the case of Imperial, Jersey Standard had held a majority of shares in Humble since the 1920s but officially maintained an arms-length relationship with that company, in part for public relations purposes. After the US Supreme Court ordered DuPont to divest itself of shares in General

Motors, however, the Jersey Standard board decided that complete legal control of Humble was necessary to avoid similar entanglements. In the wake of that merger, coordination of budgeting was expanded for all affiliates, particularly with regard to decisions about new areas of investment, which would be reviewed by a Board Advisory Committee on Investments on an annual basis.[12]

Imperial Oil was in a somewhat unusual position. After it sold International Petroleum to Jersey Standard in 1947, the company operated only in Canada and, in deference to Canadian "nationalistic political feelings," it was not subject to the intensive capital budget review imposed by Jersey Standard on other divisions and affiliates. At the same time, Imperial consulted with the executive committee of the parent company on major investment decisions, for example, in joining the oil sands consortium in the 1950s. But with the growth of new and expensive commitments in the 1960s–70s—including the move into petrochemicals, building the Strathcona refinery, participation in the Arctic Gas Pipeline initiative, and the Cold Lake project, among others—Imperial was in regular consultations with the Exxon Budget Advisory Committee about proposals for additional capital outlays, and these required reviews of performance as well as assessments of new undertakings. These presentations involved a degree of preparation of technical and financial documentation that brought the company into a much closer and regular contact with Exxon.

Meanwhile, annual meetings of Imperial Oil with its shareholders, usually held in Toronto, could be somewhat somnolent affairs. Business journalist Peter Foster described one such event in 1982, at the height of the controversies over NEP. "A venerable gathering. Widowed matrons . . . sedate elderly couples . . . small pockets of retired professional men . . . whole squadrons of former air force and navy men." The presentation by the board provided "what the shareholders came to hear," and after a few questions about the world in general, including the Falkland Islands war and its possible impact on oil prices, the recommendations of the board were "unanimously" approved. Afterwards "a buffet lunch of turkey à la king" was served. Of course, the distribution of dividends was not raised for debate.[13]

During the Great Depression, Jersey Standard had been criticized for depleting subsidiaries of capital through its dividend policies—for example Imperial. This changed in the 1940s, and in the years following the Second World War the parent company adopted an approach that ensured the stability of dividend payments to shareholders and adequate reinvestment of profits to the subsidiary. The overall growth of the industry and the economy buttressed this process. Between 1947 and 1970, dividends averaged between 50 per cent and 60 per cent of earnings per share, increasing slightly during the 1958–59 recession years when earnings sagged. In the 1970s net earnings rose faster than the dividend per share so that dividends averaged less than 50 per cent of earnings for several years.[14]

Another by-product of Jersey Standard's reorganization in 1927 was the establishment of "contact" relationships between members of its board of directors and the managers of divisions and affiliates. Each member had responsibility for maintaining contacts with one or several units in the organization, in order to facilitate the implementation of corporate policies and to represent their "contacts" on matters involving action by top management at Jersey Standard. This system was formalized in the mid-1930s. G.H. Smith, the president of Imperial and also a member of the Jersey Standard Board carried out this function until 1943. His successor was Frank W. Pierce, who had played a major role setting up Industrial Councils at Jersey Standard in the 1920s and served as board chairman of Imperial when Hewetson was president. In 1950 Hewetson was appointed to the Jersey Standard Board and acted as contact director with Imperial until 1959. In the 1960s–70s senior executives at Exxon who had experience with Imperial acted as contact directors in addition to their other tasks.[15]

The third link was the lateral movement of Jersey Standard and Imperial managers between the companies. This practice went back to the Teagle era when he brought in protégés from the US like G.W. Mayer who restructured the Canadian company's sales operations. When International Petroleum was set up, Jersey Standard dispatched geologists and pipeline engineers to help establish the infrastructure for Imperial's ventures in Peru and Colombia. A somewhat similar process took place when Hewetson took over Imperial in the 1940s and mounted a renewed effort to find oil in Alberta; Jersey Standard sent its chief geologist, L.G.

FIGURE 12.1. IOL/Exxon executives: O.B. Hopkins [far left], J.K. Jamieson [third from left], M.L. Haider [third from right], J.R. White [far right]. Glenbow Archive IP-21-1d, Imperial Oil Collection.

Weeks, and a production coordinator, L.F. McCollum, to provide advice. Perhaps the most important participant from Jersey Standard was Michael Haider, a petroleum engineer who had worked with Carter Oil Company. After Leduc, Haider remained with Imperial Oil, becoming vice president of production in the 1950s; Haider eventually returned to Jersey Standard, where he became president and chief executive in the 1960s.[16]

By this time, the exchange worked in both directions. Canadian-born Ken Jamieson, who as vice president at Imperial had played a major role in setting up the company's move into petrochemicals, went on to Jersey Standard where he too served as president and chief executive in the 1960s. In 1956 Jersey Standard "borrowed" J.A. Cogan from Imperial to help coordinate oil tanker movements during the Suez crisis; Cogan had also worked as an economic planner for Jersey Standard in New York.

During the 1920s–30s, International Petroleum had provided a kind of training ground for managers who rose to top positions later at Imperial, and this connection remained even after Imperial sold its interest in the Latin American company: Jack Armstrong, for example, spent some of his early years exploring for petroleum in Ecuador; Michael Haider was president of International Petroleum before going on to run Jersey Standard. Jamieson served as head of Humble Oil of Texas en route to being installed as chairman of the Exxon Board. These were not unusual or unique situations: by the 1970s Exxon was running more or less formal programs for aspiring managers in a variety of positions across their companies, but even earlier it was not uncommon for promising high-office candidates to spend some time with Humble Oil or Creole Petroleum or Aramco learning how to function effectively in a variety of assignments.[17]

At the same time, even though some of Imperial's chief executives spent time on assignment with other Jersey Standard companies, from Hewetson's time to the early twenty-first century, they were all Canadian-born and had for the most part risen from the ranks at Imperial Oil, including George Stewart, Bill Twaits, and Jack Armstrong. They were also a largely homogeneous group: not surprisingly most had been educated as geologists or engineers, as was the case with top managers at Exxon. Many were from the Canadian Prairies: Manitoba (Jack Armstrong and Don McIvor, who succeeded him as president) or Saskatchewan (Robert Peterson, Arden Haynes, Tim Hearn). Even as Canada was celebrating its evolution into a multicultural nation, Imperial Oil's upper ranks remained a bastion of tradition: mostly white, male, Anglo-Canadian, and Protestant. There were few women, Quebecois, or recent immigrants, and virtually no Indigenous people at this level. In the 1940s some women emerged from the ranks of geologists and research scientists: Diane Loranger, for example, began work as a field geologist for Royalite, rising to a supervisory position with Imperial, and later became an international consultant on paleontology.[18] There were some indications of change in the twenty-first century: two of the seven members of Imperial's board of directors in 2013 were women, but only one among the eight other senior managers listed in the company's annual report.[19]

FIGURE 12.2. Diane Loranger, geologist, Royalite, 1946. Glenbow Archive IP-14a-1470, Imperial Oil Collection.

The relatively benign relationship between Imperial Oil and Exxon that prevailed after the Second World War began to fray in the mid-1980s. The collapse of world oil prices in 1985–86 hit the entire industry hard, and many Canadian independents disappeared. Imperial had already instituted staff cuts in 1982 and closed down most of its western refineries when Strathcona was opened, so it avoided the worst ravages of the recession in the oil patch. But Exxon was not so fortunate: the company's revenues fell by 18 per cent in one year and earnings failed to return even to 1985 levels for six years. A new senior management team, under board chairman Lawrence Rawl and president Lee Raymond, drastically reorganized the company, paring down the complex committee systems and focusing on the most profitable product lines, particularly in petrochemicals. Inevitably the quest for savings and efficiencies led to changes in Exxon's approach to affiliates. Among other things, dividends from Imperial rose from $1.60 to $1.80/share (CAD) drawing up to 70 per cent of net earnings by 1990.[20]

Two developments, both involving mergers, would influence Imperial's relationship with Exxon after 1986. In 1984 a legal battle erupted between the US parent of Texaco Canada (formerly McColl Frontenac) and a Texas-based independent oil company, Pennzoil. Pennzoil charged that Texaco had acted illegally in a bidding contest for another large independent company, Getty Oil. In 1985 a Texas jury ruled in favour of Pennzoil and imposed a stunning $10.3 billion (USD) in damages on Texaco. Over the next two years the two companies bickered until finally reaching a settlement in 1987, after Texaco filed for bankruptcy, with Pennzoil receiving $3.5 billion (USD) as compensation. Among the assets Texaco was obliged to sell to cover these costs was its 78 per cent ownership of Texaco Canada.[21]

Texaco Canada's assets were valued at about $4 billion (CAD). It was considered a good performer, with profits in 1986 of $283 million (CAD), but like Imperial Oil, its reserves of conventional oil were declining. On the other hand, it owned a chain of 2,000 service stations nationwide, and its Nanticoke refinery was set up to produce lead-free gasoline that was required by the Canadian government. So there were many interested parties in addition to Imperial—including Husky Oil, owned by Nova Corporation (the former Alberta Gas Trunk Line) in partnership with a Hong Kong millionaire, Li ka-sheng; Gulf Canada, now controlled by the real estate entrepreneurs, the Reichmanns; Occidental Petroleum; Conoco Canada; and several entrants from outside the oil patch, such as Provigo, a Quebec supermarket conglomerate, and Bell Canada Enterprises. By the summer of 1988 share prices had risen from $35/share to 39.37/share (CAD).[22]

Imperial sold its Esso Minerals Division as a preliminary step in the contest, "to concentrate on its core energy business." By the beginning of 1989 the field had narrowed to Imperial, Shell Canada, Bond Holdings, an Australian company, and Socanov Company of Montreal, which presented itself as "the only totally Canadian group of bidders." In the end Imperial emerged victorious, paying $41/share (CAD) for 78 per cent of Texaco Canada. But its troubles were just beginning.[23]

The federal Bureau of Competition (successor to the Restricted Trade Practices Commission) indicated that Imperial would be expected to sell the Nanticoke refinery and a significant number of Texaco Canada's service outlets before the transaction would be approved. In addition the government of Quebec demanded that Imperial sell 225 of the Texaco Canada stations in that province. Nova Scotia gas station owners and employees of Texaco's Dartmouth refinery wanted assets in that province sold "as a block" with Ultramar Canada waiting in the wings to take them over. The Consumers Association of Canada opposed the merger, as did the opposition Liberals and New Democrats in Ottawa.

The Competition Bureau review dragged on into 1990. Imperial Oil's stock fell from $64/share to $60.50/share, and its net earnings fell by 9 per cent in 1990, which reflected in part the effects of a more general decline in the economy after the 1987 market "correction." Eventually the Competition Bureau accepted a plan under which Imperial would divest itself of 638 retail outlets, but would retain the Nanticoke refinery. The major beneficiary was Ultramar in Atlantic Canada.[24]

As the hearings ground on, and the value of the Texaco takeover shrank, Imperial's shareholders—including the major one, Exxon—became increasingly irked. When Imperial reported losses in its downstream business in 1990, Exxon dispatched a senior vice president, Robert Wilhelm, to assess the situation in Canada. He warned "we have a real mess on our hands," and urged major financial and staff restructuring at Imperial to address the problems. In the short run, the Canadian company—and the industry generally—benefitted from the price spike that accompanied the Gulf War, and so Imperial was able to report overall profitable performance for 1990. But it had issued $1 billion (CAD) in new equity in 1989 to help finance the Texaco Canada takeover, and its long-term obligations rose from $1.3 billion to $4.6 billion (CAD) in 1990.

Oil prices fell by $20/bbl. (USD) in the aftermath of the Gulf War and declined again in 1996. Imperial brought in a new president, Robert Peterson, in 1992 who imposed substantial cost cutting, laying off 1,700 employees and closing 1,000 service stations as well as shutting down the refinery at Port Moody, BC. Under Peterson the Texaco acquisition was paid off, and he remained as chief executive for ten years, steering the company through the oil industry doldrums of the late 1990s.[25]

Although Imperial Oil had rebounded from its troubles, the view from Exxon—headquartered in Irving, Texas near Dallas after 1990—remained skeptical. Lee Raymond, the chief executive and dominant figure in the company from 1993 to 2006, had a particularly jaundiced perspective toward Imperial: "All we heard from Imperial for years was [the need to consider] the minority shareholder," he complained. After the Exxon-Mobil merger in 1999, the parent company reassembled Mobil's operations in Canada into a new subsidiary, independent of Imperial. More changes were soon to come. In 2008 Bruce Marsh, a Mobil veteran who had held positions in the Middle East and Europe, became the first non-Canadian in more than fifty years to assume the presidency of Imperial. Marsh was succeeded in 2013 by Richard Kruger, who had worked for Exxon since 1981 in Russia, Africa, and Asia.[26]

By this time many of the issues that had preoccupied public attention—foreign ownership of Canadian industry, the role of government and private enterprise in resource management, the relative share of benefits between the federal and provincial governments—were beginning to fade. In their place the most salient concern by the early twenty-first century focused on the impact of the industry on the environment, and a debate over the effects of fossil fuel exploitation on the future of life on the planet. Inevitably Exxon and Imperial Oil were positioned at the centre of these issues.

13

A CHANGE IN THE CLIMATE

Oil has always been a dirty business. A reporter travelling through western Pennsylvania in 1865 portrayed one of the early oil fields: "The soil is black, being saturated with waste petroleum. The engine houses, pumps and tanks are black with the smoke and soot of coal fires, which raise the steam to drive the wells . . . Even the trees . . . wore the universal sooty covering. Their very leaves were black."[1] Piles of mud and pools of oil surrounded the wellheads. Oil leaked from jerry-built pipelines in the field, from wooden barrels that carried the oil by barge or wagon to refineries.

The refineries in turn contributed to the polluted scene. When kerosene was the main commercial by-product of oil refining, most of the residue, including gasoline, was dumped into nearby culverts or streams while sulphur-laden smoke poured from the chimneys. When the city of London (Ontario) was contemplating expansion in the 1870s, the refineries clustered there hastily moved to carve out a separate municipality to avoid air and water regulations that might be imposed, a tactic Imperial Oil followed when setting up refineries in locations distant from residential communities in Halifax, Montreal, and Vancouver.[2]

Oil was also a dangerous business. Drillers often encountered explosions, fires, and runaway wells, which can keep leaking or burning for weeks or months. An observer of a well explosion at Oil Creek in 1861 described the scene: "In a moment the whole air was in roaring flames . . . each drop of oil came down a blazing globe of boiling oil. Instantly the ground was in flame, increased and augmented by the falling oil."[3] Wellhead fires were a regular occurrence in the Petrolia fields, burning or smoldering for weeks on end. Refinery explosions were common as well. Jacob Englehart's first refinery in London blew up twice within seven weeks in 1873. Ten years later Imperial Oil's large Victoria refinery in London burned to the ground, leaving the company with only Englehart's Silver Star refinery in Petrolia.[4]

Between 1880 and the 1920s conditions in the industry improved to some degree, in part because of technological changes that indirectly affected pollution and safety problems. The development of "ram type blowout preventers" by James Abercrombie and Harry Cameron in the 1920s reduced the frequency of wellhead gushers that could result in runaway fires as well as extensive pollution of oil fields. Pipeline materials and design improved substantially, although these did not figure prominently in Canada until after the Second World War. The introduction of thermal cracking technology and the shift to production of gasoline and motor-vehicle related products reduced the amount of waste materials discarded by refineries. Better maintenance and measures to reduce sulphuric emissions lessened, although it did not eliminate the dangers of refinery fires.[5]

In the first half of the twentieth century, the term "conservation" was often invoked, but it could best be defined as the efficient exploitation of natural resources with an emphasis on the reduction of waste rather than protection of the environment. During debates in the US Congress in the 1920s on an Oil Pollution Act, advocates for the American Petroleum Industry argued, effectively, that improvements in thermal cracking had been so successful that refineries could be exempted from the application of the act to pollution of harbours and waterways; the law focused instead on oil tankers, requiring them to empty residual waste beyond the three-mile limit. The efficiency argument could of course work both ways. In the 1930s the Alberta Conservation Board set out to reduce gas flaring in the Turner Valley, arguing that it wasted an economic resource; it also reduced pressure on oil deposits, making them harder to locate for drilling. It took years of political manoeuvring, but the board was ultimately successful in 1938. In the 1950s the board allowed a limited amount of flaring to continue, but required that measures be taken to protect nearby land and forests.[6]

Two events during this period provide insights into Imperial Oil's approach to what would now be regarded as environmental challenges

FIGURE 13.1. Atlantic #3 Fire, 1948. Glenbow Archive PA-3478-3, Imperial Oil Collection.

during a period of transition from an emphasis on efficiency and reducing waste to one that focused more on the recovery of the environment. The first episode reviews the quashing of a runaway fire in the Leduc oilfield in 1948–49; the second focuses on the clean up of the Saint Clair River after the Second World War.

In the aftermath of Imperial success at Leduc Number 1, many other enterprises, large and small, descended on the oil field. Among these was the Atlantic Oil Company, a relatively small undertaking founded by Frank MacMahon, who later gained fame and fortune in pipeline development. On March 8, 1948, about a year after Imperial's Leduc well came in, the Atlantic Company's third well attempt erupted into a gusher, spewing oil, gas, and mud 150 feet into the air. The leaking continued for months, raising concerns that a fire could consume the Leduc field and beyond. The Alberta Conservation Board brought in Myron Kinley, an American specialist in quelling "wild wells," who tried using dynamite inside the well and then packing it with a mixture of mud, wood fibres, and lime, all to no avail. Local farmers and even residents of Edmonton demanded action.

Alberta's premier Ernest Manning, facing an upcoming election, authorized the board to close down the Leduc field, and Imperial Oil turned to Tip Moroney, the head of its western operations, and an engineer with extensive experience in Oklahoma, Peru, and Venezuela, to deal with the crisis. Moroney recruited two experienced drillers, Charlie Visser and Jim Tod from Royalite (which was in the process of separating from Imperial). They set out to relieve pressure on Atlantic Number 3 by drilling wells north and west of the runaway, which was still hurling debris into the air and leaking oil. On Labour Day the long-feared explosion and fire broke out, but fortunately water from one of the relief wells suppressed the fire after a few days. The conservation board was able to settle most liability claims from a trust fund it had set up against such a contingency. Ironically, the newspaper accounts (and dramatic photos) of the explosion brought immense publicity to Leduc and encouraged even more oil seekers to flock to Alberta. At the same time the episode enabled the conservation board to strengthen its field inspection system and preparedness for future problems. The public pressure and government action that led to the termination of the Atlantic Number 3 blowout in 1948 contrasts with the conditions that prevailed during the Royalite Number 4 well fire twenty-four years earlier.[7]

As discussed in chapter 8, during the Second World War the federal government set up Polymer Canada in Sarnia near to Imperial Oil's largest refinery, as well as Dow Chemical. After the war a number of oil refineries and petrochemical operations, including Sun Oil, DuPont, Fiberglass Canada, and Shell Canada also relocated there. Even as "Chemical Valley" was celebrated on Canada's currency, it was recognized that this was a potent source of air and water pollution on the Saint Clair River, feeding into Lake Huron and Lake Erie. In 1950 the Canada-US International Joint Commission submitted a critical report on the state of water pollution of the "boundary waters" in the Lake Erie region.[8]

In 1952 the Saint Clair River Research Committee was set up by representatives of Imperial Oil, Polymer Canada, and Dow Chemical, joined later by eight other companies in the area. By 1960 the committee had spent $14 million (CAD) conducting surveys of pollution levels and designing equipment to mitigate the effects of industrial operations. Imperial contributed $2.8 million (CAD) to this total. The committee's work led to the development of the Great Lakes Water Quality Agreement by the International Joint Commission, which was ratified in 1972.[9]

By that time there had been a sea change in public attitudes toward environmental issues in the US and Canada. Concern over the impact of pesticides, stimulated in part by the 1962 publication of Rachel Carson's *Silent Spring*, widened to cover many aspects of industrialization. The capacity of the oil industry to use technology to protect aquifers and groundwater from pollution seemed to have reached its limits. High profile disasters—such as the sinking of the tanker *Torrey Canyon* in 1968 that affected coastlines from the Bay of Biscay to the North Sea, and the fouling of beaches and marine wildlife in Santa Barbara following an oil spill by a Union Oil drilling blowout in 1969—fuelled growing demands for more intense regulation of industrial pollution. As luck would have it, Imperial Oil was to figure prominently in an episode that dramatized the dangers of oil spills in Canada in this same time period.

On the morning of February 4, 1970 the oil tanker SS *Arrow* ran aground at Chedabucto Bay in Nova Scotia during a storm. The crew was rescued but the ship remained stranded as high winds and waves impeded salvage efforts. On February 8 the ship split in half and sank, releasing over 10,000 tons (3.6 million US gallons) of bunker sea oil that the *Arrow* was carrying from Aruba to the Stora paper mill in Point Tupper. Salvaging took two months, by which time the oil slick had spread across 190 miles of the Nova Scotia shore. The clean up took more than a year, and forty years later there were still reports of oil residues in the area. The ship was registered in Liberia, owned by Sunstone Marine Co. of Panama, and managed by Olympic Maritime S.A. of Monte Carlo. Apparently Greek tycoon Aristotle Onassis controlled the vessel. It had been chartered by Imperial Oil for the voyage.[10]

Imperial had its own fleet of ships, operating since 1902. In 1945 it had fourteen coastal tankers, primarily for use on the Great Lakes, plus five deep-sea tankers. After the sale of International Petroleum, however, Imperial began to reduce its overseas fleet, although a tanker capable of ocean voyages, the *Imperial Quebec*, was launched in 1957. The company had eight ships in operation in 1970, and most of the oil imported from Venezuela and elsewhere was carried in chartered vessels like the *Arrow*.[11]

FIGURE 13.2. SS *Arrow*, Chedabucto Bay (1970). Glenbow Archive IP-14c-70-6, Imperial Oil Collection.

When Imperial's executive committee was informed about the sinking, it authorized one of its regular tankers, *Imperial Acadia*, to sail from Newfoundland to assist in the salvage, and also agreed to contribute to the clean up. At the same time, members were concerned that Imperial should not be held responsible for the accident. Two weeks later the committee heard a report from its legal counsel, J.F. Barrett, who advised them that the federal Department of Transport had agreed that the company had undertaken clean-up efforts "under extreme emergency conditions . . . to

Graham D. Taylor

minimize pollution hazards" and this did not imply "legal liability under Canadian or international law." Imperial's clean-up responsibilities would be restricted to "pools of oil in various coves." Subsequently, the company reported it had spent $500,000 (CAD) on clean-up operations, which cost over $3 million (CAD). An inquiry under a Nova Scotia judge into the accident assigned fault to the Greek captain of the *Arrow*.[12]

In terms of public relations the company escaped relatively un-scathed, in contrast to the results of the Exxon Valdez disaster in 1989. Don Jamieson, the Canadian Minister of Transport, criticized Imperial Oil because it "should have asked . . . what are we going to do if a disaster occurs?" Jamieson set up an "Oil Spill Task Force" to review the prepared-ness of oil shipping companies for accidents. Imperial followed up with a procedural manual that was regularly updated. The company retired its last regular tanker in 1998. The marine service had been an important part of Imperial's operations for almost a century, and had followed high standards of maintenance and morale throughout those years. But the expansion of pipeline systems and the move by the industry generally to contracting out transport services had been going on for a long time.[13]

At virtually the same time that Imperial's Executive Committee was informed about the *Arrow* disaster, they were notified of the likely impos-ition of emission controls on automobiles, and the prospective elimination of leaded gasoline. This was by no means a surprise, as pressure had been mounting over the previous decade, particularly in the US, for emissions regulation. Heralded in the 1920s as a breakthrough in auto fuel technol-ogy, by the 1960s leaded gasoline was seen to be a health hazard as well as a major contributor to "smog" air pollution in metropolitan areas such as Los Angeles and New York City. The Clean Air Act of 1970 in the US imposed deadlines on the auto industry (and by the extension on the oil industry) to meet reduced emission targets by the middle of the decade.[14]

Because of the Auto Pact, the Canadians might have been expected to follow in the wake of US regulations; but, interestingly, the Department of Energy, Mines and Resources under Jack Austin promoted a "Canadian" approach that would soft-pedal the imposition of the Clean Air Act stan-dards, arguing that smog was much less of a problem in Canada. Other departments, including Environment and Industry Trade and Commerce, pushed for closer integration with the US on the issue, but bureaucratic feuding hampered any action until the energy crisis shifted attention away from the environment to security of supplies. In 1980, Canadian emission requirements were lower than those in the US, and "harmonization" did not occur until after the Free Trade Agreement of 1988.[15]

Imperial Oil in 1970 was prepared, albeit reluctantly, to follow the deadlines of the US Clean Air Act, and modify their refinery facilities to meet the lead-free requirements by 1976. This was in keeping with the position of both Exxon and General Motors in Canada (as well as the United States). Not surprisingly, these costly renovations were put on hold once the position of the Canadian government was clarified (or perhaps muddied), and the company postponed action until the 1980s, at which point the Nanticoke refinery of Texaco Canada, which had moved on to developing the capabilities of producing lead-free gas, was an attractive feature in the Imperial takeover.[16]

In 1970 Imperial Oil began producing an "Environmental Protection Activities Review," which eventually was incorporated into its annual reports. A good deal of the report was devoted to refinery pollution clean ups and monitoring the impact of federal environmental policies. The degree of detail in the reviews waxed and waned with the demands from the government and the media for information, but environmental awareness did become part of the way in which the company presented itself to the public. The industry showed progress in addressing pollution generated by refineries. In an otherwise glum assessment of the effectiveness of Canadian environmental regulations, the environmental lawyer David Boyd noted that refineries had made significant reductions in emissions of phenol, ammonia nitrogen, and sulphur dioxides between 1980 and 1995—prompted, to be sure, by government regulations at the municipal as well as federal level.[17]

More frustrating for the oil industry were continuing controversies over pipeline leaks, despite major improvements in pipeline design and construction. As environmental historian Sean Kheraj has pointed out, specifically with regard to the Interprovincial Pipeline Company (now Enbridge) between 1950 and 1980: "While oil spills have been a regular occurrence . . . the volume of liquid hydrocarbons released has been proportionally small relative to the total throughput . . . That fraction of [one] per cent of a failure rate, however, led to more than 41 million litres of liquid hydrocarbon spills."[18]

The oil sands presented the greatest environmental challenges for Imperial Oil and the other companies that entered that field. The sheer scale of the operations dwarfed most conventional oil field exploration and development, but the particular features of this resource strained the technological capabilities of the industry. As Jack Armstrong said, it was a "big, tough, expensive job," and the payoff always seemed to vanish into the future.

The first major oil sands projects, those of GCOS and Syncrude, resembled strip-mining operations in the coal industry—the scraping of surface areas to reach the bitumen—and as with all mining, the tailings were left behind as too toxic to return to the existing water system. GCOS notoriously failed to meet even the minimal standards for residual recovery required by the Alberta government.

In 1973 Alberta began demanding land reclamation of the oil sands sites after use, and in 1993 banned discharges of wastewater so that tailings ponds would have to be treated before release. All of the oil sands companies made efforts to deal with land and water reclamation, but even a sympathetic observer of the industry acknowledged that these measures only covered a fraction of the problem, due in part to the renewed growth of operations in the early twenty-first century.[19]

Imperial's Cold Lake development, an *in situ* undertaking, avoided the problems of strip mining but produced its own issues. A large amount of water was required for these operations (although less than with the mining approach) and required recycling: the wastewater was injected into aquifers on the site. Although Imperial took measures to control the potential for leakages, critics claimed that bitumen was seeping into the waterways and in 2013 Canadian Natural Resources Inc. drained a lake they thought was affected.[20]

The greatest threat, not just to the oil sands but also to the petroleum industry as a whole, came from another quarter. In 1990 the Intergovernmental Panel on Climate Change, a body of scientists sponsored by the United Nations, presented a report maintaining that the earth's climate was warming at an accelerated rate, particularly since the Second World War, and that carbon emissions from human use of fossil fuels—including coal, oil, and gas—had contributed significantly to this result. In response the UN called for a Conference on Environment and Development, to be held in Rio de Janeiro in 1992.

There was precedent for this proposal. In 1987, after scientists had discovered that the ozone layer in the atmosphere that protected earth from ultraviolet radiation was being depleted, twenty-four countries signed an international agreement to restrict the use of chlorofluorocarbons, which were considered a major contributor to the problem. But when a much larger group assembled in Rio, sharp differences emerged. Industrializing nations such as China and India objected to measures that might impose restraints on carbon emissions in their countries, since the threat originated from the output of long-established industrial countries, particularly the United States and Western Europe. One hundred and fifty-three nations signed the Convention on Climate Change, which called for "the stabilization of greenhouse gas concentrations," by ensuring that by the year 2000 carbon emissions would be limited to 1990 levels. But aside from setting targets, the agreement did not commit any signer to actually doing anything. Another conference scheduled in Kyoto in 1997 was expected to identify specific carbon reduction goals.

At Kyoto the same divisions between "developed" and "developing" nations persisted. In the end a compromise was worked out that only encouraged countries such as China to undertake "clean energy" projects. The industrialized countries were to meet certain targets by 2012—Canada, for example, was assigned to cut its carbon emissions by 6 per cent by that time, while the US, Japan, and European countries would meet targets between 6 and 8 per cent. One hundred and forty-seven countries, including the US and Canada, signed on. The agreement also stipulated that it must be ratified by countries responsible for 55 per cent of global carbon emissions before going into effect.[21]

By this time, however, internal divisions were also arising, particularly in the United States, where the treaty stalled. Both the Democratic president Bill Clinton and his Republican successor, George W. Bush, declined to even present the agreement to the US Senate for ratification, and partisan divisions blocked further action, although some states such as California undertook their own emission restriction initiatives. After 2010, president Barack Obama used executive orders to enable the US

Environmental Protection Agency to impose carbon restrictions on the fossil fuel industries. Russia, where the oil and gas industry had rebounded after the collapse of the Soviet Union, was also a holdout until 2005, when its ratification brought Kyoto to the 55 per cent goal. In 2016 China and other "developing" nations agreed to participate in the Paris Protocol on carbon emission limits; but in the US a new administration under Republican president Donald Trump refused to accept the Paris accord, and rolled back emission control measures introduced by his predecessor.

Not surprisingly, the major oil and gas corporations were reluctant if not hostile observers of events preceding and following the Kyoto accord, although after 2000 BP and Shell exhibited some willingness to accept the need for controls over carbon emissions. Exxon, on the other hand, fiercely opposed the basic ideas underlying the demand for restrictions. In 1989 Exxon set up a "Global Climate Coalition" under the auspices of the US National Association of Manufacturers and sponsored speakers and organizations who criticized climate change advocates. The company's public relations strategy presented arguments that Exxon and the industry were already taking steps to limit carbon emissions, and that the cost of implementing the Kyoto targets would wreak economic hardship on the US. But much emphasis was also placed on discrediting the science on climate change—questioning the reliability of the research, and promoting the view that scientific inquiry is by its nature based on "uncertainty."[22]

Ironically, Exxon's own scientists had been conducting research on global warming trends in the 1970s. In 1979, based on concerns expressed by the research and engineering division, the company sent a supertanker carrying special measuring instruments to sail from the Gulf of Mexico to the Persian Gulf, to determine the speed and extent to which oceans acted as a "carbon sink" absorbing carbon dioxide from the atmosphere. A few years later Exxon scientists, collaborating with outside researchers, developed computer simulations of the impact of carbon emissions in increasing global temperatures: in 1983–84 the results of these studies appeared in peer-reviewed journals in atmospheric sciences.[23]

Although this research did not lead to major policy shifts by Exxon, the results did reflect a perspective that influenced senior management in the late 1970s and early 1980s. In the context of oil market instabilities, the company began looking toward a strategy of diversification in a range of fields, including nuclear power and solar power as well as synthetic fuels and non-energy related businesses. If climate change portended long-term restrictions on oil resources, this reinforced a move toward alternative energy (and other) markets. Clifford Garvin, the chief executive of Exxon in 1977, maintained: "Exxon is in the energy business, as it is most broadly defined, rather than just the oil business."[24]

The collapse of global oil prices in 1985–86 ushered in a new regime at Exxon under Lawrence Rawl and Lee Raymond, who set out to dismantle the diversification strategy and return the company to its "core business"—i.e., oil and gas. The research on global warming was terminated as part of across the board cost-cutting measures. In the 1990s, Raymond, as the dominant figure at Exxon, saw the international efforts to limit fossil fuel emissions as a direct threat to the company's "core business" and its strategy to recover leadership in the industry.[25]

Exxon's position on global warming attenuated after Raymond's retirement in 2006. By this time the company's take-no-prisoners stance had left it somewhat isolated as the other oil majors shifted: the "Global Climate Coalition" closed down in 2002, and Exxon was regularly assailed by protestors and activist shareholders at its annual meetings. Raymond's successor Rex Tillerson was a more low-key figure, with extensive experience as an oil diplomat in Russia, the Middle East, and Thailand. When he became US Secretary of State in 2017, he notably challenged President Trump's views on climate change—but also adhered quietly to the boss's decision to the contrary.[26]

Imperial Oil's challenge in the debate over climate change and carbon emission limits was in some respects greater than its parent, Exxon, had to face. With large fixed commitments both through Syncrude and at Cold Lake, it could not easily extricate itself from this strategy and although the oil sands contributed only 8 per cent of Canada's output of greenhouse gases, during the debates over Kyoto environmentalists had focused attention on this sector of the industry as the virtual embodiment of misguided economic and technological development. The *in situ* projects like Cold Lake came in for criticism, along with the strip mining operations of Suncor and Syncrude—particularly for the high energy requirements to heat water for the SAGD process. Calculations of the greenhouse gas output of the full fuel cycle (called "well to wheels") of *in situ* operations was somewhat higher than the surface mining levels and both exceeded the output of conventional oil production by 12 to 24 per cent, despite efforts to improve refining efficiencies after 2010.[27]

Imperial's shifting perspectives paralleled those of Exxon. A section on "Climatic Change, Carbon Cycle" appeared in its 1980 *Review of Environmental Protection Activities*, which included the observation that "increases in fossil fuel usage and decreased forest cover are aggravating the potential problem of increased [carbon dioxide] in the atmosphere." By the 1990s in the context of the debate over the Kyoto accord, Imperial's president Robert Peterson reiterated the arguments made by Exxon's Lee Raymond that "there is absolutely no agreement among climatologists on whether or not the planet is getting warmer, or . . . whether warming is the result of man-made factors or natural variations in the climate."[28] Also in 1998 a leaked Imperial memo, "The High Costs of Kyoto," echoed criticisms of the accord emanating from the Global Climate Coalition. But, as with Exxon, Imperial moved thereafter to accommodate environmental critics of the industry, particularly on the issue of oil sands development.[29]

In 1997 Exxon-Mobil and Imperial began laying plans for a new oil sands venture at Kearl, 40 kilometres north of Fort McMurray. It would be an open-pit mine, similar to Suncor and Syncrude, projected to cost $8 billion (CAD) to extract between 110,000 and 300,000 bbl./day, to be transported by an Enbridge pipeline to Edmonton for refining. Imperial would own 70 per cent of the project and Exxon Mobil 30 per cent.

This was Imperial's first major oil sands venture since Cold Lake in the 1970s and a kind of good-faith opportunity for Exxon and Mobil to work together pending their incipient merger. It also was devised at virtually the same time as the Kyoto Accord, and reflected Lee Raymond's defiant posture toward that initiative. It took ten years for the Kearl project to get approval from the Alberta Energy and Utilities Board, and it faced almost immediate legal challenges from the Sierra Club and the Pembina Institute in Alberta, leading to a Canadian court ruling that delayed further action until issues relating to greenhouse gas emissions were resolved. In response, Imperial mounted a public relations campaign, maintaining that the Kearl project would use "high paraffin froth" processes to reduce carbon dioxide emissions in the mining stage and would dilute the heavy bitumen with natural gas so it could be transported more readily by pipeline. The chief executive of Imperial, Bruce Marsh, maintained: "technology has been instrumental in reducing our energy consumption and greenhouse gas emissions across our company."[30]

By this time the cost of the project had escalated to $13 billion (CAD) with projected increases up to $28 billion (CAD). In 2010 an Enbridge pipeline in Michigan carrying diluted bitumen suffered a rupture, leading to an extended clean up—the incident was cited by opponents of the Keystone XL pipeline in the US and Canada. Nevertheless, Imperial began operations at the Kearl site at the end of 2011. As the costs of the technology needed to address emissions requirements mounted, the industry began pushing for subsidies from the government of Canada to support carbon-capture and storage measures and related actions so that it could "be competitive with wind power and biofuels in terms of cost per tonne for reducing greenhouse gas emissions."[31]

In 2013 Imperial and Exxon proposed a new *in situ* oil sands project christened "Aspen" that would use the SAGD technology and produce 150,000 bbl./day. Five years later, however, it was still on hold: Imperial's president Richard Kruger argued that "regulatory uncertainty"—both in the approval processes for the project and in the development of the Trans Mountain Pipeline—was responsible for the delays. By this time many of the multinational oil companies had abandoned the oil sands, and even Syncrude had cut back production.[32]

Until the 1970s, despite criticism that they took advantage of energy crises to obtain windfall profits, the large multinational oil companies were regarded as essential for the economic stability of the industrial world. By the early twenty-first century, these companies—and their local satraps like Imperial Oil—were increasingly characterized as enemies of the global environment, purveyors of pollution, and defenders of practices that could endanger the planet. They still would play an essential role in meeting the world's energy needs, but not as champions of "better things for better living."

The dilemma for Imperial Oil and the Canadian oil industry was more acute. In the 1960s–70s the oil sands were perceived (by Canadians and others) as the New Golconda, an energy source equal to—or perhaps larger than—the oil of the Middle East, and companies like Suncor and Imperial/Syncrude were hailed as hard-driving, risk-taking pioneers on the frontiers of resource development. By the second decade of the twenty-first century many Canadians (including then-prime minister Stephen Harper) might still embrace the "New Golconda," particularly as world oil prices soared in 2010–14. But the age-old problem of getting the oil sands product to market faced rising challenges.

In the US, environmentalist opponents of the Keystone XL pipeline from Alberta to the Gulf of Mexico were joined by farmers in the American Midwest worried about the impact of pipelines on their land, as well as communities reacting to reports of pipeline spills. The Keystone pipeline was ultimately approved—but only after extended and possibly unfinished controversies, by which time oil prices were once more in the doldrums. Meanwhile in Canada, a coalition of environmentalist and First Nations groups set out to block an expansion of the Trans Mountain pipeline from Alberta to the west coast of British Columbia that would carry "diluted bitumen" from oil sands production to eventually reach the markets of East Asia. In 2018 the government of Canada took over the project from Kinder Morgan while facing a court challenge from the government of British Columbia. Even Trans Canada's "all Canadian" Energy East pipeline encountered resistance in Quebec and was cancelled in 2017. As in the past, oil company executives could feel certain that ultimately energy needs would trump the opposition, but the oil sands still provided critics with prime suspects in the lineup of perpetrators of climate change; and prospective solutions through "carbon capture" measures would add costs to what was already the most expensive energy source derived from fossil fuels that the industry had developed.

In 2004 Imperial Oil announced that it was relocating its corporate headquarters from Toronto to Calgary. The company's chief executive, Thomas Hearn, explained that this move would "strengthen our focus" on Imperial's "major initiatives" in the oil sands and development of the oil and gas resources of northern Canada. In many respects it was following the lead of Exxon, which had moved its headquarters from New York to Irving, Texas (between Dallas and Fort Worth) in 1990 in order to focus on what Lee Raymond, Exxon's chief executive, designated "core business:" oil and gas.[33]

These moves were logical, even obvious, steps for the two companies. At the same time they reflected a resolute rejection of the idea that climate change would ultimately transform fossil fuel production into a "sunset" industry. As Imperial and Exxon entered their second century together, they remained committed to the course that had brought them both to leading positions in the Canadian and global petroleum industry respectively, after 1900.

CONCLUSION

The last half of the nineteenth century witnessed transformations in the technologies of extraction, production, transportation, and communications that provided opportunities for aspiring entrepreneurs to achieve economies of scale in production and expand their market reach across entire countries and abroad. In the burgeoning kerosene industry, John D. Rockefeller fashioned an empire through the vertical integration of refining, pipelines, and marketing to achieve a dominant position for Standard Oil in the United States by the 1880s and a worldwide market position over the following decade. In Canada, a group of refiners formed Imperial Oil in 1880 to establish a similar degree of dominance in the Canadian market. Imperial never achieved that goal, and lost a crucial edge in technology when the scientist Herman Frasch moved from Imperial to Standard Oil. But by the 1890s it had developed an integrated system that in many respects paralleled for Canada the much larger operations of Standard Oil across the border.[1]

The period from the 1880s to the First World War has been designated the first era of globalization as British, European, and later American companies extended their reach across much of the rest of the world. The emergence of new investment markets and expansion of existing ones, as well as the development of new financial instruments to reach a wider investing public, provided sources of capital on a much larger scale. In turn this enabled the rise of companies with national or international aspirations. The mercantilist empires of Britain and France dismantled many of their investment trade barriers by the 1860s. The establishment of the "gold standard" among major industrial nations in the following decade fostered the acceleration of capital mobility across borders.[2]

At the same time, the exponents of globalization encountered increasing resistance, particularly from emerging industrial nations including Germany, Japan, and the United States. Protective tariffs were erected and trade restrictions were developed in order to foster domestic industries. One of the by-products of these policies—anticipated or not—was that companies seeking to enter promising new markets abroad, or to access raw materials essential for industrial growth, turned to portfolio and direct investment in these protectionist countries. By the early twentieth century, the United States was host country to over $7 billion (USD) from overseas investors, of which $1.5 billion (USD) was in direct investment.[3]

Canada established its own protectionist system with the National Policy in 1879—not necessarily because it expected to become an industrial powerhouse, but rather to protect jobs at home by inviting foreign direct investment. If this was the intent, it seems to have worked: by 1914 Canada was host to $800 million (USD), equivalent to 53 per cent of FDI in the US, which had a population ten times larger. Likewise Canada's GNP more than doubled between 1880 and 1910.[4]

Imperial Oil was not so fortunate. Even before the amalgamation of the company in 1880, exports of Canadian kerosene had declined substantially, and Imperial lobbied for trade protection under the National Policy. Standard Oil's products, however, remained competitive, particularly in the Maritimes, and in the 1890s the US company embarked on a strategy familiar from its expansion ventures at home. Imperial found itself surrounded by competitors that had financing and technological support from Standard. A sharp depression in the US in the mid-1890s accelerated Standard's campaign to conquer the Canadian market. Although Imperial sought to hold its investors through generous dividend payments, by 1898–99, with prospects for a shrinking market and diminishing output from the Petrolia oil wells, the outlook was bleak. Standard offered good terms, as it had in takeovers of US competitors, and the merger was swiftly consummated.[5]

In the normal course of events, it is quite probable that Imperial would have become simply a vehicle for marketing Standard Oil products in Canada: all but one refinery was closed and the output of the Petrolia fields continued to decline. In addition, the government of Canada under the Liberal regime of Wilfrid Laurier seemed headed for some form of reciprocity in trade with the US in the first decade of the twentieth century. Three events in 1911, however, disrupted this "normal course" and transformed the relationship between Standard Oil and Imperial Oil.

At the national level, in 1911 a proposed US-Canada Reciprocity Treaty was defeated, and Canada remained protectionist for several more decades. On the industry front, Standard's greatest rival, Royal Dutch Shell, launched a beachhead in Canada, establishing an oil and gas storage facility in Montreal in 1911. This was followed with threats to embark on major exploratory ventures in Alberta a few years later. But the most significant event took place in the US when the Supreme Court upheld a ruling ordering dissolution of Standard Oil in 1911.

Small oil producers in the US, as well as populist and progressive politicians and state authorities from Pennsylvania to Texas, had been pursuing Standard Oil for more than two decades. The company had been regarded as a target of the federal Sherman Antitrust Act of 1890, but had avoided prosecution in part through various legal stratagems. In 1908, however, the US Justice Department brought a case against it, and a court-ordered dissolution was upheld three years later. Standard Oil was broken up into thirty-four companies, of which the largest were Standard Oil of New Jersey (Jersey Standard, later Exxon) and Standard Oil of New York (Socony, later Mobil). In 1999 Exxon and Mobil were reunited.[6]

Imperial Oil ended up with Jersey Standard, which proved to be providential for the Canadian company. Walter Teagle took charge of Jersey Standard's foreign sales and also became president of Imperial Oil. Combining these roles, he fashioned a strategy for both companies that would sustain them through the next thirty years, during which time he also became the chief executive of Jersey Standard.

Teagle recognized, as did other managers of Jersey Standard, that the company had immense refining assets and a strong transportation and marketing structure but virtually no direct access to crude oil, which it had to buy from other Standard remnants or independent suppliers. Standard Oil had missed an opportunity to enter the burgeoning Texas oil fields in the early 1900s, and in any case expansion into production in the US might arouse antitrust authorities. The alternative was to look for new oilfields abroad, particularly in Latin America. In that region, the British had well established commercial connections, while thanks to President Theodore Roosevelt's "Big Stick" diplomacy American companies faced hostility from local governments.

In this situation, Imperial Oil could prove useful. As part of the British Empire, the Canadian company could facilitate dealings with British companies, as was the case in Peru. In addition, it could provide cover for an American company in a hostile environment, as was the case in Colombia. In addition, Teagle regarded Imperial as a potential platform for a broader array of Jersey Standard overseas interests, shielded from scrutiny and possible further tax and antitrust measures by the US government. As it happened, this proved to be an unwarranted fear: as the US moved toward intervention in the First World War, the value of big businesses for military preparedness underwent a reconsideration. By the 1920s the US government was an enthusiastic proponent of overseas investment by the oil industry for "national defense." In the Middle East Jersey Standard acquired a foothold in the Anglo-French consortium, Iraq Petroleum, with assistance from the US State Department. In the meantime, however, Imperial Oil served Jersey Standard's purposes as a vehicle for expansion in South America through the International Petroleum Company.[7]

As president of Imperial Oil Teagle arranged for a substantial increase in capitalization—to $50 million (CAD)—to construct refineries across the country, provided Imperial with access to thermal cracking refining technology, and supported what proved to be extensive exploration for new oil resources in Alberta and the Northwest Territories. Retrospectively this might be deemed an overreaction to the threat of Royal Dutch Shell in Canada. But these measures also equipped Imperial with an updated and integrated system that enabled it to sustain its position as the leading company in the industry in Canada for much of the rest of the century.

But Imperial was also firmly embedded in Jersey Standard's international structure. While oil from Peru was carried to Imperial's market on the west coast of Canada, and Colombian oil to the Maritimes, a substantial amount of the oil from both sources went to Jersey Standard's refinery in Bayonne, New Jersey. Most of the profits from International Petroleum in the 1930s flowed ultimately as dividends to Jersey Standard. Although Imperial had established a research lab at Sarnia in the 1920s, it remained dependent on the parent company for access to the most up-to-date technology in many areas. Marketing strategies and labour relations policies drew on Jersey Standard models. International Petroleum provided opportunities for Imperial's managers, engineers, and geologists to develop their capabilities while at the top levels Imperial executives served on the Jersey Standard board of directors, and the parent company designated individual members of their executive committee to act as liaisons with Imperial Oil.[8]

As the Second World War ended, new opportunities for overseas expansion opened for Jersey Standard, particularly in the Middle East where it joined the Aramco consortium in Saudi Arabia in 1947. By that time oil production from Jersey Standard's affiliates in Venezuela had far exceeded output from Colombia and Peru, augmenting the large producing and refining operations of Humble Oil in Texas, which it had acquired in 1919. For Imperial Oil, however, the future was far less promising. During the 1920s Imperial's subsidiary, Royalite, had found gas and oil in Alberta's Turner Valley near Calgary, but by the postwar years the production rate was declining. Meanwhile, the government of Colombia was proposing to take over International Petroleum's fields by 1951. Imperial had been exploring for oil in northern Alberta and the Northwest Territories since 1921 with limited success—aside from Norman Wells, which had supplied the Canol project during the Second World War but was too distant from markets to be commercially viable.

In 1945, Henry Hewetson took over as president of Imperial. Although he was an American Hewetson had connections to Canada, having served with the Royal Flying Corps in the First World War, and he worked at the Sarnia refinery before going back to the US. Eventually Hewetson headed Standard Oil of Louisiana, then returned to Imperial Oil in 1935, where he overhauled the company's sales and marketing operations. In many respects he resembled Teagle, both physically and in his stature with the parent company, where he was appointed director in 1950.[9]

Since Alberta had plentiful reserves of natural gas, Jersey Standard contemplated providing Imperial with access to a modified version of a German patent it had acquired in the 1930s that would produce synthetic crude oil from gas. But Hewetson backed Link and other geologists seeking a "last chance effort" to strike oil, and arranged for Jersey Standard to bring in specialists and undertake research using seismic surveys to identify "anomalies" in an area of central Alberta known as the western Canadian sedimentary basin. According to one account of the events leading to the Leduc discovery, the area chosen was "geologically all wrong but [Imperial] found oil anyway."[10]

Leduc had a larger impact on the Imperial-Jersey Standard relationship than either party may have anticipated. In order to finance developing the infrastructure around Leduc, including building a pipeline to central Canada, Imperial sold International Petroleum to Jersey Standard. In effect Imperial Oil became primarily a vertically integrated Canadian operation, still linked to its US parent but increasingly oriented to the domestic Canadian market. Over the next seventy years Imperial's commitment to developing Canadian oil resources deepened as it advanced into the oil sands of Alberta and the oil and gas frontiers of northern Canada.

In 1947–48 by a curious—and unrelated—coincidence, the government of Canada contemplated, and then recoiled from, a proposed customs union and comprehensive trade agreement with the United States. During the Second World War there had been a good deal of economic cooperation between the two countries, but by 1947 Canada faced a serious imbalance in its trade and currency accounts as the British market failed to rebound and imports from the United States soared. Eventually the Marshall Plan, in which Canada was allowed to participate as a supplier of goods, mitigated these problems. But in the interim proposals for greater integration between the two countries had support, at least within the government agencies and ministries. Nevertheless their views were not endorsed by Canada's prime minister Mackenzie King, who had been a member of the Laurier cabinet during the Reciprocity Treaty debacle of 1911 and did not wish to repeat the experience.[11]

This rejection did not, then, reflect a nascent Canadian nationalism. But over the next two decades issues involving American economic (and political) influence in Canada would begin to take effect, culminating in the early 1970s when the first energy crisis focused public attention on the role of foreign-owned companies in the oil and gas industry, with Imperial Oil as exhibit number one. Even in the 1950s there was some incipient discontent: the role of Americans in financing the Trans Canada Pipe Line engendered criticism, and John Diefenbaker indulged in nationalist rhetoric during election campaigns. Generally, however, government policies reflect what later was characterized as a "continentalist" approach: the National Oil Policy, for example, supported the existing arrangements under which eastern Canada imported oil, relying on multinational suppliers—and the proposal for a pipeline to Montreal was shelved.[12]

Within the Jersey Standard system, relations with Imperial also exhibited a "continentalist" (or "corporatist") character during this period. The "Esso" oval sign towered over service stations, while the name "Imperial" diminished into the background. Generous dividends continued to flow from Imperial, although it was able to retain a somewhat greater amount of earnings for reinvestment.[13] More Canadians rose to the senior management level at Imperial, and they were also encouraged to pursue lateral promotions across other Jersey Standard divisions and affiliates: Ken Jamieson, who became president of Jersey Standard in 1965 and chairman of the board in 1969, was a prominent example of this career path.[14]

At the same time, however, Imperial was moving toward a strategy of expansion and diversification within Canada. As the company focused on new initiatives into northern Canada and the oil sands, it strengthened its research operations to support these areas. The achievements of Roger Butler and others in developing technologies to enhance *in situ* oil sands extraction and drilling for oil in Arctic conditions were the result of these measures.

Multinational oil companies, including Jersey Standard, had faced nationalism in producer states since early in the twentieth century. In 1918 Russian revolutionaries seized the Baku oil fields. During the 1930s, Bolivia and Mexico nationalized their oil, joined by Colombia in the 1950s, and Argentina, Peru, Indonesia, and Iraq in the 1960s. The floodgates opened after the first energy crisis in 1973–74 as most of the major OPEC members either nationalized their industry or set up government-owned corporations to run them.

Canada of course never experienced such upheavals, but the oil multinationals did face intense criticism in the early 1970s and again in 1979–81 in the wake of the two energy crises. The government of Canada also established a crown corporation whose initial mandate was supposed to be to promote "frontier exploration" for new oil sources. In practice it evolved into an integrated company that challenged the oil majors before being privatized in the 1990s.

The National Energy Program was an ambitious set of policies intended to encourage both new resource development and "Canadian" (not necessarily publicly owned) oil companies while enhancing federal tax revenues. It foundered in the midst of volatile oil price gyrations and feuding between the federal and provincial governments. By the end of the century, with continental free trade agreements in place, nationalist controversies over oil and other resources seemed to be vestiges of a rapidly disappearing past—except, perhaps, for Albertans with long memories.

Throughout these events, Imperial Oil was a target for criticism by Canadian nationalists. In 1981, Jack Armstrong as board chairman vigorously defended the importance of foreign investment, multinationals, and foreign technology in developing Canada's oil resources.[15] It was a forceful statement on behalf of multinationals in an era when Jersey Standard's executives and the heads of other big oil companies were being haled before committees of the US Congress, and accused of profiteering from the energy crises.

At the same time, it was a defense of the benefits the foreign-owned oil companies offered to Canada, and Armstrong presented himself as the head of a Canadian company rather than as a spokesman for Jersey Standard. This did not of course necessarily convince Canadian critics of multinationals, nor did the underlying nationalism necessarily resonate at Jersey Standard's headquarters. In 1981 Imperial was reporting record earnings levels and had promising new projects in the oil sands and northern Canada. As the historians of Exxon noted, Imperial's "independence" was respected "as long as the company remained successful."[16] Over the next two decades that perspective shifted along with the fortunes of both companies.

The events of the 1970s–80s left Jersey Standard (rechristened Exxon in 1972) in a situation reminiscent of the years following the breakup of Standard Oil. Although it retained producing fields in North America, including those of Imperial in Canada, it had lost direct access to many of its overseas production holdings. As with the other oil multinationals, it had to adapt to a world in which it processed, transported, and sold oil owned by the producer states. Beyond that role, it faced several strategic options. It could diversify into other "energy-related" fields or indeed transform itself into a kind of conglomerate. It could expand into new producing fields. Or it could accommodate to changing conditions by merging with other companies that had greater access to production or a strong market position or innovative technology.

Exxon pursued all of these options, although not simultaneously. During the 1970s–early 1980s under Clifford Garvin the company presented itself as being in "the energy business . . . rather than just the oil business."[17] To that end Exxon explored initiatives in nuclear fuel, solar power, even coal as well as supporting Imperial's oil sands ventures. Perhaps the most ambitious operation involved shale oil in Colorado; but it proved to be premature and was shut down in 1982. It was during this period that Exxon scientists were conducting research into the role of fossil fuels in climate change. As oil prices spiked up in the early 1980s, however, diversification efforts diminished; Lawrence Rawl and Lee Raymond, who by mid-decade emerged as the new leaders at Exxon, vowed to return the company to its "core business"—oil and gas.[18]

In the following decade Exxon embarked on a search for new producing fields, sometimes alone but often within a consortium or in partnership. Africa in particular looked promising, leading to ventures in Chad, Cameroon, and Angola. These undertakings sometimes presented physical risks for company employees as well as financial risks, reminiscent of exploratory operations in the early twentieth century in Latin America and Russia. The collapse of the Soviet Union seemed to present great opportunities not only in central Asian states such as Kazakhstan and Azerbaijan but also in Russia, although the complex politics and bureaucratic hurdles presented endless obstacles. Ultimately Exxon was able to mount a profitable venture on Sakhalin Island, after eleven years of manoeuvring.[19]

Given its quest for new sources of oil, a merger with another oil major with producing fields seemed logical. But there were other factors involved. After the boom and collapse of oil prices in 1981–85, the industry entered a long period of depressed prices—except for sudden episodes of volatility, as happened during the first Gulf War in 1991. The growth of the "Asian Tigers" of Southeast Asia at the end of that decade promised a larger and more enduring market for oil, but the abrupt collapse of that boom in 1998 generated a sudden rush toward consolidation among the large multinationals. This rush was initiated by BP, which sought to merge with Mobil. When that fell through, BP turned to Amoco. Soon all the other big companies were alert for further action. Exxon in particular feared losing ground to BP and Shell, two traditional rivals. This led to the quick merger of Exxon and Mobil in 1999, reuniting the two largest survivors of the breakup of Standard Oil in 1911, ironically with the blessing of the US Federal Trade Commission on the grounds that this was "a very different world."[20]

These developments at Exxon would affect the manner in which the parent company related to Imperial Oil. The oil price collapse in 1985–86 hit Exxon hard and led to a full-scale review of the company's structure by Rawls and Raymond. They concluded that Exxon had become overly bureaucratic, burdened with multiple committee reviews and reports. At the same time there was too much decentralization, so that top management lacked the capability to react in a "nimble" way to changing conditions. Imperial in particular was perceived as having too much autonomy, as did Humble (now designated Exxon USA). For the time being, both affiliates escaped the full impact of reorganization—although the reformers reoriented the company toward a renewed effort at overseas expansion of production. In 1991 Rawl orchestrated the unification of all overseas oil exploration into a new entity, undercutting Exxon USA. He and Raymond also contemplated buying out the minority shareholders in Imperial but they were reluctant to shoulder the costs and to challenge Canadian regulations of foreign takeovers.[21]

The Exxon-Mobil merger provided a new opportunity to bring Imperial Oil to heel. Raymond supported the continuation of Mobil's Canadian operations to counter those of Imperial, even though he acknowledged that this was an "inefficient arrangement."[22] Over the following years Mobil veterans were placed in managerial positions at Imperial, including the presidency of the company. This was not out of line with the policies of Exxon—or indeed of any multinational company—but still it was definitely a signal that things were changing.

Meanwhile the issue of fossil fuels and climate change loomed ever larger, both over companies and over the industry as a whole. In the 1990s Lee Raymond of Exxon adopted a position of denial and resistance to international pressures as exemplified in the Kyoto Accord. Rex Tillerson, Raymond's successor, retreated from this defiant view and Exxon Mobil announced a new initiative in biofuels, aiming at generating gasoline from algae, which received a good deal of publicity. At the same time the company continued to lobby against US measures to limit imports of oil sands products. More broadly, it took the view that world energy needs would have to rely on fossil fuels for at least another generation.[23]

Imperial Oil was, if anything, in a more difficult situation. Since the 1980s it had committed large resources to the development of the oil sands and northern Canadian oil and gas. While hopes for the latter dwindled, the company continued to place its bets on the oil sands through investments in the Kearl mine and the reopening of Cold Lake and other *in situ* ventures. But delays and resistance to pipeline development linking the oil sands to world markets and continuing volatility in oil prices made for a perpetual cycle of uncertainty about the future.

In July 2018 a *Wall Street Journal* article focusing on the new chief executive officer of Exxon, Darren Woods, noted the company's acknowledgement that a $20 billion (USD) oil sands project in Canada "was no longer profitable." The same article went on to observe: "Exxon is weighing reducing its exposure to Canada where it has operated for 130 years."[24] Imperial Oil—and for that matter Exxon—has been written off before, and risen from the dead, or at least from the sickbed. Nevertheless, this particular statement implied that a significant change in the Exxon Mobil-Imperial relationship was in the offing, although whether Exxon Mobil contemplated selling all or part of the Canadian company or just planned to scale back new investments in the oil sands was unclear.

In some respects, however, the two companies had been following different trajectories since the Leduc discovery in 1947. Exxon had lost many of its overseas production fields, then rebuilt its position. The amalgamation with Mobil had if anything made Exxon even more of a global player. Meanwhile, Imperial, while remaining part of the Exxon system, increasingly focused on serving the Canadian market and developing resources in Canada. For Exxon, Imperial's most important asset was its position in the oil sands, which was nevertheless a frustratingly expensive and controversial feature. But these conditions had been evident for more than twenty years, and while oil prices fell dramatically in 2014, they subsequently partially rebounded, rising above $74 (USD)/bbl. (West Texas Intermediate) in July 2018.[25] So it is hard to know at this time whether Darren Woods's remarks reflect a response to continuing uncertainty in the oil market or a long-term change in strategy for Exxon Mobil.

APPENDICES

APPENDIX 1

Imperial Oil Company Financial Statements, 1892–98 ($000 CAD)

Year	Assets	Surplus	Net Profit	Dividends
1892	931	297	52	32
1893	1,016	232	66	30
1894	1,094	351	69	25
1895	1,028	375	60	25
1896	1,087	447	104	36
1897	1,118	465	62	35
1898	1,055	456	n/a	30

SOURCE: Ewing, *History of Imperial Oil*, Chapter 3, Appendix II.

Imperial Oil Production, Sales, and Net Earnings, 1912–20

Year	Refining*	Sales/Mfg**	Net income***
1912	3,100	107,068	2,431
1913	3,400	119,011	3,362
1914	5,000	108,155	2,414
1915	7,000	133,620	4,784
1916	8,400	138,379	4,666
1917	13,700	227,258	5,124
1918	18,300	308,071	6,143
1919	21,200	277,877	7,174
1920	20,800	314,110	11,095

* bbl./day
** 000 imperial gallons/year
*** $000 CAD
SOURCES: Ewing, *History of Imperial Oil*, Chapter 4, Tables 6–7; Gibb & Knowlton, *History of Standard Oil (NJ): The Resurgent Years*, 677–8.

Imperial Oil Ltd., Income Received, and Dividends Paid, 1921–47 ($000 CAD)

Year	Mfg./Sales	Div. Rec'd.*	Net Income**	Div.Paid ***
1921	1,350	1,008	315	4,202
1922	7,710	2,227	9,560	4,734
1923	2,528	1,251	5,596	6,373
1924	7,927	3,246	13,089	4,837
1925	7,927	2,155	11,221	6,507
1926	14,102	3,266	17,540	8,162
1927	5,648	3,266	13,615	9,842
1928	16,775	3,098	22,963	8,693
1930	7,215	8,850	19,020	26,545
1931	8,915	8,973	18,227	13,261
1932	4,331	9,371	14,713	13,415
1933	3,927	10,279	14,101	13,415
1934	3,023	22,165	25,772	24,881
1935	2,900	23,162	25,229	33,697
1936	3,082	23,104	25,628	33,706
1937	3,572	24,406	26,452	33,706
1938	3,573	24,482	25,960	33,706
1939	5,368	17,048	19,250	33,706
1940	7,113	14,032	17,039	16,853
1941	5,496	10,635	16,144	13,482
1942	7,936	9,673	14,063	13,482
1943	8,397	9,628	15,549	13,482
1944	9,141	9,473	16,193	13,482
1945	11,902	9,415	16,617	13,482
1946	14,902	5,713	17,326	13,482
1947	15,556	5,756	20,464	13,514

* Dividends received from subsidiaries: 90% from IPC 1923–40; 80% 1940–47
** Net income after taxes
*** Standard Oil (NJ) held 78–80% of IOL shares
SOURCES: Ewing, *History of Imperial Oil*, Chapter 15, Tables 1–2; IOL Annual Reports 1932–46.

APPENDIX 2C

Imperial Oil Sales, Production, Earnings, and Dividends, 1947–80

Year	Sales 000 bbl./day	Production 000 bbl./day	Earnings $M[CAD]	Dividends $M [CAD]	%Dividends/ earnings
1947	130	6	20	14	66
1948	142	12	23	14	60
1949	154	25	25	14	54
1950	174	36	30	15	49
1951	196	63	36	17	49
1952	209	65	41	22	54
1953	212	78	48	24	50
1954	218	84	50	27	54
1955	250	93	62	29	46
1956	275	103	69	36	52
1957	276	95	75	37	52
1958	275	75	51	38	75
1959	293	82	55	38	69
1960	298	90	61	43	69
1961	295	111	68	44	65
1962	317	124	68	44	65
1963	327	126	71	49	69

Appendix 2C
Continued

Year	Sales 000 bbl./day	Production 000 bbl./day	Earnings $M[CAD]	Dividends $M [CAD]	%Dividends/ earnings
1964	342	131	79	55	70
1965	348	133	86	58	68
1966	356	146	92	63	69
1967	370	141	96	67	70
1968	383	150	100	67	67
1969	381	154	94	68	72
1970	400	170	105	68	65
1971	406	183	136	77	56
1972	417	224	151	77	51
1973	449	275	227	104	46
1974	443	224	290	104	47
1975	418	173	250	104	42
1976	441	154	264	106	40
1977	433	148	293	116	40
1978	449	147	314	124	39
1979	468	256	471	150	32
1980	449	226	601	201	33

SOURCES:
IOL and Consolidated Subsidiaries Financial Review 1959. IOL Archives, Series 4, Box 292A. Acc. 80-0021; IOL Annual Reports, 1959–81.

Canadian Oil Companies, Comparison, 1947 ($000 CAD)

	Imperial	British American *	McColl Frontenac **
Assets	241,506	71,529	44,692
Earnings	20,464	8,141	2,780
Production bbl. (000)	47,485	15,857	10,057

* British American became Gulf Canada in 1967.
** McColl Frontenac became Texaco Canada in 1941.
SOURCE: Imperial Oil Records, Series 4, Box 292A Acc. 80-0021.

Canadian Oil Companies, Comparison, 1994 ($ M. CAD)

	Imperial	Shell Canada	Petro Canada	Amoco Canada	Nova
Assets	11,928	6,113	5,912	6,076	8,257
Sales	9,019	5.034	4,730	4,270	3,724
Net Income	359	320	262	-70	575
Employees	9,470	4,391	6,209	2,800	6,600

SOURCE: Rinaldo Stefan, *Report on Imperial Oil* (1996). Appendix 1. Imperial Oil Records, IOL-pub 6-157.

Notes

Introduction

1   www.theglobeandmail.com/report-on-business/rob-magazine/top1000.

2   See Appendices 3A and 3B.

3   www.fortune.com/fortune 500/global500; Steve Coll, *Private Empire: Exxon Mobil and American Power* (New York: Penguin Press, 2012), 65–6.

4   Graham D. Taylor, *The Rise of Canadian Business* (Don Mills, ON: Oxford University Press Canada, 2009), 73.

5   Henrietta M. Larson, Evelyn H. Knowlton, and Charles S. Popple, *The History of Standard Oil (New Jersey): New Horizons 1927–1950* (New York: Harper & Row, 1971), 720–1.

6   Mira Wilkins, "The History of Multinational Enterprise," in A.M. Rugman et al., ed., *The Oxford Handbook of International Business*, 2nd edition (Oxford, UK: Oxford University Press, 2010), 3–39.

7   The volumes of *The History of Standard Oil* (New Jersey) are cited throughout this work. Other examples include Mira Wilkins and Frank Ernest Hill, *American Business Abroad: Ford on Six Continents*, 2nd edition (Cambridge, UK: Cambridge University Press 2011), and George David Smith, *From Monopoly to Competition: The Transformations of Alcoa, 1888–1986* (Cambridge, UK: Cambridge University Press, 1988).

8   Julian Birkenshaw, "Strategy and Management in MNE Subsidiaries," in Rugman et al., *the Oxford Handbook of International Business*, 367–89; Geoffrey Jones, *Multinationals and Global Capitalism* (Oxford, UK: Oxford University Press, 2005), 162–3.

9   Joseph A. Pratt and William E. Hale, *Exxon: Transforming Energy, 1973–2005* (Austin, TX: Dolph Briscoe Center for American History, University of Texas at Austin 2013).

PROLOGUE

1   Barry Broadfoot, Interviews with Vern Hunter, Doug Layer, W.D.C. MacKenzie, Vern
     Taylor. Imperial Oil Archives, Glenbow Museum and Archives, Calgary, Alberta, Series
     16: Records of the External Affairs Department [Edited versions of these interviews
     were published in Barry Broadfoot and Mark Nichols, *Memories: The Story of Imperial's
     First Century* (Toronto: Imperial Oil, 1980)]. Petroleum Industry Oral History
     Collection, Glenbow Museum and Archives: Vern Hunter [interviewed 17 Aug 1983
     by Aubrey Kerr]; Doug Layer [interviewed 12 July 1983 by Nadine Mackenzie]; Vern
     Taylor [interviewed 4 June 1981 by Aubrey Kerr]. Jacqueline Chartier, "Vern 'Dry Hole'
     Hunter: How a Preacher's Son Became an Oilpatch Legend," *Alberta History* 56, no. 3
     (Summer 2008): 2–7. "Birth of an Oil Well," *Imperial Oil Review* (Apr 1947): 3–5. Hal
     Tennant, "Leduc—Turning Point of an Industry," *Imperial Oil Review* (Feb 1958): 3–15.

2   John S. Ewing, "History of Imperial Oil," unpublished manuscript, Imperial Oil
     Archives, Glenbow Museum, chs 8, 15; Graham D. Taylor, "From Branch Operation
     to Integrated Subsidiary: The Reorganisation of Imperial Oil Under Walter Teagle,
     1911–1917," *Business History* 34, no. 3 (July 1992): 49–68.

3   "Claim Biggest Oilfield Soon Opens in North," *Globe & Mail*, 20 Oct 1920, 2.

4   George de Mille, *Oil in Canada West: The Early Years* (Calgary: Northwest Printing
     & Lithographing, 1970), 147–209. Earle Gray, *The Great Canadian Oil Patch: The
     Petroleum Era from Birth to Peak*, 2nd edition (Edmonton: June Warren Publishing,
     2004), 114–42; Aubrey Kerr, *Leduc* (Calgary: Altona, 1991), 21–32.

5   Minutes of the Board of Directors, Imperial Oil Ltd., 7 May 1947; 3 Sept 1947; 8 Sept
     1947; 7 Oct 1947. Imperial Oil Shareholders, Special General Meeting, 22 Sept 1947.
     Imperial Oil Archives, Glenbow Museum and Archives, Series 2: Corporate Services.
     Bennett H. Wall, *Growth in a Changing Environment: A History of the Standard Oil
     Company (New Jersey) 1950–1975* (New York: McGraw Hill Co., 1988), ch. 12. [Note:
     currency figures are identified as either in Canadian dollars (CAD) or US dollars
     (USD)].

CHAPTER 1

1   Joyce Barkhouse, *Abraham Gesner* (Don Mills: Fitzhenry & Whiteside, 1980), 50–60;
     Kendall Beaton, "Dr. Gesner's Kerosene: The Start of American Oil Refining," *Business
     History Review* 39 (Feb 1955): 28–53; Loris S. Russell, "Gesner, Abraham," *Dictionary
     of Canadian Biography*, vol. 9 (Toronto: University of Toronto Press, 1976), www.
     biographi.ca/en/bio/gesner_abraham; Earle Gray, "Gesner, Williams and the Birth of
     the Oil Industry," *Oil Industry History* 9 (2008): 11–23; Allison Mitcham, ed., *The Best of
     Abraham Gesner* (Hantsport, NS: Lancelot Press, 1995); Jean-Pierre Proulx, *Whaling in
     the North Atlantic: From Earliest Times to the Mid-19th Century* (Ottawa: Parks Canada
     National Historic Parks and Sites Branch, 1986), 68–9.

2   Gray, *Great Canadian Oil Patch*, 34–44; Edward Phelps, "Foundations of the Canadian
     Oil Industry, 1850–1866," in Edith Firth, ed., *Profiles of a Province: Studies in the
     History of Ontario* (Toronto: Ontario Historical Society, 1969), 156–9; Christina Burr,
     Canada's Victorian Oil Town: The Transformation of Petrolia from a Resource Town

into a Victorian Community (Montreal: McGill-Queen's University Press, 2006), 38–9, 58–66; Hope Morritt, *Rivers of Oil: The Founding of North America's Petroleum Industry* (Kingston: Quarry Press, 1993), 19–37.

3   Earle Gray, *Ontario's Petroleum Legacy* (Edmonton: Heritage Community Foundation, 2008), 38–9; Burt, 87–96; Morritt, 85–6.

4   Timothy W. Cobban, *Cities of Oil* (Toronto: University of Toronto Press, 2013), 13–24; W.B. Mack, "Oil Refining in London," 29 Nov 1948, Imperial Oil Archives, Acc. 800074/001(01).

5   W.A.E. McBryde, "Petroleum 'Deodorized': The Early Canadian History of the 'Doctor Sweetening' Process," *Annals of Science*, 1 May 1991, 102–11; Cobban, 19–21. Ewing, chapter 2, 14–15.

6   Hugh Grant and Henry Thille, "Tariffs, Strategy and Structure: Competition and Collusion in the Ontario Petroleum Industry, 1870–1880," *Journal of Economic History* 61, no. 2 (June 2001): 392–3; Ewing, ch. 2, 27–8; Ben Forster, *A Conjunction of Interests: Business, Politics and Tariffs 1825–1879* (Toronto: University of Toronto Press, 1986), 111–12.

7   Quoted in Hugh Grant, "The 'Mysterious' Jacob L. Englehart and the Early Ontario Petroleum Industry," *Ontario History* 75, no. 1 (Mar 1993): 68.

8   Grant, "The 'Mysterious' Jacob L. Englehart," 68–71; Cobban, 19–20; Morritt, 89–90, 98–100; Gray, *Great Canadian Oil Patch*, 489–92.

9   Harold F. Williamson and Arnold R. Daum, *The American Petroleum Industry: The Age of Illumination 1859–1899* (Evanston: Northwestern University Press, 1959), 337–9; *Canadian Petroleum Production, Historical Statistics of Canada* Q19-25. www.statcan. gc.ca/publ/11-516-x; Gary May, *Hard Oiler! The Story of Canadians' Quest for Oil At Home and Abroad* (Toronto: Dundurn Press, 1998), 70–5.

10   Cobban, 48–59; Gray, *Great Canadian Oil Patch*, 492–5; Grant, "The 'Mysterious' Jacob L. Englehart," 72–3; Morritt, 115–16; Albert Tucker, "Englehart, Jacob," *Dictionary of Canadian Biography*, vol. XV (Toronto: University of Toronto Press, 2005), www. biographi.ca.

11   Cobban, 29–33; Forster, 156–7; Grant and Thille, "Tariffs, Strategy and Structure," 393–4; Williamson and Daum, 209–11.

12   Imperial Oil Agreement, 30 Apr 1880. Imperial Oil Archives, Corporate Affairs, Historical File, Box 7, File 6.

13   Ewing, ch. 2, 68–9; Robert Page, "The Early History of the Canadian Oil Industry, 1860–1900," *Queen's Quarterly* 91, no. 4 (Winter 1984): 855; Imperial Oil Agreement, 30 Apr 1880.

14   Norman R. Ball and Edward Phelps, "Williams, James Miller," *Dictionary of Canadian Biography*, vol. XI (Toronto: University of Toronto Press, 1982), www.biographi.ca/en/ bio/williams_james_miller; Burt, 119–22.

CHAPTER 2

1   Williamson and Daum, 211–31, 273–9.

2   Ron Chernow, *Titan: The Life of John D. Rockefeller* (New York: Vintage, 1998), 73–95, 129–55, 157–82; Williamson and Daum, 301–8, 346–56.

3   Ralph W. Hidy and Muriel Hidy, *History of Standard Oil (New Jersey): Pioneering in Big Business* (New York: Harper & Bros, 1955), 40–68; Greene, William N., "Strategies of the Major Oil Companies," (PhD diss., Harvard University, 1982), ch. 3, 3–6.

4   Imperial Oil Profit and Loss Account, 1880–1882. Imperial Oil Archives; Williamson and Daum, Appendix D3, 747.

5   Cobban, 40–2; G.A. Purdy, *Petroleum: Prehistoric to Petrochemicals* (Toronto: Copp Clark, 1957), 32–3.

6   Hugh Grant and Henry Thille, "How Standard Oil Came to Canada: The Monopolization of Canadian Petroleum Refining, 1886–1898," (unpublished ms, July 2004), 4–5, 856.

7   W.A.E. McBryde, "Ontario: Early Pilot Plant for the Chemical Refining of Oil in North America," *Ontario History* 79, no. 3 (Sept 1987): 217–19; Cobban, 67–8; Gray, *Great Canadian Oil Patch*, 497–8; Ewing, ch. 2, 42–6.

8   McBryde, 219–24; Hidy, 160–5.

9   Imperial Oil Profit & Loss Statements, 1890–1894. Imperial Oil Archives; Ewing, ch. 2, 83–92.

10   Ewing, ch. 4, 5–6; 858–9. Samuel Rogers's son, Edward "Ted" Rogers, was one of the founders of radio broadcasting in Canada, and his son Ted Rogers Jr. became the head of the largest cable system in the country.

11   Hidy, 128–44; Daniel Yergin, *The Prize: The Epic Quest for Oil, Money and Power* (New York: Simon & Schuster, 1991), 57–63.

12   Ewing, ch. 3, 67–70.

13   Hidy, 209–25; Chernow, 330–42.

14   Grant and Thille, "How Standard Oil Came to Canada," 7–8; Cobban, 68–70.

15   See Appendix 1.

16   Ewing, ch. 4, 60–6, 862–4.

17   Ewing, ch. 4, 78–89; Cobban, 71–2; Imperial Oil, Profit and Loss Accounts 1894–1898. Imperial Oil Archives.

CHAPTER 3

1   Imperial Oil Ltd., Minutes of Board Meeting, 12–13 Jan 1899. IOL Minute Books 1899–1915. IOL Archives; Ewing, ch. 5, 1–4, 14–17.

2   Hidy, 254–6, 315–16.

3   Cobban, 71–3; Ewing, chapter 5, 18–20; John T. Saywell, "The Early History of Canadian Oil Companies: A Chapter in Canadian Business History," *Ontario History* 53, no. 1 (1961): 68–71.

4   Ewing, ch. 6, 26–39; Imperial Oil Board of Directors Minutes 16 July 1908; 8 Dec 1908.

5   Steve Weinberg, *Taking on the Trust* (New York: Norton, 2008), 208–28; Nevins, vol. 2, 519–26; Hidy, 649–52; Yergin, 96–110.

6   Hidy, 694–8; *Standard Oil of New Jersey v. United States* 221 US 1. law.cornell.edu/ supreme court/text.

7   Hidy, 711–14; Joseph A. Pratt, "Exxon and the Control of Oil," *Journal of American History* 99, no. 1 (June 2012): 147–8. By 2000, Indiana Standard, Ohio Standard, and Atlantic Refining ended up as part of British Petroleum (BP). Standard of California (Chevron) remained, along with Exxon-Mobil, as the most durable survivors of the 1911 dissolution.

8   Harold F. Williamson et al., *The American Petroleum Industry: The Age of Energy 1899–1959* (Westport, CT: Greenwood Publishers, 1959), 167–205, 242–60; Jonathan Singer, *Broken Trusts: The Texas Attorney General versus the Oil Industry 1889–1909* (Texas: A&M University Press, 2002), 57–68.

9   Yergin, 71–7, 87–95, 121–8; Hidy, 547–79.

10 Wall and Gibb, 61–9; 83–4, 94–6; George S. Gibb and E.H. Knowlton, *The History of Standard Oil of New Jersey: The Resurgent Years 1911–1917* (New York: Harper, 1956), 28–9, 76–7.

11 Walter Teagle to H.P. Chamberlain, 27 Jan 1912; Teagle to W.J. Hanna, 28 Nov 1913 Imperial Oil Archives, President's File, Box 24, File 1 (Acc. 80-0013); Hanna to Teagle, 16 Dec 1913; Teagle to Hanna, 10 Jan 1914. Imperial Oil Archives, President's File, Box 1, File 3 (Acc. 80-0028); Ewing, ch. 7, 81–2; ch. 8, 46–53; Imperial Oil Board of Directors Minutes, 29 Jan 1913, 12 Nov 1915.

12 Ewing, ch. 7, 30–4; chapter 9, 3–9; chapter 11, 96–8; Imperial Oil Board of Directors Minutes, 29 Sept 1914; 28 Aug 1916.

13 Wall and Gibb, 108–9, 113–14. The development of the Joint Industrial Committees at Imperial is described in chapter 5.

14 A.C. Bedford, Standard Oil (N.J.) to Teagle, Memorandum on Employee Stock Distribution, Feb 1916; Bedford to Teagle, 25 Sept 1916. Imperial Oil Archives, President's Files, Box 2 "Special File" (Acc. 80-0028). Imperial Oil Board of Directors Minutes, 12 Nov 1915; Ewing, ch. 8, 48–53; Wall and Gibb, 108.

15 Teagle to W.J. Davidson, 17 June 1916. Imperial Oil Archives, President's Files, Box 2, "Special File" (Acc. 80-0028).

16 Imperial Oil Board of Directors Minutes 12 Nov 1915; 9 Aug 1917; 10 Dec 1917; Dominion of Canada Income Tax Assessment Notice 27 Oct 1921. Imperial Oil Archives, Series 4 (Acc. 80-0073).

17 Wall and Gibb, 110–11.

18   Imperial Oil and International Oil Co. in South America is discussed in chapter 4. Imperial Oil's quest for oil in western Canada is discussed in chapter 6.

19   Imperial Oil Board of Directors, Board of Directors, 1 Aug 1919.

CHAPTER 4

1   Walter Teagle to W.J. Hanna, Re: Peruvian Situation, 8 Nov 1913. IOL Archives, Series 5 Corporate Affairs, Box 6, London & Pacific Petroleum Co. file; Charles Goodsell, *American Corporations and Peruvian Politics* (Cambridge, MA: Harvard University Press, 1974), 120; Gibb and Knowlton, 94–5; Wall and Gibb, 97–8.

2   W.C. Teagle to Montagu Pierce, London, 13 Dec 1913. London & Pacific Petroleum file, IOL Archives Gibb and Knowlton, 95–6.

3   Alan Hill, "Historical Foundations of Canada's Oil Industry" (MA thesis, University of Manitoba, 1979), 187.

4   M.J. Hanna, Imperial Oil Ltd., to W.T. White, Minister of Finance, Ottawa, 10 Apr 1914. London & Pacific Petroleum files, IOL Archives; Wall and Gibb, 99–100.

5   Resolution confirming the General By Laws of the International Petroleum Co. Ltd., 31 Dec 1914; "International Oil Securities Listed," 5 May 1915. London & Pacific Petroleum file, IOL Archives. IPC issued $1,039,000 in common shares on the Toronto Stock Exchange, while IOL retained majority control of the issued stock.

6   Gibb and Knowlton, 95; Rosemary Thorp and Geoffrey Bertram, *Peru 1890–1977: Growth and Policy in an Open Economy* (New York: Columbia University Press, 1978), 100–5.

7   Jonathan C. Brown, "Jersey Standard and the Politics of Latin American Oil Production, 1911–30," in John D. Wirth, ed., *Latin American Oil Companies and the Politics of Energy* (Lincoln: University of Nebraska Press, 1985), 16–17.

8   Brown, 17–18; Peter Klaren, *Peru: Society and Nationhood in the Andes* (New York: Oxford University Press, 2000), 213–18.

9   Goodsell, 120–1, 141–2; Alberto Pinelo, *The Multinational Corporation as a Force in Latin American Politics: A Case Study of the International Petroleum Company in Peru* (New York: Praeger, 1973), 13–14; Wall and Gibb, 101–4.

10   Hill, 190–3; Pinelo, 17; Harvey O'Connor, *World Crisis in Oil* (New York: Monthly Review Press, 1962), 225–31. According to Hill, based on research in the State and Military Records of the Public Archives of Canada, the Canadian government did not officially requisition the tankers, and the British minister in Lima protested against the withdrawal of the IPC tanker supplying the domestic market.

11   Gibb and Knowlton, 99–105; Brown, 19–20.

12   Brown, 20; Goodsell, 121; Gibb and Knowlton, 367–9; Thorp and Bertram, 108–11. The 1922 agreement was subsequently endorsed by an arbitration panel of the Hague International Court.

13   Marcelo Bucheli, "Multinational Oil Companies in Colombia and Mexico: Corporate Strategy, Nationalism and Local Politics," unpublished paper presented at the

International Economic History Meeting, Helsinki 2006, 9–10; Marco Palacios, *Between Legitimacy and Violence: A History of Colombia 1875–2002* (Durham: University of North Carolina Press, 2006), 85–6; Mira Wilkins, "Multinational Oil Companies in South America in the 1920s," *Business History Review* 48, no. 3 (Autumn 1974): 430.

14 Gibb and Knowlton, 369–71; Wall and Gibb, 189–93.

15 Bucheli, "Multinational Oil Companies in Mexico and Colombia," 6–9; Richard Lael, *Arrogant Diplomacy: U.S. Policy toward Colombia 1903–1922* (Wilmington: Scholarly Resources Press, 1987), 93–4; Palacios, 69–71; Wall and Gibb, 192–3.

16 Wall and Gibb, 84–5.

17 The company name appears in various iterations, including Andean and Andian. I have used the latter because it is the spelling that appears most frequently in contemporary Imperial Oil documents.

18 Teagle to Hanna, 7 Jan 1914. London & Pacific files, IOL Archives; Brown, 31–2; Hill, 194–5.

19 "Stockholders Vote for Big Oil Merger," *New York Times*, 20 Aug 1920; Gibb and Knowlton, 371–2.

20 Minutes of Annual General Meeting of Imperial Oil, Toronto, 22 Feb 1923. Annual General Meetings, Corporate Records, Series 1, IOL Archives.

21 Minutes of Imperial Oil Annual General Meeting, 26 Feb 1927. IOL Archives.

22 Edwin Lieuwen, *Petroleum in Venezuela: A History* (New York: Russell and Russell, 1954), 84–5.

23 Henrietta Larson, Evelyn Knowlton, and Charles Popple, *History of Standard Oil (New Jersey): New Horizons 1927–1950* (New York: Harper & Row, 1971), 58–9, 132–8; Greene, "Strategies of the Major Oil Companies," ch. 4, 22–3.

24 Frederick Pike, *The Modern History of Peru* (New York: Praeger, 1967), 268–76; Goodsell, 142; Thorp and Bertram, 165–6.

25 Rene De La Pedraja, *Energy Politics in Colombia* (Boulder, CO: Westview Press, 1989), 5–11, 25–6, 36–8; Palacios, 99–103; Stephen Randall, *The Diplomacy of Modernization: Colombian-American Relations 1920–1940* (Toronto: University of Toronto Press, 1971), 90–4.

26 Gibb and Knowlton, 372.

27 *Imperial Oil Review*, June 1933, 6–7, 12–13; Gibb and Knowlton, 103–4.

28 Imperial Oil Co., Annual General Meeting, 22 Feb 1923. IOL Archives.

29 Bucheli (2008), 80.

30 Brown, 29–30.

31 Imperial Oil President Charles O. Stillman, Report to Annual General Meeting, Toronto, 15 Mar 1928. IOL Archives; Bucheli, (2006) 81–2; Palacios, 86. The main target of political ire at this point was the Colombian Oil Company, a subsidiary of Gulf Oil,

which had acquired the "Banco concession" in eastern Colombia but had failed to develop the field: De La Pedraja, 12–14; Randall, 98–9.

32   "Petroleum Transport in the Tropics," *Imperial Oil Review* (Sept 1927).

33   Xavier Duran, "Oil in Colombia 1900–1950: Speculators and Multinational Companies," *Ecopetrol: Energia limpia para el future.* www.ecopetrol.com.co/especiales, n16. During the 1930s–40s the average Bayonne refinery output was about twice the volume of all the Imperial refineries in Canada. Larson et al., 200–1.

34   Imperial Oil, Minutes of the Annual General Meeting, 1922, 1924, 1927. IOL Archives.

35   Gibb and Knowlton, 458–9; Larson et al., 115, 474, 720.

36   Ewing, ch. 15, Tables 1–2; ch. 20, Tables 1–2. International Petroleum Company Annual Reports 1932–46. IOL Archives. See Appendix 1].

37   Ewing, ch. 20, 6–7.

38   See Appendix 2A.

39   Ewing, ch. 20, 4–5;

40   Duran, 4–5; De La Pedraja, 36–8.

41   Larson et al., 726–7; Bennett H. Wall, *History of Standard Oil (New Jersey: Growth in a Changing Environment 1950–1975* (New York: McGraw Hill, 1988), 431–44.

42   Victor Bulmer Thomas, *The Economic History of Latin America since Independence* (Cambridge: Cambridge University Press, 2003), 156–60, 424–5; Palacios, 14–15.

43   Palacios, 58.

44   Thorp and Bertram, 164.

45   Wilkins (1974), 422–3. Gibb and Knowlton, 503–6.

46   Wall, 435.

CHAPTER 5

1   Wall and Gibb, *Teagle*, 120–2.

2   Ewing, chapter 8, 83–4; *Imperial Oil Review* (August 1919): 13; February 1922, 3; "G. Harrison Smith the New President," *Imperial Oil Review* (June/July 1933): 12–13; Thelma LeCocq, "LeSueur: Imperial's President," *Canadian Business* (July 1944): 28–9.

3   Wall and Gibb, 71.

4   Wall and Gibb, 202–10; Gibb and Knowlton, 279–307; Yergin, 197–204.

5   Wall and Gibb, 258–60; Yergin, 260–5; Anthony Sampson, *The Seven Sisters*, 86–7.

6   Wall and Gibb, 236–45; Alfred D. Chandler Jr., *Strategy and Structure: Chapters in the History of American Industrial Enterprise* (Cambridge, MA: MIT Press, 1962), 164–225.

7   *Historical Statistics of Canada*, T147-194a; Ewing, ch. 6, 5–6; Robert Ankli et al., "Adoption of the Gas Tractor in Western Canada," *Canadian Papers in Rural History* 2 (1980): 9–39; Steve Penfold, "Petroleum Liquids," in R.W. Sandwell, *Powering Up*

Canada: A History of Power, Fuel and Energy from 1600 (Montreal: McGill-Queen's University Press, 2016), 276–9.

8   Gibb and Knowlton, 113–16; Purdy, *Petroleum*, 157–9.

9   Gibb and Knowlton, 115–18.

10   Ewing, ch. 11, 63–71; Gibb and Knowlton, 532–6; "Imperial Oil Announces New 3 Star Gasoline," *Globe & Mail*, 3 Sept 1931, 15. Imperial's research and development operations are reviewed in more detail in chapter 8.

11   Ewing, ch. 9, 22–3. One of these independent distributors was Kenneth Irving in New Brunswick, who leveraged his "partnership" with Imperial in the 1920s into a full-fledged integrated oil company (with offshoots in shipbuilding and numerous other industries) in the years after 1948. Irving became one of the richest individuals in Canada, while hiding his wealth overseas.

12   Gibb and Knowlton, 487–9, 502–3; Ewing, ch. 9, 26–33, 71–2.

13   Ewing, ch. 9, 24–5, 66; *Imperial Oil Review* (February 1922): 3, 17; March 1934, 27. Union Oil of California (later Unocal) was acquired by Standard of California (Chevron) in 2005.

14   Saywell, "Early History of Canadian Oil Companies," 71–2; Earle Gray, "How Shell Bought the No. 3 Spot," *Oilweek*, 27 Nov 1967, 19–25.

15   Earle Gray, "BA Poised for Dynamic Growth," *Oilweek*, 9 Oct 1967, 24–8; "A.L. Ellsworth," *Globe & Mail*, 7 June 1929, 21. In 1965 Gulf Oil acquired British American Oil.

16   Charles Law, "Trust Texaco to Go Where the Most Profits Flow," *Oilweek* 1 Nov 1968, 21–4, 30; "McColl Brothers Oil Sale is Completed," *Globe & Mail*, 7 Dec 1927, 7; "Texaco Buys into McColl Frontenac," *Globe & Mail*, 27 Apr 1938, 18; "Texaco Corporation Wins McColl Fight," *Globe & Mail*, 3 June 1938, 20. In 1994 Imperial Oil acquired Texaco Canada during the chaotic aftermath of Texaco's bankruptcy.

17   Ewing, ch. 15, 14–16; "Imperial Oil Ltd. Will Split Common Stock Four-One," *Globe & Mail*, 2 Apr 1929, 7; "Imperial Oil Soars to New High 119 ½ under Heavy Buying," *Globe & Mail*, 15 Apr 1929; "Losses Predominate Among Active Issues on Exchange," *Globe & Mail*, 16 Oct 1929, 6.

18   "Imperial Oil Limited and Consolidated Subsidiaries Financial Review: Twenty Year Statistics," [1952, 8]. IOL Records, Series 4 [Comptrollers Records], Box 292A Acc. 80-0021.

19   C.D. Crichton, "'Exclusive Rights Agreement' Newfoundland Petroleum Monopoly, 1932–34," 5 Dec 1960; G.H. Smith, Vice President IOL, to Sir Wilfred Grenfell, 27 May 1932 (Attachment No. 5); Victor Ross to G.H. Smith, 3 Apr 1932 (Attachment No. 6); Victor Ross, "Newfoundland Exclusive Rights" [re: Amulree Commission report], 28 Nov 1933 (Attachment No. 12). Imperial Oil Ltd. Vertical File: History, Misc. Glenbow Archive. See Peter Neary, *Newfoundland in the North Atlantic World 1929–1949* (Montreal: McGill-Queen's University Press, 1988), 12–28, on the background to this episode. Newfoundland joined Canada in 1948.

20   Ewing, ch. 15, 31–2, 36.

21   G.A. Purdy, *Petroleum: Prehistoric to Petrochemical* (Toronto: Copp Clark, 1957), 125–30, 153–5; Hugh M. Grant, "The Petroleum Industry and Canadian Economic Development: An Economic History 1900–1960" (PhD diss., University of Toronto, 1987), ch. 3.

22   Gibb and Knowlton, 141–52, 575–77; Howard M. Gitelman, *The Legacy of the Ludlow Massacre: A Chapter in American Industrial Relations* (Philadelphia: University of Pennsylvania Press, 1988); Paul Craven, *An Impartial Umpire: Industrial Relations and the Canadian State 1900–1911* (Toronto: University of Toronto Press, 1980).

23   "The Industrial Representation Plan," *Imperial Oil Review* (January 1919); H.M. Grant, "Solving the Labour Problem at Imperial Oil: Welfare Capitalism in the Canadian Petroleum Industry 1919–1929," *Labour/Le Travail* 41 (Spring 1998): 81–3; Ewing, ch. 8, 72–3.

24   "In Quebec," *Imperial Oil Review* 4 (1971); East Montreal Refinery, IOL Vertical File.

25   Grant, "Solving the Labour Problem," 79–81.

26   All references are from the Montreal East Refinery Joint Industrial Council Minutes. IOL Archives, Series 18, Human Relations Acc 80002, Box 02.

27   "Pacific Pioneer," *Imperial Oil Review* 5 (1971).

28   All references are from the Ioco Refinery Joint Industrial Council Minutes, IOL Archives, Series 18, Human Resources, Box 2, Acc. 90-0001.

29   "History of Ioco Strike, 24 Sept–26 Nov 1957." Imperial Oil Archives, IOLpub 6-12. Glenbow Archives; Imperial Oil Executive Committee Minutes, 19 Sept 1957; 11 Nov 1957; 26 Nov 1957. Imperial Oil Archives, Series 2, Executive Committee Minutes. [Hereafter cited as IOL Exec. Cte. Minutes], Glenbow Archives.

30   IOL Exec. Cte. Minutes, 29 May 1969; 6 Oct 1969.

31   "Joint Industrial Councils and Committees in I.O.L.," 11 Jan 1977. IOL Archive, Vertical Files, Industrial Relations.

CHAPTER 6

1   Peter McKenzie Brown, *Bitumen: The People, Passions and Performance behind Alberta's Oil Sands* (Calgary: Create Space Independent Publishing Platform, 2017), 29–30.

2   David H. Breen, *Alberta's Petroleum Industry and the Conservation Board* (Edmonton: University of Alberta Press, 1993), 8–15; F.K. Beach and J.L. Irwin, "The History of Alberta Oil," (Edmonton: Alberta Department of Lands and Mines, 1939), 8–13.

3   David H. Breen "Anglo-American Rivalry and the Evolution of Canadian Petroleum Policy to 1930," *Canadian Historical Review* 62, no. 3 (1981): 283–6.

4   David Finch, *Hell's Half Acre: Early Days in the Great Alberta Oil Patch* (Surrey, BC: Heritage House Publishing, 2005), 18–23; "Herron's Gas Seep Started in All," *Oilweek* 14, 18 May 1964; Gray, *Great Canadian Oil Patch*, 71–80; Colin A.M. Duncan and R.W. Sandwell, "Manufactured and Natural Gas," in Sandwell, ed., *Powering Up Canada*, 318–25.

5   Bosworth's report on his 1914 expedition into Alberta may have influenced Shell in its 1917 bid for a monopoly in the exploitation of oil development in the region. Peter McKenzie-Brown, *Bitumen*, 59–61, 67–8.

6   "Claim Biggest Oilfield Soon Opens in North," *Globe & Mail*, 20 Oct 1920, 2.

7   Ewing, ch. 12, 8–22; De Mille, *Oil in Canada West*, 151–5, 185–99; John Ness, "The Story That Can Never Be Told," IOL Archive, Vertical Files, IOL History 1948–55; Gray, *Great Canadian Oil Patch*, 119–20.

8   Sarah Lawley, "The Link of History," *Imperial Oil Review* (Spring 1989): 17–19; Frank H. Ellis, "Bold Venture into Northern Winter," *Imperial Oil Review* (April 1971): 130–3; J.M. Smallwood, "Oil in the Frozen North," *American Review of Reviews* (1921): 639–44. IOL Archives, Vertical Files, Industry & Trade: Canadian North File.

9   J.H. McLeod, "A Factual Memorandum Concerning the History of the Incorporation and Development of Royalite Oil Company Limited," 13 Dec 1938. Royalite Archives, Glenbow Museum and Archives, Series 9: M6891/File 197, 5–6; Ewing, ch. 12, 28–30; Finch, 25–6; Gibb and Knowlton, 659; Timothy Le Riche, *Alberta's Oil Patch* (Calgary: Folklore Publishing, 2006), 46–7. McLeod had also headed the Dalhousie Company in 1925–28.

10   Breen, *Alberta's Petroleum Industry*, 36–7; Patricia Barry, "The Canol Project: An Adventure of the U.S. War Department in Canada's Northwest" (Edmonton: P.S. Barry, 1985), 242–5.

11   Finch, 38–42; Gray, *Great Canadian Oil Patch*, 82–4.

12   "Royalite Oil Takeovers," Royalite Archives, Series 9, File 1; McLeod, "Factual Memorandum," 11–15; Ewing, ch. 12, 34–5.

13   Ewing, ch. 12, 38; James Gray, *R.B. Bennett: The Calgary Years* (Toronto: University of Toronto Press, 1991), 119–29; Peter B. Waite, *In Search of R.B. Bennett* (Montreal: McGill-Queen's University Press, 2012), 12–13.

14   "Eugene Lacoste Deplores Wasting of Alberta's Gas," *Toronto Globe*, 9 Dec 1929, 6; Larson et al., *New Horizons*, 110–11.

15   Royalite Annual Meetings 5 Apr 1927; 30 Apr 1929; 18 Apr 1933; 30 Apr 1935. Royalite Archives, M6891, File #8; Breen, *Alberta's Petroleum Industry*, 51–8, 72–3; McLeod, "Factual Memorandum," 6; Le Riche, 46–8.

16   Earle Gray, *Great Canadian Oil Patch*, 85–7; Gray, "Home Oil Built on Turner Valley," *Oilweek* 15, no. 1, 18 May 1964; Le Riche, 77–9.

17   Gray, *Great Canadian Oil Patch*, 100–5.

18   Gray, *Great Canadian Oil Patch*, 108–9.

19   Breen, *Alberta's Petroleum Industry*, 110–19, 138–45; Gray, *Great Canadian Oil Patch*, 106–10.

20   "Alberta's Oil Industry: Report of a Royal Commission to Inquire into Matters Connected with Petroleum and Petroleum Products," 266–71. IOL Archives, McGillvray Commission; "Alberta Royal Commission Reports on the Oil Industry,"

Imperial Oil Review (Summer 1940): 23–9; Breen, *Alberta's Petroleum Industry*, 169–87; Finch, 81–2.

21   "Imperial Oil Contribution to the War Effort," n.d. (c. 1944), Vertical Files, Petroleum in War, IOL Archives; Larson et al., *New Horizons*, 392–8; Purdy, *Petroleum*, 51–2.

22   Larson et al., 161–6.

23   R.K. Stratford, "The Canadian Petroleum Industry's Contribution to the War," 1944, Petroleum in War, Vertical Files, IOL Archives; Stratford, "Post War Advantages Expected to Result From Processes and Products Developed for Wartime Purposes," 1945, Petroleum in War, Vertical Files, IOL Archives; Larson et al., 507–12; Purdy, *Petroleum*, 52. Chapter 8 provides more details on Imperial Oil research and the development of petrochemicals.

24   Stetson Conn and Byron Fairchild, *The Framework of Hemispheric Defense* (Washington, DC: US Department of the Army, 1960), 390–408; Brian Garfield, *The Thousand Mile War: World War II in Alaska and the Aleutians* (Fairbanks: University of Alaska Press, 1995).

25   *Life*, 13 Apr 1942, 20.

26   Philip Fradkin, "The First and Forgotten Pipeline," *Audubon News*, November 1977, 59–67; Patricia Barry, "The Prolific Pipeline: Getting Canol Under Way," *Dalhousie Review* 56, no. 2 (Summer 1976): 252–67; Charles R. O'Brien, "The Canol Project: A Study in Emergency Planning," *Pacific Northwest Quarterly* 61, no. 2 (April 1970): 101–8; Ian Kerr Kelly, "The Canol Project: Defence, Politics and Oil" (MA thesis, Trent University, 1977), 18–45. Gray, *Great Canadian Oil Patch*, 121–4. The term "Canol" is usually interpreted to stand for "Canadian Oil" but has also been presented as an acronym for "Canadian American Norman Oil Line."

27   Kelly, 47.

28   Ewing, ch. 16, 17–20; Kelly, 44–5. Ewing noted that at this time the cost of transporting crude oil to the Norman Wells region would be $6.00 (CN) per bbl., while the average cost of crude oil in the US was $1.25/bbl.

29   Patricia Barry, "The Canol Project: An Adventure of the U.S. War Department in Canada's Northwest" (Edmonton: P.S. Barry, 1985), 253–4.

30   Barry, "Canol Project," 261.

31   Patricia Barry, "The Prolific Pipeline: Finding Oil for Canol," *Dalhousie Review* 57, no. 2 (Summer 1977): 205–23; Ewing, ch. 16, 21–4; Stephen J. Randall, *United States Foreign Oil Policy Since World War I* (Montreal: McGill-Queen's University Press, 2005), 160–5.

32   W.D.C. Mackenzie, interview. IOL Archives, Oral History Collection.

33   Fradkin, 75–6; Kelly, 102–6.

34   Kelly, 150–3; Ewing, ch. 16, 24–5; Gray, *Great Canadian Oil Patch*, 130–1.

35   Ewing, ch. 10, 70–6; Larson et al., 323–4.

36   Ewing, ch. 17, 13–19, 31–45, 85–6.

37 "Discovery at Jumping Pond," *Nickle's Daily Oil Bulletin*, 15 Dec 1944; "Sun Oil of Philadelphia Enters Alberta," *Nickle's Daily Oil Bulletin*, 16 Jan 1945.

38 Ewing, ch. 17, 9–13. The US had introduced an oil depletion allowance in 1926, and expanded it during the Second World War.

39 Gray, *Great Canadian Oil Patch*, 134.

40 Larson et al., 723–4; Breen, *Alberta Petroleum*, 248–9.

41 Gray, *The Great Canadian Oil Patch*, 136–41; Breen, *Alberta Petroleum*, 250–1; Hal Tennant, "Leduc—Turning Point of an Industry," *Imperial Oil Review* (February 1957): 3–7; "Imperial-Leduc: It's an Oil Discovery!," *Nickle's Daily Oil Bulletin*, 14 Feb 1947. The events on 13 Feb 1947 are recounted in the prologue to this book.

CHAPTER 7

1 W.G. Charlton, "Imperial Oil Limited History 1950–1975," 4–5. Imperial Oil Archives, Series 5. Glenbow Museum & Archives; Eric J. Hanson, *Dynamic Decade: The Evolution and Effects of the Oil Industry in Alberta* (Toronto: McClelland & Stewart, 1958), 66–83; Oliver Knight, "Oil—Canada's New Wealth," *Business History Review* 30, no. 2 (September 1956): 297–328.

2 Erik Lisee, "Betrayed: Leduc, Manning and Surface Rights in Alberta, 1947–55," *Prairie Forum* 35, no. 1 (Spring 2010): 77–100.

3 "Report of an Assessment of Farmers' Opinions in the Leduc Area Pertaining to Drilling Operations," 23 Oct–5 Nov 1947. Imperial Oil Archives Acc 80-0039, Box 27, File 2. Glenbow Archives.

4 Hanson, 79–83.

5 See chapter 13 for a more detailed account of the Atlantic #3 fire.

6 Gray, *Great Canadian Oil Patch*, 150–2, 215–18; Hanson, 101–9.

7 Breen, *Alberta's Petroleum Industry and the Conservation Board* (Edmonton: University of Alberta Press, 1993), 252–84; Hanson, 93–109.

8 The purchasing power of the Canadian dollar in 1946 was 25 to 30 per cent less than it had been in 1935–40. The exchange rate affected not only the costs of importing US crude, but also the purchase of new equipment for production and distribution. The Canadian government did not lift price controls on domestic petroleum products until 1947 so Imperial and other oil importers had to absorb the gap. Ewing, ch. 20, 2–3; Larson et al., *New Horizons*, 561–2.

9 Imperial Oil Board of Directors, Minutes 3 Sept 1947; 8 Sept 1947; Minutes of Special Shareholder's Meeting, 22 Sept 1947. Imperial Oil Archives, Series 1, Glenbow Archives. Ewing, ch. 20, 3–6.

10 Ewing, ch. 20, 18–20; Larson et al., 726–32.

11 Imperial Oil board of directors, minutes 16 June 1947; 7 Oct 1947. Imperial Oil Archives, Series 1. Glenbow Archives. Royalite board of directors minutes 13 Nov 1948; 17 Dec 1948; 14 Jan 1949. Royalite Archives. Glenbow Archives. Ewing, ch. 20, 24–5.

"Royalite Co. Now Independent," *Western Oil Examiner*, 22 Jan 1949, 1, 3; Wellington Jeffers, "Finance At Large," *Globe & Mail*, 17 Jan 1949, 20. When Royalite reorganized its board it 1950, two of its new members included Allan and Samuel Bronfman, of Seagram fame.

12   "Imperial Oil Ltd. Investments in Canadian Marketing Companies," 8 Sept 1946. Imperial Oil Archives, Acc. 80-0028, Box 005. Glenbow Archives. The General Manager of Champlain Oil in 1932–35 was Charley Trudeau, who had sold his chain of thirty service stations in Quebec, the Automobile Owners Association, to Champlain in 1932 for $1 million [CAD]. Charley's son, Pierre, and his grandson, Justin, both became prime ministers of Canada.

13   D.L. McCarthy to the President and Directors of Imperial Oil Ltd., 26 Oct 1946; Imperial Oil board of directors, Minutes 27 Jan 1947. Imperial Oil Archives, Series 1, Glenbow Museum.

14   Memorandum re: K.C. Irving, 27 Feb 1945; Memorandum for Mr. Hewetson re: Maritime Situation, 18 Jan 1946 [This document has the intriguing heading: "To be destroyed on consummation of plan"]; Draft Agreement between Kenneth C. Irving and Imperial Oil Ltd., 1 Feb 1946. Imperial Oil Archive, Series, Acc. 80-0028, Box 005, Irving File, Glenbow Archives.

15   Douglas How and Ralph Costello, *KC: The Biography of K.C. Irving* (Toronto: King Porter Books, 1993), 29–31, 44–56, 140–1.

16   H.H. Hewetson, Meeting re: P.J.B.D. proposal, 22 Sept 1946. Imperial Oil Archives, Series 3, Corporate Affairs, Acc. 80-0028, Box 005, Joint Defence Board file. Glenbow Archives; Barry, 142–3.

17   "Refineries: Edmonton Refinery (1950). Imperial Oil Archives, Series, Vertical File: Refineries. Glenbow Archives; Charlton, 6.

18   Hanson, 143–7; B.H. Wall, *Growth in a Changing Environment*, 352, 282–3.

19   W.J. Davenport, "The Imperial Pipe Line," *Imperial Oil Review* (January 1918): 9–10; Larson et al., *New Horizons*, 228–32, 744–50; Imperial Oil board, Minutes, 12 April 1946. Imperial Oil Archives, Series 1, Glenbow Archives.

20   Gray, *Great Canadian Oil Patch*, 250–1; Charlton, 6–7; J.D. White, Vice Pres., Imperial Oil to A.I. Levorsen, Dean of School of Mineral Science, Stanford University, Palo Alto, California, 20 July 1949; W.O. Twaits, "Board Review of Pipe Line Status," 24 Feb 1949; Interprovincial Pipe Line Co., First Shareholders Meeting, 6 May 1949. Imperial Oil Archives, Glenbow Archives.

21   Gray, *Great Canadian Oil Patch*, 250–1. O.B. Hopkins, Memorandum re: Duty and Sales Tax on Pipe Line Material, 20 May 1949; G.L. Stewart, president, Imperial Oil to Hon. C.D. Howe, Minister of Trade & Commerce, 3 Aug 1949; Howe to Stewart, 8 Aug 1949. Imperial Oil Archives, Glenbow Archives.

22   C.D. Crichton, Interprovincial Pipeline Co. to W.F. Prendergast et al., Memorandum re: Public Relations program, 18 July 1949; W.F. Prendergast to A.A. Turner, Imperial Oil Ltd., Regina, Sask., 23 June 1949. Imperial Oil Archives, Glenbow Archives.

23 Imperial Oil board, Minutes, 6 Oct 1949. Imperial Oil archives, Series 1, Glenbow Museum; Hanson, 155–8. A similar "Throughput Agreement" was made by Imperial and other Canadian oil companies in 1950 to help finance the expansion of the Portland to Montreal pipeline.

24 D. Murie, Manager, Fort William Chamber of Commerce to I.W. Mackerath, Imperial Oil Co., Fort William, 9 June 1949; "Plan for Oil Pipe Line Points to Canadian Wealth" *Port Arthur News Chronicle*, 27 May 1949; "Oil Pipe Line Routes," *Winnipeg Tribune*, 8 Sept 1949. Imperial Oil Archive, Glenbow Archives.

25 "Canadian Shield Diverts Pipeline to Northern U.S.," *Globe & Mail*, 9 Sept 1949, 9; Wall, *Growth in a Changing Environment*, 354–5.

26 Quoted in Gray, *Great Canadian Oil Patch*, 254.

27 "Lakehead Groups Want Oil Pipeline Kept in Canada," *Globe & Mail*, 7 Sept 1949, 2; G.L. Stewart, pres., Imperial Oil to Hewetson, 28 Sept 1949. Imperial Oil Archive, Glenbow Archives.

28 O.B. Hopkins, pres. Interprovincial Pipeline Co., to Mayor C.O. Robinson, Port Arthur, Ontario, 21 September 1947; "Oil Men Defend Pipe Line Decision," *Fort William Daily Times*, 27 Sept 1949. Imperial Oil Archives, Glenbow Archives.

29 Hanson, 157–8; Gray, *Great Canadian Oil Patch*, 254; Hopkins to T.B. Sexton, Transit Co. Ltd., 25 May 1949; "Comparison of 50,000 B/D Movement to Sarnia via P/L and Lake Tanker versus Direct Pipeline," 28 June 1949; J.R. White to Hon. Douglas Abbott, Minister of Finance, 23 Sept 1949. Imperial Oil Archive, Glenbow Archives.

30 L.F. Kahle to O.B. Hopkins, pres., Interprovincial Pipeline Co. 28 Oct 1949; L.F. Kahle, "Memorandum on discussion with I.N. McKinnon, Deputy Minister of Mines and Minerals and J.L. Oberholtzer, Deputy Minister of Industries and Labour, 2 Nov 1949." Imperial Oil Archive, Glenbow Archives; "Pipeline Contracts Let Now Total $41,000,000," *Globe & Mail*, 3 Nov 1949, 22.

31 "Western Oil Reaches Ontario," *Imperial Oil Review*; Gray, *Great Canadian Oil Patch*, 256–7.

32 Charlton, 32–3.

33 Hanson, 249–64.

CHAPTER 8

1 Gibb and Knowlton, *The Resurgent Years*, 520–33; Larson et al., 150–1.

2 "Biographical Information Dr. R.K. Stratford"; "Chronology of the Technical and Research Department." Exxon Mobil Records, General Subject Files: Research Imperial Oil, Call No. 2.207 G220. Dolph Briscoe Center for American History, University of Texas, Austin TX.

3 Ewing, ch. 11, 63–5; Larson et al., 151–2.

4 Larson et al., 153–6;

5 Ewing, ch. 11, 66–8.

6   Larson et al., 165–6; Purdy, *Petroleum*, 164–6.

7   Larson et al., 433–42; Wall, *Teagle*, 314–15; "German-Held Patents Freed to Industry," *Globe & Mail*, 26 Mar 1942, 3.

8   Larson et al., 412–16, 507–13; Matthew Bellamy, *Profiting the Crown: Canada's Polymer Corporation 1942–1990* (Montreal: McGill-Queen's University Press, 2005), 16–21; Paul A.C. Koistinen, *Arsenal of World War II: The Political Economy of American Warfare 1940–45* (Lawrence: University Press of Kansas, 2004), 148–58.

9   Bellamy, 28-37; Cobban, *Cities of Oil*, 64–6, 92–8; Purdy, *Petroleum*, 52, 442–4.

10 Cobban, 98–100; Larson et al., *New Horizons*, 512; E.R. Rowzee, "Sarnia, the Birthplace of Canada's Petro-Chemical Industry," *Chemistry and Industry*, 10 Dec 1949, 864–5. Exxon Mobil Archives, Call No. 2.207/G220. Dolph Briscoe Center.

11 F.C. Lantz, "Memorandum: Outline of Scope of St. Clair's Activities in Relation to Imperial, Standard Oil Development, and Polymer Organization," 3 Jan 1944. Imperial Oil Archives, Acc. 80-0013, Box 3; Series, 1m-14, Box 12g. Glenbow Archives.

12 Bellamy, 65–70; Cobban, 98–104; Peter McKenzie-Brown, Gordon Jaremko, and David Finch, *The Great Oil Age: The Petroleum Industry in Canada* (Calgary: Detselig Enterprises Ltd., 1993), 117–18.

13 John L. Tiedje, "International Technology Transfer through a Multinational Corporation," Address to the World Congress on Chemical Engineering, 6 Oct 1981; J.L. Livingstone, "Imperial's Research," 10 Feb 1981. Imperial Oil Archives, Vertical Files, Research/Glenbow Archives; Mark Nichols, "Fifty Years of Men and Ideas," *Imperial Oil Review* 4 (1979): 6–13.

14 Larson et al., 768.

15 Wall, *Growth in a Changing Environment*, 175–86.

16 "The Man From Medicine Hat," *Time*, 18 Feb 1974; Wall, *Growth in a Changing Environment*, 189–90; Le Riche, *Alberta's Oil Patch*, 180.

17 Imperial Oil *Annual Report*, 1956, 9; IOL Exec. Cte. Minutes, 15 Dec 1955; 12 Feb 1957; 5 March 1957.

18 IOL Exec. Cte. Minutes, 26 Nov 1959.

19 IOL Exec. Cte. Minutes, 16 March 1961; D.A. Foster to C.S. Lindsley Re: Imperial-Redwater Fertilizer Manufacturing Project, 1 Dec 1966. Esso Chemical Canada Business Plan Studies: Notes and Correspondence. Imperial Oil Archives, Series, 1M-14-Box 15. Glenbow Archives.

20 Wall, *Growth in a Changing Environment*, 359–60; Charlton, 21–2; "Imperial Enters Petrochemical Field," *Imperial Oil Review* (Dec 1955): 14; Patricia Clarke, "Made of Oil," *Imperial Oil Review* 4 (1981): 18–22.

21 Wall, *Growth in a Changing Environment*, 55–6; IOL Exec. Cte. Minutes, 5 April 1962.

22 Wall, *Growth in a Changing Environment*, 56-7, 260. IOL Exec. Cte. Minutes, 19 May 1964; 21 Sept 1965; 3 Mar 1966; 17 July 1969.

23   IOL Exec. Cte., 4 March 1965. On Deuterium and Industrial Estates, see Roy George, *The Life and Times of Industrial Estates Ltd.* (Halifax: Dalhousie University Institute of Public Affairs, 1974), 77–8.

24   Interview with W.O. Twaits, 10 July 1979. Imperial Oil Archives.

Chapter 9

1   Robert J. Bertrand, *Canada's Oil Monopoly* (Toronto: Lorimer, 1981), 589–614. This volume, an abridgement of a seven-volume government document prepared by Bertrand as part of a Combines Investigation, engendered its own controversy as the Canadian government tried, unsuccessfully, to block Lorimer from publishing it as a "commercial" book.

2   David L. Jackson, "A Study of Imperial Oil Limited," 1964. Imperial Oil Archives, IOL pub-6-24, 18, 26.

3   Jackson, 20, 23; Bertrand, 444–53.

4   W.O. Twaits to IOL Executive Committee, 20 Apr 1955.

5   IOL Exec. Cte. Minutes, 26 July 1955; 26 Sept 1958; 4 July 1968. Wall, *Growth in a Changing Environment*, 132–3.

6   IOL Exec. Cte. Minutes, 3 Apr 1962.

7   "Hockey Night Across Canada," *Imperial Oil Review* (March/April 1952): 12–13.

8   IOL Exec. Cte. Minutes, 12 Sept 1953; 28 Sept 1961. J.L. Potts, "Saturday Night Hockey," Canadian Communications Foundation, Jan 2002; Paul Patskovy, "Hockey Night in Canada—The Television Years," Canadian Communications Foundation, Aug 2007.

9   IOL Exec. Cte. Minutes, 8 Jan 1953; 10 Mar 1953; 22 Dec 1953.

10   IOL Exec. Cte. Mintes, 4 Jan 1962; 2 July 1963; 11 Feb 1964.

11   IOL Exec. Cte. Minutes, 29 Apr 1971; 27 Feb 1973; 12 Sept 1975; 14 Oct 1975.

12   "Here is How Imperial Protects Its Dealers and Customers in a Price War," IOL Exec. Cte. Minutes, 25 June 1959.

13   IOL Exec. Cte. Minutes, 7 Nov 1957; 20 Mar 1958; 8 Sept 1958; 28 Mar 1959.

14   IOL Exec. Cte. Minutes, 5 Sept 1961; 7 Sept 1972.

15   Bertrand, 91–6.

16   "A Program for Dealer Relations, 1962"; V.B. Cervin, "Analysis of Dealer Problems, 1958," Marketing Research Dept. Acc. 80-0039, Box 27, Files 7, 8, IOL Archives.

17   Brian Brennan, *The Good Steward: The Ernest C. Manning Story* (Calgary: Fitzhenry & Whiteside, 2008), 88–92.

18   Breen, *Alberta's Petroleum Industry*, 305.

19   Breen, *Alberta's Petroleum Industry*, 312.

20   Breen, *Alberta's Petroleum Industry*, 313–17; Earle Gray, document on "Prorationing" to author, 13 June 2016; "Oil Allowable for Redwater Again Discussed," *Globe & Mail*, 25 Apr 1949, 30.

21   Wall, *Growth in A Changing Environment*, 379; IOL Exec. Cte., 11 Aug 1964; "Big Producers Win Point, Alberta Slashes Well Minimums," *Globe & Mail*, 27 July 1964, 22.

22   IOL Exec. Cte. Minutes, 15 Dec 1960.

23   IOL Exec. Cte. Minutes, 10 Jan 1961; 17 Oct 1961.

24   IOL Exec. Cte. Minutes, 3 Sept 1962.

25   IOL Exec. Cte. Minutes, 24 Sept 1963; 3 Oct 1963, 1 Oct 1964.

26   Ruth Worth, "Gasoline Price Prober on Safari in 2,600,000-word Tiger Infested Jungle," *Globe & Mail*, 20 July 1965, B12; IOL Exec. Cte. Minutes, 2 Jan 1964; 4 June 1964.

27   IOL Exec. Cte. Minutes, 19 June 1966; George MacFarlane, "Gas Price Report Gains Approval of Imperial Oil," *Globe & Mail*, 7 Apr 1966, B10.

28   Gray, *Great Canadian Oil Patch*, 297–330.

29   William Kilbourn, *Pipeline: Transcanada and the Great Debate, A History of Business and Politics* (Toronto: Clarke Irwin, 1970), 94–113; John Duffy, *Fights of Our Lives: Elections, Leadership and the Making of Canada* (Toronto: Harper Collins, 2002), 196–9.

30   Breen, *Alberta's Petroleum Industry*, 424–5, 465–8; Riche, 80–1; Gray, *Great Canadian Oil Patch*, 420–1.

31   Breen, *Alberta's Petroleum Industry*, 437–8; "Imperial Oil Opposes Pipeline to Montreal," *Globe & Mail*, 6 May 1958, 24; Earle Gray, *Forty Years in the Public Interest: A History of the National Energy Board* (Toronto: Douglas & McIntyre, 2000), 9–10.

32   Ron Anderson, "Refining in Canada: Alberta Oil Seeks Wider Markets," *Globe & Mail*, 7 Aug 1958, 24.

33   Gray, *National Energy Board*, 28–9; Tammy Nemeth, "Canada-U.S. Oil and Gas Relations 1958 to 1974," (PhD diss., University of British Columbia, 2007), 55–65; IOL Exec. Cte. Minutes, 4 Mar 1959.

34   Breen, *Alberta's Petroleum Industry*, 398–419; John N. McDougall, *Fuels and the National Policy* (Toronto: Butterworths, 1982), 90.

35   Nemeth, "Canada-U.S. Oil and Gas Relations," 126–7; Nemeth, "Consolidating the Continental Drift: American Influence on Diefenbaker's National Oil Policy," *Journal of Canadian History* 13, no. 1 (2002): 202–3.

36   Nemeth, "Canada-U.S. Oil and Gas Relations," 156–9; G. Bruce Doern and Glen Toner, *The Politics of Energy* (Toronto: Methuen, 1985), 80–2.

37   See, for example, David Crane, *Controlling Interest: The Canadian Gas and Oil Stakes* (Toronto: McClelland & Stewart, 1982), 55–6; Melissa Clark-Jones, *A Staple State: Canadian Industrial Resources in Cold War* (Toronto: University of Toronto Press, 1987), 42–9. For a critique see Nemeth, "Canada-U.S. Oil and Gas Relations," 143–6.

38 Wall, *Growth in a Changing Environment*, 399–402, 425–8; George Philip, *Oil and Politics in Latin America: Nationalist Movements and State Companies* (Cambridge: Cambridge University Press, 1982), 294–9.

39 Nemeth, "Canada-U.S. Oil and Gas Relations," 156–61.

40 De Mille, *Oil in Canada West*, 159–60; Ewing, ch. 19; Peter A. Shulman, "The Making of a Tax Break: The Oil Depletion Allowance, Scientific Taxation and Natural Resource Policy in the Early Twentieth Century," *Journal of Policy History* 23, no. 3 (June 2011): 281–322.

41 Twaits quoted in Clark-Jones, 38; Carl Nickle, *Daily Oil Bulletin*, 31 Dec 1957.

42 Supreme Court of Canada, *Home Oil v. Minister of National Revenue*, SCR 733 (10 Oct 1955).

43 "Imperial Oil Enters Tax Appeal Test Case," *Globe & Mail*, 26 Sept 1957, 17; Bruce MacDonald, "4-3 Tax Ruling Costs Oil Firms $60,000,000," *Globe & Mail*, 5 Oct 1960, 21; Supreme Court of Canada, *Minister of National Revenue v. Imperial Oil Co. Ltd.*, SCR 735 (4 Oct 1960).

44 IOL Exec. Cte. Minutes, 27 Sept 1962.

45 IOL Exec. Cte. Minutes, 30 Oct 1962; 9 Nov 1962; 11 Dec 1962.

46 IOL Exec. Cte. Minutes, 22 Feb 1968.

47 "B-A Urges Exploration Incentives," *Globe & Mail*, 9 Nov 1963, 34; "Participation Plan," *Globe & Mail*, 11 Dec 1963, B5; "Stop Importing Tax Plans, Imperial Oil Urges Canada," *Globe & Mail*, 8 Oct 1963, B4.

48 Report of the Royal Commission on Taxation, Feb 1967, vol. 4, 322–7, 356–7. Publications.gc.ca/collections 2014; John F. Helliwell et al., "Oil and Gas Taxation," *Osgoode Hall Law Journal* 26, no. 3 (Fall 1988): 455–6.

49 Kenneth Smith, "Could Have Disastrous Effects, Mining Group Says Angrily," *Globe & Mail*, 27 Feb 1967, 25; "Carter Report Misguided, Deficient: Twaits," *Globe & Mail*, 19 April 1967, B1; "Carter Prospects Devastating for Oil Industry, Twaits Says," *Globe & Mail*, 25 May 1967, 28. Interestingly, Peter Munk, later to head Canada's largest gold mining companies, supported the report; at the time he was heading a company called Clairtone, in the stereo equipment business.

50 Linda McQuaig, *Behind Closed Doors* (Markham: Penguin Books Canada, 1987), 154–8; "Position Overstated, Carter Says: Tax Report Author Backtracks on Complete Implementation," *Globe & Mail*, 25 Apr 1967, B1; Ronald Anderson, "Carter Plan Dead But Gains Tax Likely Result, Economists Predict," *Globe & Mail*, 21 Dec 1967.

51 "Tighter Depletion Allowances for Oil, Gas, Mining Companies," *Globe & Mail*, 23 Oct 1968, B12; "Imperial Oil Profit Lower by $2 Million," *Globe & Mail*, 22 Oct 1969, B7; McQuaig, 158–9.

52 Halliwell, et al., 457–8.

53 "Imperial and the Tax White Paper," *Imperial Oil Review*, June 1970, 29–31; "White Paper Threat to Syncrude Stressed by Imperial Oil Head," *Globe & Mail*, 9 Apr 1970, B1.

CHAPTER 10

1 Denis Smith, *Rogue Tory: The Life and Legend of John G. Diefenbaker* (Toronto: MacFarlane Walter and Ross, 1995), 224–7; John Duffy, *Fights of Our Lives: Elections, Leadership and the Making of Canada* (Toronto: Harper Collins, 2002), 196–9.

2 IOL Exec. Cte., Minutes, 25 July 1963; Peter Foster, *The Blue Eyed Sheiks: The Canadian Oil Establishment* (Toronto: Collins, 1979), 66–7.

3 Wall, *Growth in a Changing Environment*, 137–46; Charles Emmerson, *The Future History of the Arctic* (New York: Public Affairs Press, 2010), 177–9. As in the case of Leduc, the North Slope exploration that began in the early 1960s proved fruitless until the Prudhoe Bay discovery.

4 Quoted in Peter McKenzie Brown, *Bitumen*, 60; Joyce E. Hunt, *Local Push, Global Pull: The Untold History of the Athabasca Oil Sands, 1910–30* (Calgary: J.E. Hunt, 2011), 269–71. The bituminous oil fields were often interchangeably designated the "tar sands" and "oil sands" in the early references up to the subject, but in the 1960s the term "oil sands" became the preferred usage in government and business circles, while environmental critics continued to use "tar sands" to highlight their views emphasizing the industry's pollution and association with climate change, e.g., Andrew Nikiforuk, *Tar Sands: Dirty Oil and the Future of a Continent* (Vancouver: Greystone Books, 2010), 12–14; Tony Clarke, *Tar Sands Showdown: Canada and the Politics of Oil in an Age of Climate Change* (Toronto: Lorimer, 2008).

5 Hunt, 273–7.

6 Quoted in Paul Chastko, *Developing Alberta's Oil Sands: From Karl Clark to Kyoto* (Calgary: University of Calgary Press, 2004), 1.

7 McKenzie Brown, *Bitumen*, 29–30, 47–8; Steve Lynett, "Digging for Oil," *Imperial Oil Review* 4 (1973): 18–21.

8 McKenzie Brown, *Bitumen*, 77–88; Michael Pengelly, "The Enigma of the Oil Sands," *Imperial Oil Review* (Apr 1960): 16–18; Gray, *Great Canadian Oil Patch*, 335–41.

9 Chastko, *Developing Alberta's Oil Sands*, 31–45.

10 McKenzie Brown, *Bitumen*, 93–108; Gray, *Great Canadian Oil Patch*, 342–4.

11 Chastko, 81–90.

12 Brian Brennan, *The Good Steward: The Ernest C. Manning Story* (Calgary: Fifth House, 2008), 110–14; Chastko, 103–12; Graham D. Taylor, "Sun Oil and Great Canadian Oil Sands Ltd.: The Financing and Management of a 'Pioneer' Enterprise 1962–1974," *Journal of Canadian Studies* 20, no. 2 (Autumn 1985): 106–8; Breen, *Alberta Conservation Board*, 439–40.

13 McKenzie Brown, *Bitumen*, 116–17.

14 IOL Exec. Cte. Minutes, 9 July 1959; 4 Aug 1959.

15 "The Tar Sands of Alberta, Canada," 31–5. Exxon-Mobil Archives, Box 2.207.G236. Briscoe Center, Austin Texas; Wall, *Growth in a Changing Environment*, 943, fn63.

16 Breen, *Alberta Conservation Board*, 447–8.

17   IOL Exec. Cte. Minutes, 9 Mar 1959.

18   "Project Oilsand," Alberta Energy Heritage. Alberta.ca/energyheritage/sands/mega-projects; J.R. Walker, "Oil Sands A-bomb Seen Great Danger," *Calgary Herald*, 29 Jan 1959, 1.

19   IOL Exec. Cte. Minutes, 1 Oct 1959; McKenzie Brown, *Bitumen*, 119.

20   IOL Exec. Cte. Minutes, 8 Sept 1959; *Nickle's Daily Oil Bulletin*, 15 Jan 1960.

21   IOL Exec. Cte. Minutes, 14 Mar 1961; 18 July 1961; "Report on Athabasca Technical and Policy Committees," 1 July 1, 1961. IOL Archives.

22   IOL Exec. Cte, Minutes, 2 Feb 1960, 11 Sept 1962; Pengelly, "The Enigma of Athabasca," 15–16; "The Tar Sands of Alberta," 30–1, 36–8.

23   Taylor, "Sun Oil," 108–9; Breen, *Alberta Conservation Board*, 455–7.

24   Taylor, "Sun Oil," 109–10; IOL Exec. Cte., 22 May 1962; 13 Jan 1963.

25   McKenzie Brown, *Bitumen*, 155–8; IOL Exec. Cte. Minutes, 4 Dec 1963; 7 Jan 1965; 19 Jan 1965.

26   Taylor, "Sun Oil," 104.

27   Gray, *Great Canadian Oil Patch*, 346–7.

28   "Tar Sands of Alberta," 68–71; IOL Exec. Cte. Minutes, 13 May 1966; 16 Sept 1969; "Syncrude Proposes 80,000 b/d Production from Alta. Tar sands," *Oilweek* 19, no. 1 (13 May 1968): 21–2; Chastko, 127–32.

29   IOL Exec. Cte. Minutes, 10 Dec 1968; 16 Sept 1969.

30   IOL Exec. Cte. Minutes, 8 May 1973, 8 Aug 1973; Gray, *Great Canadian Oil Patch*, 350–1; David Wood, *The Lougheed Legacy* (Toronto: Key Porter, 1985), 112–19; Erik Lizee, "Rhetoric and Reality: Albertans and Their Oil Industry under Peter Lougheed" (MA thesis, University of Alberta, 2010), 96–7.

31   Larry Pratt, *The Tar Sands: Syncrude and the Politics of Oil* (Toronto: Hurtig Press, 1976); Foster, *Blue Eyed Sheiks*, 83–4; Lizee, 99–100.

32   IOL Exec. Cte. Minutes, 6 Dec 1974; Gray, *Great Canadian Oil Sands*, 351–2; McKenzie Brown, *Bitumen*, 160–2; Chastko, 160–1. In 1966 Imperial, Cities Service and Richfield had diluted their Syncrude commitment to enable Royalite to increase its share to 30 per cent. Subsequently Gulf Oil of Canada (which had already taken over British American Oil Co.) absorbed Royalite.

33   Gray, *Great Canadian Oil Patch*, 352–3; McKenzie Brown, *Bitumen*, 167–8.

34   Gray, *Great Canadian Oil Patch*, 353–4; "Jacob Absher," www.history.alberta.ca/energyheritage/sands.

35   Roger M. Butler, "Energy From Cold Lake," 10 Feb 1981. IOL Archive, Vertical File, Research; "Reaching the Heavy Oil," *Imperial Oil Review* 3 (1975): 27. Butler was the chief developer of the process, which was patented by Imperial in 1969. McKenzie Brown, *Bitumen*, 190.

36   IOL Exec. Cte. Minutes, 7 June 1966; "Reaching the Heavy Oil," 28–9; Steve Lynett, "Cold Lake," *Imperial Oil Review* 4, 1974, 5–7; Dominion Securities, "The Heavy Oil Deposits of Western Canada," Oct 1974, 9–11. IOL-pub-6-74.

37   Paul Murray, "Miracle at Cold Lake," *Imperial Oil Review* 6 (1979): 17–19; Sandford Brown, "Wringing Oil from Sand," *The Lamp* (Spring 1985): 17–18; Foster, *Blue Eyed Sheiks*, 86–7.

38   McKenzie Brown, *Bitumen*, 191–3; Gray, *Great Canadian Oil Patch*, 258–9; "Dr. Roger M. Butler," www.canadianpetroleumhalloffame.ca/roger_butler.

39   Gray, *Great Canadian Oil Patch*, 362–4; Emmerson, *The Future History of the Arctic*, 172–5; J.G. Thomson, "Development of North Hampered by Muskegs," *Oilweek*, 11 Dec 1959, 21–2.

40   IOL Production Department, "Notes on Northwest Territories Land Play," IOL Exec. Cte. Minutes, 1 Apr 1958; *Nickle's Daily Oil Bulletin*, 18 June 1961; Gray, *Great Canadian Oil Patch*, 364–5; Peter Foster, *Other People's Money: The Banks, the Government and Dome* (Don Mills, ON: Collins, 1983), 35–7.

41   IOL Exec. Cte. Minutes, 16 Jan 1964; 17 Apr 1964.

42   Gray, *Great Canadian Oil Patch*, 367–72; "Energy From the Frontiers," *Imperial Oil Review* 1 (1974): 28–9; *Nickle's Daily Oil Bulletin*, 30 June 1967, 3–5; IOL Exec. Cte., Minutes, 5 May 1971.

43   Wall, *Growth in a Changing Environment*, 134–5.

44   Wall, *Growth in a Changing Environment*, 135–40; Emmerson, *The Future History of the Arctic*, 178–9.

45   IOL Exec. Cte. Minutes, 9 Apr 1970; "Energy From the Frontiers," 29–31; J.A. Armstrong, "Notes for a Panel Discussion, N.Y. Security Analysts," 6 Feb 1973. IOL Vertical Files, Petroleum Industry & Trade—Canadian North. Imperial Oil Archives; "The Search," *Imperial Oil Review* 1 (1975): 16–19.

46   W.G. Charlton, "Imperial Oil Limited History 1950–75," 41–2; Gray, *Great Canadian Oil Patch*, 402.

47   Robert Page, *Northern Development: The Canadian Dilemma* (Toronto: McClelland & Stewart, 1986), 172–6; McKenzie Brown and Finch, *The Great Oil Age*, 91–2. Exxon moved the Glomar Beaufort Sea platform to its offshore operations near Russian Sakhalin Island in 2001.

48   Earle Gray, *Unfamiliar History: Canada @150* (Toronto: Civil Sector Press, 2017), 342–57; Emmerson, 95–6. By the second decade of the twenty-first century, with Arctic warming, hundreds of vessels had travelled through the Northwest Passage.

49   IOL Exec. Cte., Minutes, 21 Aug 1969; 16 Dec 1969; *Nickle's Daily Oil Bulletin*, 14 July 1969, 6; Gray, *Great Canadian Oil Patch*, 385–6. The consortium's argument about tanker safety may have been influenced by the sinking of Imperial Oil's tanker, *Arrow*, off Nova Scotia in February 1970.

50   Wall, *Growth in a Changing Environment*, 376–7; Page, *Northern Development*, 75–88; Foster, *Blue Eyed Sheiks*, 112–18.

51   Page, *Northern Development*, 155–65.

52   IOL Exec. Cte., Minutes, 25 June 1974; 4 Mar 1975; Foster, *Blue Eyed Sheiks*, 120–1.

53   IOL Exec. Cte., Minutes, 18 July 1972.

54   Page, *Northern Development*, 66–8; Foster, *Blue Eyed Sheiks*, 116.

55   Page, *Northern Development*, 103–21.

56   Charlton, "Imperial Oil History 1950–75," 38–9; Earle Gray, *Forty Years in the Public Interest: A History of the National Energy Board* (Toronto: Douglas & McIntyre, 2000), 66–70; Page, *Northern Development*, 124–54.

57   Earle Gray, *National Energy Board*, 71–4; Page, *Northern Development*, 268–81. The energy crises and the National Energy Program are discussed in chapter 11.

58   Foster, *Blue Eyed Sheiks*, 67–9, 212–13.

59   Sean Kheraj, "An Environmental History of the Hearings on the Norman Wells Pipeline in the 1980s," Riley Fellowship Lecture, University of Winnipeg, 27 Oct 2017.

60   Page, *Northern Development*, 230–5; Robert Bone and Robert Mahnic, "Norman Wells: The Oil Center of the Northwest Territories," *Arctic* 37, no. 1 (March 1984): 55–7; *Nickle's Daily Oil Bulletin*, 17 May 1985.

61   Robert Huston and Ashish George Sam, "The Mackenzie Valley Pipeline." www.utexas.edu/energy.com/thinkcorner/Mackenzie.

62   Jason Unrau et al., "Timeline: The Mackenzie Valley Saga," *Globe & Mail*, 30 Dec 2009; 23 Aug 2012; "Trans Canada and Exxon Mobil to Work Together On Alaska Pipe Line Project," 11 June 2009. www.transcanada.com/announcements.

63   Jeffrey Jones, "Imperial Oil weighs Mackenzie gas project revamp," *Globe & Mail*, 18 Oct 2013; Lauren Krugel, "Imperial Oil Seeks Sunset-Clause Extension for Mackenzie Gas Project," *Globe & Mail*, 27 Aug 2015; "Mackenzie Gas Project Extended," *Oil & Gas Journal*, 3 June 2016; Joseph A. Pratt and William E. Hale, *Exxon: Transforming Energy 1973–2005* (Austin: University of Texas Dolph Briscoe Center, 2013), 490–1.

64   Guy Quenneville, CBC News, "Imperial Oil to Suspend Norman Wells Oil Production Due to Continuing Pipeline Shutdown," 26 Jan 2017; Gary Park, "Adieu to Norman Wells," *Petroleum News* 21, no. 38 (18 Sept 2016).

CHAPTER 11

1   Daniel Yergin, *The Prize*, 244–68; Mira Wilkins, *The Maturing of Multinational Enterprise*, 238–41; William R. Childs, *The Texas Railroad Commission: Understanding Regulation to the Mid-Twentieth Century* (College Station, TX: Texas A&M University Press, 2005), 199–228; William R. McNally, *Crude Volatility: The History and Future of Boom-Bust Oil Prices* (New York: Columbia University Press, 2017), 67–112.

2 Wilkins, *Maturing of Multinational Enterprise*, 365–70; Yergin, *The Prize*, 563–87; Robert Fitzgerald, *The Rise of the Global Company*, 386–97.

3 Yergin, *The Prize*, 588–632; Andrew Scott Cooper, *The Oil Kings* (New York: Simon & Schuster, 2012), 137–68.

4 Yergin, *The Prize*, 674–98, 711–14; McNally, *Crude Volatility*, 123–44.

5 McNally, *Crude Volatility*, 145–59; Randall, *United States Foreign Oil Policy*, 295–318.

6 McNally, *Crude Volatility*, 160–9; Yergin, *The Quest: Energy, Security, and the Remaking of the Modern World* (New York: Penguin Press, 2011), 285–311.

7 McNally, *Crude Volatility*, 170–224; Yergin, *The Quest*, 327–45.

8 Steve Coll, *Private Empire: Exxon Mobil and American Power* (New York: Penguin Books, 2013), 51–5, 157–70, 452–67.

9 Pratt and Hale, *Exxon*, 12–22, 310–61; Yergin, *The Quest*, 84–107.

10 Gray, *National Energy Board*, 58–9, Appendix B; "Western Canadian Select Explained," *Oil Sands Magazine*, 20 Feb 2016; Kevin McCormack, "Canadian Oil and Gas Production: Older Than the Country Itself," *BOE Report*, 17 Oct 2016.

11 Paul Sabin, "Crisis and Continuity in U.S. Oil Politics, 1965–80," *Journal of American History* 99, no. 1 (June 2012): 177–86; Randall, *United States Foreign Oil Policy*, 260–5; Robert Sherrill, *The Oil Follies of 1970–80* (New York: Anchor Press, 1983), 77–8.

12 Peter Foster, *Self Serve* (Toronto: MacFarlane Walter & Ross, 1992), 39–53; Nemeth, "Canada-U.S. Oil and Gas," 261–73. The EMR was established in 1966 but expanded its role, at the expense of the NEB, during the Trudeau era.

13 Gray, *Great Canadian Oil Patch*, 442–5.

14 "Energy Statement by Donald MacDonald, Nov. 1, 1973," *Nickle's Daily Oil Bulletin*, 8 Nov 1973.

15 Gray, *Great Canadian Oil Patch*, 445–8; John English, *Just Watch Me: The Life of Pierre Elliott Trudeau*, volume 2 (Toronto: Knopf Canada, 2009), 231–2, 240.

16 IOL Exec. Cte. Minutes 3 Jan 1974; 15 Jan 1974; Aug. 13, 1974; Nemeth, "Canada- U.S. Oil and Gas," 275–81; Gray, *National Energy Board*, 52–4.

17 Quoted in Wall, *Growth in a Changing Environment*, 386.

18 "Ten Year Financial and Operating Summary, 1966–75," *IOL Annual Report* 1976, 20.

19 Foster, *Self Serve*, 57–63; John Fossum, *Oil, the State and Federalism: The Rise and Demise of Petro Canada as a Statist Impulse* (Toronto: University of Toronto Press, 1997), 73–84.

20 Fossum, 99–100; Helliwell et al., "Oil and Gas Taxation," *Osgoode Hall Law Journal* 26, no. 3 (Fall 1988): 463–4.

21 English, 482.

22 Gray, *National Energy Board*, 60–1; Peter Foster, *The Sorcerer's Apprentices* (Toronto: Collins, 1982), 143–50; G. Bruce Doern, *The Politics of Energy* (Toronto: Methuen, 1985), ch. 6.

23 Doern, 207–9; Foster, *Sorcerer's Apprentices*, 158–9; Helliwell et al., "Oil and Gas Taxation," 467–8.

24 Geoffrey Stevens, "The Politics of Energy," *Globe & Mail*, 20 Nov 1980, 6; Jeff Carruthers, "Imperial Oil Stops Judy Creek Project Because of Federal Pricing Plan," *Globe & Mail*, 1 Dec 1980, B1; Anthony McCallum, "Imperial Oil Sees Need to Adapt to Energy Rules," *Globe & Mail*, 6 Jan 1981, B2.

25 Doern, 210–11; English, 488–92; Andrew Brown, "IPAC Members React Strongly to National Energy Policy," *Nickle's Daily Oil Bulletin*, 7 Nov 1980; "Trudeau, Lougheed Sign Five Year Agreement," *Nickle's Daily Oil Bulletin*, 2 Sept 1981.

26 Gray, *Great Canadian Oil Patch*, 450–4; Tammy Nemeth, "Pat Carney and the Dismantling of the National Energy Program," *Past Imperfect* 7, 1998: 87–123.

27 IOL *Annual Report* 1981, 44–5; IOL *Annual Report* 1986, 42–3.

28 IOL *Annual Report* 1981, 46–7; "Imperial Oil Limited—Historical Highlights 1978 –86." IOL Public Affairs and Secretary's Department, IOL Archives, Acc. 80-0074/001(01).

29 Gillian Steward, "The Age of Imperialism Comes to an End," *Canadian Business*, August 1982, 61–71; Foster, *The Sorcerer's Apprentices*, 257–9.

30 Foster, *Sorcerer's Apprentices*, 254; "Imperial Oil—Historical Highlights 1978–86"; Rinaldo Stefan, "Report on Imperial Oil Ltd." 1996. IOL-pub-6-157. IOL Archives. See Appendix 3B.

CHAPTER 12

1 Canada Bureau of Competition Policy, *The State of Competition in the Canadian Petroleum Industry*, volume 1: Findings, Issues and Remedies (Ottawa: Bureau of Competition Policy, 1981), 16–33.

2 "Major Oil Companies Issue Denials of Conspiracy to Fix 1970s Prices," *Globe & Mail*, 5 Mar 1981, 8; "Oil Firms Profited from Tax, PC Says," *Globe & Mail*, 13 Mar 1981, 10.

3 James Lorimer, ed., *Canada's Oil Monopoly* (Toronto: James Lorimer & Company, 1981)

4 William Johnson, "Executives Take Stand in Oil Combines Case," *Globe & Mail*, 22 Apr 1975, 8; "Oil Price Fixing Investigation Nears End," *Globe & Mail*, 17 Dec 1976, 8; Edward Clifford, "'Invisible' Combines Watchdog Turns Media Star," *Globe & Mail*, 19 Mar 1979, B5.

5 Robert Stephens, "Oil Giants' Control of Supply under Fire," *Globe & Mail*, 20 Oct 1981, 2; Stephens, "Chairman Denies Ottawa Managing Oil Industry Probe," *Globe & Mail*, 1 Dec 1981, 19; Jennifer Lewington, "Combines Investigation Distorted, Imperial says," *Globe & Mail*, 8 Sept 1982, 8.

6 Christopher Waddell, "Ottawa Proposes New Bill to Alter Competition Laws," *Globe & Mail*, 18 Dec 1985, B1; Moya K. Mason, "From Mackenzie King's 1923 Combines Investigation Act to the Competition Act of 1986," www.moyak.com/papers/combines-investigation-act.

7 *Canada's Oil Monopoly*, 4.

8   Foster, *Blue Eyed Sheiks*, 64–5.

9   Yves Lavigne, "Exxon-Imperial Pact on Technology is Bleeding the Country Dry: Broadbent," *Globe & Mail*, 22 Nov 1980, A13. Broadbent's charges were based on material from James Laxer, *The Big, Tough Expensive Job: Imperial Oil and the Canadian Economy* (Montreal: Press Porcepic, 1976), x.

10   Paul Taylor, "Imperial's Exxon Ties Held Benefit Not Drain," *Globe & Mail*, 27 March 1981, B2; "The Myth of Foreign Control," *Imperial Oil Review* (June 1964).

11   Gibb and Knowlton, *The Resurgent Years*, 617–21; Larson et al., *New Horizons*, 20–1, 32–4.

12   Wall, *Growth in a Changing Environment*, 65–70.

13   Lyman H. Fraser, Assistant General Secretary, IOL, to Prof. A.E. Safarian, University of Saskatchewan, 4 Oct 1960. IOL Archives, Acc. 80.0079/001 (01); Wall, *Growth in a Changing Environment*, 72, 943; Foster, *The Sorcerer's Apprentices*, 238–42.

14   "Imperial Oil Limited and Consolidated Subsidiaries Financial Review: Twenty Year Statistics," IOL archives, Series 4, Box 292A, Acc. 80-0021; Ten Year Financial Operating Summary, IOL *Annual Report* 1976, 20–1.

15   Larson et al., *New Horizons*, 465–7; Ewing, ch. 20, 72–3.

16   Larson et al., *New Horizons*, 723–4.

17   Wall, *Growth in a Changing Environment*, 392; Nicholas Lemann, "So You Want to be Chairman of Exxon?" *Texas Monthly*, Dec 1978, www.texasmonthly.com/arti cles; "The Long-Term View from the 29th Floor," *Time*, 29 Dec 1967.

18   R. Kelland, "Claiming Their Ground: Three Pioneering Women in Their Profession," 19 Oct 2006. albertashistoricplaces.com.

19   IOL *Annual Report*, 2013, 6; Foster, *The Sorcerer's Apprentices*, 248–53.

20   Pratt and Hale, *Exxon*, 217–25; IOL *Annual Report* 1990, 28–9.

21   Thomas Petzinger Jr., *Oil and Honor: The Texaco-Pennzoil Wars* (1988).

22   Sean McCarthy, "Texaco Canada May Play Key Role in U.S. Plan," *Globe & Mail*, 16 Dec 1987, B9; Leonard Zehr, "Sale Could Make Texaco Canada Hot Stock," *Globe & Mail*, 17 Sept 1988, B2.

23   Leonard Zehr and Martin Middlestaedt, "Imperial Wins Bidding for Texaco Canada," *Globe & Mail*, Jan. 18, 1989, B1.

24   John Kohut, "Imperial-Texaco Takeover Stalled," *Globe & Mail*, May 12, 1989, B1; Clyde Graham, "Texaco Takeover Faces Opposition before Tribunal," *Globe & Mail*, Aug. 1, 1989, B5; Drew Fagan, "Tribunal Allows Texaco Deal, "*Globe & Mail*, Feb. 17, 1990, B1.

25   Deirdre McMurdy, "Imperial Shareholders Still Steaming," *Globe & Mail*, 25 Apr 1990, B1; Pratt and Hale, *Exxon*, 368–9, 554; Stefan, "Report on Imperial Oil," 1996.

26   Pratt and Hale, *Exxon*, 369–70; IOL, *Annual Report* 2013.

CHAPTER 13

1   Quoted in Chris J. Magoc, "Reflections on the Public Interpretation of Regional Environmental History in Western Pennsylvania," *Public Historian* 36, no. 3 (Aug 2014): 59.

2   Cobban, *Cities of Oil*, 15,17, 24–5.

3   Quoted in Brian Black, *Petrolia: The Landscape of America's First Oil Boom* (Baltimore: Johns Hopkins University Press, 2000), 65.

4   Gray, *Great Canadian Oil Patch*, 352–3.

5   Hugh S. Gorman, *Redefining Efficiency: Pollution Concerns, Regulatory Mechanisms and Technological Change in the U.S. Petroleum Industry* (Akron: University of Akron Press, 2001), 162–3; "Ending Oil Gushers—BOP," American Oil & Gas History, www.aogh.org/technology.

6   David Finch, "The History of the Conservation Board," *Alberta Oil Magazine*, 29 July 2008; Breen, *Conservation Board*, 645–7.

7   David Breen, "Atlantic No. 3 Disaster: From Raging Inferno to 'Beacon of Promise,'" in Anthony Rasporich, ed., *Harm's Way: Disasters in Western Canada* (Calgary: University of Calgary Press, 2004), 157–75.

8   Jamie Benidickson, "The Evolution of Canadian Water Law and Policy: Securing Safe and Sustainable Abundance," *Water Policy History* 13, no. 1 (2017): 73–4.

9   "Control of Industrial Pollution in the Sarnia Area," IOL-pub-6-16. Acc. 628.509713. Imperial Oil Archives; Cobban, *Cities of Oil*, 93, 111–12.

10 "On the Rocks: Shipwrecks of Nova Scotia," Maritime Museum of the Atlantic, Halifax, NS, novascotia.com/museum/wrecks/shipwrecks.

11 Mac MacKay, "Imperial Oil Tankers—Part I: Imperial Quebec," *Shipfax*, 28 Apr 2015. Shipfax.blogspot.ca/2015/imperial-oil-tankers-part1; Wall, *Growth in a Changing Environment*, 381–2.

12 IOL Executive Committee, Minutes, 17 Feb 1970, 3 Mar 1970; Brenda Large, "Costs from Arrow Cleanup Are Hard to Recover, Lawyers Say," *Globe & Mail*, 27 July 1970, 3.

13 "Jamieson Criticizes Businesses for Irresponsibility on Pollution," *Globe & Mail*, 14 Mar 1970, 2.

14 Joseph Pratt, "Letting the Grandchildren Do It: Environmental Planning during the Ascent of Oil as a Major Energy Source," *Public Historian* 2, no. 4 (Summer 1980): 43–50.

15 Dimitry Anastakis, "A 'War on Pollution?' Canadian Responses to the Automotive Emissions Problem, 1970–1980," *Canadian Historical Review* 90, no. 1 (Mar 2009): 99–137.

16 IOL Executive Committee, 22 Dec 1970: "Motor Gas Lead Elimination Studies"; IOL Executive Committee Minutes, 18 July 1970.

17 David R. Boyd, *Unnatural Law: Rethinking Canadian Environmental Law and Policy* (Vancouver: University of British Columbia Press, 2003), 31–2, 97.

18 Sean Kheraj, "Manifold Destiny: A History of Oil Pipelines in Canada," unpublished lecture, Riley Lectures on Canadian History, University of Winnipeg, 26 Oct 2017, 16.

19 Chastko, 161–3; McKenzie Brown, *Bitumen*, 215–24; Canadian Energy Research Institute, *Oil Sands Environmental Impacts: Study #143* (Calgary 2014), 3–4; John Cotter, "Environmental Health Risks of Oil Sands Likely Underestimated: Study," *Globe & Mail*, 3 Feb 2014.

20 CERI, *Oil Sands Environmental Impacts*, 5–6; John Cotter, "Environmental Health Risks of Oil Sands Likely Underestimated: Study," *Globe & Mail*, 3 Feb 2014; Kelly Cryderman, "CNRL Ordered to Drain a Lake in Alberta, Stop Oil Spill," *Globe & Mail*, 24 Sept 2013.

21 Boyd, 80–94; Yergin, *The Quest*, 493–525.

22 Pratt and Hale, *Exxon*, 461–6; Steve Coll, *Private Empire: Exxon Mobil and American Power* (New York: Penguin Press, 2012), 79–92.

23 Neela Banerjee et al., "Exxon: The Road Not Taken," *Inside Climate News*, 2015, 4–6.

24 Pratt and Hale, *Exxon*, 185.

25 Pratt and Hale, *Exxon*, 219–22; Tom Bower, *Oil: Money, Politics and Power in the 21st Century* (New York: Grand Central Publishing, 2009), 161–2.

26 Pratt and Hale, *Exxon*, 471–6; Coll, *Private Empire*, 594–8.

27 Alex D. Charpentier et al., "Understanding the Canadian Oil Sands Industry's Greenhouse Gas Emissions," *Environmental Research Letter* 4 (2009): 1–2; Jacob G. Englander et al., "Historical Trends in Greenhouse Gas Emissions of the Alberta Oil Sands (1970–2010)," *Environmental Research Letter* 8 (2013): 1–2; John P. Giesy et al., "Alberta Oil Sands Development," *Publications of the [U.S.] National Academy of Science*, 19 Jan 2010, 951–2. www.pnas.org/cgi/doi/10.1073/pnas.0912880107.

28 Imperial Oil, "Review of Environmental Protection Activities for 1978–1979," 1–2. IOLpub-6-117; Robert Peterson, "A Cleaner Canada," *Imperial Oil Review* (Summer 1998): 29. These documents were cited in Brendan DeMelle and Kevin Grandia, "'There Is No Doubt': Exxon Knew CO2 Pollution Was a Global Threat by the Late 1970s," www.desmogblog/com/2016/04/26.

29 Philip Hope, "No Kudos for Kyoto from Imperial Oil," *Alberta Report* 25, issue 50, 30 Nov 1998.

30 David Ebner, "Imperial Oil's Kearl Project Gets Green Light," *Globe & Mail*, 1 Mar 2007, B5; Ebner, "Imperial Suffers Kearl Defeat," *Globe & Mail*, 15 May 2018, B1; Bruce Marsh, "Technology Holds the Key to Responsible Oil Sands Development," *Imperial Oil Review* (Winter 2010): 4–5.

31 McKenzie-Brown, *Bitumen*, 171–2; Shawn McCarthy, "Big Oil Makes Case for Carbon-Capture Subsidies," *Globe & Mail*, 9 Nov 2009, B4.

32 Kelly Cryderman, "Imperial Turns Off Taps on New Growth Opportunities," *Globe & Mail*, 18 July 2018, B1.

33 "Imperial Oil Moving Head Office to Calgary: Report," *Globe & Mail*, 29 Sept 2004, A6. Pratt and Hale, *Exxon*, 256–9.

Conclusion

1   William N. Greene, "Strategies of Major Oil Companies," ch. 3, 2–21; Grant and Thille, "Tariffs, Strategy and Structure: Competition and Collusion in the Ontario Petroleum Industry," 392–413.

2   Jeffry A. Frieden, *Global Capitalism* (New York: Norton, 2006), 2–20; Geoffrey Jones, *Multinationals and Global Capitalism* (Oxford, UK: Oxford University Press, 2005), 18–22.

3   Robert Fitzgerald, *The Rise of the Global Company* (Cambridge, UK: Cambridge University Press, 2015), 44–54; Mira Wilkins, *The History of Foreign Investment in the United States 1914–1945* (Cambridge, MA: Harvard University Press, 2004), 8.

4   Michael Bliss, "Canadianizing American Business: The Roots of the Branch Plant," in Ian Lumsden, ed., *Close the 49th Parallel, etc.: The Americanization of Canada* (Toronto: University of Toronto Press, 1972), 26-42; Kenneth Norrie and Douglas Owram, *A History of the Canadian Economy* (Toronto: Harcourt Brace Jovanovich, 1991), 293–5.

5   Greene, ch. 3, 22–6; Grant and Thille, "How Standard Oil Came to Canada: The Monopolization of Petroleum Refining, 1886–98," 4–5; Ewing, "History of Imperial Oil," ch. 4.

6   James May, "The Story of Standard Oil Co. v. United States," in Eleanor M. Fox and Daniel A. Crane, ed., *Antitrust Stories* (New York: Foundation Press, 2007), 1–59; Daniel Yergin, *The Prize*, 96–113.

7   Wall and Gibb, *Teagle of Jersey Standard*, chs 6, 11; Greene, ch. 4, 2–18; Stephen Randall, *United States Foreign Oil Policy*, 13–44.

8   Ewing, ch. 20; Larson et al., *The History of Standard Oil (New Jersey): New Horizons*, 619, 809–10.

9   Ewing, ch. 10; Larson, 584, 619.

10 Gray, *Great Canadian Oil Patch*, 137–8; Aubrey Kerr, *Corridors of Time* (Calgary: S.A. Kerr, 1988), 108–9.

11 Robert Bothwell, *Canada and the United States* (Toronto: University of Toronto Press, 1992), 28–34.

12 Clark-Jones, *A Staple State*, 58–64; Nemeth, "Consolidating the Continental Drift," 191–215.

13 See Appendix 2.

14 Earle Gray, "John Kenneth Jamieson," *The Canadian Encyclopedia*, 20 Sept 2007. www.thecanadianencyclopedia.ca.

15 See chapter 12.

16 Pratt and Hale, *Exxon*, 223.

17 Pratt and Hale, *Exxon*, 185.

18 Yergin, *The Prize*, 715–16; Pratt and Hale, *Exxon*, 185–214.

19   Pratt and Hale, *Exxon*, 310–61; Coll, *Private Empire*, 154–93, 349–70; Yergin, *The Quest*, 33–5.

20   Yergin, *The Quest*, 93–9; Fitzgerald, *Rise of the Global Company*, 471–3.

21   Pratt and Hale, *Exxon*, 238–40, 447–8.

22   Pratt and Hale, *Exxon*, 448.

23   Coll, *Private Empire*, 544–9.

24   Bradley Olson, "Exxon, Once a 'Perfect Machine,' is Running Dry," *Wall Street Journal*, 13 July 2018.

25   www.http.oilprice.com/oil-price-charts.

Bibliography

Archival Sources

Exxon/Mobil Records, Dolph Briscoe Center for American History, University of Texas at Austin

Imperial Oil Archives, Glenbow Museum and Archives, Calgary

Imperial Oil Annual Reports, 1927–2016. Imperial Oil Archives

Royalite Records, Glenbow Museum and Archives, Calgary

Newspapers and Journals

Globe and Mail

Imperial Oil Review

Monetary Times

Nickle's Daily Oil Bulletin

Oil Week

Books

Barkhouse, Joyce. *Abraham Gesner.* Don Mills: Fitzhenry & Whiteside, 1980.

Bellamy, Matthew. *Profiting the Crown: Canada's Polymer Corporation 1942–1990.* Montreal: McGill-Queen's University Press, 2005.

Bertrand, Robert. *Canada's Oil Monopoly.* Toronto: James Lorimer, 1981.

Black, Brian. *Petrolia: The Landscape of America's First Oil Boom.* Baltimore: Johns Hopkins University Press, 2000.

Bower, Tom. *Oil: Money, Politics and Power in the 21st Century.* New York: Grand Central Publishing, 2009.

Boyd, David R. *Unnatural Law: Rethinking Canadian Environmental Law and Policy.* Vancouver: University of British Columbia Press, 2003.

Breen, David H. *Alberta's Petroleum Industry and the Conservation Board.* Edmonton: University of Alberta Press, 1993.

Brennan, Brian. *The Good Steward: The Ernest C. Manning Story.* Calgary: Fitzhenry & Whiteside, 2008.

Burr, Christina. *Canada's Victorian Oil Town: The Transformation of Petrolia from a Resource Town into a Victorian Community.* Montreal: McGill-Queen's University Press, 2006.

Chastko, Paul. *Developing Alberta's Oil Sands from Karl Clark to Kyoto.* Calgary: University of Calgary Press, 2004.

Chernow, Ron. *Titan: The Life of John D. Rockefeller.* New York: Vintage Press, 1998.

Childs, William R. *The Texas Railroad Commission: Understanding Regulation in the Mid-20th Century.* College Station, TX: Texas A&M University Press, 2005.

Clark-Jones, Melissa. *A Staple State: Canadian Industrial Resources in Cold War.* Toronto: University of Toronto Press, 1987.

Clarke, Tony. *Tar Sands Showdown: Canada and the Politics of Oil in an Age of Climate Change.* Toronto: Lorimer, 2008.

Cobban, Timothy W. *Cities of Oil.* Toronto: University of Toronto Press, 2013.

Coll, Steve. *Private Empire: Exxon Mobil and American Power.* New York: Penguin Books, 2013.

Crane, David. *Controlling Interest: The Canadian Oil and Gas Stakes.* Toronto: McClelland & Stewart, 1982.

Craven, Paul. *An Impartial Umpire: Industrial Relations and the Canadian State 1900–1911.* Toronto: University of Toronto Press, 1980.

De La Pedraja, René. *Energy Politics in Colombia.* Boulder, CO: Westview Press, 1989.

DeMille, George. *Oil in Canada West: The Early Years.* Calgary: Northwest Printing and Lithographing, 1970.

Doern, G. Bruce. *The Politics of Energy: The Development and Implementation of the National Energy Policy.* Toronto: Methuen, 1985.

Finch, David. *Hell's Half Acre: Early Days in the Great Alberta Oil Patch.* Surrey, BC: Heritage House, 2005.

Fitzgerald, Robert. *The Rise of the Global Company: Multinationals and the Making of the Modern World.* Cambridge, UK: Cambridge University Press, 2015.

Forster, Ben. *A Conjunction of Interests: Business, Politics and Tariffs 1825–1879.* Toronto: University of Toronto Press, 1986.

Fossum, John. *Oil, the State and Federalism: The Rise and Demise of Petro Canada as a Statist Impulse.* Toronto: University of Toronto Press, 1997.

Foster, Peter. *The Blue Eyed Sheikhs: The Canadian Oil Establishment.* Toronto: Collins, 1979.

———. *The Sorcerer's Apprentices: Canada's Super-Bureaucrats and the Energy Mess.* Toronto: Collins, 1982.

———. *Self Serve: How Petro Canada Pumped Canadians Dry*. Toronto: MacFarlane Walter & Ross, 1992.

———. *Other People's Money: The Banks, The Government and Dome*. Don Mills, ON: Collins, 1983.

Gibb, George S., and Evelyn H. Knowlton. *The History of Standard Oil (New Jersey): The Resurgent Years 1911–1927*. New York: Harper & Row, 1956.

Gitelman, Howard. *The Legacy of the Ludlow Massacre: A Chapter in American Industrial Relations*. Philadelphia: University of Pennsylvania Press, 1988.

Goodsell, Charles. *American Corporations and Peruvian Politics*. Cambridge, MA: Harvard University Press, 1974.

Gorman, Hugh S. *Redefining Efficiency: Pollution Concerns, Regulatory Mechanisms and Technological Change in the U.S. Petroleum Industry*. Akron: University of Akron Press, 2001.

Gray, Earle. *Super Pipe: The Arctic Pipeline – World's Greatest Fiasco?* Toronto: Griffin House, 1979.

———. *Forty Years in the Public Interest: A History of the National Energy Board*. Toronto: Douglas & McIntyre, 2000.

———. *The Great Canadian Oil Patch: The Petroleum Era from Birth to Peak*, 2nd ed. Edmonton: June Warren Publishers, 2004.

———. *Ontario's Petroleum Legacy*. Edmonton: Heritage Community Foundation, 2008.

Gray, James R. *R.B. Bennett: The Calgary Years*. Toronto: University of Toronto Press, 1991.

Hanson, Eric J. *Dynamic Decade: The Evolution and Effects of the Oil Industry in Alberta*. Toronto: McClelland & Stewart, 1958.

Hidy, Ralph W., and Muriel Hidy. *The History of Standard Oil (New Jersey): Pioneering in Big Business*. New York: Harper & Row, 1955.

Hunt, Joyce E. *Local Push, Global Pull: The Untold History of the Athabasca Oil Sands 1910–30*. Calgary: J.E. Hunt, 2011.

Jones, Geoffrey. *Multinationals and Global Capitalism: From the Nineteenth to the Twenty-First Century*. Oxford, UK: Oxford University Press, 2005.

Kerr, Aubrey. *Leduc*. Calgary: Altona, 1991.

Kilbourn, William. *Pipeline: Transcanada and the Great Debate, A History of Business and Politics*. Toronto: Clarke Irwin, 1970.

Klaren, Peter. *Peru: Society and Nationhood in the Andes*. New York: Oxford University Press, 2000.

Lael, Richard. *Arrogant Diplomacy: U.S. Policy toward Colombia 1903–1922*. Wilmington: Scholarly Resources Press, 1987.

Larson, Henrietta, Evelyn H. Knowlton, and Charles Popple. *History of Standard Oil (New Jersey): New Horizons 1927–1950*. New York: Harper & Row, 1971.

LeRiche, Timothy. *Alberta's Oil Patch: The People, Politics and Companies.* Calgary: Folklore Publishing, 2006.

Lieuwen, Edward. *Petroleum in Venezuela: A History.* New York: Russell and Russell, 1954.

May, Gary. *Hard Oiler!: The Story of Canadians Quest for Oil at Home and Abroad.* Toronto: Dundurn Press, 1998.

McKenzie Brown, Peter. *Bitumen: The People, Performance and Passion behind Alberta's Oil Sands.* Calgary: Create Space Independent Publishing Platform, 2017.

McKenzie Brown, Peter, David Finch, and Gordon Jarenko. *The Great Oil Age: The Petroleum Industry in Canada.* Calgary: Detselig Enterprises, 1993.

McNally, Robert. *Crude Volatility: The History and Future of Boom-Bust Oil Prices.* New York: Columbia University Press, 2017.

McQuaig, Linda. *Behind Closed Doors.* Markham: Penguin Books Canada, 1987.

Morritt, Hope. *Rivers of Oil: The Founding of North America's Petroleum Industry.* Kingston: Quarry Press, 1993.

Nikiforuk, Andrew. *Tar Sands: Dirty Oil and the Future of a Continent.* Vancouver: Greystone Books, 2010.

O'Connor, Harvey. *World Crisis in Oil.* New York: Monthly Review Press, 1962.

Page, Robert. *Northern Development: The Canadian Dilemma.* Toronto: McClelland & Stewart, 1986.

Palacios, Marco. *Between Legitimacy and Violence: A History of Colombia 1875–2002.* Durham: University of North Carolina Press, 2006.

Philip, George. *Oil and Politics in Latin America: Nationalist Movements and State Companies.* Cambridge, UK: Cambridge University Press, 1982.

Pike, Frederick. *The Modern History of Peru.* New York: Praeger, 1967.

Pineto, Alberto. *The Multinational Corporation as a Force in Latin American Politics: A Case Study of the International Petroleum Company in Peru.* New York: Praeger, 1973.

Pratt, Joseph A., and William E. Hale. *Exxon: Transforming Energy 1973–2005.* Austin, TX: Dolph Briscoe Center for American History, 2009.

Purdy, G.A. *Petroleum: Prehistoric to Petrochemicals.* Toronto: Copp Clark, 1957.

Randall, Stephen J. *The Diplomacy of Modernization: Colombian-American Relations 1920–1940.* Toronto: University of Toronto Press, 1971.

———. *United States Foreign Oil Policy since World War I,* 2nd ed. Montreal: McGill-Queen's University Press, 2005.

Sampson, Anthony. *The Seven Sisters: The Great Oil Companies and the World They Made.* New York: Viking Press, 1975.

Sandwell, R.W., ed. *Powering Up Canada: A History of Power, Fuel, and Energy from 1600.* Montreal: McGill-Queen's University Press, 2016.

Sherrill, Robert. *The Oil Follies of 1970–1980*. New York: Anchor Press, 1983.

Singer, Jonathan. *Broken Trusts: The Texas Attorney General versus the Oil Industry 1889–1909*. College Station, TX: Texas A&M University Press, 2002.

Thomas, Victor Bulmer. *The Economic History of Latin America since Independence*. Cambridge, UK: Cambridge University Press, 2003.

Thorp, Rosemary, and Geoffrey Bartram. *Peru 1890–1977: Growth and Policy in an Open Economy*. New York: Columbia University Press, 1978.

Waite, Peter B. *In Search of R.B. Bennett*. Montreal and Kingston: McGill-Queen's University Press, 2012.

Wall, Bennett H. *Growth in a Changing Environment: A History of Standard Oil (New Jersey) 1950–1972*. New York: McGraw Hill, 1988.

Wall, Bennett H., and George S. Gibb. *Teagle of Jersey Standard*. New Orleans: Tulane University Press, 1974.

Weinberg, Steve. *Taking on the Trust*. New York: Norton, 2008.

Wilkins, Mira. *The Emergence of Multinational Enterprise: American Business Abroad from the Colonial Era to 1914*. Cambridge, MA: Harvard University Press, 1970.

———. *The Maturing of Multinational Enterprise: American Business Abroad from 1914 to 1970*. Cambridge, MA: Harvard University Press, 1974.

———. *The History of Foreign Investment in the United States 1914–1945*. Cambridge, MA: Harvard University Press, 2004.

Williamson, Harold F., and Arnold R. Daum. *The American Petroleum Industry: The Age of Illumination 1859–1899*. Evanston: Northwestern University Press, 1955.

Williamson, Harold F., Ralph L. Andreano, Arnold R. Daum, and Gilbert C. Klose. *The American Petroleum Industry: The Age of Energy 1899–1959*. Westport, CT: Greenwood & Publishers, 1959.

Wirth, John D., ed. *Latin American Oil Companies and the Politics of Energy*. Lincoln: University of Nebraska Press, 1985.

Yergin, Daniel. *The Prize: The Epic Quest for Oil, Money and Power*. New York: Simon & Schuster, 1991.

Articles and Chapters

Anastakis, Dimitry. "A War on Pollution? Canadian Responses to the Automotive Emissions Problem, 1970–80." *Canadian Historical Review* 90, no. 1 (March 2009): 99–137.

Ankli, Robert W. "Adoption of the Gas Tractor in Western Canada." *Canadian Papers in Rural History* 2 (1980): 9–39.

Barry, Patricia. "The Prolific Pipeline: Getting Canol under Way." *Dalhousie Review* 56, no. 2 (Summer 1976): 252–67.

Beaton, Kendall. "Dr. Gesner's Kerosene: The Start of American Oil Refining." *Business History Review* 39 (February 1955): 28–53.

Benidickson, Jamie. "The Evolution of Canadian Water Law and Policy: Securing Safe and Sustainable Abundance." *McGill Journal of Sustainable Development* 13, no. 1 (2017): 61–103.

Birkenshaw, Julian, and Torben Petersen. "Strategy and Management in MNE Subsidiaries." In *Oxford Handbook of International Business*, 2nd edition, edited by A.M. Rugman and T.L. Brewer, 367–88. New York: Oxford University Press, 2010.

Breen, David. "Atlantic No. 3 Disaster: From Raging Inferno to 'Beacon of Promise.'" In *Harm's Way: Disasters in Western Canada*, edited by Anthony Rasporich, 157–75. Calgary: University of Calgary Press, 2004.

Brown, Jonathan C. "Jersey Standard and the Politics of Latin American Oil Production, 1911–1930." In *Latin American Oil Companies and the Politics of Energy*, edited by John D. Wirth, 1–50. Lincoln, NE: University of Nebraska Press, 1985.

Bucheli, Marcelo. "Canadian Multinational Corporations and Economic Nationalism: The Case of Imperial Oil Ltd. in Alberta (Canada) and Colombia, 1899–1938." *Enterprise and History* 54 (April 2009): 67–85.

Chastko, Paul. "Anonymity and Ambivalence: The Canadian and American Oil Industries and the Emergence of Continental Oil." *Journal of American History* 99, no. 1 (June 2012): 166–76.

Finch, David. "The History of the Conservation Board." *Alberta Oil Magazine*, 29 July 2008.

Grant, Hugh. "The 'Mysterious' Jacob L. Englehart and the Early Ontario Petroleum Industry." *Ontario History* 85, no. 1 (March 1993): 65–75.

———. "Solving the Labour Problem at Imperial Oil: Welfare Capitalism in the Canadian Petroleum Industry, 1919–1929." *Labour/Le Travail* 41 (Spring 1998): 69–95.

Grant, Hugh, and Henry Thille. "Tariffs, Strategy and Structure: Competition and Collusion in the Ontario Petroleum Industry, 1870–1880." *Journal of Economic History* 61, no. 2 (June 2001): 390–413.

Gray, Earle. "Gesner, Williams and the Birth of the Oil Industry." *Oil Industry History* 9 (2003): 11–23.

Helliwell, John F., Mary E. MacGregor, Robert N. MacRae, and Andre Plourde. "Oil and Gas Taxation." *Osgoode Hall Law Journal* 26, no. 3 (Fall 1988): 453–94.

Knight, Oliver. "Oil – Canada's New Wealth." *Business History Review* 30, no. 2 (September 1956): 297–329.

Lemann, Nicholas. "So You Want to be Chairman of Exxon?" *Texas Monthly*, December 1978. www.texasmonthly.com/articles.

Lissee, Erik. "Betrayed: Leduc, Manning and Surface Rights in Alberta 1947–55." *Prairie Forum* 35, no. 1 (Spring 2010): 77–100.

Magoc, Chris J. "Reflections on the Public Interpretation of Environmental History in Western Pennsylvania." *Public Historian* 36, no. 3 (August 2014): 50–69.

McBryde, W.A.E. "Ontario Early Pilot Plant for the Chemical Refining of Oil in North America." *Ontario History* 79, no. 3 (September 1987): 203–29.

———. "Petroleum 'Deodorized': The Early Canadian History of the 'Doctor Sweetening Process.'" *Annals of Science* 48, no. 2 (1991): 103–11.

Nemeth, Tammy. "Pat Carney and the Dismantling of the National Energy Program." *Past Imperfect* 7 (1998): 87–123.

———. "Consolidating the Continental Drift: American Influence on Diefenbaker's National Oil Policy." *Journal of Canadian History* 13, no. 1 (2002): 191–215.

Page, Robert. "The Early History of the Canadian Oil Industry 1860–1900." *Queen's Quarterly* 91, no. 4 (Winter 1984): 849–66.

Phelps, Edward. "Foundations of the Canadian Oil Industry 1850–1866." In *Profiles of a Province: Studies in the History of Ontario*, edited by Edith Firth, 156–9. Toronto: Ontario Historical Society, 1969.

Pratt, Joseph A. "Letting the Grandchildren Do It: Environmental Planning during the Ascent of Oil as a Major Energy Source." *Public Historian* 2, no. 4 (Summer 1980): 28–61.

———. "Exxon and the Control of Oil." *Journal of American History* 99, no. 1 (June 2012): 145–54.

Saywell, John T. "The Early History of Canadian Oil Companies: A Chapter in Canadian Business History." *Ontario History* 53, no. 1 (1961): 68–71.

Shulman, Peter. "The Making of a Tax Break: The Oil Depletion Allowance, Scientific Taxation and Natural Resource Policy in the Early Twentieth Century." *Journal of Policy History* 23, no. 3 (June 2011): 281–322.

Steward, Gillian. "The Age of Imperialism Comes to an End." *Canadian Business*, August 1982, 61–71.

Taylor, Graham D. "Sun Oil and Great Canadian Oil Sands Ltd.: The Financing and Management of a 'Pioneer' Enterprise 1962–74." *Journal of Canadian Studies* 20, no. 2 (Autumn 1985): 102–21.

———. "From Branch Operation to Integrated Subsidiary: The Reorganisation of Imperial Oil under Walter Teagle, 1911–1917." *Business History* 34, no. 3 (July 1994): 49–69.

———. "Under (Canadian) Cover: Standard Oil (New Jersey) and the International Petroleum Company in Peru and Colombia 1914–1948." *Management and Organizational History* 10, no. 2 (2015): 153–69.

Wilkins, Mira. "Multinational Oil Companies in South America in the 1920s." *Business History Review* 48, no. 3 (1974): 414–46.

———. "The History of Multinational Enterprise." In *The Oxford Handbook of International Business*, 2nd edition, edited by A.M. Rugman and T.L. Brewer, 3–38. New York: Oxford University Press, 2010.

Unpublished

Barry, Patricia. "The Canol Project: An Adventure of the U.S. War Department in Canada's Northwest." Edmonton: P.A. Barry, 1985. Trent University Archives, Peterborough, Ontario.

Bucheli, Marcelo. "Multinational Oil Companies in Colombia and Mexico: Corporate Strategy, Nationalism and Local Politics." Paper presented at the International Economic Meeting, Helsinki, 2006.

Charlton, W.G. "Imperial Oil History 1950–1975" (ca. 1981). IOL pub 1a-22. Imperial Oil Archives.

"Esso Mariners – A History of Imperial Oil's Fleet Operations, 1899 to 1980." IOL pub 1a-20. Imperial Oil Archives.

Ewing, John S. *History of Imperial Oil* (ca. 1951), 4 volumes. IOL pub 1a-8. Imperial Oil Archives, Glenbow Museum and Archives, Calgary, Alberta.

Finch, David. "Leduc – A Living History." 2007. IOL pub 1a-27. Imperial Oil Archives.

Grant, Hugh. "The Petroleum Industry and Canadian Economic Development: An Economic History 1900–1961." PhD diss., University of Toronto, 1986.

Grant, Hugh, and Henry Thille. "How Standard Oil Came to Canada: The Monopolization of Canadian Petroleum Refining, 1886–1898." Working Paper, 2004. http://EconPapers.repec.org/RePEc.gue.guelph.2004-4.

Greene, William N. "Strategies of the Major Oil Companies." PhD diss., Harvard University, 1982.

Jackson, David L. "A Study of Imperial Oil Limited." 1964. IOL pub 6-24. Imperial Oil Archives.

Kheraj, Sean. "Manifold Destiny: A History of Oil Pipelines in Canada." Riley Fellowship Lecture on Canadian History, University of Winnipeg, 26 October 2017.

———. "An Environmental History of the Hearings on the Norman Wells Pipeline in the 1980s." Riley Fellowship Lecture on Canadian History, University of Winnipeg, 27 October 2017.

Little, Edward J.H. "Fixed Asset Accounting for an Integrated Oil Company." 1968. IOL pub 6-31. Imperial Oil Archives.

Mason, Moya K. "From Mackenzie King's 1923 Combines Investigation Act to the Competition Act of 1986." www.moyak.com/papers/combines-investigation-act.

Nemeth, Tammy. "Canada-U.S. Oil and Gas Relations 1958 to 1974." PhD diss., University of British Columbia, 2007.

Stefan, Rinaldo. "Report on Imperial Oil Ltd." 1996. IOL pub 6-157. Imperial Oil Archives.

Index

Page numbers in italics refer to figures.

C

Calder, William, 128, 129
Calgary Development & Producers Ltd., 126
Calgary Natural Gas Company, 118, 119
Calgary Petroleum Products Company, 119, 123
Cameron, Harry, 282
Canada: chemical companies, 178; Clean Air Act, 287–88; demand for fertilizer, 182; Department of Energy, Mines and Resources (EMR), 257; gross national product, 298; Interprovincial Pipeline system, 257; kerosene export, 298; National Energy Program (NEP), 5, 230, 261, 304; National Oil Policy, 203, 204, 257, 298, 303; Oil and Gas Resources Conservation Act, 195; Oil Import Compensation Program, 261; participation in Marshall Plan, 302; Petroleum and Gas Revenue Tax (PGRT), 261; Pipe Line Act, 195; protectionism, 298; tax laws, 66, 72, 257–58; Western Accord, 256
Canada's Bank Act (1871), 34
Canada's War Bonds, 65–66
Canada-United States Free Trade Agreement, 288
Canada-US International Joint Commission, 284, 285
Canadian Arctic Gas project, 238
Canadian Arctic Resources Committee (CARC), 240
Canadian Congress of Labour, 115
Canadian crude oil: distillation process, 27, 44–45; domestic reserves, 143; export of, 27; problem of sulphur, 13, 27, 43; transportation of, 31, 169
Canadian Natural Resources Inc., 289
Canadian Oil Company, 24, 36
Canadian oil industry: cartel arrangements, 29; challenges to, 192; companies in, 1, 186, 270–71, 316; depletion allowances, 210, 260–61; export market of, 30,

202–3; history of, 5–6; post-Second World War, 143; price regulation in, 255–56, 258, 267; protectionism of, 13, 27, 32–33, 46, 50, 261; regulatory system, 195; rise of oil production, 30; "Rockefeller plan" for, 34; taxation of, 205, 206–10, 264
Canadian Pacific Railway, 43, 117–18
Canadian Polysar, 94, 134
Canadian Victory Loan Bond, 65
Canadian Western company, 125–26
Canadian Western Natural Gas, Light, Heat & Power Company, 118
Canol Project, 134, 137–38, 140, 160
carbon emissions, 5–6, 289–90, 291
Carbon Oil Company, 29, 30, 32
Carling, John, 26
Carney, Patricia, 263
Carpenter, A.A., 127
Carson, C.E., 161, 177
Carson, Rachel, 285
Carter, John H., 71
Carter, Kenneth, 208, 210
Carter Oil, 106, 144
Caspian Sea oil fields, 47
Chamberlain, Horace, 54, 56, 60, 63
Champlain Oil Company, 158, 330n12
Chandler, Alfred, Jr., 95
Charles Pratt Company, 38
Charlton, W.G., 241
China National Petroleum Company, 2
China's economic growth, 253
Cities Service consortium, 220, 221, 223, 224, 226
Clark, Edgar M., 171
Clark, Joe, 261
Clark, Karl, 216, 218, 220
climate change, 291–92, 295–96
Clinton, Bill, 290
Coakley, George, 11
coal hydrogenation process, 174
Cochrane, Thomas, 22
Cogan, J.A., 274–75
Cold Lake oil fields, 229–30, 265, 289, 292

254; merger with Humble Oil, 271–72; offshore drilling, 255; organizational structure, 271; programs for managers, 275; relations with Imperial Oil, 270, 278–79; reorganization of, 306; research on global warming trends, 291, 292; revenue, 276; search for new oil fields, 305; *See also* Jersey Standard; Standard Oil Company

Exxon Mobil: affiliates, 2–3; creation of, 6–7, 279, 306; global operations, 2, 89; oil sands exploration, 227; ownership of Imperial Oil, 17; studies of, 6; *See also* Jersey Standard; Standard Oil Company

Exxon Valdez disaster, 255, 287

F

Fairbank, John H., 25, 29, 31, 36, 51
Fall, Albert B., 80
Fallows, Joseph, 35
Farish, William, 175
Fischer-Tropsch process, 15
Fisher, William, 228
Fitzgerald, Frederick A., 31, 34, *35*, 35–36, 48, 54, 56
Fitzsimmons, Robert, 216, 217, 221
Flagler, Henry, 38
Flanagan, James, 79, *80*
flash test, 33
Fluid Iron Ore Reduction (FIOR), 114, 183
Folger, Henry, 56
Foothills Oil & Gas Ltd., 126
Ford, Henry, 97
Fordson Tractor, 97
Fort McMurray, 120, 215, 216–17, 218, 226
Fort Norman, 14–15, 121, 122–23
Foster, Peter, 264, 265, 272
"fracking" technology, 254
Frasch, Herman, 43, 44, *44*, 45, 97–98, 171, 297
Frontenac Oil, 103
Frost, Leslie, 169

G

Gallagher, Jack, 232, 233
"Gallagher allowance," 261
Garvin, Clifford, 292, 305
Gas-Arctic Northwest Project Study Group, 237
Gas Arctic Study Group, 241
gasoline: advertising, *189*; demand for, 97; import duties on, 99; lead-free, 287, 288; market for, 98–99, 101, 191; price wars, 196; production of high-octane, 133
Geary, John, 31, 35
General Motors of Canada, 97
Geological Survey of Canada, 118
Gesner, Abraham, 21, 22
Getty, Don, 226, 230
Gilliland, E.R., 179
"Global Climate Coalition," 291, 292
globalization, 297–98
global oil companies, 251, 255
Gordon, Walter, 199, 260
Gordon Commission report, 201
Gould, Jay, 39
Graham, James, 136–37
Grand Trunk Railway, 31
Grattan Oil, 120
Great Canadian Oil Sands (GCOS), 218, 223–24, 289
Great Depression: impact on petroleum industry, 86, 104–5, 128
Great Lakes Water Quality Agreement, 285
Great Western Railway, 25, 31
Green, Howard, 221
Greenfield, Herbert, 127
Gretna-Superior pipeline, 166, 167
Guggenheim, Isaac, 32, 34
Gulf Canada, 236
Gulf Oil Corporation, 82, 95, 186
Gulf Refining Company in Texas, 61
Guthrie, H.J., 56, 63

H

Haider, Michael, 144, *274*, 275
Hale, William, 6
Halifax Gas Company, 22
Hall, Frank G., 163
Halvorsen, A.E., 101, 163
Hamilton, J.W., 165
Hanna, William J., 54, 63, 74, 79, 92, 120
Harkness, Samuel, 38
Heard, S.F., 157
Hearn, Thomas, 295
Hearst, William Randolph, 57
Herrera, Enrique, 82
Herron, William S., 119, 123, 128, 129, 157
Hewetson, Henry, 11, 15, 16, 142–43, 144, *154*, 165, 273, 301
Hewitt, Edward, 111
Hicks, Clarence, 108, 109
Higgins, Ebenezer, 29
Hodgins, Edward, 31, 35
Hodgins, Thomas, 31, 35, 36
Holman, Eugene, 136, 137
Holt, Herbert, 79, 85
Home Oil, 206–7
Hopkins, O.B., 15, 121, 122, 144, 163, 165, *274*
Hopper, Wilbert, 260
Houdry, Eugene, 175
Howard, Frank, 171, 174, 180
Howe, C.D., 137, 163, 166, 176–77, 178, 199
Hubbert, M. King, 214
Hudson's Bay Company, 117
Humble Oil, 93, 96, 172, 233, 236
Humphreys, Claude, 217
Humphreys, R.E., 97
Hunt, Thomas Sterry, 22
Hunter, Vern, 9
Husky Oil, 230
Husky Refining Company, 186

I

Ickes, Harold, 140
I.G. Farben, 94, 132, 134, 143, 174, 175

Imperial Acadia (tanker), 286
Imperial Oil Company: access to oil reserve, 72, 214–15; acquisitions, 51, 123–24, 126; advertising, *102*, *189*, 190; affiliate companies, 162; Alberta operations, 87, 94, 146, 149, 196; archival materials on, 5; Arctic exploration, 235–36; assets, 141; bank loans, 46, 154; Bertrand investigation of, 267–68, 269; board of directors, 36; branches, 43; business strategy, 183; in Canada's petroleum industry, role of, 1, 3, 270–71; Canadian war effort and, 65; Canol Project, 134, 137–38; capitalization, 63, 300; capital spending cut, 263; centralization of, 191; challenges of, 12–13, 46, 48; chemical production plant, 181; chief executives, 275; climate change strategy, 292; Cold Lake operations, 230, 265; competitors, 1, 2–3, 101, 103, 143, 186–87; control over distributors, 157–58; cracking process license, 98; creation of, 6, 12, 34–35, 107, 297; criticism of, 304; debt of, 55; decentralization of, 194; diversification of, 183–84; dividends, 42, 46, 51, 86–87, 153, 276–77, 314–15; drilling operations, 14, 153; employee stock purchase program, 112; energy crisis of 1973–74 and, 260; "enhanced oil recovery" project, 263; environmental challenges, 282–83; expansion of, 1–2, 6, 11, 154, 163–64; expedition to Fort Norman, 215; Exxon's relations with, 6–7, 270–71, 272, 276, 278–79; fertilizer operation, 182; financial restructuring, 153–59; financial statements of, 311; fleet of ships, 285; full service gas stations, 100, *100*, 191–92; gasoline production, 98, 99, 100; golden age for, 169–70; governments' relations with, 6, 194–95, 198–99; during Great Depression, 103–4; headquarter relocation, 295; heavy water

project, 184; infrastructure, 160–70; international business operations, 180, 300; International Petroleum Company and, 90, 302; investments, 85, 129, 169–70, 184; Judy Creek operations, 263, 265; labour relations in, 64, 107, 114–15, 115–16; leadership, 141; lease of mineral rights on Crown lands by, 124; management of, 13, 273; marketing strategy, 99, 188, 191; motor oil production, 187–88; National Energy Program and, 262–63; Newfoundland operations, 105–6; oil exploration, 14–15, 17, 120, 143, 153–54; oil sands development, 228–29, 293, 294, 307; oil transportation, 16; operating capital, 156; parent company, 13–14, 17, 154–55, 299; patents, 1, 174, 270; pipelines, 2, 12; pricing policy, 192, 193; profit, 42, 46, 66, 153, 312, 314–15; public relations, 190–91; recapitalization of, 104; refineries, 12, 16, 42, 107, 124, 140, 153, 161, 272; reorganization of, 13, 91–92, 142, 207–8; research operations, 171–72, 175, 178; revenue, 1, 2, 43, 46, 51, 260, 264; royalties, 152, 260; sales operations, 56, 64, 104, 196–97, 312; during Second World War, 132–33, 134, 137–38, 139–41, 140; shareholders, 35, 43, 272; size of, 12; South American investments, 72, 74, 86, 87, 155–56; spending on drilling, 205–6; staff cuts, 276; Standard Oil's control of, 51–52, 53–54, 106; stocks, 53, 141, 277, 278; subsidiary companies, 16–17, 134; support of professional hockey, 190; surplus inventory problem, 99; taxation of, 206–7, 264; Teagle's tenure at, 60–68, 91–92; technological developments, 55–56, 171, 244; Texaco Canada takeover, 6, 277–78; "The High Costs of Kyoto" memo, 293; value of, 104, 106; vulnerability of, 186–87;

wages at, 114–15; weaknesses of, 43; western market, 48; women in, 275
Imperial Oil Ltd., 63, 313
Imperial Oil Resources Ventures Ltd., 227
Imperial Oil Review, 64, 85, 92, 109, 110, 114
Imperial Pipe Line Company in Alberta, 164
Imperial Quebec (tanker), 285
Indigenous people, 238–39
Industrial Estates Ltd., 184
Industry and Humanity (King), 108
Intergovernmental Panel on Climate Change, 289
International Bitumen Co., 216
International Mining and Manufacturing Company, 23
International Petroleum Company (IPC): acquisition of Tropical Oil, 80–81; Canadian press on, 84–85; capital, 74, 80; concessions, 76, 81, 89; connection to Imperial Oil, 90, 156; construction of pipelines, 162; creation of, 67, 72, 74, 88; dividends, 86–87; Jersey Standard's control of, 83, 87–88, 156; labour relations, 85; loans, 76; oil production, 81, 86; opportunity for Imperial's employees in, 301; South American operations, 13, 16, 74–76, 78–79, 81–84, 85, 88–89, 90, 156; training ground for managers, 275; transportation issues, 81
Interprovincial Pipeline Company (Enbridge), 16, 163, 165, 167
Ioco refinery, 109–10, 113, 114, 115
Iraq oil fields, 94
Irving, Kenneth C., 158–59
Irving Oil, 158, 159, 186

J

Jamieson, Don, 287
Jamieson, J. Kenneth, 181, 254, 274, *274*, 303
Jersey Standard (Standard Oil Company of New Jersey): access to oil reserve, 72, 214; antitrust investigation of, 158; Board of Directors, 273; budgeting, 271;

business strategy, 90, 180; challenges of, 93; competitors, 61, 93–94; control of International Petroleum, 87–88; creation of, 58, 59; criticism of, 204; diversification, 183; dividend payments, 273; expansion of, 6; forty-hour work week, adoption of, 64; in the global oil markets, 92–94; lawsuit against, 95; management of, 54, 273; mergers, 59; oil exploration in Alberta, 119; overseas expansion, 301; patents, 175, 177; pipeline construction, 85, 162; production of aviation fuel, 133; profits, 300–301; relations with Imperial Oil, 12, 16, 303; renaming, 304; reorganization of, 49, 57, 96, 271, 273; research and development, 144, 179; South American operations, 71–72, 82, 85, 204; stock ownership plan, 65; subsidiaries of, 60, 180; synthetic rubber development, 134, 176, 180; Teagle's tenure at, 83; *See also* Exxon Corporation; Exxon Mobil; Standard Oil Company

Johnson, Lyndon, 257

Joint American Study Committee (Jasco), 174

joint industrial councils, 109, *110*, 110–12, 113, 116

Jones, Jesse, 176

Joseph Bullock & Sons, 48; *See also* Eastern Oil Company

K

Kearl project, 293, 294

kerosene: commercial production of, 22, 97; demand for, 30; import of, 27, 29, 32; market for, 60; price for, 32; quality of, 43; use of, 97

Kerwin, Patrick Grandcourt, 207

Keswick, William, 71

Kevin-Sunburst oilfield, 125

Keystone XL pipeline, 294, 295

Kheraj, Sean, 288

King, Benjamin, 25

King, William Lyon Mackenzie, 108, 137, 166

King, William R., 54

King-Hicks program, 109–10

Kinley, Myron, 283

Klein, Ralph, 227

Knode, William, 130

Knox, Frank, 140

Kruger, Richard, 279, 294

Kyoto accord, 290–91, 292, 293

L

labour relations, 107, 109–10, 114; *See also* strikes

La Brea y Parinas oil fields, 71, 74, 76

Lalonde, Marc, 262, 270

Lambton County: drilling operations in, *24*

Lambton Crude Oil Partnership, 29

Lantz, F.C., 177

Laurier, Wilfrid, 50, 299

Leaver, Charles, 174

Leduc Number One site, 9, *10*, 11

Leduc Number Two site, 151

Leduc oil fields: competition in, 185; exploration of, 146; explosion and fire in, 283–84; oil discovery in, 87, 89, 144, 149, 302; strike, 67

Lee, Ivy, 166

Leguia, Augusto, 76, 82

LeSueur, R.V., 68, 83, 92, 96, 137, 139, 140, 141, 142

Levy, Walter, 201

Lewis, W.K., 179

Li, Ka-sheng, 277

Limits to Growth, The (report), 240

Link, Theodore, 14, 15, 121, 122, *135*, 136, 138, 144

liquefied natural gas (LGN) technology, 244

Livingstone, J.R., 179, 262, 268

Lloyd, Henry Demarest, 49

Lloyd Champion, 217, 218

Lodge, Henry Cabot, 80

London & Pacific Petroleum Company, 71, 89
London Refining Company, 30–31, 32, 34, 281
London Union Oils Ltd., 126
Loranger, Diane, 275, *276*
Lougheed, James, 119, 124, 225
Lougheed, Peter, 225, 263
Lougheed Terminal, 115
Loughney, Ed, 208
Lowery Petroleum Ltd., 126
Ludlow Massacre, 108

M

MacDonald, Donald, 226, 258, 260, 269
Macdonald, John A., 33
Mackenzie, Alexander, 33, 117, 216
Mackenzie Valley Gas Project, 243, 244
Mackenzie Valley highway, 243
Mackenzie Valley pipeline, 240, 241, 244, 245
Mackenzie Valley Pipe Line Research Ltd., 236
MacKinnon, Ronald, 136
MacMahon, Frank, 283
Manning, Ernest, 130, 152, 169, 195, 201, 225, 284
Marcus Hook refinery, 218
Marsh, Bruce, 279, 294
Marshall, George, 136
Mathieson, Kenneth, 71
Maximum Permissible Rate of Recovery (MPR), 196
Mayer, G.W., 64, 68, 92, 273
Mayland Oil Co., 126
McClave, James, 217
McCloskey, Leo, 177
McColl Brothers Ltd., 103
McColl Frontenac, 103, 151, 161, 316
McCollum, L.F., 274
McGillvray, A.A., 131
McGregor, Duncan, 97
McKinley, William, 57, 58

McLaughlin, Robert, 97
McLeod, John H., 123, 130
McMahon, Frank, 163, 237
McMurray Oil & Asphaltum Co., 216
McQueen, Alexander, 68, 83, 120, 123, 124, 127
Mechin, G.C., 112, 113, 114
Mellons family, 60–61
Mene Grande Oil Company, 82
Menzies, Merrill, 213
Mexican oil industry, 82, 93, 203, 303
Midwest Petroleums Ltd., 126
Midwest Refining Co., 67
Mildred Lake mine site, 221
Minhinnick, John, 31, 35, 43, 44
Mining Association of Canada, 209
Mitchell, George, 254
Monnett, Frank, 57
Montalvo, José Antonio, 82
Montreal East refinery, 111, 112–13, 114
Montreal Pipeline, 201, 203, 204, 205
Moroney, Tip, 152, 195, 284
Morrow, Charles W., 198
Moyer, John, 129
Mulroney, Brian, 263
Murchison, Clint, 199
Murray, Alexander, 23
Mutual Oil Company, 32

N

National Energy Board, 203, 240, 241, 242, 244, 245, 257, 263
Natland, Manfred, 220
natural gas: prices of, 244; problem of wastage of, 127–28, 130
Nesbitt Thomson, 103
Newfoundland's "Prosperity Loan," 105
New Jersey's corporate reform act, 72
New York Life Insurance Company, 76
Nickle, C.J., 152, 206
Nixon, Richard, 257
Nobel group, 93

Norman Wells: establishment of, 231; expansion of, 136, 138; Imperial operations at, 136, 245; oil production capacity, 137–38, 140, 242; pipeline from, 139, 140; during wartime, 137

North American Free Trade Agreement (NAFTA), 264

North American Gas Light Company, 22

North Atlantic: oil exploration in, 235–36; specialized vessels in, 236

Northern Border Pipeline Agreement, 241

Northern Frontier, Northern Homeland (report), 241

Northwest Company, 120, 121–22

North West Company, 117

Northwest Pipeline Corporation, 237

Northwest Territories: oil exploration in, 14, 117

Nova Corporation, 265, 277, 316

O

Obama, Barack, 290

Ohio oil fields, 45

Oil, Chemical and Atomic Workers Union (OCAW), 115

Oil and Gas Wells Act, 127

Oil Creek well explosion, 281

oil prices: global politics and, 278; impact on oil industry, 254; volatility of, 227, 242–43, 255, 276, 305, 306

oil producing countries, 253, 303

oil sands: Cold Lake venture, 229–30; companies involved in exploration of, 223–24, 227; environmental challenges of, 289; history of discovery of, 215–16; Imperial's venture in, 293; location of, 16; map of, *219*; Mildred Lake project, 224; mining technology, 223, 224–25; oil extraction from, 220; Peace River and a Japanese group (JACOS) project, 230; pilot plant, 221–22, *222*; profitability of, 307; public perception of, 294–95; refining technology, 231,

292; terminology, 336n4; transportation problem, 230

oil spills, 281, 285, 287

Oil Springs, 24–25

Okalta Oils Ltd., 128

Onassis, Aristotle, 285

"Operation Franklin" geological survey, 232

"Operation Oil Sands," 220–21

Organization of Petroleum Exporting Countries (OPEC), 95, 251–52, 253

ozone layer, 290

P

Panamanian "revolution," 78–79

Panarctic Oils Ltd., 233

Pardo y Barreda, José, 75

Paris accord, 291

Parsons, Silas, 103

Pearson & Son company, 78

Pennsylvania crude, 27

Pennsylvania oil fields, 30, 37, 281

Pennsylvania Railroad, 40

Pennzoil oil company, 277

Perez Alfonso, Juan, 204

Peru: internal oil consumption in, 89; oil exports from, 86, 88; oil fields in, 71, *73*; policy toward foreign companies, 75, 76, 82; political turmoil in, 75, 76, 82; taxation system in, 75

Peters, William, 27

Peterson, Robert, 278, 293

Petro Canada, 260, 262, 316

petroleum conservation legislation, 130–31

petroleum industry: Asian market, 305; boom and bust cycles, 249; era of optimism, 38; expansion of, 98–99, 250; global politics and, 251–52, 253; government regulations of, 124; marketing organizations, 158; military and, 93; new producers in, 250; price wars, 192–93, 194; reaction to climate change, 291–92, 295–96; system of transportation, 50; technological

changes and, 282; in the US and
Canada, map of, *39*; *See also* refining
industry
Petrolia fields in Ontario, 12–13, 25–26, 55,
56, 143, 281–82
Petrolia-London pipeline, 42
Petro Peru, 88
Pew, J. Howard, 60, 218, 224
Phillips, Lazarus, 207, 210
Pierce, Frank W., 273
Pipe Line Act, 163
pipelines: construction of, 31–32, 161–62,
164, 165–67, 169; incidents at, 294;
interprovincial, 164–66, 200; leaks of,
288–89; map of, *168*; opposition to, 294,
295; technological changes and, 282;
See also individual pipelines
pollution, 281, 284, 287, 288
Polymer Corporation, 177, 178, 181, 284
Pond, Peter, 117, 216
Port Arthur city, 165, 166
Portland-Montreal pipeline, 142, 155, 162
*Practical Treatise on Petroleum, Coal and
Other Distilled Oils, A* (Gesner), 22
Pratt, Joseph, 6
Pratt, Wallace, 233
Pratt, William, 54
Premier Oil Company, 48
Project Plowshare, 218
Pulitzer, Joseph, 57
Pure Oil, 78

Q

Qadaffi, Muammar, 251
Queen City Oil Company, 51, 55

R

railways, 31, 32, 39–40
Rawl, Lawrence, 276, 292, 305, 306
Raymond, Lee, 255, 276, 278, 292, 293, 295,
305, 306
Redwater oil field, 11, 155, 163, 164, 182, 195

refining industry: centres of, 26–27, 29, 38,
66; competition in, 111; consolidation
of, 26, 29, 34; expansion of, 63–64,
161; hazards of, 26, 33, 281–82; labour
relations in, 108–10, 111–12; pollution
emission, 281, 288; safety problems,
282; technological processes, 37–38,
97–98, 107, 133, 171, 175–76, 178–79
Regina-Gretna pipeline, 169
Restrictive Trade Practices Commission,
268, 269
*Review of Environmental Protection
Activities*, 293
Reyes Prieto, Rafael, 78
Richfield Oil Company, 220, 225, 234
Ritchie, Ronald, 198
Robinson, C.O., 166
Rockefeller, John D., 12, 33, 38–39, 40–41, 57,
58, 297
Rockefeller, John D., Jr., 108–9, 166
Rockefeller Foundation, 108
Rogers, Henry H., 41, 58
Rogers, Samuel, 46, 47, 51, 55
Romanian oil fields, 185
Roosevelt, Theodore, 58
Ross, Victor, 92, 101, 105, 142
Royal Commission on Canada's Economic
Prospects, 199
Royal Commission on Energy (Borden
Commission), 200
Royal Commission on Taxation (Carter
Commission), 208–11
Royal Commission on the Economic Union
and Development Prospects for
Canada, 268–69
Royal Dutch Shell: competitors of, 2, 13;
early history of, 61; as international
power, 93; oil sands exploration, 227;
penetration into Canadian market, 14,
67, 101, 103, 120, 121, 300
Royalite Number 4 site, 124, 125
Royalite Oil Co.: acquisition of CPPL, 128;
business operations in Alberta, 17,
125–26, 301; business strategy, 130;

Turner Valley Royalties, 103, 129

Twaits, Bill: career, 187; on government tax policy, 206, 208, 210, 211; meetings with government officials, 197, 201; personality, 197; photograph, *188*; public relations, 190

U

Ultramar, 185

Union Oil Company of California, 101, 113, 285

Union Oil of Canada, 143

United Farmers of Alberta (UFA), 123–24, 127, 129

United States: antitrust legislation, 49, 58, 74, 299; "Big Stick" diplomacy, 75, 300; Clean Air Act, 287, 288; corporate income tax, 72; depression in, 49; economic policy, 257; foreign affairs, 78–79, 257, 300; foreign investments in, 298; Mandatory Oil Import Program, 202, 203; oil industry, 30, 205, 251, 300; Oil Pollution Act, 282; Panamanian "revolution" and, 78; real-estate bubble, 253; strategic petroleum reserve, 233; Trans Alaska Pipeline Act, 236–37; Wagner Act, 116; Webb-Pomerene Act, 92

Urrutia, Carlos, 79

Urrutia-Thomson Treaty, 79, 80

US Atomic Energy Commission, 220

US-Canada relations, 160, 299, 302

US Environmental Protection Agency, 291

V

Vacuum Oil Company, 42

Venezuela's oil industry, 82, 204–5

Victor refinery, 34, 42

Viking-Kinsella field, 120, 144

Visser, Charlie, 284

Voluntary Oil Import Program, 202

W

Walker, John, 35, 36

wars and revolutions: impact on oil market, 252, 253, 278

Waterman, Herman, 29, 35

Waterman, Isaac, 29, 35, 36

Wealth against Commonwealth (Lloyd), 49

Weeks, L.G., 144, 273–74

welfare capitalism, 109

Western Select Crude (WSC), 256

West Texas Intermediate (WTI) light crude, 256

whale oil: utilitarian use of, 21–22

White, Edward D., 59

White, Frederick, 51

White, Jack, 181, 270

White, John R., 163, *274*

White, T.H., 72

Whitehorse refinery, 15, 16, 137, 138–39, 140, 161

White Paper on Carter Commission recommendation, 209, 210, 211

Wilhelm, Robert, 278

Williams, Charles James, 36

Williams, James Miller, 23, 24, 26, 36

Williamson, Archibald, 71

Wilson, Woodrow, 72, 79

Winnipeg General Strike, 107

Woods, Darren, 307

W.W. Barnes, 161

Y

Yost, Raymond, 119

Young, James, 22, 23

Yukon geological surveys, 231

www.ingramcontent.com/pod-product-compliance
Lightning Source LLC
Chambersburg PA
CBHW040146270326
41929CB00025B/3389